From Victoria to Vladivostok

STUDIES IN CANADIAN MILITARY HISTORY
Series editor: Dean F. Oliver, Canadian War Museum

The Canadian War Museum, Canada's national museum of military history, has a threefold mandate: to remember, to preserve, and to educate. Studies in Canadian Military History, published by UBC Press in association with the Museum, extends this mandate by presenting the best of contemporary scholarship to provide new insights into all aspects of Canadian military history, from earliest times to recent events. The work of a new generation of scholars is especially encouraged and the books employ a variety of approaches – cultural, social, intellectual, economic, political, and comparative – to investigate gaps in the existing historiography. The books in the series feed immediately into future exhibitions, programs, and outreach efforts by the Canadian War Museum. A list of the titles in the series appears at the end of the book.

From Victoria to Vladivostok:
Canada's Siberian Expedition, 1917-19

Benjamin Isitt

UBCPress · Vancouver · Toronto

20 19 18 17 16 15 14 13 12 11   5 4 3

Printed in Canada on FSC-certified ancient-forest-free paper (100% post-consumer recycled) that is processed chlorine- and acid-free.

Library and Archives Canada Cataloguing in Publication

Isitt, Benjamin, 1978-
   From Victoria to Vladivostok: Canada's Siberian Expedition, 1917-19 / Benjamin Isitt.

(Studies in Canadian military history, 1449-6251)
Includes bibliographical references and index.
ISBN 978-0-7748-1801-8 (bound); ISBN 978-0-7748-1802-5

   1. Canada. Canadian Army. Canadian Expeditionary Force (Siberia) – History. 2. Soviet Union – History – Allied intervention, 1918-1920. 3. Canada – Foreign relations – Soviet Union. 4. Soviet Union – Foreign relations – Canada. 5. Siberia (Russia) – History – Revolution, 1917-1921. I. Title. II. Series: Studies in Canadian military history.

DK265.42.C2I85 2010   947.084'1   C2010-900464-7

e-book ISBNs: 978-0-7748-1803-2 (pdf); 978-0-7748-5947-9 (epub)

Canada

UBC Press gratefully acknowledges the financial support for our publishing program of the Government of Canada (through the Canada Book Fund), the Canada Council for the Arts, and the British Columbia Arts Council.

This book has been published with the help of a grant from the Canadian Federation for the Humanities and Social Sciences, through the Aid to Scholarly Publications Programme, using funds provided by the Social Sciences and Humanities Research Council of Canada.

Publication of this book has been financially supported by the Canadian War Museum.

UBC Press
The University of British Columbia
2029 West Mall
Vancouver, BC V6T 1Z2
www.ubcpress.ca

For my family – and for those who speak truth to power

So we grow up thinking there were no struggles to engage in, no obstacles to be overcome.

We suppose now that the new text books will tell children that the world was set free in 1914-1918 – with no hint that autocracy is not yet out of the saddle, no suggestion that there are other fields to be won.

– "History Teaching All Wrong,"
Semi-Weekly Tribune (Victoria),
22 September 1919

Contents

List of Maps, Illustrations, and Appendices

Maps

Illustrations

After page 108

Appendices

Preface

CANADA'S WEST COAST and the Russian Far East often seem worlds apart. Separated by barriers of language, culture, geography, and political economy, their trajectories rarely cross in the public mind. However, for a few months in 1918-19, the histories of Canada and Russia coincided: Canada deployed 4,200 troops to engage an amorphous opponent – Bolshevism – part of an undeclared four-front war that included thirteen Allied countries, half a million White Russian fighters, and the anomalous sixty thousand-strong Czecho-Slovak Legion. The Siberian Expedition (or Canadian Expeditionary Force [Siberia] as it was officially known), like campaigns at Murmansk, Arkhangelsk, and Baku, was designed to replace the Bolshevik Party of V.I. Lenin with a government more sympathetic to Western interests.[1] As Admiral Aleksandr Kolchak, Canada's White ally and supreme dictator of the "All-Russian" government at Omsk, told a Canadian officer in spring 1919: "The principal aim of the campaign is to destroy the Bolshevik armies. After that it would prove an easy matter to restore law and order in the country."[2]

Canada was defeated in Russia. In a strange irony, few of the Canadian soldiers ever reached Siberia, a vast region in the Russian interior far removed from the port of Vladivostok on the Pacific coast (see Map 1). The Bolsheviks retained and consolidated power, cementing Soviet-style Communism as a world force and foreshadowing the hot and cold wars of the twentieth century. The Siberian Expedition was a particularly poignant defeat, coinciding with the first military expedition in Canadian history organized independently of the British military and the country's first foray in the Far East. The failure of Canada and its Allies to wipe out the Soviet Union at its inception helps explain the historiographic black hole. Military history has been inclined towards jingoism, amplifying victories and ignoring losses in marginal theatres of war. The layer of historians who have looked at Allied Intervention have left no mark on how most Canadians remember the First World War. My primary motivation in telling this story is to raise these troubling questions of Canadian policy in 1918-19, to give voice to soldiers and workers who advocated a different course, and to force a rethinking of how the war is remembered.

I arrived at the Siberian Expedition through a circuitous path, by way of an undergraduate paper on Victoria's labour movement during the First World

War. As I read through the records of the Victoria Trades and Labor Council, opposition to the Siberian Expedition became apparent after the armistice of 11 November 1918. Labour entered into a dialogue with soldiers, many of whom were conscripts under the Military Service Act, 1917; large numbers of troops attended protest meetings where labour speakers offered an interpretation starkly different from that of the Canadian government and the military command. Guided by vague sources, I uncovered the Victoria mutiny of 21 December 1918, where French-Canadian conscripts broke from a march before boarding the SS *Teesta* at the point of bayonets. Gradually, I pulled together the diverse pieces of the Siberian puzzle, through military records at Ottawa and a journey across Russia in spring 2008.

A dozen Russian scholars made this a truly memorable and productive trip. In Vladivostok, I was hosted at the Institute of History, Ethnography and Archeology of the Far Eastern Peoples, an affiliate of the Russian Academy of Science. I wish to thank Sergey Vradiy, Boris Mukhachev, Lidia Fetisova, Liudmila Galliamova, Oleg Sergeev, Tamara Troyakova, and Amir Khisamutdinov for sharing their insights into the history of their region. Sergey Ivanov provided stellar interpretive services during rambles around Vladivostok, Churkin, Gornostai, and Shkotovo. In Irkutsk, I met Victor Dyatlov at Irkutsk State University, toured monuments to Kolchak's fall with Vladimir Yurasov, and conversed with Pavel Novikov, a specialist in the civil war period. At Kemerovo, a coal-mining region in the centre of Siberia, I was welcomed into the home of Sergei Pavlovich Zviagin, an expert in the history of White Siberia. Elena Semibratova and Aleksey Ilyasov provided interpretive services. At Omsk, where Canadian and British troops propped up the White government of Admiral Kolchak, I enjoyed a walking tour with Vladimir Shuldyakov and Dennis Plugarev. Tamara Karnagova helped acquaint me with academic contacts in Moscow and Boris Kolonitskii discussed the mechanics of revolution during a visit to the St. Petersburg Institute of History. These scholars, and dozens of other Russians whom I met along the ten thousand-kilometre length of the Trans-Siberian Railroad, provided a glimpse into the warm Russian spirit.

Histories are like building blocks, with one work building off those that precede it. I wish to acknowledge scholars whose research has shone light on the chaotic events in Canada and Russia at the end of the First World War – particularly John Swettenham, Roy MacLaren, and John Skuce. I am also indebted to colleagues who supported this work through its various stages. Eric W. Sager, Phyllis Senese, and Jennifer Evans supervised early research, and a number of colleagues read drafts: Gregory S. Kealey, David Frank, Margaret Conrad, Marc Milner, Foster Griezic, Kirk Niergarth, Janis Thiessen, Lee Windsor, Glen Leonard, Amy O'Reilly, Matthew Baglole, Janet Mullin, Heidi Coombs,

Heather Molyneaux, Patrick Webber, and readers at the *Canadian Historical Review* and UBC Press. Gwen Stephenson provided access to the Stephenson Family Papers and her uncle Edwin's photographs from Siberia; Sidney Rodger, Jim Neis, and Dona Crawford shared their fathers' diaries and photographs; Viateur Beaulieu and Mireille Lagacé provided valuable insight into the service of men from St-Épiphane, Quebec. Larry Black opened up the records of the Centre for Research on Canadian-Russian Relations, while Norman Pereira, Patricia Polansky, and Jennifer Polk helped connect me with Russian scholars and archivists, including Maxim Yakovenko, who shared original research on the Canadian occupation of Vladivostok. Irina Gavrilova and Mathieu Rioux assisted with translation.

This book has been published with the help of a grant from the Canadian Federation for the Humanities and Social Sciences, through the Aid to Scholarly Publications Programme, using funds provided by the Social Sciences and Humanities Research Council of Canada. Additional funds, including SSHRCC doctoral and postdoctoral fellowships and institutional grants from the University of Victoria and the University of New Brunswick, facilitated the research and writing, as did archivists and administrative staff. UNB's Gregg Centre for the Study of War and Society provided a generous travel grant for my trip across Russia. The team at UBC Press, particularly Emily Andrew, Melissa Pitts, Jean Wilson, Holly Keller, Peter Milroy, and Dean Oliver, helped steer this work to completion with a blend of efficiency, kindness, and precision. Finally, I wish to thank family, particularly Melissa and Aviva, my parents Linda and Julian, and friends for supporting me throughout this project. Without your assistance, I would not be telling this important story.

Abbreviations

AEF	American Expeditionary Force
AFL	American Federation of Labor
BCFL	British Columbia Federation of Labor
CAMC	Canadian Army Medical Corps
CASC	Canadian Army Service Corps
CAVC	Canadian Army Veterinary Corps
CE	Canadian Engineers
CEF	Canadian Expeditionary Force
CEFS	Canadian Expeditionary Force (Siberia)
CGA	Canadian Garrison Artillery
CGS	Chief of General Staff, Ottawa
CMGC	Canadian Machine Gun Corps
COC	Canadian Ordnance Corps
CPOS	Canadian Pacific Ocean Services
CPR	Canadian Pacific Railway
FLP	Federated Labor Party
IWW	Industrial Workers of the World
OBU	One Big Union
RCMP	Royal Canadian Mounted Police
RNWMP	Royal North-West Mounted Police
RSDWP	Russian Social Democratic Workers' Party
RSDWP(b)	Russian Social Democratic Workers' Party (Bolshevik)
SPC	Socialist Party of Canada
SR	Socialist Revolutionary Party
TLC	Trades and Labor Congress of Canada
VTLC	Victoria Trades and Labor Council

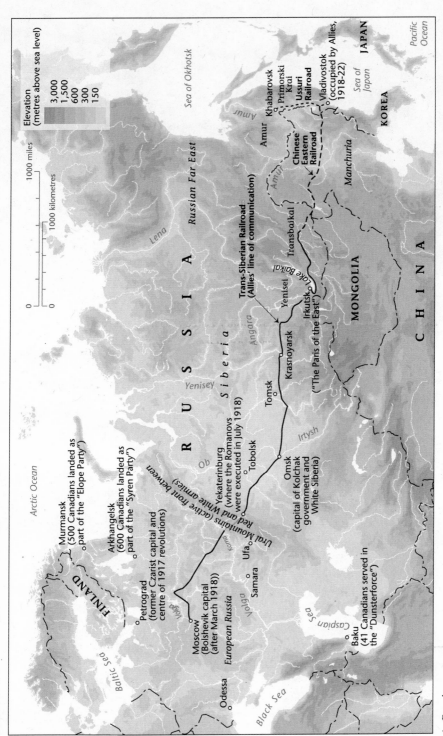

Elevation
(metres above sea level)
3,000
1,500
600
300
150

1000 miles

1000 kilometres

Arctic Ocean

FINLAND

Murmansk
(500 Canadians landed as
part of the "Elope Party")

Arkhangelsk
(600 Canadians landed as
part of the "Syren Party")

Petrograd
(former Czarist capital and
centre of 1917 revolutions)

Moscow
(Bolshevik capital
(after March 1918))

Odessa

Black Sea

Baltic Sea

Volga

Samara

Ufa

Kama

Ural Mountains (active front between
Red and White armies)

Yekaterinburg
(where the Romanovs
were executed in July 1918)

Tobolsk

Ob

Caspian
Sea

Baku
(41 Canadians served in
the "Dunsterforce")

European Russia

R   U   S   S   I   A

Yenisey

Siberia

Angara

Lena

Russian Far East

Sea of Okhotsk

Omsk
(capital of Kolchak
government and
White Siberia)

Irtysh

Tomsk

Krasnoyarsk

Yenisei

Irkutsk
("The Paris of the East")

Trans-Siberian Railroad
(Allies' line of communication)

Lake Baikal

Transbaikal

MONGOLIA

C   H   I   N   A

Amur

Amur

Amur

Khabarovsk

Primorski
Krai

Ussuri
Railroad

Chinese
Eastern
Railroad

Manchuria

Vladivostok
(occupied by Allies,
1918-22)

Sea of Japan

JAPAN

KOREA

Pacific
Ocean

1   Russia, 1918

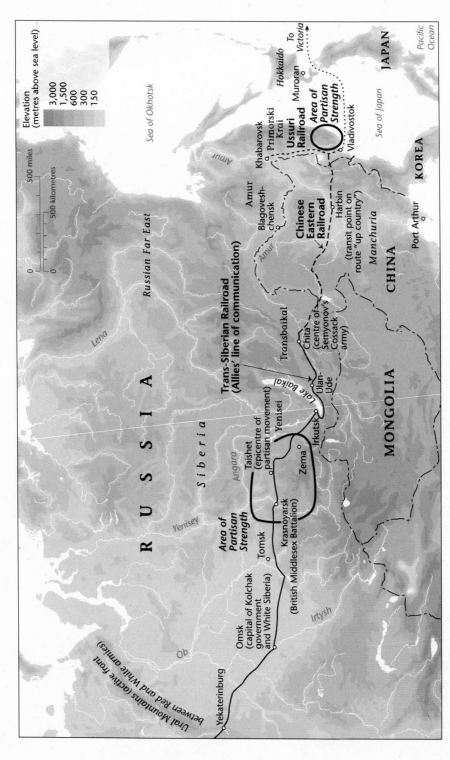

2 Siberia and the Russian Far East, 1918

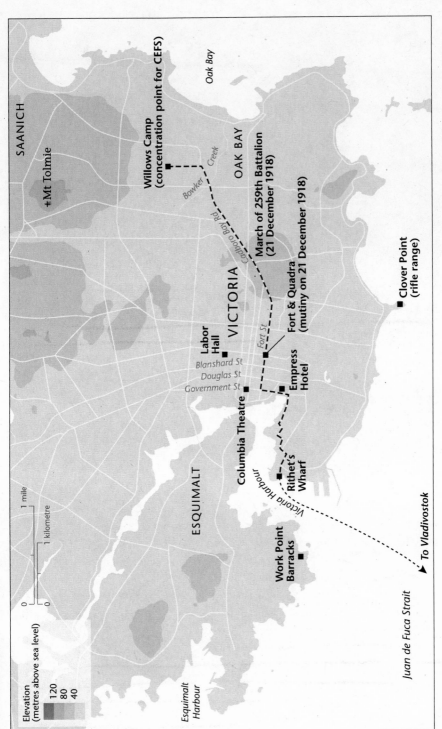

Elevation
(metres above sea level)
120
80
40

SAANICH

+ Mt Tolmie

Oak Bay

Willows Camp
(concentration point for CEFS)

OAK BAY

Bowker Creek

VICTORIA

Cadboro Bay Rd

March of 259th Battalion
(21 December 1918)

Fort & Quadra
(mutiny on 21 December 1918)

Fort St

Labor Hall

Blanshard St
Douglas St
Government St

Columbia Theatre

Empress Hotel

Clover Point
(rifle range)

ESQUIMALT

Rithet's Wharf

Victoria Harbour

Esquimalt Harbour

Work Point Barracks

To Vladivostok

Juan de Fuca Strait

0   1 mile
0   1 kilometre

3 Victoria, 1918

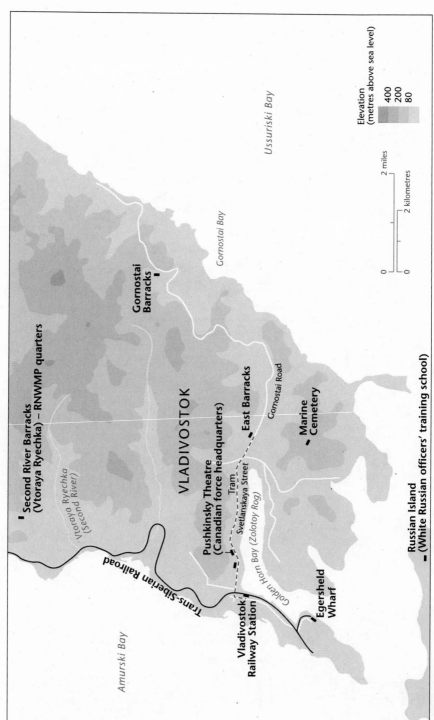

Elevation
(metres above sea level)
400
200
80

2 miles

2 kilometres

0

0

Second River Barracks
(Vtoraya Ryechka) – RNWMP quarters

Vtoraya Ryechka
(Second River)

Gornostai
Barracks

Ussuriski Bay

Gornostai Bay

Amurski Bay

Trans-Siberian Railroad

VLADIVOSTOK

Pushkinsky Theatre
(Canadian force headquarters)   **East Barracks**

Tram

Svetlanskaya Street

Cornostai Road

Marine
Cemetery

Golden Horn Bay (Zolotoy Rog)

Vladivostok
Railway Station

Egersheld
Wharf

Russian Island
(White Russian officers' training school)

4 Vladivostok, 1919

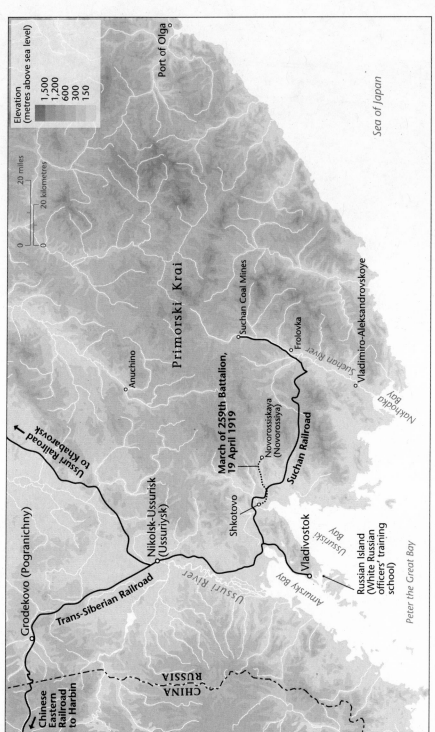

5 Partisan strength around Vladivostok, 1919

From Victoria to Vladivostok

Introduction: Why Siberia?

They are taking us to Russia,
As soldiers of the King,
And if we see a Bolshevist,
We will shout, "You horrid thing."[1]

— DAWN FRASER, "THE MUD-RED
VOLUNTEERS," *SONGS OF SIBERIA AND
RHYMES OF THE ROAD* (C. 1919)

IT WAS THE SHORTEST day of the year – and the first day of winter – when the soldiers began their six-kilometre march from the Willows Camp to the troopship *Teesta* on Victoria's outer wharves. Saturday, 21 December 1918. The Armistice had been signed six weeks earlier, ending four years of bloody warfare on the Western Front. But peace evaded these men. The troops belonged to the 259th Battalion, 16th Infantry Brigade, Canadian Expeditionary Force (Siberia) (CEFS). They were bound for Vladivostok, a beachhead of Western interests in Russia's Far East, where Canada and a dozen Allies were opening a new terrain of battle against an amorphous enemy – Bolshevism.

Dissent was palpable in the 259th Battalion. War weariness sapped morale as a wet BC autumn and the outbreak of the Spanish Flu combined with misgivings over the purposes of the Siberian Expedition. Trade-union organizers and socialists had fanned such doubts at protest meetings attended by hundreds of members of the force. Speakers invoked the demand "Hands Off Russia," questioning Allied intervention on the four fronts encircling Russia, while propagandists sold pamphlets entitled *The Soviet at Work* and *The Siberian Expedition*.[2] "We are going to be railroaded to Siberia, and we cannot do a thing to help ourselves," a soldier wrote to his sister in New Westminster. "They started to dish out our clothes to us the first day, and out of 78 of us 77 refused to take them."[3] As a court martial later concluded, "the trouble appears to have started at the date when the men were asked whether they were willing to volunteer for service in Siberia."[4]

Within the 259th Battalion, two-thirds of the troops – many from Quebec – were conscripts, compelled to serve under the Military Service Act, 1917. Questions later arose over the legality of deploying "MSA men," hinging on whether or not the Siberian Expedition qualified as "the defence of the realm."[5] Changes in company organization disrupted existing patterns of leadership and authority. "Owing to the requirements of the Record Office the men were marched to the Wharf in Alphabetical order," the court martial found. "This completely changed the company organization so that the men were not under the command of their own Platoon officers and NCOs. There was one case of an officer who could not speak French being in charge of a platoon of men who could not understand English."[6]

The troops, 856 enlisted men and forty-two officers under the command of Lieutenant-Colonel Albert "Dolly" Swift, proceeded up Fort Street towards downtown Victoria (see Map 3). Midway through the march, at the intersection with Quadra Street, a group of conscripts near the front halted. "There was a plan among them that they would refuse to go," a trade unionist by the name of Flewin recalled. "There was one man chosen to lead them, but when he struck down one of the officers the rest didn't give him support."[7] A lieutenant from Toronto described the events that followed:

> the colonel drew his revolver and fired a shot over their heads – in the main street of Victoria – when some more got into line, though there were still a large number who would not, so the other two companies from Ontario were ordered to take off their belts and whip the poor devils into line, and they did it with a will, and we proceeded.[8]

Subdued by canvas belts and revolver fire, most of the rebels fell into line. However, several continued to shout defiantly "Outwards Turn" – proposing a return to the Willows Camp – while others bellowed *"On y va pas à Siberia!"*[9] A guard of honour formed, "fifty men in close formation, with rifles and fixed bayonets on either side of the road," who escorted the mutinous company ("the French-Canadian company") to the wharf "at the point of the bayonet, they being far more closely guarded than any group of German prisoners I ever saw."[10] Twenty hours passed before the last dissenters were herded aboard the *Teesta*. "When we proceeded to our quarters below, the natural feeling was one of indescribable disgust," Lance-Corporal Erskine Ireland wrote in his diary, "especially when the hammocks were up side by side, as close together as sardines in a tin."[11] In the ship's hold, along with twenty-one tons of gear for the YMCA and seventeen hundred tons of ammunition, a dozen ringleaders were detained in cells, the two worst handcuffed together. At 4:15 AM on 22 December 1918, the 259th Battalion of the Canadian Expeditionary Force (Siberia) set sail for Vladivostok.[12]

The Real Story of Intervention

"Time will reveal some strange things in the great Siberian drama," the *Semi-Weekly Tribune*, newspaper of the Victoria Trades and Labor Council, declared two days before the mutiny.[13] This forgotten chapter of the First World War presents several challenges of research and interpretation. Straddling military history, working-class history, and the social history of Canada, Quebec, and Russia, this story fits uneasily into any one field. The Canadian experience of war has been temporally, geographically, and thematically bounded by the assassination of Archduke Ferdinand and the signing of the Armistice on 11 November 1918.[14] A handful of historians have examined Canada's intervention in Russia, but these studies underestimate the dissent among the troops and the unique dialogue between conscripts and organized labour.[15] Absent is a serious inquiry of the social movement that emerged within the Canadian working class to force their return home. Within the field of working-class history, domestic expressions of industrial unrest have been privileged over local responses to international events such as the Russian Revolution. No work has focused on Canadian labour's response to the Siberian Expedition. This topic raises important questions, such as the dual role of soldiers as workers and the way class tensions were manifested within the armed forces, providing fertile ground for expanding our understanding of the working-class experience in Canada.[16] As William Rodney observed in 1968, "the real story of intervention and Canada's role in it has still to be written."[17]

As the last guns sounded on the Western Front, more than four thousand Canadian troops assembled at Victoria, New Westminster, and Coquitlam for deployment to Siberia. Born at a meeting of the Imperial War Cabinet in London in July 1918, the CEFS was plagued from the outset by lack of clarity about its aims. A month after the main body of the force arrived in Vladivostok, the order was issued from Ottawa to begin preparations for evacuation. Few troops in the CEFS ever saw direct fighting. Ambivalence in Allied strategy prevented their deployment into the interior of Siberia, "up country" to the Ural Front, where White Russian and Czecho-Slovak troops fought the Red Army. Most of their time was spent training White Russian officers and conducting guard duty and routine security operations around Vladivostok – responding to looting, theft, assault, and murder in the port city. The threat of Bolshevik insurgency and a burgeoning partisan movement precipitated countermeasures by the Canadian command and the deployment of a small number of troops to the village of Shkotovo. An attempt to move a body of troops up the Trans-Siberian

CEFS – Canadian Expeditionary Force Siberia

Railroad was thwarted by a strike of Russian rail-workers, while another train carrying the horses and men of the Royal North-West Mounted Police (RNWMP) was wrecked near Irkutsk. By June 1919, all but a handful of troops had returned to Canada.

The Siberian Expedition was part of a larger Allied campaign to alter the outcome of the Russian Revolution and to install a more sympathetic government in Russia. From Murmansk and Arkhangelsk to Baku and Vladivostok, Canadian troops joined soldiers from thirteen countries in a multi-front strategy of encirclement designed to isolate and defeat the Bolshevik regime in Moscow – a "cordon sanitaire," in the words of Winston Churchill.[18] In Siberia and the Russian Far East, the Canadians backed a succession of White Russian governments, headed by General Dmitri Horvath, Grigori Semyonov, and, finally, Aleksander Kolchak, former admiral of the czar's Black Sea Fleet, who seized power at Omsk in November 1918. The Armistice on the Western Front liberated Allied forces for battle against the nascent Soviet state. The *British Columbia Federationist* (hereafter cited as *BC Federationist*), newspaper of the BC Federation of Labour, quoted G.W. Tschitcherin, Soviet commissar of foreign affairs, who presented a Bolshevik interpretation of the conflict:

> A handful of capitalists who desired to repossess themselves of the factories and banks taken from them on behalf of the people; a handful of landowners who want to take again from the peasants the land they now hold; a handful of generals who again want to teach docility to the workers and peasants with a whip ... have betrayed Russia in the north, in the south, and in the east to foreign imperialist states, by calling foreign bayonets from wherever they could get them.[19]

The failure of Canada and its allies to defeat the Bolsheviks consigned this story to the margins of history, far removed from the heroism of the Canadian Corps in the trenches of France and Flanders.[20]

Dissent among the troops, graphically displayed in the Victoria mutiny of 21 December 1918, provides a compelling window into persistent tensions in Canadian society - tensions that were amplified in the heat of wartime. The historic antagonism between French and English, heightened around the issue of conscription, combined with the political radicalism of British Columbia's working class. The French-Canadian conscripts who arrived in Victoria were mustered from the districts around Quebec City and Montreal, which had experienced rioting in opposition to the Military Service Act; in the British Columbia capital, they encountered a robust socialist movement that identified with the aims of the Russian Revolution and launched a determined campaign to prevent their deployment to Siberia. In street-corner meetings and in packed auditoriums, working-class leaders of the Socialist Party of Canada and Federated Labor Party provided a vocal critique that transformed latent discontent among the troops into collective resistance.[21] Both class *and* ethnicity drove the conscripts towards mutiny; neither can sufficiently explain the complex motivations behind an event that military and press censors did their best to conceal at the time. At this junction of social forces – the converging interests of working-class Québécois and BC socialists – a violent standoff erupted in Victoria.

The working-class response to the Siberian Expedition revealed bonds of solidarity that transcended national borders. The First World War had amplified class antagonisms in all belligerent countries as conscription, the high cost of living, profiteering, and censorship aggravated existing tensions between workers, employers, and the state. These tensions intensified after 1917. The class position of Canadian workers provided a framework through which they interpreted the Russian Revolution, which, in turn, provided a framework for understanding Canadian class relations. This reciprocal relationship – between domestic conditions and international events – motivated the Allied decision to embark on the Siberian Expedition and shaped the working-class response. As the *BC Federationist* noted in July 1917:

> The Russian revolution has everywhere heartened the foes of present-day society. It has given them a territorial focus, a base of operations, and if the "Reds" overthrow the provisional government of Russia and replace the liberal leaders, Miliukov, Lvov, etc. by chiefs of really crimson hue, we shall see a wave of syndicalist unrest sweep over the whole earth.[22]

This prediction hit home in June 1919, as the last Canadians returned from the Russian Far East. From Victoria to Winnipeg to Amherst, Nova Scotia, workers gravitated behind the idea of One Big Union and the tactic of the general strike. The Russian revolution had provided an interpretive framework, and an example of agency, to challenge the authority of employers and the legitimacy of the state. Controversy over Canada's Siberian Expedition prefigured foreign policy debates that persisted into the closing decade of the twentieth century.

Why Siberia?

To understand the working-class response, and the growth of discontent among the troops, it is essential to understand the rationale behind the Siberian Expedition. From the beginning, Canada's aims in Russia were complex, fluid, and confused. Military strategy, international diplomacy, economic opportunity, and ideology influenced the decision of Canada and its allies to intervene in the Russian Civil War.

Czar
=
emperor

Militarily, the Siberian Expedition must be understood in the context of Russia's transition from trusted ally to de facto enemy. In March 1917, as unrest mounted in Petrograd and the Romanov three-hundred-year rule neared its end, a group of Canadian military officers toured Russia, meeting with Czar Nicholas II and other Russian leaders. "Russia is now thoroughly supplied with munitions," Victoria's *Daily Times* reported: "The Czar's huge armies are prepared ... industries and transportation are fully organized ... everything is in readiness for a great offensive, simultaneously with a similar move by the Western Allies."[23] Within a week of this optimistic report, the czar abdicated the throne. By November, under V.I. Lenin, the Bolshevik Party had displaced the pro-war provisional government and entered into negotiations with Germany and other belligerent nations, which ultimately removed Russia from the war – and liberated German forces for battle on the Western Front. The Allied Supreme War Council, meeting in London in December 1917, pledged support to those elements in Russia committed to a continuation of war against Germany.[24] The stage was set for Allied intervention.

In a speech to the Canadian Club and the Women's Canadian Club in Victoria's Empress Hotel in September 1918, Newton Rowell, president of the Privy Council, described the loss of Russia as the most "tragic surprise" of the war. The Siberian Expedition was necessary, he said, "to reestablish the Eastern front" and "support the elements and governments of the Russian people, which are battling against German armed force and intrigue."[25] This theme of Germanic influence on the Bolshevik side tapped into public fear of "Hun" aggression and harked back to Lenin's famed passage through Germany in a sealed railcar; it provided justification for opening fronts far removed from Germany and for continuing to fight after Germany's surrender. Allegations of Bolshevik atrocities, including the supposed "nationalization of women," were amplified to bolster public support for the Siberian campaign.[26] A final component of this military rationale was the presence in Siberia of the Czecho-Slovak Legion, an anomalous body of sixty thousand troops that was marooned in Russia from 1917 to 1920 and that, in a desperate bid for national recognition, formed the advance party of the Allied campaign.[27]

Diplomacy also shaped Canadian policy in Russia. The Bolsheviks had inflamed Allied leaders in December 1917 by publishing the terms of the secret treaties, signed by the former czar and dividing the spoils of the German and Ottoman empires between Russia, Britain, France, Italy, Serbia, Romania, and Japan.[28] Canada's political and military leaders sought greater power and independence within the British Empire. As Rowell told the Canadian Club, the achievements of Canadian troops during the war had won for the country "a new place among the nations," obliging Canada to do its part on the world

Treaty between Nations that is not revealed to other Nations.

*major
military
formation*

stage. He informed Parliament that, after refusing a request from the British War Office to send another contingent to France, Canadian leaders felt obliged to provide a brigade for Siberia. Borden underscored this diplomatic motivation in a letter to a sceptical colleague as domestic opposition to the Siberian Expedition mounted: "I think we must go on with this as we have agreed to do so ... [I]t will be of some distinction to have all the British Forces in Siberia under the command of a Canadian Officer."[29] Soviet historian M.I. Svetachev elaborates on this point: "The Canadian bourgeoisie, which became rich during the world war, tried to gain independence, especially in foreign policy. It believed that Canadian participation in the intervention would help to reach this goal."[30] According to Gaddis Smith, the Siberian Expedition was "the initial episode in Canada's struggle for complete control of her foreign policy after World War I."[31]

More significant than diplomacy, however, was the economic motivation. For decades Canadian, American, Japanese, British, and German investors had eyed the resource wealth of Russia's Far East and the region's consumer market. The German-owned Kunst and Albers Company had established a vast retail-wholesale network in the Russian Far East before the war, an enterprise similar to that of the Hudson's Bay Company in Canada. When Russia's provisional government ordered that the firm be sold, a Canadian intelligence officer saw "a wonderful chance for Canada." Trade commissioners had been posted to Petrograd and Omsk in 1916, and a Russian purchasing mission was established in Canada; exports to Russia reached $16 million, making it the seventh largest market for Canadian goods.[32] In June 1917, Russia's consul-general to Britain, Baron Alphonse Heyking, described Siberia as "the granary of the world" and urged: "Let capitalism come in. It will develop quickly."[33] The Bolshevik Revolution interrupted these efforts to develop the Russian economy along capitalist lines. Rather than welcome foreign investment and trade, the new regime nationalized the assets of Russians and foreigners. "This vast country is in a very precarious position from the standpoint of trade and commerce," Rowell warned. "She needs capital and expert guidance in the work of reconstruction ... [With] more intimate relations the greatest benefit may result both to Canada and Siberia."[34] In October 1918, as Canadian troops were mustered to Victoria, the Privy Council authorized the formation of a Canadian Siberian Economic Commission, including representatives of the Canadian Pacific Railway (CPR) and the Royal Bank of Canada (the latter opened a branch in Vladivostok in early 1919).[35]

The Allied countries also had a direct financial interest in the defeat of the Lenin regime. An estimated 13 billion rubles in war loans had been repudiated by the Bolsheviks in January 1918.[36] This "caused quite a flutter of alarm" among "ruling class thieves," noted the *BC Federationist*, which welcomed the move in the hope that "the entire superstructure of bourgeois flimflam and swindle would crash to the ground."[37] Against this outstanding debt stood the Imperial Russian Gold Reserve, the largest holdings of the precious metal in the world. Valued at over 1.6 billion gold rubles, one-quarter of this gold had been shipped from Vladivostok to Vancouver in December 1915, June 1916, November 1916, and February 1917 to guarantee British war credits. The gold was then transported on the CPR and stored for several months in a Bank of England vault in Ottawa. The portion remaining in Siberia has its own intriguing story, moving from one train to another, and from town to town, as the czar and an array of White generals retreated eastward.[38] As a military officer told a December 1918 meeting of the Federated Labor Party in Victoria: "We are going to Siberia as far as I know because Britain has loaned a great amount of money to Russia. I don't know how much, and the Bolsheviki has repudiated the loan money. This is as much ours as anybody's, and we are going there to get it."[39]

The final motivation behind the Siberian Expedition was ideological. In all industrialized countries, the events of 1917 amplified divisions between the social classes. As working-class grievances against profiteering and conscription mounted in Canada, with labour demanding the "conscription of wealth," the Russian Revolution provided a powerful symbol of resistance. Fear of revolution informed Allied policy from the start. An editorial in the *BC Federationist* summed up a growing sentiment among BC workers: "There is no other sign post upon the social horizon pointing the way to peace than the movement which is now typified in the Russian Bolsheviki. Well may rulers and robbers hail its advent with terrified squawks and bourgeois souls quake with terror at its probable triumph. For with that triumph their game of loot and plunder will end."[40] To radical sections of BC labour, the Bolshevik insurrection was celebrated as a bold response to the twofold scourges of war and capitalism: it provided a framework through which BC workers came to interpret their own class position. Within the Canadian elite, however, the Bolshevik Revolution was received with grave misgivings, viewed as a catalyst to domestic unrest and an example of radical movements that were left unchecked. The *Siberian Sapper*, newspaper of the CEFS, warned that "Bolshevik missionaries are spreading their doctrines in every country in the world ... There is a mad dog running loose among the nations, and it would seem to be the duty of the nations to handle it as mad dogs are usually handled."[41] This fear of domestic Bolshevism was intensified by statements such as those of Joseph Naylor, president of the BC Federation of Labour and a socialist leader of the Vancouver Island coal miners: "Is it not high time that the workers of the western world take action similar to that of the Russian Bolsheviki and dispose of their masters as those brave Russians are now doing?"[42]

This complex array of Canadian motives – military, diplomatic, economic, ideological – is reflected in a cryptic letter, received by the Victoria Trades and Labor Council from the deputy minister of militia and defence, Ottawa, "acknowledging a letter from the Council opposing the Siberian expedition":

> The Department does not consider Canada at war with the Russian people, but that they, the Government of Canada, are supporting certain governments in Russia, such as that organized at Omsk and Archangel, which governments are, by the way, quite socialist. At any rate no aggression is meant by the Dom. Govnt, rather an economic development.[43]

This official statement of Canadian policy, despite its confusing syntax, reveals not only implicit opposition to the spread of socialism but also a clear intent to alleviate labour's fear that Canada was acting on purely ideological grounds.

A More Complete Picture

The work that follows provides a brigade history of the Canadian Expeditionary Force (Siberia), immersed in the social and political climate of the years 1917 to 1919. It draws from military and labour sources to reconstruct the experiences of the Canadians who served in the Russian Far East as well as the perceptions of those on the Home Front. The events in Canada and Russia are the subject of heated scholarly controversy, a reflection of the political tension that shaped the course of twentieth-century history. Both partisans and opponents of the Russian Revolution fashioned accounts to suit their purposes – in the immediate aftermath of 1917 and in later historical studies. *From Victoria to Vladivostok* draws from a diverse body of source material to navigate between these conflicting biases, relying heavily on the daily press, which, though oriented towards an elite viewpoint, offers a clarity undiluted by historical hindsight.

Part 1 is entitled "Canada's Road to Siberia" and consists of five chapters. Chapter 1 examines the backdrop to the Siberian Expedition, mounting domestic problems, and the revolution that removed Russia from the war; Chapter 2 explores events in Vladivostok in 1917; Chapter 3 follows diplomatic manoeuvres on the world stage that culminated in Allied intervention and the "Red Scare"; Chapter 4 details the mobilization of the Siberian Expedition from across Canada and the growth of dissent at the Willows Camp; and Chapter 5 illuminates the Victoria mutiny of 21 December 1918, the day the SS *Teesta* departed for Vladivostok. Part 2 is entitled "To Vladivostok and Back" and takes us across the Pacific with the troops. Chapter 6 sheds light on the Canadian experience in Vladivostok and the partisan movement that wreaked havoc on the Allied command; Chapter 7 discusses the situation up country and the evacuation of the Canadian forces; and Chapter 8 surveys developments in Siberia and Canada in the aftermath of the Siberian Expedition.

Taken as a whole, *From Victoria to Vladivostok* tells an important story that has long lingered on the margins of Canadian history. To be sure, the Western Front – the locus of battle where sixty-six thousand Canadians perished – deserves attention. However, our understanding of Canada during the First World War is incomplete if we fail to look beyond Western Europe and Armistice Day. The Siberian Expedition is a complex subject that straddles the military, labour, and political history of Canada and Russia. Obscured by press and military censorship in 1918-19, it has been dismissed as a side note to the war (if, indeed, it is mentioned at all). This book strives to correct this imbalance. Working-class history can and should enter into a closer dialogue with military history. The Siberian Expedition offers fertile ground for such an approach, highlighting the interaction of social pressures on the Home Front and military engagement overseas. The pages that follow challenge and complicate prevailing approaches, pointing towards a more complete picture of this unstable moment in Canada's past.

PART 1

Canada's Road to Siberia

1917: A Breach in the Allied Front

*If the combined bodies of the dead and wounded were laid head to foot
we could form with their bodies a human bracelet around the entire
world, with enough bodies left over to line every foot of the Canadian
Pacific railroad from Vancouver to Montreal.*[1]

– "The Trifling Cost of Three Years of War,"
British Columbia Federationist, 19 October 1917

On 10 March 1917, three hundred munitions workers at the Canadian Explosives Ltd. plant on James Island, off Victoria, went on strike. They demanded
shorter hours, the six-day work week, safer working and living conditions, and
a reduction in the daily food levy charged by the company. The strikers boarded
two special trains for the twenty-five-kilometre journey to the BC legislature,
where they lobbied the Liberal premier, Harlan Brewster, to advocate on their
behalf. The James Island plant, opened in 1913, was a linchpin in the Allied war
effort, providing one-twelfth of Britain's TNT during the war. "The manufacture
of munitions in unending quantities at the present time is vital to the success
of the British armies in the field," Victoria's *Daily Colonist* reported.[2] While the
strike was settled after two weeks, in a compromise brokered by the province,
it foreshadowed a growing concern in Canada and the Allied countries: the
spectre of labour unrest on the Home Front.[3]

War polarized relations between the classes. Shortages of food and other
necessities of life fuelled allegations of hoarding and profiteering by manufacturers and drove up living costs. The Victoria Trades and Labor Council (VTLC)
wrote the premier (Conservative William Bowser, who preceded Brewster) in
November 1916 pointing to "the impossibility of a man with an average family
existing on $2.25 a day," and it advised union members to remember Conserva-
tive and Liberal neglect in upcoming provincial elections.[4] In February 1917, the
council protested "the unnecessary increased cost of food commodities," which
imposed "hardship on the working class and the families of the men away serving the Empire."[5] Labour's newspaper, the *BC Federationist*, noted that, "if the
war lasts six months longer, Dominion Steel, a Canadian company, will finish

the year's business with cash holdings of $15,000,000."[6] The war was increasingly viewed as benefiting employers to the detriment of workers.

Unrest mounted across the globe. In Cuba, four hundred US Marines landed at Santiago to crush a rebel uprising. "The cane fields and the Union Sugar Mill at San Luis, ten miles north of Santiago, are burning," the *Daily Colonist* reported. Rebel leader and former president José Miguel Goméz was arrested in Havana after a fierce gun battle with US-backed government forces.[7] In Sweden, the king and government were in a state of crisis as the Social Demokraten counted the days to parliamentary rule.[8] In Britain, a strong pacifist current emerged in the Labour Party caucus, forcing the pro-war majority to pull out of a Paris conference of Entente Socialists.[9] In Germany, socialist deputy Herr Hofer warned the Reichstag: "If you insist on carrying on war you must see that the people are adequately fed. Does it not suffice for the government to incur the hatred of the whole world, or does it also want revolution at home?"[10]

Sharp Allied losses on the Western Front intensified social conflict on the Home Front, as voluntary enlistments dried up and pressure mounted for compulsory military service. The British offensive at the Somme River in autumn 1916 left 24,029 Canadians dead or wounded, part of 600,000 Allied casualties that pushed the lines six kilometres to the northeast.[11] Frederick Carne, a twenty-six-year-old Victoria salesman who served as a stretcher-bearer in the 8th Field Ambulance and took a piece of shrapnel to the cheek, recalls "that hell hole called the Somme ... an infernal war every minute of the day":

> That preliminary bombardment was something awful, the thousands of shell holes in around the village amply testify. And it is over similar obstacles that every foot of the way back to the Rhine will have to be fought.[12]

When the British halted the offensive, Carne noted: "The question of leave is once more agitating the unit." Back in Victoria, the *Colonist* noted: "Considerable numbers of Canadian soldiers ... are asking for their discharge so that they may return home."[13] A total of 31,358 Canadians were killed or wounded from August to November 1916, while only 26,279 enlisted voluntarily.[14] Moreover, the Dominion government sought to "keep enough troops in Canada to guard against invasion or insurrection," devoting sixteen thousand troops to the task.[15] An acute troop shortage loomed, prompting Prime Minister Robert Borden to introduce a national-service registration system at the end of 1916, requiring all adult men to register with the state. R.F. Green, MP for Victoria and director of the National Registration Service for Military District 11, informed the VTLC executive that the "failure to answer the questions re National registration would mean fine or imprisonment."[16] Registration, and the prospect of conscription, drove a wedge between Canadian workers and the state, providing an opening for radical working-class leadership.[17]

Owing to the pattern of colonization on the province's industrial frontier, British Columbia's working class had a tradition of political independence and industrial militancy. The Socialist Party of Canada had elected members to the Legislative Assembly from coal-mining districts at the turn of the century, and radical unions such as the Industrial Workers of the World (IWW) sunk roots in resource sectors that tended towards industrial, rather than craft, organization.[18] Such trends were manifest prior to the war and were exemplified in a bitter two-year strike involving Vancouver Island miners – a strike that resulted in the military occupation of the coal fields and the arrest and imprisonment of 179 miners. However, according to George Hardy, an IWW organizer in Victoria who later played a prominent role in Britain's Communist Party: "The outbreak of World War to the accompaniment of wholesale treachery in the leading ranks of Labour had a stunning effect on the socialist movement in British Columbia."[19] The collapse of internationalism – which saw European socialists support the war because they believed that German kaiserism was the antithesis of democracy – had parallels in Victoria. In August 1914, an attempt to organize a protest meeting at the Victoria Labour Hall against the summons to the militia was denounced by a VTLC official, who said that labour would "not countenance any attempt to interfere with the garrison."[20]

Wartime conditions moved British Columbia's working class from a position of weakness to a position of strength. Death on the battlefields in Europe, the erosion of living standards at home, and the growing conscription crisis widened the breach between workers, the Dominion government, and conciliatory labour leaders.[21] In January 1917, a delegation from the BC Federation of Labor (BCFL) met with Borden during a visit to the west coast. The prime minister said that conscription was unlikely, but he added: "A man may decide that he will not mortgage his house, but may afterwards have to change his mind."[22] A meeting of labour leaders from Victoria, Vancouver, and New Westminster disagreed on the prospects of mounting an anti-registration campaign "in view of the censorship of the press, mails and telegraph service." However, "spontaneously,"

all the Western Trades Councils, without any common understanding, took action against the registration scheme. Resolutions were passed; mass meetings were held, and the working people advised to ignore the cards, a policy that was followed to a large extent in the larger centres of the province.[23]

In Victoria, labour delegates described registration as "a prelude to conscription" and pledged to "oppose any description of registration until some action is taken to Nationalize the Industries of the Dominion," a move Borden said was impossible without Parliament's consent.[24] A group of Vancouver women in the Pioneer Political Equality League also debated registration, with their president, Mary McConkey, declaring:

> The men who were going to the front were endangering their lives not only for the protection of their homes, but also for the protection of capital. This condition made it only fair that there should be a registration and conscription of war profits, and also of wealth.[25]

The war generally, and conscription in particular, fuelled radicalization in working-class ranks. At the BCFL's 1917 convention, held in Revelstoke in January, a slate of Socialist Party members captured executive positions. President-elect Joseph Naylor was a coal miner from Cumberland on Vancouver Island who had been blacklisted for his role in the 1912-14 strike. Naylor's friend and ally Albert "Ginger" Goodwin, a union official at the Consolidated Mining and Smelting Company smelter in Trail, was elected vice-president for the West Kootenay region. Other Socialists on the new executive included Vancouver union official Victor Midgley, South Wellington miner Walter Head, carpenters' official Albert Wells, and Joseph Taylor, a Victoria longshoreman.[26] At the convention, Taylor had successfully moved "a vote of non-confidence in the Dominion government" with regard to its registration scheme.[27] Delegates also approved a referendum of affiliated members on a general strike against conscription, which workers endorsed by a three-to-one margin.[28] This dissent arose organically out of wartime conditions in Canada. However, events on the international stage soon caused working-class unrest to be viewed – by both workers and the elite – through the lens of one of Canada's allies: Russia.

The March Revolution

In March 1917, ties between Canada and Russia were strong. A group of Canadian military officers toured Russia with an Allied delegation, meeting with political and military leaders and visiting the famous health spas in the Caucasian Spur. "Mud and mineral baths there are excellent for rheumatism and kindred complaints, and the climate is mild, like the French Riviera," the *Daily Colonist* noted: "All expenses will be paid, including the first class accommodation and meals."[29] The Canadians were hosted in the Caucasus by Duke Aleksander Oldenburg, a confidant of the czar, and later attended meetings with Russian premier Georges K. Lvov, leaders of the Duma, and Czar Nicholas II (a first cousin to British King George V).[30]

This visit coincided with a Russian offensive on the Eastern Front, which the Allies hoped would relieve pressure on their forces in France and Flanders:

> Russia is now thoroughly supplied with munitions ... the Czar's huge armies are prepared ... industries and transportation are fully organized ... everything is in readiness for a great offensive, simultaneously with a similar move by the Western Allies.[31]

The Arras campaign loomed on the Western Front, as British forces occupied Baghdad and Russian armies advanced from Hamadan, preparing for an "advance up towards Armenia."[32] Reconnaissance missions on the Russo-Galician and Romanian fronts proceeded, a Russian airship withstood German fire and bombed the town of Balanovichi, and near the Volchek station on the Sarny-Jevel railway, Russian aviators downed a German plane:

> On no fewer than five fronts in all – on four fronts in Europe, and one front in Asia – Russia is taking her part in the battle-line, in the closest concert with the Allies ... One powerful Russian contingent is fighting in France, on the Western front. A large and constantly increasing Russian army is helping the Roumanians, and its presence in the war-area will assuredly, before long, turn the scales decisively along the Danube. There is a Russian contingent with General Sarrail's Salonica army ... In the Baltic, the Russian fleet is master of the northern inland sea ...

> Not for one moment has Russia flinched. Nothing, indeed, also could be finer, or more inspiring, than the firm, outspoken expression of her determination to see the war through to a completely victorious finish, as voiced by the Emperor Nicholas ..., the Russian Premier, and the Leaders of the Duma, to the Allied delegates now visiting Russia.[33]

However, appearances of strength concealed growing internal strife. Russia's working class, which numbered about 3 percent of the agrarian country's 134 million people, had radicalized since the failed revolt of 1905, when czarist troops killed several hundred protesters outside the Winter Palace in Petrograd.[34] Skilled metalworkers in the capital were the locus of militancy, emboldened by the wartime labour shortage, increased demand for their goods, and an infusion of class-conscious young workers.[35] Embodying the growing radicalism were the *Soviets*, councils of workers', peasants', and soldiers' deputies that had emerged in 1905 and increasingly challenged the authority of the czar and Duma during the war.[36] In February 1917, the *BC Federationist* reported: "Eleven members of the workmen's group of the Central Military and Industrial committee of Petrograd have been arrested, charged with belonging to revolutionary parties and fomenting a labor movement with the ultimate aim of transforming Russia into a Social-Democratic republic." The newspaper commented: "the move of the Petrograd workmen does not meet with the approval of either the Russian government or that of the daily press of this glorious capitalist Dominion." It further noted:

> It would indicate a disposition upon the part of at least a section of the Russian workers to act along class lines in a manner that would indeed portend trouble for that class that lives by the art of ruling and robbing. This could not be expected to bring joy to the hearts of rulers and swag gatherers in any land, be it a despotic Russia or a democratic Britain or France.[37]

On International Women's Day, Thursday, 8 March 1917,[38] five thousand female textile workers went on strike in Petrograd protesting the high cost of food. They were joined by women and children in bread lines, and they marched to the Putilov metalworks, where thirty-six thousand strikers joined them. Demonstrators flooded out of the working-class Vyborg district into the city's imperial core, their numbers swelling to the hundreds of thousands. Police fired machine guns from rooftops, killing and wounding three hundred, but the czar's Cossack guards refused orders and joined the protests, as did Petrograd's 100,000-strong military garrison and reinforcements rushed to the Russian capital. Prisoners were freed from the city's prisons, one of which was razed to the ground along with the Law Courts and two police stations. The Winter Palace was occupied by revolutionists and declared national property. Mass strikes paralyzed Petrograd and the streetcars stopped running.[39]

Members of the Imperial Duma, or Parliament, struggled to retain control of the Russian state from the ascendant Soviets. A twelve-member provisional committee of the Duma formed, with Prince Lvov as premier and Aleksandr Kerensky (a member of the Socialist Revolutionary Party) as justice minister. On 13 March, radicals issued "a most seditious proclamation," according to the *Colonist*, forcing the provisional committee to consent to elections for a constituent assembly.[40] An armed band of workers, soldiers, and sailors marched through the regal Astoria military hotel, disarming Russian officers and terrifying the Allied officers then in Petrograd.[41] A telegraph from the city reported: "A steady flood of socialist pamphlets has been poured out ... All government buildings are displaying red flags."[42] The next day, the czar's train was stopped in the town of Pskoff en route to the capital, and Nicholas II received the following message from the Duma committee:

Unless Your Majesty complies with the moderate element of influence at present exercised by the provisional committee of the Imperial Duma, it will pass whole-sale into the hands of the Socialists, who want to see a republic established, but who are unable to institute any kind of an orderly Government, and must inevit-ably precipitate the country into anarchy within and disaster without.[43]

[handwritten: L Society w/out enforced gov.]

At midnight, 15 March, Czar Nicholas II abdicated the throne on behalf of himself and his hemophiliac son Aleksei, naming his brother Michael as suc-cessor.[44] However, on the afternoon of Friday, 16 March 1917, Grand Duke Michael Aleksandrovitch himself abdicated, marking the end of the Romanov dynasty's three-hundred-year rule.[45] The Duma's provisional committee declared Russia a republic and named itself the new government, a move promptly recognized by Great Britain, France, and Italy – and also by the Petrograd Soviet, on the condition that they share power.[46]

[handwritten margin notes: a hard rule / + his pain / old rule / for 300yrs]

Across the globe in Victoria, the daily press reported belatedly and selectively on these developments in Russia. No mention of the Petrograd disturbances appeared until 14 March, and even then the *Colonist* cited only "mild demon-strations," "small demonstrations by a small portion of the inhabitants ... composed mostly of students and boys" that were "dispersed without violence" by Cossack troops.[47] However, two days later, the newspaper changed its tune, suggesting in a banner headline that the "Russian Revolt Was Expected," a point reiterated in a story claiming that the "real basis of the revolution" was to weed out German sympathizers in the Russian government and rule out the possibil-ity of the country's signing a separate peace with Germany.[48] The day Nicholas II abdicated the throne, the *Colonist* expressed nothing but optimism for the rapid changes unfolding in Allied Russia:

[handwritten margin note: Place in Russia]

> The Revolution in Russia, culminating in the abdication of the Czar, is the climax of unrest many decades old ... The outcome of the revolution will mean consti-tutional government in the Empire, an extended process of economic readjust-ment, and lastly, and what is of highest import to the Entente cause, a rejuvenation of the vast energies which Russia is putting forth to secure peace with victory.[49]

However, after Michael's abdication and the proclamation of the Russian re-public, the paper's editorial tone shifted again. The revolution was now blamed on the personal failings of the czar: "The ex-Czar was never a strong man from an intellectual point of view, and instances might easily be recalled when he exhibited a lack of ordinary personal courage." Nicholas should never have abandoned Petrograd to lead the army at the front, the paper claimed, and "there was no public animosity towards him up to the time when he foolishly dissolved the Duma." It was highly probable that order would be fully restored "in a day or two," the *Colonist* maintained, and that "a stronger and fully united Russia [would] face the Teutonic enemies of civilization."[50] A new stage of the First World War had begun.

Ambivalent Ally

On 25 March 1917, Leon Trotsky, a Russian intellectual who, like Vladimir Lenin, lived in exile due to his radical activity, boarded the SS *Christianiafjord* in New York for the journey back to Russia. Six days later, during a stop in Halifax, Trotsky, his wife and two young sons, and several associates were detained by British authorities. The Russian revolutionist was transported to the town of Amherst, two hundred kilometres distant, and confined in a military internment camp for twenty-six days.[51] "Here we were subjected to a search such as I did not have to go through even in my confinement in the fortress of Peter and Paul," claimed Trotsky, who described his detention as "shameful" in a letter to Lvov's minister of foreign affairs.[52] He opposed efforts by British officers to fingerprint him and developed bonds with the 850 detainees, most of whom were German prisoners-of-war and political internees. When Colonel A. Morris banned meetings midway through his stay, Trotsky collected a petition bearing 530 signatures. When he was escorted out of the camp on 29 April, the prisoners provided a rousing send-off, their makeshift orchestra playing the "Revolutionary March." Captain F.C. Whiteman, an officer in the camp, would later describe Trotsky as having "quite the most powerful personality of any man [he had] ever met before or since."[53]

The circumstances surrounding the future Soviet foreign minister and Red Army chief's detention in Canada remain vague. According to Trotsky, Colonel Morris said that the Russians were detained because they "were dangerous to the present Russian government."[54] Britain's ambassador to Russia confirmed this view, implicating Trotsky in a German-financed plot to overthrow the provisional government and suggesting that he had been detained with the consent of that government.[55] Documents later surfaced that pointed to the involvement of a British agent from the MI5 security service, who tracked the Bolshevik's movements and ordered his arrest at Halifax.[56] Days after Trotsky's Military Revolutionary Committee seized power in November, the *Halifax Herald* described surveillance of his wife Natalia Sedova and their nine- and twelve-year-old sons in Halifax. "If ever I get back to my own country, I will talk, I will write, I will let my country people know that Canada is not free, that the United States is not free, that there is as much slavery in these countries as there is in Siberia," Sedova said at the time.[57] Following their release at the end of April 1917, Trotsky and his family boarded the Danish steamer *Helig Olaf,* sailing to Norway and Finland then travelling overland to Petrograd. Four months later, he was elected president of the Petrograd Soviet and, in November, headed the Military Revolutionary Committee that propelled the Bolsheviks to power. Early in 1918, Trotsky helped to form the Red Army.[58]

In the intervening months, the struggle had intensified between Russia's provisional government and the Soviets, the councils of workers', peasants', and soldiers' deputies that had been resuscitated during the March Revolution and that provided the springboard for the Bolsheviks. In the unstable political environment known as "dual power," debate raged over Russia's involvement in the war. While the provisional government pledged to continue the war against Germany, the Bolsheviks and many workers in the Soviets favoured a separate peace. The government policy of "revolutionary defencism" was predicated on defending the revolution's gains from the menace of kaiserism. In contrast, "revolutionary defeatism" called for soldiers to lay down their arms, fraternize with the enemy, and pave the way for peace at any cost, a position endorsed by Lenin upon his return to Russia from Switzerland in a sealed train in April 1917. In the famous April Theses, the Bolshevik called for the "abolition of the police, the army, the bureaucracy" and declared: "We are for permanent revolution. We will not stop halfway."[59] That month, conflict between the government and the Soviets erupted when a leaked memo revealed the government's intent to "pursue the war to a victorious conclusion."[60] According to William Rosenberg and Diane Koekner, "Direct action had toppled the Czarist regime, and the experience clearly taught Petrograd workers that the streets offered an opportunity to change governmental policies."[61] When the militant arm of the rightist Kadet Party fired on a crowd, killing several workers and injuring dozens, the recently formed Red Guards saw a surge in support. A Petrograd conference of Red Guards at the end of April consisted of ninety delegates representing 170,000 workers.[62]

The April Crisis was settled by an uneasy truce between the government and the Soviets, illuminated by a *BC Federationist* report:

> Advices from Petrograd indicate that the governmental crisis is over. A new cabinet has been formed and accepted by representatives of the Council of Workmen's and Soldiers' delegates. Six representatives of socialist groups are to sit in the cabinet and share in the government. One of them, A.F. Kerensky, is to assume the war portfolio.[63]

The labour paper reported on huge May Day demonstrations, "the marching of fully a million men and women in various parades in the city of Petrograd, on May 1st, under the red banner of International Labor, and singing the songs of liberty."[64] The same newspaper noted that the provisional government had "taken over the entire trade in grain and flour."[65] However, tension persisted. In June, a Petrograd conference of factory committees voted 73 percent in favour of Soviet power and 400,000 workers rallied behind this demand.[66] Economic hardship combined with discontent over a new Russian offensive on the Eastern Front. Bread, meat, and butter rations were cut by 15 percent, provoking the "July Days" demonstrations, in which Red Guardsmen and armed trucks led throngs of workers and soldiers through Petrograd's streets, and four hundred demonstrators were killed or wounded by government fire. Bolshevik Party headquarters were ransacked and party officials arrested, amid calls for a reinstatement of the death penalty.[67] Kerensky, who had been appointed minister of war in May, succeeded Lvov as the second prime minister of the provisional government. He appointed former czarist general Lavr Kornilov supreme commander of Russia's military, oversaw the evacuation of the Romanov family to Tobolsk, Siberia, and confirmed the final break between the moderate and radical arms of the working-class movement: "there can be no other economic order in Russia besides capitalism."[68]

As Russia lurched towards civil war, there were other ominous signs on the Allies' horizon. In May, following the Canadian victory at Vimy Ridge and the American declaration of war against Germany, fifty-four divisions (one-half of all units) in the French Army mutinied, with twenty thousand soldiers refusing orders to advance.[69] Betraying the fears of other Allied leaders, Borden warned: "If this war should end in defeat, Canada, in all years to come, would be under the shadow of German military domination."[70] The British War Cabinet was in regular communication with Russia's top military commander, Kornilov, who asked the Allies to ramp up pressure on the Western Front and proposed shooting troops to restore discipline on the Eastern Front. Several Allied diplomats and military envoys in Russia favoured such an approach. On the night of 17 August 1917, British general Alfred Knox met with Kornilov before leaving Petrograd for London.[71]

In September, desperate Russian leaders endorsed Kornilov's ill-fated coup. According to historian David Mandel, Kornilov and Kerensky allowed Riga to fall to the Germans in order to discredit Petrograd's Bolshevik-controlled Soviet and military garrison and to fuel the perception that the capital was vulnerable to attack. Loyal military units suppressed the Bolshevik press and occupied working-class districts, and, on 9 September 1917 (under a previous agreement with Kerensky), Kornilov disbanded the provisional government and placed Petrograd under military rule.[72] However, the general's reinforcements never reached the capital. Railway and telegraph workers disrupted lines of communication as trains and rail-lines were sabotaged. Kornilov's defeat paved the way for the Bolshevik victory.

November

Canada's daily and labour presses offered predictably divergent accounts of events in Russia in autumn 1917, prefiguring later scholarly debates. While the mainstream press equated revolution with anarchy, tyranny, and destruction, labour described it as a natural outgrowth of social conditions, "merely a change from the old to the new."[73] This disparity widened as the Bolshevik Party and Soviets gained strength. Outlying provinces had not seen the same upheavals as Petrograd; however, in October and November these areas experienced an unprecedented strike wave involving 1.5 million workers.[74] The struggle was no longer over wages or material conditions but, in Lenin's words, over who would control whom.[75] Isabel Tirado attributes the Bolsheviks' popularity "to the capacity of its leadership, particularly at the grassroots, to articulate and champion the demands of the radicalized sectors of the working class."[76] By November, thirty-four thousand Petrograd workers belonged to the Red Guards and, at a historic meeting chaired by Trotsky, pledged loyalty to the Soviet. A military revolutionary committee was established, under Trotsky's command, proclaiming authority over the Petrograd garrison. The Kerensky government responded by summoning outside troops, suppressing the Bolshevik press, and raising bridges to the working-class districts in the capital, but the end was near.[77]

On 7 November 1917, the *Colonist* ran the story "Trouble Looms in Petrograd":

PETROGRAD. Nov. 6 – Negotiations between the general staff in the Petrograd district and the military revolution committee of the Council of Workmen's and Soldiers' Delegates ... has been broken off. The military committee, learning that the military governor during the night had summoned troops in the environs of the capital to Petrograd ordered these troops to disobey the Government. The city is now guarded by loyal troops. The situation is complicated by the action of Premier Kerensky in suspending three Maximalist [Bolshevik] and two Conservative newspapers.

The authorities tonight ordered a disconnection of bridges between the quarters of the city inhabited by the working classes and the centre of the capital ... At this afternoon's preliminary session of the preliminary parliament Premier Kerensky, referring to the Maximalist attempt to seize power and provoke civil war, said amid applause from the right, centre and part of the left: "The people who dare

to raise their hands against the will of the Russian people are at the same time
· threatening to open the front to Germany."[78]

The following day, the *Colonist* reported on "Another Russian Crisis":

Premier Kerensky has at last awakened to the realization that the organization
known as the Soldiers' and Workmen's Council is subversive of law and order in
the country. It is questionable if the repressive measures he has undertaken have
come in time. Already a Maximalist revolt is beginning to take shape. Kronstadt
apparently is siding with M. [sic] Lenine[79] for a naval guard has taken forcible
possession of offices of the official Petrograd Telegraph Agency. This step would
be preliminary to preventing any news of what is happening going beyond Petrograd. It is apparent from the occurrences of the past few days, that the Russian
capital is once more the scene of an uprising against existing authority, though
how far the disaffection goes cannot be estimated.

If the time has not been reached now, its coming is inevitable when the Provisional
Government will have to get to grips with the Soviet, and between them they will
have to decide which is to have sovereignty in the country ... By virtue of the
Revolution Russia has recast her ideas on the war and has practically admitted
that the Declarations regarding peace, signed by Great Britain, France, Italy, Japan
and herself, is no better than a scrap of paper. The other nations of the Entente
must regard Russia's actions from the viewpoint of international honour. When
the honour of an Ally is besmirched faith in that Ally must waver and break.[80]

Russia had become an ambivalent ally of Canada. As the *Colonist* lamented: "If
General Korniloff's revolt had been successful it is probable conditions would
have been vastly different today. But General Korniloff's failure has given M.
Lenine and his Bolshevik following their second chance."[81]

On 7 November, Red Guardsmen under the direction of the Petrograd Soviet's
Military Revolutionary Committee wrested control of the Russian capital from
the Kerensky government. Bridges spanning the Neva River and Nevsky Prospekt
– the city's main thoroughfare – were seized from government troops, along
with key buildings (such as the telegraph). As evening fell, the naval cruiser
Aurora was unmoored from the Nikolai Bridge and sailed within range of the
Winter Palace, where the provisional government ministers had holed up. The
Soviet issued an ultimatum demanding their surrender and, after a twenty-
minute grace period, laid siege to the imperial landmark. Armed cars pulled in
front of the palace gates as cannon from the *Aurora* and the St. Peter and St.

Paul Fortress pummelled the palace from across the Neva. After four hours of fighting, during which the elite Women's Battalion of Death made a last stand against Bolshevism, the ministers surrendered. Kerensky fled the capital. The Soviet ruled Petrograd.[82]

The revolt coincided with the opening of the All-Russian Congress of Soviets, where 560 delegates converged on Petrograd. According to the *Colonist*, 250 were Bolshevik, 150 were Socialist Revolutionary (a peasant-based party), 60 were Menshevik, 14 were Menshevik-Internationalist, 6 were National-Socialist, 3 were non-party socialist, and the remainder were independent. A Menshevik resolution to negotiate with the provisional government was defeated. Delegates elected a twenty-one-member executive, consisting of fourteen Bolsheviks, including Lenin and Trotsky, and seven Socialist Revolutionaries. The Military Revolutionary Committee issued a proclamation outlining the program of the new authority:

> First, the offer of an immediate democratic peace; Second, the immediate handing over of all large proprietorial lands to the peasants; Third, the transference of all authority to the Council of Soldiers' and Workmen's Delegates; Fourth, the honest convocation of a constituent assembly.[83]

The proclamation included a message for the front, instructing "the revolutionary soldiers to watch the conduct of the men in command. Officers who do not join the accomplished revolution immediately and openly must be arrested at once as enemies." Troops were instructed to prevent "uncertain military detachments" from leaving the front for Petrograd "by force without mercy." Any attempt to prevent the proclamation being read to rank-and-file troops constituted "a great crime against the revolution, and [would] be punished by all the strength of the revolutionary law." The proclamation ended simply: "Soldiers: For the peace, for bread, for land and for the power of the people."[84]

Russia had severed ties with the old regime and had lurched towards an untested model of political, economic, and military power. Back in Victoria, the press reacted harshly. Under the headline "M. Lenine's Coup D'Etat," the *Colonist* called the Bolsheviks "the enthronement of anarchy at Petrograd" and declared:

> The new authority in Petrograd, which has secured power by a coup d'etat, cannot last, because it is the centralized force of all the disruption which has brought Russia to her present pass. No government among the Allied Powers will recognize the sovereignty of M. Lenine and his followers ...

The latest developments are the most sinister for the Allies since the outbreak of the war. The Leninites are going to enter into negotiations with all the Powers for an armistice. That means they will have pourparlers with the enemy alone, for none of the Allies will recognize their authority ... If the army, as it appears, is supporting the Extremists of Petrograd, Germany can withdraw a score or two score more divisions from her Eastern front and use them as she thinks best. For the time being Russia has ceased to be a factor in the war ... *dues live up to — not a contract -*

Since the certainty exists that the Leninites will repudiate all the obligations of their predecessors in office, the Allies have no longer any guarantees for the loans they have made to Russia. Presumably no further aid will be given. In the event of Russia concluding a separate peace with the enemy, the Allies will have to decide jointly on what their course of action will be. If Russia becomes an active friend of Germany and supplies her with foodstuffs and munitions, some drastic measures will have to be adopted.[85]

Russia was now, for all intents and purposes, an enemy of Canada, on a trajectory towards abandoning its military obligations and repudiating $13 billion rubles in war loans owed to Britain and France. The stage was set for intervention.

British Columbia Workers and the Russian Revolution

For a population weary of compulsory military service and desperate for economic improvement, Bolshevism emerged as a potent alternative to militarism and exploitation. A growing layer of Canadian workers was drawn to the radical tactics of its Russian counterparts, while businesspeople and politicians identified with White Russian forces and sought to quash what they considered to be Canadian incarnations of Bolshevism. "There is not and never was a matter ... which had evoked as much interest among the workers as the situation in Russia is doing at this present moment," declared Joe Taylor, a socialist longshoreman from Victoria and vice-president of the BCFL.[86] Labour unrest in Canada was increasingly viewed – by both workers and the elite – through the lens of the Russian Revolution. These allegiances shaped Canadian responses to the Siberian Expedition and prefigured the contours of the labour upheavals of 1919.[87]

The overthrow of czarism in March 1917 had provoked discussion among BC workers regarding how far the revolution would go – a question that mirrored debates in Russia and struck at the root of Marxist theories of history and the role of the working class as an agent of social change. A week after the czar abdicated the throne, the *BC Federationist* equated the March Revolution with the French Revolution of 1789:

BCFL = British Columbia Federation of Labour.

the Russian revolution marks the downfall of autocracy, and the uprise of the bourgeoisie, the capitalist class, to power... [T]he workers have been used to bring this about, but even so it is distinctly a working class victory in the sense that the triumph of the bourgeoisie over autocracy is but a prelude to the eventual triumph of the working class over its master and exploiter, the capitalist class.[88]

Another article asked: "Were the Russian Revolutionists fighting merely for the privilege of exchanging tyrants? Have they overthrown the Romanoffs for the purpose of putting the Russian Rockefellers and Morgans on their necks?"[89] From the outset, a layer of British Columbia workers believed the March Revolution was "but a prelude" to a more overtly proletarian revolution, anticipating the upheaval of November 1917.

Russian workers were emerging as the vanguard of an international working-class movement, which was distinguished by national variations but shared common responses to wartime privation. "All hail to the Russian people," the *BC Federationist* declared: "They have indeed set the world an example in patriotism that may well be followed by the people of other lands who may be in any manner threatened by the forces of reaction and tyranny." Such "sinister influences" proliferated during wartime, with the common people "called upon to forego their privileges and surrender their liberties in order that the war may be successfully carried on." Liberties that were lost would never be regained without a fight: "When ruling classes want war, then is the time for those over whom their rule is exercised to demand and take, if possible, whatever extension of their liberties they may deem advisable. Either that or refuse to shed any blood." The Russian Revolution was held up as a model to be emulated, a roadmap for peace: "If the German people would but follow the lead of the Russians ... peace would return to Europe forthwith.[90] BC workers were cognizant of the prospect of counter-revolution in Russia. "Let it be hoped that the forces of reaction in Russia will be unable to nullify the gains of the liberty-loving Russian people by means of any counter-revolution," the *BC Federationist* opined. Anticipating the bloody civil war, the newspaper sanctioned the slaughter of reactionary forces: "may all that has been gained be held, even though it necessitates the lopping off of the heads of all the bureaucrats and reactionaries in Russia."[91] While the revolution had been achieved with "very little bloodshed," sections of Canadian workers favoured the spilling of blood to defend its gains.

In spring 1917, as the struggle intensified between the Russian Soviets and the provisional government and the Allies grappled with the French army mutinies and heavy losses on the Western Front, the tensions between Canadian workers and the state intensified. In April, the BCFL released a "Labor Programme" for the Dominion, which included a radically democratic view of military organization that bore parallels to reforms being implemented by rank-and-file Russian troops on the faltering Eastern Front: "No distinction should be made between officers and men, either in pay or pensions."[92] International Labour Day, 1 May 1917, was celebrated from the coal mines of Vancouver Island to the streets of Petrograd and Vladivostok, demonstrating bonds of solidarity that transcended national borders. In South Wellington, near Nanaimo, coal miners downed tools in a one-day strike that paralyzed the operations of Canadian Collieries Ltd. "I will always look back on that day with joy, as one of the days when the workers made a demonstration of the power that they possess, but never, as a class, use," reflected miners' leader Walter Head.[93] In Petrograd, huge May Day celebrations clogged Nevsky Prospekt: "To the tottering thrones and the trembling capitalists of the world, the marching of fully a million men and women in various parades in the city of Petrograd, on May 1st, under the red banner of International Labor, and singing the songs of liberty, could not have been a pleasing and inspiring spectacle."[94] The *BC Federationist*'s banner headline proclaimed: "The Oncoming Tread of the Proletariat Is Now Heard – Increasing Labor Unrest Presages the Collapse of Capitalism."[95]

BC workers closely followed developments in Russia over the course of 1917, contrasting bold social policies with enduring inequality in Canada. When the provisional government nationalized the trade of grain, eliminating "the graft of the speculator," the *BC Federationist* lamented: "The 'graft of the speculator' has not even been threatened here in Canada as yet. He is still perfectly safe to go the limit. The people of Canada are too highly civilized to cut off profit gambling."[96] When the April Crisis forced the shuffling of the provisional government cabinet, with six socialist ministers and Kerensky's promotion to minister of war, the *BC Federationist* celebrated "the advanced intelligence of the Russian working class" with "the heavy representation of the socialist movement in the government":

In no other country in the world can a similar representation be found. It is a distinct challenge to the intelligence of the workers in those countries that have long boasted of democracy and freedom, and whose labor movements have professed to constitute the vanguard of human progress. It is now up to the Russian working class to send cablegrams of cheer and wise counsel to the labor movement of Canada, the United States and other backward lands.[97]

Responding to political tensions in Sweden, the *BC Federationist* postulated that the Russian Revolution had provided "foes of present-day society" with "a territorial focus, a base of operations," anticipating a "wave of syndicalist unrest":

Sweden, Russia's neighbour, is caught first by the revolutionary ground-swell. It is not against this or that political abuse that the Swedish Social-Democrats are raising their heads; it is against the whole fabric of modern society, whose basis is both Sweden's and ours. Russia and Sweden lie geographically far away, but in the more ethereal realm of thought and emotion they may stand closer than we dream. The Russian revolution may be the beginning of great and terrible things. We would do well to prepare against a coming storm.[98]

This prophetic statement foreshadowed the horror of Russia's civil war as well as the industrial strife that paralyzed Canadian cities from Victoria to Winnipeg to Amherst at war's end.

In June 1917, the Military Service Act was introduced in the Canadian Parliament, authorizing compulsory military service and provoking rioting in Quebec.[99] At a protest meeting organized by the Social Democratic Party (an organization that would be deemed "unlawful" in 1918), Victoria workers unanimously endorsed a resolution for a national referendum on conscription. Local labour council delegates also endorsed the conduct of longshoreman Joe Taylor, whose anti-conscription stance had inflamed a Montreal conference intended to drum up support for Borden's war policies.[100] The BCFL conducted its own referendum, polling affiliated workers on whether they favoured a general strike against conscription.[101] At a meeting in Vancouver's Empress Theatre, socialist William Pritchard (who would be jailed for sedition during the Winnipeg General Strike) told a working-class crowd that war was caused by "the desire of capitalists to place their extra wealth in countries where capital has not yet penetrated." He offered a home-grown theory of imperialism to match the views expounded by Lenin from the balcony of Petrograd's Kshesinskaya Mansion and invoked the memory of the Paris Commune of 1871, which saw thirty thousand French workers slaughtered defending an ephemeral workers' republic: "If proletarian Russia becomes strong enough to constitute a menace to militarism, the latter would immediately lay itself out to wipe out that proletariat, as happened in France in the bygone days." As Pritchard reminded his audience: "The army serves not only to act against foreign powers, but has a domestic duty to fulfill. When the police fail the army must be active at times of great strikes, when free labor must be protected. There is a call to war, and to this war the Socialist Party of Canada calls you all, for it is a war for the wiping out of all conditions which make war possible, a war against those who fatten and batten on the bodies of the workers."[102]

Wartime conditions fuelled social strife across the industrialized world, energizing local movements that increasingly looked to Russia as a symbol of peace and working-class emancipation. In August 1917, ten thousand British workers packed a huge mass meeting at Albert Hall, London, and "gave hearty greetings to the Russian revolutionists."[103] In Japan, eight hundred kilometres from Vladivostok, a conference of socialists hailed "the Russian revolution as the beginning of a series of revolutions which [would] end in the downfall of capitalism." A resolution called on the "proletariat of the belligerent countries" to "turn the guns ... at once on the ruling classes of their own respective countries. This is the responsibility of Russian socialists as well as international socialists."[104] From Vancouver, the BC *Federationist* offered a similar view: "Plainly the peoples of the world must take the affairs of the world out of the hands of the kaisers ... and see whether with these greedy profit-mongers out of the way, the world cannot have permanent peace. And this is what the Russian revolutionists are just now asking themselves and the world."[105]

Bolshevism gained strength in Russia as conscription amplified tensions between Canadian workers and the state. George Stirling, a socialist from Salmon Arm, British Columbia, and newly appointed Dominion organizer of the Social Democratic Party, linked the fight against conscription with developments in Russia:

Our comrades in Russia have made a stand against imperialism; against the machinations of politicians; against the greed of ambitious potentates; and the heartless profiteering of capitalists. In Italy and France and Great Britain, the power of the Social Democracy is growing so rapidly that its bitterest foes are now mouthing phrases about Liberty and Democracy. In Canada our forces have been disorganized since the outbreak of the war, with the result that our rulers have passed the iniquitous conscription measure in flagrant contempt of the wishes of the majority ... Organization is imperative.[106]

This spirit imbued a special convention of the BCFL, which met in Vancouver over Labour Day weekend in September 1917, to devise means for opposing the Military Service Act. Affiliated workers had voted by a wide margin in favour of a "down tools" policy, empowering the BCFL's executive to call a general strike against conscription. Of 2,417 ballots cast, 1,841 favoured a strike, with only 576 opposed. The labour convention ratified this policy, empowering the executive to call a strike when the first unwilling conscript was forced into service.[107] Labour's only position, longshoreman Jack Kavanagh said, was to say to the master class, "If you touch a man of us, we will touch your industries."[108]

Albert "Ginger" Goodwin, the BCFL's vice-president from the West Kootenays and business manager of the smelterworkers' union in the town of Trail, attended the convention and described the war and conscription in class terms, declaring that "conscription meant life or death to the workers." He pledged to "do all in his power to prove to the workers that the war was none of their business." Goodwin believed that "there was a great force of opinion against conscription, and [that] the idea of striking and otherwise opposing it was not confined to Quebec by a long shot."[109] By November 1917, on the eve of the Bolshevik insurrection, Goodwin wrote a pointed letter to the *BC Federationist*, in which he hoped that capitalism would "fang itself to death":

> What is to become of the present capitalist system of production and distribution? There are signs on the horizon that portend of basic and fundamental changes in the future. Just at what time this is to be, there is no telling, but if the circumstances to which the master class are resorting to are considered it seems as if the end is in sight … War is simply a part of the process of capitalism … Whether the capitalist system can survive this cataclysm remains to be seen. It is the hope of the writer that capitalism will fang itself to death, and out of its carcass spring the life of the new age with its blossoms of economic freedom, happiness and joy for the world's workers.[110]

The change occurred far sooner than Goodwin imagined, as the Bolsheviks seized power in Petrograd before the next issue of the newspaper went to press.

Demonstrating the domestic conditions driving working-class unrest in Canada, fifteen hundred Trail smelterworkers, led by Ginger Goodwin, went on strike on 15 November 1917 against the Consolidated Mining and Smelting Company, a CPR subsidiary, demanding the eight-hour workday and union recognition.[111] The smelter produced twenty to fifty tonnes of zinc per day for the Imperial Munitions Board, an essential ingredient for Allied munitions bound for the Western Front.[112] Goodwin's message from Trail was brief and to the point: "Strike on at Trail. Advise all men to keep away."[113] The strike disrupted "practically all mines" in the Kootenays, but the company and the state had powerful tools to undermine the smelterworkers' union. Consolidated Mining and Smelting Company manager Selwyn Blaylock exercised influence with the local judiciary to remove Goodwin from the picture. The union leader was recalled before the local Exemptions Board and classified "fit for military service," despite a chronic lung condition. The smelterworkers' strike weakened and was called off after five weeks. Goodwin first fled to Vancouver, then to the wooded hills of Vancouver Island.[114]

Throughout autumn 1917, the breach between radical sections of British Columbia's working class and the Canadian elite widened, as grievances against conscription, profiteering, and the hoarding of foodstuffs mounted. At a meeting of the Vancouver Trades and Labor Council, socialist Helena Gutteridge, leader of the garment workers' union, reported: "The cold storage plants were groaning with piled-up food ... One concern on Water Street has so much butter in storage it was necessary to brace the floors to hold it." Delegates called on Canada's food controller to order the release of food "so there would be enough to eat."[115] In line with a decision at the special September convention, the BCFL fielded eight labour candidates against Borden's Unionist ticket in the Dominion election of December 1917, which was triggered by the prime minister's dissolution of the six-year Parliament.[116] The "Conscription Election," which returned Borden by a wide majority against Laurier's anti-conscription Liberals, confirmed the Military Service Act while revealing schisms in political alignments. The campaign was notable for the selective extension of the franchise to women. The wives, mothers, and sisters of soldiers – those believed most likely to favour Borden's policies – were granted the vote.[117] The BC labour candidates, meanwhile, ran on the pledge "to abolish profit-making."[118] However, the thirty labour candidates across Canada received a paltry 8 percent of the vote in the seats they contested, mirroring the result in British Columbia; Borden's Unionist candidates took all thirteen BC seats.[119] During the campaign, a *BC Federationist* correspondent identified as "A. Rebel" urged support for working-class candidates and linked the election to the political upheaval in Russia: "You can be on one side or the other, there is no room between ... The other side has but to follow the destiny of the Romanoffs, Siberia, and receive a taste of their own philosophy."[120]

The year 1917 closed as BC socialists gravitated towards the Bolsheviks and the Canadian elite grew hostile. "There is no other sign post upon the social horizon pointing the way to peace than the movement which is now typified in the Russian Bolsheviki," the *Federationist* opined: "Well may rulers and robbers hail its advent with terrified squawks and bourgeois souls quake with terror at its probable triumph. For with that triumph their game of loot and plunder will end."[121] A month later, the labour newspaper serialized Lenin's essay *Political Parties in Russia* (a tract banned by the Canadian state six months later).[122] Joseph Naylor, a Cumberland coal miner, friend of Ginger Goodwin, and president of the BCFL, claimed that "clear-thinking socialists [had] all along been convinced that Kerensky was only a tool of ... financial interests" and that the overthrow of the czar had been intended "to oust an autocracy and enshrine a capitalist plutocracy, such as we so loyally uphold here in Canada." Naylor urged Canadian workers to "take action similar to that of the Russian Bolsheviki and dispose of their masters as those brave Russians [were then] doing."[123]

Sympathy for Bolshevism was not confined to manual workers. Dr. W.J. Curry, a Vancouver dentist, ridiculed the contortions of British Columbia's "kept" press:

Our kept press hates and fears the turn the revolution of Russia is now taking ... Well, we remember when Nicholas, "our gallant ally," entered the ring with John Bull and France, to avenge martyred Belgium and crush the brutal Huns ... Then suddenly, the rotten old aristocracy fell to pieces and the duma was no more. But it was days after this greatest of social miracles that our press reluctantly recorded the fact ... Kerensky was now the heaven-sent saviour of Russian democracy.

But alas! News came of the regiments deserting to go home, and of peasants firing their landlords and actually taking possession of the land they worked, of industrial workers seizing mills and factories and producing for use instead of dividends for social parasites. This was the last straw. This violated the "sacred rights of property" and if lauded and tolerated in Russia, the workers some day might turn the same trick in Canada or with the great landowners of Britain and the Land of the Free. So the mental guardians of plutocracy grasped at Korniloff ... But alas, Korniloff soon stumbled and fell down and even a move to bring law and order once more to Russia by replacing Nick or placing his uncle upon the throne was hailed with inward satisfaction by our press since anything is better than social democracy and the rule of the common people.

The worst has now happened for Russia ... The extreme rebels, those who would actually conscript land and all social property, and who have abolished titles, are on top and apparently there to stay.[124]

Dr. Curry concluded that Canada's political and financial rulers were "profit-mad and war-mad" and belonged to the "same class" as Russia's deposed elite: "The time has come for the common people of Canada and elsewhere to unite for the purpose of doing to their rulers what the workers of Russia did to theirs – fire them off their backs and establish a real democracy."[125]

Radicalization in British Columbia's working class coincided with renewed attention on independent political action. On the heals of the federal "conscription election," coal miners in Newcastle, near Nanaimo, elected James H. Hawthornthwaite in a provincial by-election in January 1918, while Mary Ellen Smith, a Liberal running as an independent in Vancouver, was elected as the province's first woman legislator.[126] During the campaign, Hawthornthwaite, a prominent socialist politician prior to the war, discussed the "striking beneficial results" of the war in Europe: "Russia has, in a carnival of destruction, got rid of the Romanoff autocracy that for generations foully oppressed the working people of that country."[127] On polling day, Hawthornthwaite defeated his Liberal opponent by a two-to-one margin. "The Bolsheviki triumphs!" proclaimed the *Federationist*.[128] While Hawthornthwaite later broke from radical labour and condemned the Bolsheviks, he initially celebrated the social changes unfolding in Russia.[129]

Two weeks after Hawthornthwaite's victory, delegates at the BCFL's annual convention voted to form a new political party, the Federated Labor Party of British Columbia (FLP), to "secure industrial legislation for the collective ownership and democratic operation of the means of wealth production."[130] At the party's inaugural meeting, held in the Vancouver Labor Temple on 23 February 1918, Hawthornthwaite declared: "We can abolish capitalism by special acts in the province of British Columbia, in Canada, or any part of the British empire." He predicted:

> The day is coming when class rule shall no longer prevail ... when the downfall of capitalism is at hand. The workers the world over are aroused and thinking. They are looking over the world and thinking what is in this war for them, nothing but misery, hunger, want and degradation. But they intend to have no more of that. Listen to the tramp of the revolutionary workers of the world marching to the front. Yes, marching on to war, and marching on to victory, victory for their class.[131]

As FLP branches sprouted around the province, Hawthornthwaite elaborated on the party's socialization objective, lauding the Zapatista movement in Mexico and insisting that, in British Columbia, "we can take over the mills, mines and factories; by paying for them, if necessary, and then operat[ing] them for the common good and giv[ing] to each the product of his or her toil."[132] He warned South Wellington miners of an Allied plot against the Russian workers' republic:

> The capitalist press in this country is out-lying each other in vilifying the Bolsheviki, but we cannot believe one word we read. A close observer is forced to the conclusion that the Allies are standing by to allow the Germans to overwhelm Russia and steal from them the fruits of the revolution. The Allies have a majority of three to two in men and two to one in guns and ammunition and yet they do not start the spring offensive, which has been so well advertised and which started much earlier last year. The Russians have large stores of supplies in Vladivostok and Petervolosky, which to all appearances the Japs are about to cut off. So we are forced to the conclusion that the Allies are liberating the Germans on the western front, and allowing them to devastate the Russian workers' republic.[133]

The events of 1917 catapulted the Bolsheviks into the leadership of an international working-class movement. However murky the details, a layer of BC workers viewed the insurrection of November 1917 as a successful challenge to the twofold scourges of war and capitalism. They drew inspiration from the agency of Russian workers, navigating between the half-truths and distortions of the censored mainstream press. Domestic class relations shaped BC workers' attitudes towards the Russian Revolution in a reciprocal relationship that saw workers (and the elite) view Canadian conditions through a Russian lens. Fearing domestic radicalism, Prime Minister Robert Borden appointed his friend C.H. Cahan, a Montreal lawyer and financier, to investigate the proliferation of Bolshevism in Canada (Cahan's clients included the Canadian Car Company, which had filled munitions contracts for the czar's government).[134] Meanwhile, the prime minister entered into high-level talks that resulted in the deployment of Canadian troops to Vladivostok.

Vladivostok: 1917

NESTLED ON THE HILLY shores of Golden Horn Bay, on a peninsula in the Sea of Japan, a scant fifty kilometres from China and 120 kilometres from North Korea, the port of Vladivostok – Russian for "Ruler of the East" – has been a gateway to the Pacific since the nineteenth century, a focal point of competing imperial claims.[1] The city is a strategically important place, the terminus of the world's longest railroad. During the 1905 revolution, a mutiny of sailors and soldiers in Vladivostok, combined with a railworkers' strike, spiralled into the wholesale rejection of czarist authority in eastern Siberia and the Russian Far East. After the 1917 revolution, the city was the beachhead of Western intervention in Russia's civil war. From 1948 until the fall of communism in 1991, the Soviet Union declared it a "closed city," guarding its nuclear submarine fleet and restricting access to Russians and foreigners alike. Today, Vladivostok is a magnet for foreign investment, afflicted with all the ills of "cowboy capitalism" and major ecological and social strains.[2] Geopolitics shaped Vladivostok's history as rival powers sought access to and from Asia – and control of Far Eastern markets and resource wealth.

Imperialism in the Russian Far East before 1917

Between the seventeenth and nineteenth centuries, the area was ruled by China's Qing dynasty and occupied by the Jurchen and Manchu people. Russia looked north, to Okhotsk and the Kamchatka Peninsula, the departure points for Danish-born Vitus Bering and Russian navigators who plied the North American coast from Alaska to California. In the 1850s, Russia revived claims to the Sea of Japan, as Qing China decayed and French and British merchant ships probed Golden Horn Bay (then known by the Chinese name *Gamat*). The Russian governor of eastern Siberia, Nikolai Muraviev, secured the territory from China in the Treaty of Aigun, 1858, and landed with thirty-one settlers and two cannon in 1859, establishing a fortress that he called Vladivostok.[3] The military ship *Manchur* protected the outpost, which became a port in 1862 and was connected by telegraph to Shanghai and Nagasaki in 1871. From surrounding Asian ports and distant St. Petersburg and Odessa, settlers arrived by steamer to populate the hilly shores of Golden Horn Bay. Vladivostok became a city in 1880 and the capital of the new Primorsky Krai (Maritime Province).[4]

Treaty between Russian Empire and Qing dynasty that established borders.

In these early years, Vladivostok was oriented towards Asia, and, after the opening of the Trans-Siberian Railroad in 1903, European Russia. Railroad expansion was driven by the demand of Russian industry for raw materials and concern over Japan's growing commercial and military clout in the Far East. Construction began in 1891 at a Vladivostok ceremony at which Crown Prince Nicholas II (the future czar and chairman of the Siberian Railroad Committee) turned the inaugural shovel of soil.[5] Count Sergei Witte, finance minister and confidant to the czars, oversaw construction, which spanned 9,230 kilometres and seven time zones and cost the Russian state 1.45 billion rubles.[6] A deal with China cemented Russian influence in Manchuria, the territory south of the Transbaikal region that offered the shortest route from Moscow to Vladivostok. Though technically part of China, the Chinese Eastern Railway zone came under de facto Russian control (see Map 2).

Japan's victory in the first Sino-Japanese War (1894-95) had established it as the regional power, with naval supremacy over the Sea of Japan and control of the Korean peninsula; the country's industrialized economy and modern military (which included British- and French-built warships and an army organized along Prussian lines) clashed with Russian imperial designs. In 1904, the two countries went to war when Japan attacked Port Arthur, a warm-water Manchurian port that Russia leased from China.[7] The war exposed the defects of czarism as Japanese forces routed Russia's Far Eastern Fleet, defeated its Manchurian Army, and sunk thirty-three of thirty-eight ships in the Baltic Sea Fleet (rechristened the Second Pacific Squadron and deployed 29,000 kilometres around the Cape of Good Hope to re-establish a naval presence in the Far East). Port Arthur fell in January 1905 as revolution erupted in Russia. On Bloody Sunday, the czar's Cossack guards gunned down hundreds of demonstrators in St. Petersburg, and revolt spread through the hinterland.[8]

The Trans-Siberian Railroad was an epicentre of worker unrest during the 1905 revolution. As Henry Reichman observed, "East of Krasnoiarsk, Siberia experienced the most serious breakdown of authority, culminating in de facto seizures of power by revolutionaries in several cities and towns."[9] At the outbreak of hostilities with Japan, the railroad was "still a flimsily constructed, inadequate and accident-ridden experiment" capable of moving only thirteen trainloads of troops and supplies per day. Its infrastructure and administrative apparatus deteriorated the further one moved eastward, and though the eastern Siberian railworkers were better paid than their counterparts elsewhere in Russia, their estrangement from a regional middle class strengthened the appeal of radical socialist parties.[10] The Bloody Sunday massacre provoked strikes and demonstrations in Siberia and the Russian Far East, consolidating a stable network of Bolshevik railworkers "at every major depot" along the Siberian line.[11]

Throughout spring and summer 1905, the radicals gave direction to a growing general strike movement against czarism and for the eight-hour day. By November, when the czar announced a new reform-oriented constitution, "virtually all [rail] traffic and most official telegraph communication had come to a halt." The governor of eastern Siberia described the situation as "desperate."[12]

In this rebellious climate, sailors and soldiers in Vladivostok mutinied on 12 November 1905. The commanding officer in the city, General Kazbek, was beheaded and "nearly half the city was burned," according to the *New York Times*, including the Naval Club, the Girls Gymnasium, and the entire Chinese quarter. "The city and the port form a mass of smoldering ruins," reported the *International Herald Tribune:* "The women and children have taken refuge on board the steamers."[13] Dissent was concentrated among reserve troops, many from Harbin, China, who resented their delayed return to European Russia and drew inspiration from a mutiny of Kronstadt sailors days earlier. The military command responded rapidly and ruthlessly to the Vladivostok uprising, summoning one thousand Ussuri Cossacks to patrol the streets and quell disorder. Three hundred soldiers and sailors were killed or wounded in the first twenty-four hours, the *New York Times* reported. At sea, Russian prisoners-of-war (released by Japan and destined for Vladivostok aboard the steamers *Vladimir* and *Boronej*) seized control of the vessels until Japanese police intervened on behalf of Russian officers. Another ship, the naval cruiser *Lena*, approached Vladivostok but received a wireless message warning it to "keep away unless in sympathy with the people." While the crew was reportedly in "sympathy with the uprising," the captain chose to retreat to Honolulu.[14] News of the Vladivostok mutiny spread rapidly along the Trans-Siberian Railroad, provoking unrest among scores of demobilized units; locomotives were commandeered as mobs of troops ransacked train stations and railcars, particularly those of the upper classes. Striking railworkers at Krasnoyarsk began dispatching troop-trains back to Europe, without authorization from railroad officials or the military command. The unauthorized movements reached eleven trains per day and "cemented a practical alliance" between soldiers and workers.[15] "In effect, all 500,000 of the Manchurian reserves mutinied en masse and for two months," Bushnell wrote.[16] Railworkers' strike committees transformed into local Soviets, with special defence committees to guard against vigilante attacks. Armed workers and soldiers assumed de facto control of several Siberian cities and, in Krasnoyarsk and Chita, proclaimed "republics" independent of the czar. However, the rebellion was short-lived. Loyal military units were dispatched from Moscow in the west and Harbin in the east, executing hundreds of workers and soldiers without trial. Martial law was proclaimed as the Trans-Siberian Railroad fell under military control until 1908.[17]

[handwritten] Military Rule by Military Authorities over designated Regions on an emergency basis

Unrest continued to percolate in Vladivostok. On 23 January 1906, the one-year anniversary of Bloody Sunday, loyal government troops fired on a procession of workers, soldiers, and sailors, leaving thirty dead. Armed soldiers and sailors responded by storming the city's fortress and executing the commanding officer, General Selivanov. Order was restored four days later when a Cossack division entered Vladivostok from Manchuria, arresting two thousand mutineers, fifty of whom were executed.[18] A year later, in October 1907, another mutiny erupted in Vladivostok, this time among sailors aboard the Russian torpedo-boat destroyer *Sukurni*. Eye-witnesses, who landed in Victoria a month later, attributed the disturbance to the agitation of four women revolutionaries, while another report suggested the crew had been "incited by agitators, including some Jews."[19] The women apparently boarded the *Sukurni* and persuaded the crew to seize the officers and the ship, and then to sail for Japan. However, before leaving Golden Horn Bay, the rebels decided to turn their guns on Vladivostok. They hoisted the Red Flag and opened fire on the admiralty building and the fortifications guarding the harbour, along with four Russian warships. A shell fired from the city's fort hit the *Sukurni*'s engine room, prompting the rebels to run the ship ashore to prevent it from sinking. According to the *New York Times*, "the four girls who instigated the mutiny were killed" in the battle, along with military officers, some civilians hit by errant shells, and a number of rebel sailors. The surviving mutineers were arrested, as military authorities declared a state of siege and cracked down on Vladivostok's revolutionary movement. When the British steamer *Mary* departed on 21 October 1907, it was thronged with refugees fleeing for Japan.[20] Reflecting the broader current of unrest, seven revolutionists were hanged in St. Petersburg, including Ragozinnikova, a woman who shot Russia's director of prisons.[21]

Czarism reasserted its authority in the Russian Far East against the backdrop of growing commercial ties, as foreign capitalists sought to tap the region's markets and resource wealth. In 1900, an earlier Siberian Expedition had departed from North America for the Russian Far East. As Victoria's *Daily Colonist* reported at the time, San Francisco speculator George D. Roberts, backed by British and French capital and a Russian syndicate led by Colonel Vladimir Vonliariarsky, won a concession from the czar's government to mine gold along a 1,600-kilometre stretch of Russia's North Pacific coast. Roberts' "Siberian Expedition" ended in disarray, when dissension erupted between American and Russian crew members on the ship *Samoa*, en route to the Russian Far East from Nome, Alaska.[22] A second trip, in summer 1902, failed to generate the anticipated windfall.[23] However, such setbacks were overshadowed by growing commercial ties. The German-owned Kunst and Albers Company, founded in Vladivostok in 1864 and, as mentioned earlier, described by historian Robert

Murby as an enterprise akin "in scope of activities and importance" to the Hudson's Bay Company in Canada, emerged as eastern Russia's leading retailer-wholesaler prior to the First World War. Kunst and Albers benefited from a growing market for consumer goods, buoyed by 1,105,800 European Russians who migrated to Siberia and the Russian Far East in the decade between 1895 and 1904. All goods were of German origin, shipped through the parent house in Hamburg. With a network of branches across the Far East, and enterprises ranging from sawmills and a coal mine to the chief bunkering facility at Vladivostok, Kunst and Albers recorded sales of 150 million rubles in 1913.[24] It was, according to Canadian trade commissioner Constantin F. Just, "the greatest stronghold of German commercial influence in the Russian Far East and along the Eastern Asiatic Coast."[25]

Canada's trade in the region paled in comparison, but it grew during the war as the British Empire moved closer to its Russian ally, and German assets, such as Kunst and Albers, were ordered sold. In 1896, Canadian exports to Russia had totalled a meagre $16,000.[26] Early efforts to expand trade floundered in the face of strong German influence, Canadian ambivalence, and restrictions on foreign ownership. In 1901, the British Columbia Board of Trade had proposed an expansion of pan-Pacific exports, requesting that a Canadian trade commissioner be sent to Siberia.[27] Instead, the CPR sent its own representative, William Whyte, who travelled from St. Petersburg to Vladivostok in the summer of 1901, assessing the condition of the Trans-Siberian Railroad and "the probability of doing business with Siberia."[28] Canadian Pacific steamers made occasional trips to Vladivostok in subsequent years, but it was not until the outbreak of hostilities that Canadian trade with Russia saw rapid growth.

Canadian manufacturers, under the administration of the Imperial Munitions Board, began filling war contracts for the Russian government and seconded contracts from British firms.[29] Five steel submarines were built on Vancouver's Burrard Inlet in autumn 1915 (followed by six other boats built in Montreal) and were shipped in crates to Vladivostok for transport across Russia and service in the Baltic and Black seas.[30] A confidant of Robert Borden, Montreal lawyer and financier Charles Hazlitt Cahan (later appointed director of public safety to combat Bolshevism), wrote of "a war of unprecedented violence between rival financial and commercial interests."[31] As mentioned in Chapter 1, Cahan represented the Canadian Car and Foundry Company, which held munitions contracts for the czar's government. In 1916, two Canadian trade commissioners were posted to Russia – Constantin F. Just in Petrograd and L. Dana Wilgress in Omsk. A Russian consulate opened in Vancouver and a Russian purchasing mission was established in Canada, with Colonel Kovalev arriving in Ottawa days before the czar's fall to oversee "the purchase of war materials for Russia."[32]

Canadian exports to Russia rose from $1.4 million in 1914 to $4.9 million in
1916, making it the seventh largest market for Canadian goods. Submarines,
rifles, ammunition, saddles, railroad cars, and agricultural implements flowed
from Canadian factories to Vladivostok.[33]

These growing commercial ties coincided with the closing of the final gap
along the Trans-Siberian Railroad, over the Amur River near Khabarovsk, eight
hundred kilometres north of Vladivostok. Since 1903, all rail traffic between
Vladivostok and European Russia had followed the Chinese Eastern Railroad
through Manchuria, meeting the main Siberian line near Lake Baikal. The
Russian government resumed construction of the Amur Line in 1913, but the
project was halted when a German naval cruiser sank two of the massive steel
spans in the Indian Ocean en route from Warsaw to Vladivostok. New spans
were hastily manufactured in Canada and shipped to Russia. In October 1916,
the 2,590-metre-long Alekseyevsky Bridge (named after the crown prince)
opened. For the first time, the Pacific was linked to Moscow and Petrograd by
an all-Russian route, buffered from Japanese intrigue in Manchuria but simultaneously "a lightening rod for revolution."[34] Vladivostok's population surged,
from sixty-five thousand people in 1914 to about 170,000 by the time of the
Allied intervention. One-third of the city's population was Chinese, with a
large number of Koreans and Eastern Europeans.[35]

Vladivostok served as the transit point for the shipments of arms and other
war materials from North America to Russia as well as for gold moving in the
opposite direction to guarantee British and French loans.[36] One-quarter of
the Imperial Russian Gold Reserve, the largest holding of the precious metal in
the world, was shipped through Vladivostok to Vancouver in four shipments,
in December 1915, June 1916, November 1916, and February 1917, respectively. A
month prior to the czar's fall, 187 million rubles of Russian gold left the Far East
for the BC port aboard the SS *Hazel Dollar*.[37] It arrived in Vancouver in mid-
March, at which time an acute labour shortage impeded the unloading of cargo.
"The additional freight from the *Hazel Dollar* which is unloading a heavy
Vladivostok consignment at the Great Northern docks is proving a serious
incumbrance," the *Colonist* reported: "Handling firms are energetically scouring
the city for additional help."[38] The czar's gold reached Vancouver as the March
Revolution forced his abdication in Russia.

The Russian Revolution in Vladivostok

The Russian Far East was subject to the same political pressures as elsewhere
in Russia, but distance from the centre "caused delays in political events," historian Boris Mukhachev suggests.[39] It took two weeks for newspapers from Petrograd to reach Vladivostok, and telegraph reports lacked detail and were easily

suppressed. On 12 March 1917, the czar's governor general in the Priamur territory, Nikolay Lvovich Gondatti, banned the dissemination of information
regarding the political upheavals in the capital. Vague reports reached the Far
East from abroad, but detailed news was not forthcoming until the czar had
abdicated and the provisional government had taken power. The censorship
order was lifted on 16 March 1917 as Gondatti retreated to Khabarovsk. There
he was arrested by local revolutionaries.[40]

With the collapse of czarism, the revolutionary situation developed rapidly.
Factory owners, state bureaucrats, and high-ranking military officials gravitated
towards local committees for public safety, while workers, soldiers, sailors, and
peasants gravitated towards nascent Soviets. This process was uneven across
the Far East, foreshadowing later events, and the balance of power shifted between Menshevik, Bolshevik, and Socialist Revolutionary (SR) factions. The
March Revolution had "removed only the apex" of czarist authority: "Atamans,
army officers, and civil servants remained in their posts."[41] Aboriginal people
were ambivalent, John Stephan noted, while "most peasants, Cossacks, merchants,
teachers, workers, exiles, soldiers, and sailors welcomed the end of Romanov
rule ... Each Far Eastern constituency thought it saw the imminent fulfillment
of its own aspirations."[42] The *zemstvos*, village councils formed by affluent peasants in 1916, became organs of self-government with responsibility for policing,
health services, education, and pubic works. The urban middle class favoured
the strengthening of local dumas.[43]

In Vladivostok, parallel meetings of workers and businesspeople on 16 March
1917 inaugurated the Far Eastern equivalent of "dual power." A large meeting
of workers voted to form a local soviet, inviting all labour organizations and
military departments to send delegates. The first meeting of the Vladivostok
Soviet of Workers', Soldiers', and Sailors' Deputies convened the following day,
electing a Bolshevik soldier, S.M. Goldbreikh, as chairman of its executive committee. Order No. 1 of the Soviet set its first priority as democratization of the
armed forces. Konstantin Sukhanov, a twenty-three-year-old student with strong
ties to organized labour and past experience with the Petrograd Bolsheviks, was
elected chairman of the Vladivostok Soviet's Workers' Commission. Just prior
to the March Revolution, Sukhanov, the son of a former czarist official, had
been released from prison, where he had been sent for distributing anti-war
propaganda among Vladivostok port workers.[44] The Soviet began to sink roots
in the city, organizing a commission on port security and assistance for released
political prisoners. As the representative body of wide sections of Vladivostok
workers and soldiers, the Soviet was a powerful force that could not be ignored
by the local elite. Concurrently, delegates of the Vladivostok City Duma held

their own emergency meeting on 16 March, at which they decided to form a committee for public safety, with representatives from commercial, industrial, financial, and military sectors. The committee grew to several hundred members in a matter of days.[45]

As czarist authority disintegrated in the Russian Far East, the provisional government struggled to maintain a semblance of central power. It appointed the chairman of the Vladivostok Committee of Public Safety, I.A. Yushenkov, as commissar of Primorsky Krai, with the mandate of military governor. However, the more radical Khabarovsk Committee of Public Safety warned that its Vladivostok counterpart was assuming "a dangerous counter-revolutionary character" and was seeking to usurp power.[46] Under pressure from the local Soviet, the Vladivostok committee reorganized, with ten delegates from the City Duma, twenty-five Soviet delegates, and twenty-five delegates from social organizations. The czarist-era gendarmes were disarmed and disbanded and replaced with a security force responsible to the reformed committee. A Menshevik, F.E. Manaev, was elected head of the new Primorsky Committee of Public Safety. In May, the provisional government vested its authority in a People's Commissariat of the Far East, based in Khabarovsk.[47] Continuity with the old regime was apparent, however, when the provisional government appointed General Dmitri Horvath, director of the Chinese Eastern Railway, as its commissar in the Russian-controlled railway zone. While Bolsheviks and other revolutionaries vigorously challenged Horvath, the general – "a very cautious and diplomatic old gentleman" who was "accustomed to being the recipient of large political favors from the old regime" – enjoyed support among Russian and Chinese property owners and Allied consular representatives in Harbin.[48]

The provisional government in Petrograd sought to assure Allied governments and investors that the Russian Far East and Siberia were open for business. It lifted controls on foreign ownership of land and property and, in May 1917, passed an order-in-council mandating the sale of the Kunst and Albers Company (because it was German-owned), making it clear that Allied nationals were welcome to purchase the firm's vast assets and operations.[49] "This revolution is conservative," declared Baron Alphonse Heyking, the provisional government's consul general in Britain, in June 1917, elaborating on investment opportunities in eastern Russia:

In Siberia, which as yet has hardly been developed at all, she possesses the granary of the world ... There is no mineral wealth which is not to be found there, and the conditions for carrying on industry are there also ... We have been kept out of the capitalist system, but I do not see how we can avoid it any longer ... We are a rich country but we are short of capital ... Let capitalism come in; it will develop quickly.[50]

In summer 1917, the CPR sent Vice-President George Bury and William Winterrowd to Russia to pursue commercial ties. Another Canadian, Harvard-trained geologist James Mackintosh Bell, who enlisted in the CEF and served in Russia as an intelligence officer with the British Military Mission, travelled from Petrograd to Vladivostok in July 1917, describing the commercial ventures of sundry businesspeople aboard the Trans-Siberian Railroad: "Some had obtained concessions from the new Government for exclusive rights to trade in furs, or prospect for gold in remote islands of the Sea of Okhotsk, others ... aspired to obtain possession of enemy holdings in the Far East which had been appropriated though not sold by the late Government."[51] The sale of Kunst and Albers presented "a wonderful chance for Canada," Mackintosh Bell informed Borden.[52] However, in July 1917, the Provisional Government cancelled an order with the British Pacific Construction and Engineering Company for submarines from Vancouver.[53] Growing radicalization in Russia disrupted commercial ties and undermined efforts to develop the Siberian and Far Eastern economies along capitalist lines.

When the ice broke on the Sea of Japan in spring 1917, a flood of Russian radicals returned to Vladivostok from exile in Canada, the United States, and other countries. More than eight hundred political émigrés landed at the port in May and June 1917.[54] Allied and Russian officials took steps to stem this migration. In June, the British consul at Pittsburgh, in the United States, advised Canada's minister of militia and defence that "a party of Russian anarchists left Pittsburgh ... for Russia via Vancouver taking with them as personal baggage a large quantity of anarchist literature and other propaganda which they plan to disseminate upon their arrival in Russia. They also have a small printing press." When the Russians, numbering forty-six women and men, reached the Canadian Pacific Steamship offices at the port of Vancouver on 21 June 1917, they were searched and detained. The Russians fought their way past CPR police and, following the intervention of the Russian consul in the city, were permitted to board the *Empress of Japan*. However, during a stop at Victoria, the CPR officials surreptitiously removed the crates of offensive literature and equipment, hidden in bags of sugar and laundry - a plan hatched by the chief commissioner of the Dominion Police. The Russians proceeded across the Pacific, faced further questioning in Yokohama (at the instigation of the Canadians), and eventually reached Vladivostok. Around this time, the parcel post service between Vancouver and Russia was discontinued amid reports of "small parties" of Russians crossing the American border into Canada by car to board CPR ships. Despite

such episodes (and the earlier internment of Leon Trotsky), Canada's super-
intendent of immigration did not anticipate "any strong movement of Bolsheviks from Canadian ports."[55]

At the mouth of Golden Horn Bay, a Russian patrol boat guarded the harbour,
boarding trans-Pacific ships to inspect the passports of the returning émigrés.
Canadian intelligence officer James Mackintosh Bell, who worked as the Allied
passport control officer aboard the patrol, recalls the "mixed feelings of rage
and admiration" that greeted the passengers, "not infrequently to the accompaniment of a fierce revolutionary song, which fairly rocked the little craft as
it ambled across the harbour."[56] The mood in Vladivostok in 1917 is conveyed
in a poem by N.P. Matveev, written in the wake of the March Revolution and
entitled "To the Fighters for the Motherland":

Brothers, let's build a cathedral
To the forces that coalesce to freedom
Eternal memory to our perished comrades
Eternal memory to those who still live
Terrible years are gone, forever
And the sun of freedom
Shines above our motherland.[57]

Alongside political radicalization, the end of czarism produced an outpouring
of cultural activity and creative energy. Diverse youth organizations sprouted,
such as the Union of Students, the Youth Union, the Self-Education Circle, and
the Children's Society. Many youth organizations published their own journals,
such as *Mysli Uchachshikhsya* (*Thoughts of Students*) in Khabarovsk and *Edinenie*
(*Unification*) in the city of Blagoveshchensk.[58]

Trade unions also flourished in the wake of the czar's fall. By April, there were
thirty unions operating in Vladivostok, including the powerful Machinist and
Shipyard Workers, with five thousand members; the Temporary Car Assembly
Workers, with six thousand members; and the Port and Construction Workers,
with four thousand members. Vladivostok woodworkers and machinists waged
successful strikes for increases in pay, paralyzing operations at the Kunst and
Albers Company, the Vasiliev furniture factory, the Skidelski plywood plant, the
Piankov shops, and other establishments in the city. Transportation workers,
meanwhile, forced a settlement with local employers that included a pay scale
based on the weight and type of cargo and a ban on overtime work without the
consent of the workers' committee. The Temporary Car Assembly Workers
began firing supervisors, replacing them with the most popular workers in the
shops. In April 1917, the Central Bureau of Vladivostok Trade Unions was formed,

headed by Bolshevik S.Y. Grosman. Also that month, the First Congress of Teachers of the Far East convened in Khabarovsk. Working-class organizations extended to all major centres in the Primorsky and Amur regions as workers came to play an increasingly active role in social and political life.[59]

In March, the Russian Social Democratic Workers' Party (RSDWP) had formed a Vladivostok organization, attracting a hundred workers in a matter of days. The organization elected a temporary provisional committee headed by the Bolshevik Vasily Antonov, who had been a member of the party since 1901 and had worked in Vladivostok since 1912. He was a devout Marxist who had met with Lenin in exile. Unlike branches in European Russia, the Vladivostok branch of the RSDWP was a united party with adherents of both Bolshevik and Menshevik factions.[60] Exiles returning from abroad rapidly rose to prominent positions in the Vladivostok organization, a process mirrored across Russia. At a meeting in May 1917, Arnold Neibut was elected chairman of the Vladivostok RSDWP, having served on the National Executive Committee of the Socialist Party of America at the time of the March Revolution. Konstantin Sukhanov – then a Menshevik-Internationalist who would join the Bolsheviks in the fall – was elected chairman. The Vladivostok RSDWP distributed the organ *Krasnoe Znamya* (*Red Banner*) among port workers and soldiers from the local garrison. A small Socialist Revolutionary group issued the rival *Sotsialist-Revolyutsioner* (*Socialist Revolutionary*), while the centrist Labour Party of Peoples' Socialism maintained a base of strength at the local Oriental Institute, the largest educational institution in the region. At Khabarovsk, a conference of anarchists took place, which included representatives of the influential Group of Anarchist Communists, which called for "the destruction of state power and the organization of a federation of free communes."[61]

The Vladivostok elite responded to the growing radicalization as Siberia and the Russian Far East emerged as a refuge for displaced members of the old regime. In April 1917, the *Kadet* party formed a Vladivostok organization called the Union of Free Russia and began issuing the newspaper *Golos Primor'a* (*Voice of Primorye*).[62] Landowners, wealthy bureaucrats, and military officers began migrating east as their social standing in European Russia evaporated. In August 1917, as the balance of power tipped towards the workers' councils and the fragile Kerensky government in Petrograd assented to Kornilov's failed coup, the *BC Federationist* reported:

> Mr. Nicholas Romanoff and family have left Petrograd and taken up their residence in Siberia. It has been suggested that the Romanoff purpose in so doing is to establish the nucleus of a colony to be built up solely by erstwhile royal

throne-sitters and crown-toters who have been repudiated by the vulgar and irreverential commonality. It is expected the colony will rapidly increase in membership during the years immediately following the ending of the present royal row in Europe.[63]

Kerensky personally oversaw the secret evacuation of the Romanovs from Petrograd. Pressure had mounted since the czar's abdication in March, with a failed attack on the family's quarters at Aleksandrovsky Palace, amid rumours of a rightist plot to liberate the czar and a growing thirst for vengeance among revolutionists. "Only five or six persons in all Petrograd" were informed of the plans, Kerensky wrote in his memoirs. In the early dawn of 14 August 1917, the czar and his family were spirited in motor cars under Cossack guard to the Nikolayevsky Station, where they boarded a special train to the Siberian city of Tobolsk, a "really remote place" on the banks of the Irtysh River north of Omsk. The family was quartered in the governor's house, "fairly comfortable" accommodations by Kerensky's account, with a regimental guard posted on the grounds.[64] They were later moved to the city of Yekaterinburg as the civil war developed, foreshadowing a grisly death by firing squad in the summer of 1918.

Throughout the summer and autumn of 1917, social unrest intensified through Siberia and the Russian Far East, mirroring polarization in European Russia. Peasants formed themselves into village committees (*sel'soviets*), which had come together at a regional congress at the end of May and proclaimed in favour of self-governing *zemstovo* and peasant Soviets.[65] Soviets also banded together, into a People's Commissariat of Far Eastern Soviets (*Dalsovnarkom*), based in Khabarovsk.[66] According to Canadian intelligence officer James Mackintosh Bell, "the real power in Vladivostok" rested with the executive committee of the local Soviet.[67] This committee strengthened its organizational fibre, drafting a constitution and bylaws as a succession of Bolsheviks, Mensheviks, and SRs occupied leading positions in its executive committee.[68] The Soviet also formed a commission on port security and coordinated assistance for released political prisoners, sinking roots among port and railway workers, miners, sailors, and garrison troops.[69] Large meetings were held nightly in the *Narodyi Dom* (People's House) on Svetlanskaya Street, notable for the radically egalitarian participation of working-class women and men.[70]

While the Soviets of Vladivostok, Khabarovsk, and Blagoveshchensk had denounced Petrograd Bolsheviks for "betraying the revolution" during the July Days uprising, Far Eastern Bolsheviks saw their support grow during the summer of 1917.[71] Historian John Stephan attributes this process to the ability of Bolsheviks to adapt to local conditions as well as to the influence of the Russian exiles who had returned from abroad, such as Aleksandr Krasnoshchekov and five others from Chicago.[72] The Kornilov coup provided the opportunity for Far Eastern revolutionists to strengthen their hold on the levers of administrative and political power, and it tipped the scales further in favour of the Bolsheviks. When word of the coup reached the Vladivostok Soviet in mid-September 1917, the organization called on "all the Soviets to take power ... to save the revolution." A day later, the Soviet formed the United Executive Committee (*Ob'edinennyi Ispolnitel'nyi Komitet*), a "compromise between Bolsheviks and moderate socialists," with representatives of peasant Soviets and local governments. The committee took measures to defend the city, deploying envoys to local military divisions and to guard the telegraph and post office. The counter-revolutionary newspaper *Dalny Vostok* (*Far East*) was suppressed, and the United Executive Committee began issuing instructions to local industry.[73]

However, the Vladivostok Soviet's executive committee was soon embroiled by a split within RSDWP ranks. In September 1917, in the wake of the Kornilov coup, Vladivostok Bolsheviks split from the Mensheviks at the Second Far Eastern Conference of the RSDWP, forming the RSDWP (b).[74] Eight Bolshevik delegates narrowly out-voted seven Mensheviks, who stormed out of the Congress in the town of Nikolsk-Ussuriisk. The Congress had adopted the Bolshevik platform for upcoming elections to the Constituent Assembly and approved a resolution calling for the conversion of Soviets into organs of state power. The final meeting of the Congress empowered the Bolshevik-dominated Vladivostok Soviet to perform the role of the Far Eastern Krai Bureau (*Kraevoe buro*) of the RSDWP(b). The Nikolsk-Ussuriisk Congress represented the first step towards independent Bolshevik organization in the Far East. Emissaries were sent to Khabarovsk, Blagoveshchensk, and Harbin, and the Vladivostok committee oversaw the distribution of the newspaper *Krasnoe Znamya* as Bolshevik groups were established in all major centres, organizing three thousand members by November 1917.[75]

When the provisional government's commissar in the Far East, the Menshevik Meneev, published an order from Kerensky that the revolutionary organizations were to be dissolved, tensions in the Vladivostok Soviet's United Executive Committee exploded. A majority of the committee's members voted to ignore the order, prompting the chairman, a Socialist Revolutionist named Mikhail'ov, to resign and the peasant Soviets to recall their delegates. While the provisional government had hoped to subordinate organs of local self-government to central power, the Vladivostok Soviet retained its strength. Elections to the Constituent Assembly, which allocated six deputies for the Far East, demonstrated not only rising Bolshevik strength but also an urban-rural divide. In Vladivostok, Bolshevik candidates captured 49 percent of the vote, one of the highest results in all of Russia. Across the Far East, Bolsheviks took 19 percent of the vote, including 37 percent in the cities, 32 percent in the military garrisons, and 9 percent in rural areas. The second strongest party, the Socialist Revolutionaries, took 14.5 percent of the regional vote, with 19 percent in the cities, 47 percent in the garrisons, and 65 percent in rural areas.[76]

Meanwhile, the labour situation deteriorated. Foreshadowing future strife, railworkers on the Amur and Ussuri lines joined a national strike in September 1917, called by Vikzhel, the all-union committee of railworkers, to protest the provisional government's refusal to grant wage increases commensurate with the rising cost of living. "This strike was supported by thousands of workers in railcar assembly shops in Vladivostok and railway construction workers on the eastern part of Amur Railway near Khabarovsk," historian Boris Mukhachev writes. In the face of this pressure, the provisional government was forced to relent, releasing an additional 235 million rubles for railworkers' wages for 1917 and pledging a larger sum for 1918. In the Amur River goldfields near Blagoveshchensk, miners waged a militant strike against twelve-hour working days, low wages, and poor camp conditions.[77]

Workers' grievances were aggravated by a sharp increase in prices as the value of the ruble fell, contributing to spiralling costs for food and transportation. The provisional government imposed a 150 percent increase on passenger transportation tariffs and a 300 percent increase on cargo in mid-1917. Despite a bumper agricultural crop in the Russian Far East in 1917, food riots erupted as food prices soared. The provisional government had introduced a state monopoly on grain production and had formed a food committee for Primorsky Krai, which set prices for grain growers and determined the retail price of bread. The area under cultivation expanded from 630,000 *desyatina* (690,000 hectares) to 810,000 *desyatina* (880,000 hectares) in the year 1917, while total grain output increased from 41 million *pood* (670,000 tons) to 42.4 million *pood* (695,000 tons).[78] However, in the Amur region, three-quarters of the grain supply was imported from Manchuria, and incentives to Russian grain growers only spurred price inflation. A desperate mob ransacked bread stores in Blagoveshchensk, on the Manchurian border, in September 1917. A week later, the provisional government imposed a state monopoly on sugar. Attempts were made to regulate the price of *keta* and *gorbusha* salmon, while peasants and workers banded together into consumer cooperative societies to weather the economic storm.[79] According to Mukhachev, "the food crisis played a major role in the coming crisis of power."[80]

Radicalization was also widespread within the armed forces. The military commission of the Vladivostok Soviet, formed in March, rose in power, issuing orders to the military command in Vladivostok and throughout the Priamur

disavow : claim responsibility

territory. This commission implemented radical reforms, including the election of officers, a process that intensified after the Kornilov coup. According to Mukhachev: "Soldiers stopped obeying the officers, and soldier committees forced the officers to sign declarations disavowing Kornilov and his supporters and declaring their loyalty to the soldier committees." Concurrently, a process of "self-demobilization" arose, "almost always armed," with soldiers abandoning their units to return to their villages and towns: "Bolsheviks sought to enlist into their ranks these ex-soldiers having these arms in their possession."[81] In Vladivostok, a meeting of soldiers in the 4th Vladivostok Artillery Regiment voted to release three hundred guns to local workers, while the Fortress Miners Regiment released an additional one thousand guns. Propaganda extended to the Pacific fleet, which had a large Bolshevik following by November 1917.[82]

Radicalization in the armed forces generated misgivings among foreign citizens and Allied diplomats residing in Vladivostok. Canadian intelligence officer James Mackintosh Bell caught a train to Khabarovsk, where he met with Kerensky's regional chief of military staff, General Domanyevsky, to propose a training scheme for "the thousands of idle troops in and around Vladivostok" based on "a class of picked men." Upon returning to Vladivostok, Mackintosh Bell addressed the 4th Artillery Regiment, "explaining the necessity of Russia sticking by her allies." These remarks provoked a heated exchange of words with several soldiers in the crowd. Owing to the unsettled state of affairs, Mackintosh Bell's plan languished and he was recalled to England.[83]

In Allied capitals, political and military leaders viewed with growing concern the massive quantity of war matériel at the port of Vladivostok, which spilled out of the city's warehouses and lay unprotected along the wharves – exposed to the elements and a progressively more hostile population. Deterioration of the Trans-Siberian Railroad had created a bottleneck for nearly 700,000 tons of arms, ammunition, and other supplies shipped from Allied ports for the czar's flagging forces. As *New York Times* correspondent Carl Akerman observed:

> during the war scores of great warehouses were constructed to house the perishable goods, and when these were stacked to the rafters it became impossible to erect buildings as fast as the supplies came, everything from cotton to unassembled motor-lorries, were piled in open fields and lots and covered with tarpaulins. Outside the city ... are hills and fields of munitions and materials, rotting, rusting, decaying, wasting ... There are 37,000 railway truck-wheels and heavy steel rails in such quantities as to make it possible to build a third track from the Pacific to Petrograd. There is enough barbed wire to fence Siberia. There are field guns, millions of rounds of ammunition, and a submarine; automobiles, shoes, copper and lead ingots.[84]

On 4 October 1917, the American consul at Vladivostok wired the secretary of state in Washington, warning of Bolshevik activity in Primorsky Krai and the danger of unrest in Vladivostok. He suggested that American warships pay regular visits to the port, "not in order to suppress unrest, but to prevent the possibility of unrest."[85] Meanwhile, the American ambassador in Petrograd publicly mused over sending two divisions of troops to Russia (either through Sweden or Vladivostok) and claimed to have preliminary approval from the Kerensky government.[86] Later in October 1917, the Allied consular corps in Vladivostok sent an urgent letter to the provisional government's acting commissar, F. Skachkov, warning of an upcoming meeting of Vladivostok workers, soldiers, and sailors. Previous meetings of the garrison and the fleet had endorsed resolutions encouraging "confiscation of private property": "It becomes obvious that such feeling is predominant among a big portion of the population, and it possibly can lead to unrest which will cause damage to life and property of the population, including foreign communities situated in Vladivostok."[87]

Soviet Power in the Russian Far East

One the eve of the October Revolution in Petrograd, an important meeting of trade unionists convened in Vladivostok. The First Congress of Unions of the Far East met from 2 November to 8 November 1917, with delegates from the Bolshevik, Menshevik, SR, and other parties vying for influence among the region's organized workers, who were viewed as an integral source of power. The Bolshevik Grosman served as chair of the presidium of the Congress, alongside Vice-Chairman (and fellow Bolshevik) Krasnoshchekov. A resolution from Neibut provoked strong "polemical" debate, proposing that fraternal greetings be sent to the Second All-Union Congress of Soviets, then being held in Petrograd, and that the Vladivostok Congress promise its "full support in the creation of strong Soviet power." The leader of the Menshevik delegation, Agarev, said he considered social revolution in Russia impossible because of the country's incomplete economic development. Neibut disagreed: "The Russian revolution is at the forefront of the world revolution. This is why we demand power in our hands." Neibut's resolution was adopted by a slim majority, demonstrating the ongoing schism within the labour movement of the Russian Far East. The Congress also adopted resolutions calling for the immediate introduction of the eight-hour working day, a ban on overtime work without permission of workers' committees, and the strengthening of cultural-educational work as an essential means of developing the working-class movement. Another resolution, of import to later events, called upon "all unions to support Soviets and defend them from counter-revolutionary forces." By the end of the Congress, the delegates had received word of the events in Petrograd.[88]

The Bolshevik insurrection of 7 November 1917 "only ruffled the Far East," John Stephan suggests, but power arrangements shifted in important ways.[89] At Nikolsk-Ussuriisk, one hundred kilometres north of Vladivostok on the main rail line, the return of Soviet delegates from Petrograd on 11-12 November prompted the local Soviet, chaired by Krasnoshchekov, to proclaim Soviet power and adopt "Soviet laws."[90] In Harbin, the commercial city in Manchuria that fell within Russia's Chinese Eastern Railway zone, Bolsheviks challenged the authority of General Dmitri Horvath, governor of the railway zone.[91] At Irkutsk, the largest city in eastern Siberia, the Bolsheviks gained control of the local Soviet on 28 November and began occupying government buildings in mid-December, triggering ten days of bloody fighting in which more than one thousand people were killed or wounded.[92] Less blood was spilled at Khabarovsk, eight hundred kilometres north of Vladivostok on the Amur River, where a Bolshevik-led coalition won a majority on the Soviet on 19 December and immediately organized a Red Guard. On 24 December, the guard arrested the provisional government's commissar in the city, with the assistance of "Internationalists" – German and Austro-Hungarian prisoners-of-war who joined the revolution. Three days later, the Third Far Eastern Regional Congress of Soviets, meeting in Khabarovsk, proclaimed Soviet authority over the entire Russian Far East, appointing the Chicago émigré Krasnoshchekov as chairman of *Dalsovnarkom*.[93]

In Vladivostok, local Bolsheviks seized power on 18 November 1917 and won a majority on the Soviet on 3 December.[94] The twenty-four-year-old university student Konstantin Sukhanov, son of a former czarist official and a Bolshevik, was elected president of the Soviet and exercised de facto power over Russia's Pacific gateway. Well-heeled Russians fled Vladivostok for Japan as Allied emissaries eyed with apprehension the 650,000 tons of war matériel piled on Vladivostok's wharves. On 30 November 1918, the British government banned the shipment of further strategic goods, preventing 31,700 tons of Canadian Car Company railroad cars from leaving the port of Vancouver. Six weeks later, the Lenin government decreed a state monopoly on gold. Events had gotten out of hand. The Allies moved.[95]

authoritive
order.

3
The Road to Intervention

THE DAY THE BOLSHEVIKS seized power in Petrograd, 7 November 1917, Victoria's *Daily Colonist* reported: "Premier Kerensky is planning a visit to England on official business ... and it is expected he will leave Petrograd for England within a few days."[1] Kerensky was forced from power as the newspaper went to press, but deliberations proceeded with new-found urgency. Talks opened between Allied and Russian leaders that culminated in the deployment of Canadian and Allied troops to Vladivostok, Arkhangelsk, Murmansk, and Baku.[2] According to Raymond Massey, an officer in the Siberian Expedition whose father, Chester, owned the Massey-Harris tractor company and whose brother, Vincent, served as secretary to the Cabinet (and later as governor general):

> The expedition was to help complete what Winston Churchill had termed the "Cordon Sanitaire," which was to contain the Bolshevik revolution. Specifically, the Canadians and any allies would operate in support of the White Russians who, Vincent said, were more or less in control of Siberia as far west as Omsk.[3]

Mary Nicolaeff, a fifty-seven-year-old Russian émigré and self-described "rebel," offered a more pointed analysis in a letter to the Victoria *Semi-Weekly Tribune*: "Capitalists of the whole world joined hands to crush the Russian working masses."[4]

Talks and Manoeuvres
In March, days after the czar abdicated, the Imperial War Cabinet was formed in London, consisting of British prime minister David Lloyd George, Canadian prime minister Robert Borden, and political and military leaders from Britain, Canada, New Zealand, Australia, South Africa, and Newfoundland.[5] The Allied leaders closely followed developments in Russia, receiving regular reports from their emissaries in Petrograd, who consulted with Korlinov in advance of his failed coup. They watched with apprehension as the Bolsheviks toppled the Kerensky government in November and repelled a Cossack attempt to retake the capital from Pulkovskiye Heights.[6] The Allied leaders found solace in reports from the south of Russia, in the region between the Black Sea and the River Don, where generals Kornilov, Alekseyev, and Kaledin raised an anti-Bolshevik

volunteer army, inaugurating the Russian Civil War. Meeting in London in December 1917, the Imperial War Cabinet pledged support to those governments in Russia committed to a continuation of war against Germany. And, in January, it discreetly channelled 15 million rubles to the nascent White forces on the Don.[7]

Canada, like other Allied powers, refused to recognize the Bolshevik government. As longshoreman Ernest Winch told the January 1918 convention of the BCFL, "a number of Russians are marooned here [in Vancouver], and not permitted to return to their homes ... The Canadian government will not permit them to leave for Russia unless sure they can enter Russia. But the Bolsheviki government has abolished passports, and the Canadian government does not recognize the Bolsheviki."[8] Despite the official policy of "non-recognition," Allied diplomats worked discreetly in Petrograd, maintaining contact with Trotsky and other Bolshevik leaders, in the hope of establishing Allied-Soviet cooperation against Germany.[9]

In the Russian Far East, the Allies moved quickly but inconsistently to protect their stores at Vladivostok and to prop up anti-Bolshevik forces. These moves were stymied by suspicion between Britain, the United States, and Japan, the latter having joined the Allies in 1914 and being best positioned to land forces at Vladivostok. Fully aware of the quantity of Allied war materials on the city's wharves, Britain proposed a joint operation at Vladivostok in early December, suggesting that Japan provide "principal forces" alongside "token" British forces from Hong Kong and American troops from the Philippines. The war office claimed such action was necessary to prevent the matériel at Vladivostok "from falling into German hands."[10] However, the Japanese government balked, insisting on its right to act unilaterally, and sent the naval cruisers *Iwami* and *Asahi* to Golden Horn Bay.[11] Britain responded by deploying the HMS *Suffolk* from Hong Kong and considered taking action with the Americans alone, a plan that was rejected due to fears that it would drive the Bolsheviks into an open alliance with Germany. The Japanese and British warships reached Vladivostok in January 1918 and lay at anchor in the harbour, followed by the American cruiser USS *Brooklyn* in February.[12] Alongside high-level talks, Allied diplomats in Harbin sent an urgent request to the Chinese government for military assistance against pro-Bolshevik forces that were challenging the authority of General Dmitri Horvath, director of the Chinese Eastern Railway and former governor of Russia's railway zone in Manchuria. On 26 December 1917, Chinese troops entered Harbin from Kirin Province and disarmed pro-Bolshevik Russian troops.[13]

Britain, Canada, and the Allies wavered over the appropriate strategy in the Russian Far East, demonstrating an ambivalence that characterized the Siberian

Expedition from beginning to end. Conflicting imperial motives impeded unified action against the Bolsheviks. Japan was the only country with the capacity to anchor an intervention in the Far East, but its imperial designs clashed with those of the West. Britain and France were generally more "hawkish" than the United States, particularly after President Wilson's storied support for national self-determination in his Fourteen Points of January 1918. On 1 January, the British Cabinet had responded to reports of Bolshevik atrocities at Irkutsk with a telegram to Washington urging reconsideration of the proposed ground force for Vladivostok. A week later, France formally proposed sending an expeditionary force to Siberia. However, the United States rejected this proposal, believing foreign intervention would unify Russians against the Allies.[14]

This vacillating Allied strategy is illuminated in the memoirs of British Lieutenant-Colonel John Ward, a Labour MP and commander of the 25th Battalion, Middlesex Regiment, which had been performing garrison duty at Hong Kong. "I answered a summons from Headquarters at Hong-Kong, one morning in November, 1917, and received the instruction to hold myself and my battalion in readiness to proceed to a destination unknown," Lieutenant-Colonel Ward writes.[15] The troops were destined for "a very cold climate," which the commander later learned was Siberia. With preparations nearly complete, the departure was postponed, and in January 1918 it was cancelled. "Like all Allied efforts," Ward recalled, the decision to intervene "had been frustrated by divided counsels and stupid national jealousy."[16] Seven months passed before the 25th Battalion landed at Vladivostok.

In the intervening period, Allied leaders debated their response to the Russian Revolution as the Bolsheviks invited all belligerent nations to negotiate an immediate peace. On 22 November 1917, Trotsky, the peoples' commissar of foreign affairs, had published the terms of the Allies' secret treaties, signed by the czar and uncovered in Russian archives. "The Russian people, as well as the peoples of Europe and of the whole world, must know the documentary truth about those plots which were hatched in secret by financiers and industrialists, together with their Parliamentary and diplomatic agents," Trotsky declared.[17] The treaties divided the spoils of the German and Ottoman empires between Russia, Britain, France, Italy, Serbia, and Romania; however, in line with the policy of national self-determination, the Bolsheviks repudiated these obligations. The Allies refused any consideration of peace talks with the Bolsheviks, honouring a clause in the treaties that proscribed a separate peace. The Bolshevik regime was determined to remove Russia from the war, signing first an armistice in December 1917 and then the Brest-Litovsk Treaty with Germany in March 1918. The treaty surrendered huge swaths of territory, including Poland, Belarus, the Baltic states, and the Ukraine (including 90 percent of Russian coal mines);

armistice: parties agree to stop fighting.

provided Germany with 25 percent of the oil from the Baku fields; and relinquished 6 billion German marks in reparations.[18] This was seized upon by the Allies as proof of collusion between Lenin and the German kaiser – and as grounds for military intervention in Russia as part of the wider war against Germany.

As high-level diplomacy unfolded, Japanese, British, and American warships lay at anchor in Vladivostok's Golden Horn Bay. By March, local Bolsheviks were growing "increasingly resentful of the inhibitions placed upon them by the spectacle of the foreign warships in the harbour," and Allied consular representatives were "increasingly irritated by the harassment of their nationals and the suppression of normal business activity in the port."[19] An active military front had opened near the town of Grodekovo, on the Manchurian border 150 kilometres northwest of Vladivostok. The Vladivostok Soviet raised a Red Guard, which repelled anti-Bolshevik Cossack units under the command of Ataman Ivan Kalmykov.[20] Meanwhile, a flood of refugees from the Russian interior swelled the city's 1917 population of seventy thousand to nearly 200,000.[21] American journalist Albert Rhys Williams describes the chaotic class structure of revolutionary Vladivostok, where he spent seven weeks in 1918:

> The city was thronged with evicted landowners, dreaming of their estates, their retinue of servants and the idle feasting of bygone days; officers telling of the former discipline, when soldiers jumped into the gutter at their presence and stood rigid in salute while beaten in the face ... As a port of exit, Vladivostok was full of Russian émigrés coming out. As a port of entry, it was full of Allied capitalists going in. It was a key to the El Dorado beyond ... From London and Tokio, from the Paris Bourse and Wall Street, they came flocking hither, lured by dazzling prospects. But between them and the fisheries, gold-mines and forests they found a big barrier. They found the Soviet.[22]

In the months following the Bolshevik seizure of power, the Vladivostok Soviet had sunk roots in the city's working class, particularly among miners, railway workers, longshore workers, and port workers. Under the leadership of Konstantin Sukhanov, the twenty-four-year-old student who was "small in stature, but great in energy," and three young Bolshevik women from upper-class backgrounds, the Soviet set out to democratize Vladivostok industry. Workers' committees ramped up production of railway rolling stock and re-tooled the city's Military Port to build and refurbish civilian ships and machines. Working-class housing was built closer to industry in order to increase workers' leisure time, and the Soviet opened a peoples' university, three theatres, and two daily newspapers.[23] Fearful of such changes, the American and Japanese ambassadors and British and French consuls fled Vladivostok for Japan in March.[24] "Only the presence of the Allied warships in the harbour kept the Bolshevik-led Soviet from seizing complete control of the city," historian James Morley writes.[25] The German threat was invoked as grounds for Allied intervention in the Far East, with the *New York Times* citing the presence of ninety-four thousand German prisoners-of-war east of Lake Baikal who were "beyond control and ... trying to get arms."[26]

Allied concern reflected the rapid pace of economic reform in Russia. The Bolsheviks nationalized land and industry and, in February, repudiated 13 billion rubles in Allied loans to Russia.[27] The Bolshevik regime – rebranded the Russian Communist Party in March 1918, with a newly minted capital in Moscow – felt no obligation to honour the financial commitments of the czar. Allied embassies in Petrograd responded with an ominous statement, refusing to recognize either the repudiation or the confiscation of Allied property, which they said would be reclaimed at an "opportune time."[28] Canadian socialists, however, applauded repudiation:

> The intimated intention of the Russian Bolsheviki to repudiate the debt contracted by previous governments of that country has caused quite a flutter of alarm in the dove-cote of the ruling class thieves. And that alarm is amply justified, for if such a precedent were once established and followed out to its logical conclusion, the entire superstructure of bourgeois flimflam and swindle would crash to the ground, and the soft sand of living on the plunder taken from slaves under the pretense of payment and the humbug of money, be brought to an end.[29]

Another writer, J. Galitzky from the mining town of Hedley in British Columbia's southern interior, argued: "it would be unjust if the Russian people would have to pay interest on money loaned to the Czar's government for the purpose of conquest, war profit and wholesale murder."[30] The extent of British commercial interests in Russia was outlined in a report to the Foreign Office in London. British firms controlled "the grain trade on the Volga and in southern Russia ... the whole sugar trade in the Ukraine, 1.25 million acres of 'easily accessible' forest, 300,000 acres of irrigated cotton land in central Asia, nearly all the Russian insurance business, besides large coal, oil, cement and other concerns."[31] The British government responded to the report by purchasing the Siberian Bank.[32]

On 5 April 1918, five hundred Japanese marines landed in Vladivostok from the warships in the harbour.[33] The killing of three Japanese nationals a day earlier provided a pretext for intervention, which was officially justified as necessary in order to "protect [the] life and property of Japanese."[34] In tandem with this move, fifty Royal Marines were deployed from the cruiser *Suffolk* to guard the British Consulate.[35] The Bolshevik leadership in Moscow responded with a directive from Lenin to the Vladivostok Soviet:

> We consider the situation very serious and issue the most categorical warning to the comrades. Do not harbour any illusions: the Japanese will certainly attack. That is inevitable. Probably all the Allies without exception will help them. Hence it is necessary to begin preparations without the least delay and to prepare seriously, exerting every effort. Above all, attention must be devoted to correct withdrawal, retreat, and removal of stores and railway materials.
>
> Do not set yourselves unrealisable aims. Prepare to sap and blow up railway lines, and to remove rolling stock and locomotives; prepare minefields around Irkutsk or in the Transbaikal area. Twice every week inform us exactly how many locomotives and how much rolling stock have been removed, and how much remains. Otherwise we do not and shall not believe anything. We have no currency notes now, but we shall have plenty as from the second half of April, but our help is conditional on your practical success in removing rolling stock and locomotives from Vladivostok, in preparing to blow up bridges and so forth.[36]

Later that month, on a trans-Atlantic steamer, Canadian intelligence officer James Mackintosh Bell confided that "a proposal then under discussion in London had every prospect of culminating in a force being sent from Canada to Siberia."[37] The war for Siberia was on.

Across the Pacific, Japan's incursion at Vladivostok provoked discussion among BC trade unionists. The *BC Federationist* published a statement from the International Bureau of the Council of Workmen's, Soldiers', and Peasants' delegates declaring that the "Russian working classes are not striving for a republic of the type of the American trust magnates, or of the French Stock Exchange sharks ... These republics view with complacency the impudent intervention of feudal Japan into Russian affairs. A bourgeois republic in Russia would be quite acceptable to all the remaining ancient tyrannies on earth, but a Worker's Republic, never."[38] The newspaper quoted Viscount Uchida, Japan's ambassador to Russia, who appeared to oppose his country's interference in Russia's internal affairs:

> The Soviets are gaining enormous power in Russia. The people feel that they are the rulers of the country and it is wonderful to observe them. Germany may

destroy the Lenine government but Bolshevikism will permeate the world. Any other pronouncement would be false.

Uchida went on to say that every foreigner who did not have large commercial interests "leaves Russia fairly committed to the Bolshevist view of life."[39]
Throughout Russia, opponents of the Bolsheviks were coalescing into White armies to challenge the new regime and its revolutionary program. In the south, an army was formed under Colonel Anton Denikin, Kornilov's chief of staff during the ill-fated 1917 coup.[40] In the northwest, along the border with Finland, General Mannerheim repelled Bolshevik forces, capturing eight thousand Red Guards in March.[41] At Murmansk and Arkhangelsk on the shores of the White Sea, supporters of the old regime rallied their forces in anticipation of a German U-boat attack; General Eugene Miller, a Russian émigré who had been living in Rome prior to the war, spearheaded the defence of stockpiled Allied arms.[42] Several Cossack armies rose up across the country, with the ataman generals Grigori Semyonov and Ivan Kalmykov leading the charge in eastern Siberia and the Russian Far East and General Vladimir Kappel spearheading the White campaign near the Ural Mountains in western Siberia.[43]
The White generals in eastern Russia lacked cohesion and suffered from the same rival ambitions that impeded the Allied intervention. In January 1918, an "All-Siberian" constituent assembly had convened at the city of Tomsk and, though broken up by local Bolsheviks, pledged to pursue Siberian "autonomy" and elected a seventeen-member cabinet.[44] By spring, several members of this Cabinet made their way to Vladivostok. They proclaimed the Provisional Government of Autonomous Siberia, led by Socialist Revolutionary Pyotr Derber, courted Allied support, and attempted to consolidate power. However, the American consular representative in Vladivostok had concluded by mid-1918 that Derber "ha[d] no authority for claiming to be the government of Russia." General Dmitri Horvath, former director of the Chinese Eastern Railway, developed a rival administration based in Harbin, with the backing of Chinese troops, and garnered more favourable attention from the Allies. The *New York Times* described Horvath as "a representative of the old regime, having been one of the Czar's favourites."[45] Another correspondent observed that "no Government in Siberia can hope to remain solidly in being unless temporarily at least based on effective allied support, giving it the necessary power to endure."[46]

The Fall of the Vladivostok Soviet
The Allies made common cause with the White Russians and benefited from the auspicious presence of the Czecho-Slovak Legion in the Russian Far East.

The sixty thousand troops that comprised this Legion consisted of prisoners-of-war and deserters from the Austro-Hungarian army who had joined the czar's forces midway through the war to bolster their nationalist cause. After the March Revolution, the Czecho-Slovak Legion won recognition as an official Allied army under the red and white flag of Bohemia. Led by General Radola Gaida, Mikhail Dieterichs, Milan Štefánik, and Tomáš Masaryk (a professor who had been exiled in London), the seasoned soldiers in the Czech units stood in stark contrast to the irregular White Russian troops. The Czecho-Slovaks had demonstrated their military prowess in June 1917, capturing four thousand Austrians as part of General Brussilov's offensive after Russian troops deserted and left the front. The collapse of the Russian army produced a windfall of machine guns, rifles, and ammunition for the Czechs, but the ongoing war against Germany prevented their return home. Following the November Revolution, Masaryk negotiated a deal with the Bolsheviks to evacuate the Czecho-Slovaks through Vladivostok; he arrived in Vancouver on 29 April 1918 en route to Washington and Europe.[47] However, before the main body of the troops departed Russia, conflict erupted along the Trans-Siberian Railroad. On 14 May 1918, an argument with a pro-Austrian Czech in a passing train at Chelyabinsk culminated in the Czecho-Slovaks' seizing control of the town. Leon Trotsky, people's commissar of war and commander of the Red Army, ordered the entire Legion disarmed, but the Czechs intercepted the message and took control of the rails.[48] By June 1918, the Czecho-Slovak Legion had seized Samara and Omsk, western Siberia's largest city, and controlled a seven thousand-kilometre span of the Trans-Siberian Railroad from the Volga to Vladivostok. Czech units were ordered to lead the Allied offensive against the Bolsheviks in western Siberia and northern Russia, while a force of fifteen thousand deployed to Vladivostok.[49]

On 26 June 1918, Czech leaders met with the Allied consuls in Vladivostok, requesting the immediate deployment of an Allied force of 100,000 troops and large quantities of arms.[50] Three days later, on 29 June, fifteen thousand Czechs, along with Japanese, British, Chinese, and American units, toppled the Vladivostok Soviet and established the Provisional Government of Autonomous Siberia.[51] Albert Rhys Williams, the American journalist who was in Vladivostok at the time, described the Allied operation:

> The Japanese seize the powder-magazine, the British the railroad station. The Americans throw a cordon around the consulate. The Chinese and others take up lesser points. The Czechs converge upon the Soviet building. They encircle it from all sides. With a loud "Hurrah," – they rush forward, and go crashing thru the doors. The Red Flag of the Socialist Republic is pulled down, and the red,

white and blue flag of autocracy is run up. Vladivostok passes into the hands of the Imperialists.[52]

William's account, published in the *BC Federationist*, describes the revolutionists' last stand:

> When the Czechoslovaks, aided by Japanese and British troops, suddenly seized the Soviet and its officers, throwing confusion and terror into the ranks of the workers, the gruzshchiki (longshoremen) rushed into the Red Staff building, and, though outnumbered forty to one, refused to surrender until the building was fired by an incendiary bomb.[53]

Local Bolsheviks were rounded up in the streets and jeered by shouting crowds. On 1 July, the Soviet People's Commissariat for the Russian Far East issued a petition stating that the "White Czechs managed to surprise the Vladivostok Soviet and reinstate the dictatorship of the bourgeoisie" and called on workers, peasants, and Cossacks to take up arms "to protect the Soviets."[54] Vladivostok Bolsheviks retreated north to Nikolsk-Ussuriisk, at the junction of the Chinese Eastern and Ussuri railroads, clashing with Czech forces in ugly hand-to-hand combat.[55]

On 4 July 1918, a mass funeral was held for the fallen *gruzshchiki*. According to Williams, seventeen thousand Vladivostok workers joined the procession, "jamming the street not from curb to curb, but from wall to wall." At the head of the march four men carried a huge red banner proclaiming: "Long live the Soviet of Workmen's and Peasants' Deputies! Hail to the International Brotherhood of the Toilers!" One hundred young women dressed in white, carrying green wreaths from forty-four unions in the city, accompanied the freshly painted red coffins of the fallen longshoremen. The music of the Red Fleet Band was drowned out by the singing of the "Internationale." A group of Czech troops offered the procession a guard of honour, but they were flatly refused. In the main square, in front of the surrendered Red Staff building and "fifty feet" from the British Consulate, speakers mounted a platform on the back of a truck. Konstantin Sukhanov, the deposed president of the Vladivostok Soviet – paroled for the day by the new authorities – told the crowd:

> Here before the Red Staff building where our comrades gruzshchiki were slain, we swear by these red coffins that hold them, by their wives and children that weep for them, by the red banners which float over them, that the Soviet for which they died shall be the thing for which we live – or if need be – like them, die.[56]

Two days later, British, French, American, Japanese, and Czechoslovak officials placed the city under their "temporary protection."[57]

A power struggle ensued in Vladivostok between warring White Russian factions. Pyotr Derber's moderately socialist Provisional Government of Autonomous Siberia sought to consolidate power, while the more reactionary General Dmitri Horvath, director of the Chinese Eastern Railway, proclaimed himself "temporary" dictator of all Russia on 10 July 1918 and issued a decree calling for "firm discipline" in the army and abolition of "socialization, nationalization, and anarcho-syndicalism" in industry. From Harbin, Horvath mobilized an army of two thousand Chinese and White Russian troops and entered Vladivostok, ensconcing himself on a railway siding in the city centre and assuming judicial, administrative, and financial control. Horvath's cabinet – which promised "to be acceptable to nine-tenths of the population of Siberia," according to the *New York Times* – included financiers and politicians from the old czarist regime, two socialists, and two military officers: General Vasily Egorovich Flug, the czar's military commander for Vladivostok, and Admiral Aleksandr Kolchak, commander of the czar's Black Sea Fleet and leader of the White Russian forces at Harbin.[58]

Canada's Intervention

According to historian Steuart Beattie, Canadian participation in the Siberian Intervention was motivated by two myths: that invention was "essential to victory over Germany" and that "those who intervened would profit from trade with Siberia."[59] Beneath these official justifications was the growing bogey of Bolshevism. On 24 June 1918, Aleksander Kerensky, former prime minister of Russia, met for several hours with British prime minister David Lloyd George, discussing the Bolsheviks' hold on power and prospects for the future. Kerensky had travelled to London in the wake of the November Revolution and expressed the view that Trotsky was pro-German and that Lenin "lived in the clouds."[60] Following this meeting, Lloyd George provided a full report to the Imperial War Cabinet, which held sessions in London from June to August 1918. The War Cabinet debated the merits of intervention, with Canadian prime minister Borden suggesting: "we ought to have Allied intervention and not Japanese intervention."[61]

In the weeks that followed, Allied troops seized Vladivostok as the Allied leaders in London thrashed out a military strategy for defeating the Moscow government. Developments on the Western Front lent urgency to Allied deliberations as Germany's swift victory over Romania in spring 1918 fuelled fears of a fresh offensive in the west. At the beginning of July, the Supreme Allied War Council agreed to the principle of Siberian intervention. US president Woodrow

Wilson authorized the deployment of seven thousand American troops (later expanded to twelve thousand).[62] On 9 July, the British War Office sent a formal request to Borden asking if Canadian troops could be made available to "restore order and a stable government" in Siberia, provide assistance to the Czechoslovaks, and help reopen an Eastern Front against Germany.[63] Major-General Sir Thomas Bridges, British military envoy in Washington, travelled to Ottawa to further the War Office request as military officials in Ottawa began preparations for a Canadian contingent.[64] Lord Balfour, Britain's foreign secretary, suggested that the destination of the force be kept secret, given the "delicate situation as regards negotiation for intervention in Siberia."[65] When Czecho-Slovak troops advanced on the Siberian city of Yekaterinburg in mid-July, local Soviet officials executed former Czar Nicholas II and his family.[66] Another propaganda weapon had been handed to the Allies.

In his memoirs, on 27 July 1918, Borden writes: "we discussed our contingent for the Siberian expedition." The next day, the prime minister received a wire stating: "[the Privy Council] approves principle of sending expedition, leaving you to arrange cost and other detail."[67] Reports of the Siberian Expedition made their way into the labour press. In late July, the BC Federationist speculated on Allied motives:

It is reported from Shankhai [sic] that the Allies have decided on joint intervention in Siberia. British, French, American and Japanese contingents are to occupy Vladivostok, it seems, in the interests of the Czecho-Slovaks. We can't quite make things out. If the Czecho-Slovaks are not strong enough to win control by themselves, they must surely be in the minority, and, therefore, not entitled to run the country ... If, on the other hand, the Czecho-Slovaks are the strong party, there doesn't seem much need to assist them. Of course, the opponents of the Czecho-Slovaks are the Bolsheviki – mere working people. That may explain matters somewhat.[68]

The Allies disavowed any suggestion they were intruding on Russian sovereignty. According to a dispatch from London published in the Victoria Daily Colonist: "The aim of His Majesty's Government is to secure the political and economical restoration of Russia without internal interference of any kind and bring about the expulsion of enemy forces from Russian soil. His majesty's government categorically declares that it has no intention of infringing to the slightest degree the territorial integrity of Russia."[69] In early August, the Bolshevik military stronghold of Kazan fell to the Whites, who transferred 651 million rubles of the czar's gold reserve to the State Bank in Omsk. Trotsky travelled to the Ural Front to direct the Red Army campaign and issued a communiqué that highlighted the strategic importance of Siberia: "More than ever before, the Urals are the backbone of Soviet Russia. We cannot tolerate for one more day the presence there of bands which bar our access to Siberian grain. In order that Soviet Russia may live, develop, and give a firm rebuff to aggression from without we must ruthlessly smash the Czechoslovak and White-Guard revolt on our territory."[70]

Allied leaders assented to the Siberian campaign as one thousand troops in Britain's 25th Battalion, Middlesex Regiment, made their way from Hong Kong to Vladivostok to serve under the Canadian command. They landed on 3 August, "the first contingent of Allied troops to arrive," escorted into Golden Horn Bay by two Japanese destroyers. A Czech band and Britain's consul greeted the British troops, pejoratively described as the "Hernia Battalion" because of the preponderance of "B1" class men (older soldiers released from service on other fronts). However, before the Middlesex troops settled into their barracks, they were deployed up country to repel Bolshevik forces on the precarious Ussuri Front. Meeting with other Allied commanders, British lieutenant-colonel Ward emphasized the inferior fighting abilities of his men but pledged to "render every assistance," given the "desperate circumstances" at Ussuri. Bolsheviks were overpowering three thousand "indifferently armed" Czech and Cossack troops, threatening the Trans-Siberian Railroad. Ward left Vladivostok with half his force – 550 troops – on 5 August and, alongside Japanese troops, thwarted the Bolshevik advance: "The enemy were entirely demoralized, and never made another stand east of Lake Baikal."[71] On the opposite side of Russia, near the Finnish border, Allied troops landed at the port of Arkhangelsk on 8-9 August 1918, seizing the city from eight thousand Bolsheviks and catapulting a White "Government of the North" into power.[72]

As Bolshevik authorities in Moscow placed the British consul-general under arrest, Trotsky declared: "our troops are fighting against the British invaders and a declaration of war can hardly be avoided"; Lenin issued an ultimatum to the Japanese consul demanding the withdrawal of troops from eastern Russia.[73] "The Bolsheviki are mobilizing their forces, and ... they do not intend to submit to foreign rule without a struggle," *The Nation* magazine reported from New York.[74] However, rather than withdraw, Japan intensified its involvement. By the end of August, fifteen thousand of seventy-three thousand Japanese troops had landed in Vladivostok. American soldiers sailed from the Philippines as an array of foreign armies made its way to Siberia and the Russian Far East: 2,000 Italians, 12,000 Poles, 4,000 Serbs, 4,000 Romanians, 5,000 Chinese, and 1,850 French troops (mainly Annamites from Vietnam). When combined with the Czecho-Slovak Legion and White Russian forces, the total Allied troop strength between the Pacific and the Urals exceeded 350,000.[75]

On 13 August 1918, details of the Canadian Expeditionary Force (Siberia) was revealed publicly: "Canada to Send Force 4,000 Strong to Help Russia in Siberia," the Victoria *Daily Colonist* announced. A day earlier, the Privy Council had approved order-in-council PC 1983 authorizing the deployment of the force.[76] Victoria was selected as the principal assembly point, along with New Westminster and Coquitlam. Brigadier-General James H. "Gentleman Jim" Elmsley, commander of the 8th Brigade of the Canadian Expeditionary Force on the Western Front, was recalled from Europe to lead Canada's Siberian Expedition and was promoted to the rank of major-general. Military officials arranged for the shipment of 3,000,000 rounds of ammunition from Vancouver to Vladivostok.[77] When Borden returned to Canada on 24 August, he confirmed that troops were destined for Siberia and announced that, henceforth, the Canadian army would be organized independently of the British army.[78] This important step towards Canadian sovereignty – independent military organization – was helped along by the unlikely conflict in the Russian Far East.

Even at its inception, however, the CEFS was plagued by indecision in senior ranks. General Sydney C. Mewburn, minister of militia and defence, questioned whether the troops could be raised voluntarily. He asked Borden: "How will the public of Canada view the raising of another Force to be sent to another theatre of war ... in view of the present unrest in Canada?"[79]

Red Scare at Home

Canada's Privy Council approved the Siberian Expedition as labour unrest erupted on the Home Front. Strikes paralyzed key industries, new unions emerged, and socialist parties enjoyed a surge of support. The killing of one prominent labour leader, Albert "Ginger" Goodwin, prompted Canada's first city-wide general strike and contributed to the divide between workers and the state. Reflecting a "Red Scare" that developed across the Western world, the Canadian state responded with a firm hand. By September 1918, the socialist labour leadership in western Canada had broken from the moderate labour leadership in the east. While radicalism and militancy extended across the country, British Columbia and other western provinces were notable for the ascendancy of radicals in working-class ranks. These radicals were the primary target of state repression. With growing frequency, worker militancy and radicalism in Canada were viewed through a Russian lens. The same attitudes that shaped Allied strategy in Russia – the use of force to quash Bolshevism – informed domestic responses to labour unrest.

On the night of 26-27 July 1918, Albert "Ginger" Goodwin, the socialist labour leader who had been recalled for military service in the midst of the Trail smelterworkers' strike, was shot by Dominion Police constable Dan Campbell in the wooded hills near Comox Lake on Vancouver Island.[80] While the police officer claimed to have fired his weapon in self-defence, trade unionists alleged murder. The Vancouver Trades and Labor Council sent a delegate to the Comox Valley to investigate as Cumberland coal miners stood watch over Goodwin's body awaiting the local coroner. The day of Goodwin's funeral, 2 August 1918, Vancouver trade unionists staged the first city-wide general strike in Canada's history, shutting down shipyards and streetcar operations. "German or British–Which?" blared the *Vancouver Sun* in a front-page editorial.[81] A vigilante mob of three hundred returned soldiers attacked the Labor Temple and forced union officers to kiss the Union Jack. At a mass meeting that evening, local politicians and businesspeople called for immediate conscription of the strike leaders and demanded "strong and stern measures to suppress all seditious and anti-war movements or language."[82] On Vancouver Island, coal miners took a "general holiday," halting Canadian Collieries Ltd. operations at Cumberland, as the chief of police ordered Dominion Police out of the district, suggesting that "he would not be responsible for the results unless this was done." A kilometre-long procession, headed by the town band, wound its way to Cumberland cemetery where the Socialist Party organized a funeral – "the most largely attended in the history of Cumberland" – and socialist luminaries William Pritchard and Wallis Lefeaux addressed the crowd.[83]

The killing of Ginger Goodwin and the sympathy strikes reflected the militant mood of BC workers in the late stages of the First World War. Wartime conditions and conscription fuelled support for radical political alternatives and contributed to the divide between workers, employers, and the state. While not advocating the armed seizure of power, a layer of BC workers was hindering Canada's war effort, expressing opposition to capitalism and solidarity with Russian Bolsheviks. Burgeoning colonies of draft resisters took shape on Vancouver Island and near Howe Sound on the Lower Mainland as workers refused to fight in what they viewed as a "bosses' war." On both the industrial and political fields, BC labour developed organizational muscle. The FLP formed branches across the province, backed by a team of organizers that included J.S. Woodsworth.[84] Aided by wartime labour shortages, new unions took root among shipyard workers, longshoremen, sawmill workers, civic workers, telephone operators, teamsters, school teachers, firefighters, police officers, and laundry workers.[85] Women workers led a sit-down strike on the steps of the BC Legislature, demanding a minimum wage law.[86] Led by militants in the Socialist Party of Canada (SPC), British Columbia's labour movement was entering a period of unprecedented unrest, preparing to mount a challenge to the moderate leadership of the Trades and Labor Congress of Canada (TLC).

The Canadian government sought to suppress BC labour's radical turn. In late July 1918, the VTLC-backed newspaper *The Week* was suppressed by government order and its editor W.E. Peirce jailed for publishing excerpts from the Allies' secret treaties. Copies of the errant issue were seized from city newsstands.[87] Two weeks later, on 7 August, the chief press censor of Canada, Ernest J. Chambers, visited *BC Federationist* offices, threatening to suppress the paper unless its directors signed a written undertaking promising "that in the future no objectionable matter ... [would] be printed."[88] Government regulations defined as objectionable "any statement, report or opinion which may tend to weaken or in any way detract from the united effort of the people of Canada in the prosecution of the war."[89] The Canadian state jailed other working-class leaders. On 14 August 1918, Joe Naylor – the blacklisted coal miner, past president of the BCFL, SPC member, and personal friend of Ginger Goodwin – was arrested and detained in Courtenay jail for aiding draft resisters. While he was later acquitted, another worker, David Aitken, faced jail time. The treatment of Aitken and Naylor, who had served as labour's representative on the coroner's inquest into the Goodwin killing, revealed apprehension in ruling circles.[90]

These fears were heightened by moves towards unity between unionized workers and returned soldiers – a potentially powerful combination of forces. As early as January 1917, VTLC delegates had shown interest in the plight of returned soldiers, particularly on matters relating to working conditions and postwar reconstruction.[91] The prospect of soldier-labour unity was demonstrated in June 1918, when ex-soldier Francis Giolma won a Victoria provincial by-election, defeating the Liberal candidate with almost 60 percent of ballots cast.[92] The following month, as the prospect of postwar unemployment loomed, the Victoria Metal Trades Council and returned soldiers' organizations put together a parade and demonstration in support of local shipbuilding.[93] Vocational training was considered essential to the integration of returned soldiers into the workforce and postwar society. In mid-1918, the provincial labour federation's Committee on Returned Soldiers drafted a plan outlining the governance and operation of vocational training schools, a plan endorsed by Victoria delegates from the Great War Veterans' Association and Comrades of the Great War. In September 1918, Victoria unions and returned soldier organizations formed a special joint committee to provide recommendations on reconstruction after the war.[94]

Resolutions submitted by Victoria's labour council to the 1918 TLC convention reveal this concern for soldiers' interests. One resolution demanded that the Dominion government provide "free medical attention to the wives and children and dependents of our men now fighting overseas," while another demanded "a living wage of $100.00 monthly to the women folk of our fighting men" in light of increasing living costs with the approaching "Canadian winter." A third resolution challenged the hierarchy within the Canadian armed forces, declaring:

> Whereas the Canadian army is recruited without regard to social rank, to fight in the cause of democracy; Be it resolved that all pensions paid to Canadian solders, whether of commissioned rank or not be paid only in proportion to the disabilities incurred without regard to rank.[95]

The volatility of the returned soldier question was exposed in August 1918, when returned soldiers rioted alongside civilians and police in Toronto, ransacking local businesses and prompting a declaration of martial law and the deployment of five hundred troops from the Niagara Camp.[96]

In September 1918, the radical turn of the Canadian working class erupted on the floor of the annual TLC convention in Quebec City – a rupture between craft-union leaders centred in the eastern provinces and radical industrial unionists centred in the western provinces.[97] The radicals were defeated on a host of issues, from demands for the six-hour working day to a VTLC-sponsored resolution proposing a travel pool to congress meetings. James Watters, a Victoria carpenter, socialist, and congress president since 1911, lost the presidency to Tom Moore, a member of the Conservative Party from Niagara Falls who led the carpenters' union in eastern Canada.[98] Midway through the convention, delegates debated Resolution 32, proposed by the Toronto machinists, on the issue of "Allied Intervention in Russia." As a Vancouver delegate later reported:

> Delegate Koldofsky of Toronto, in supporting the resolution, stated that he was not a Bolsheviki and that he did not agree with them altogether. He had taken part in the 1905 revolt and was personally acquainted with Lenine, though not by any means in accord with his ideas. From his personal knowledge of Lenine, however, he was convinced that under no consideration could he be guilty of the crimes toward the working class in Russia such as were being charged in the daily press. He was strongly opposed to Allied intervention in Russia. In order to conceal their ignorance of the matter, the Eastern delegates shut off debate by tabling the resolution.[99]

Angered over what they considered the conservatism of eastern delegates, the forty-five representatives of unions "from Winnipeg and points west of that city" nearly walked out in protest. They caucused twice during the convention and decided to hold their own meeting before the TLC met again: this would evolve into the Western Labour Conference of March 1919 that endorsed the breakaway One Big Union. While the *BC Federationist* insisted that developments at Quebec "did not represent a secessionist or separatist movement," events were leading in that direction.[100] British Columbia's working-class leadership had broken from the conciliatory policies of the mainstream of Canadian labour.

The Canadian state escalated its campaign against working-class radicalism within days of the labour split in Quebec. This response was strongly informed by the report of Montreal lawyer and financier C.H. Cahan on Bolshevism in Canada, which was submitted to Borden on 14 September 1918. Cahan had been defeated as a Unionist candidate in Maisonneuve in the 1917 conscription election and was subsequently appointed as Borden's director of public safety, heading a new branch within the federal Department of Justice with the mandate of "extirpating" Bolshevism in Canada.[101] Cahan warned that tensions manifested during the war – among workers angered by profiteering and farmers outraged over conscription – were being exploited by the Industrial Workers of the World and kindred radical groups to foment discord among otherwise peaceful Russian, Ukrainian, and Finnish immigrants. These radical societies promoted "the destruction of all state authority, the subversion of religions and the obliteration of all property rights." Borden instructed his Cabinet to take "immediate and vigorous action" on Cahan's recommendations.[102]

On 28 September 1918, a few days after the TLC convention adjourned, the Borden government approved Privy Council Order 2384, which declared fourteen working-class organizations to be unlawful associations "while Canada is engaged in war." The list of banned organizations confirms that Bolshevism was viewed as the primary threat:

The Industrial Workers of the World;
The Russian Social Democratic Party;
The Russian Revolutionary Group;
The Russian Workers Union;
The Ukrainian Revolutionary Group;
The Finnish Social Democratic Party;
The Social Democratic Party;
The Social Labor Party;
Group of Social Democrats of Bolsheviki;
Group of Social Democrats of Anarchists;
The Revolutionary Socialist Party of North America;
The Workers International Industrial Union;
Chinese Nationalist League;
Chinese Labor Association.[103]

The order-in-council stipulated a prison sentence of "not less than one year and not more than five years" for anyone who belonged to these groups or who possessed their literature, wore their buttons or insignia, or attempted to "sell, speak, write or publish anything" on their behalf.[104] The bias against Russian and Slavic radicals was evident in another clause, which decreed: "No public meeting or assemblage of any kind except church meetings or meetings for religious services, shall be held in Canada during the present war at which the proceedings or any part thereby are conducted in ... the language or any of the languages of Russia, Ukraine, or Finland." Attendees at such meetings could be apprehended without warrant and subjected to a $5,000 fine and five years in prison.[105] Germany faded as Canada's foe as the threat of Bolshevism in Russia and Canada mounted.

The notorious order-in-council 2384 was accompanied by a string of government censorship notices that targeted socialist and radical literature. On 28 September, the secretary of state of Canada issued a censorship notice deeming Lenin's essay "Political Parties in Russia" to be "objectionable matter" and prohibiting its possession in Canada – an offence punishable by a $5,000 fine or five years' imprisonment.[106] Six months earlier, the *BC Federationist* had serialized the Bolshevik tract.[107] In October 1918, the Canadian government banned the *Western Clarion*, newspaper of the Socialist Party of Canada (published at 401 Pender Street East, Vancouver), prompting the appearance of the underground organ *Red Flag*.[108] Other publications banned by the Canadian state in September and October 1918 included:

"The Canadian Forward," 397 Spadina Avenue, Toronto
"Rabotchyj Narod" (The Working People), printed in Russian,
   664 Pritchard Avenue, Winnipeg
"The World Tomorrow," Fellowship Press, New York
"The International Socialist Review," Charles H. Kerr & Co., Chicago
"After War," Charles H. Kerr & Co., Chicago
"To the Young Workers," printed in Russian, Union of Russian Workmen,
   New York
"Anarchism and Communism," printed in Russian; location unknown
"Defense News Bulletin," Industrial Workers of the World, Chicago
"Men and Mules," W.F. Ries, Girard, Kansas
"World Problems – The Solution," Pacific Press Publishing Association,
   Mountain View, California
"Komy Potribna Wyjna" (Who Wants War), translated from Russian into
   Ukrainian by T. Stefanicky, Toronto
"Do Not Chain the Living Soul," printed in Ukrainian, Chicago.[109]

Highlighting the government's anti-Bolshevik crusade, two additional publications deserve mention: a leaflet entitled *The Bolshevist Declaration of Rights* and a pamphlet published by the Alberta Provincial Executive Committee of the Socialist Party of Canada entitled *A Reply to the Press Lies Concerning the Russian Situation.*[110]

On 11 October 1918, a month before the Armistice ended fighting on the Western Front, the Canadian government banned labour strikes in most industries. Prompted by a dispute of Calgary freight-handlers and threats of sympathy strikes, the order-in-council declared: "any person who during the continuance of the present war shall incite, order or participate in a lockout or strike ... shall be guilty of an offence punishable" by six months' imprisonment and a $10,000 fine. The legislation included a "work-or-fight" clause, empowering the government to conscript strikers into the armed forces.[111] The *Semi-Weekly Tribune*, newspaper of the VTLC, described "government by order-in-council" as a "menace to our national life." Freedom of thought was "a safety valve against violence and lawbreaking" that was "all the more necessary" during wartime. The newspaper, edited by the moderate union official Eugene Woodward, said that the Social Democratic Party was the "least radical and most reasonable of all the Socialist societies in Canada" and protested "emphatically" against "unwise, unnecessary and dangerous attempts ... to rivet the shackles of Prussianism on this country."[112]

The war against Germany neared its end as the Canadian state declared war on radical labour in Canada and Russia. The string of orders-in-council and censorship notices coincided with the mobilization of the CEFS to British Columbia. The government's actions of autumn 1918 were motivated by domestic class relations and by events in Russia and responses within the Canadian working class. Bolshevism would be wiped out by banning radical parties and newspapers, jailing dissident workers, and invading Soviet Russia from the Siberian front. However, inadvertently, the Borden government strengthened ties between Canadian workers and Russian Bolsheviks. The two-pronged strategy of domestic repression and foreign intervention appeared to confirm a commonality of interests, drawing parallels between conditions in revolutionary Russia and wartime Canada and strengthening the appeal of the Russian model as a vehicle for social change. Canadian incarnations of Bolshevism, rather than being crushed, would come to play an important role in the unravelling of Canada's Siberian Expedition.

4
Mobilization

THE WAR IN EUROPE drew to a close as a force of five thousand soldiers mobilized to Canada's West Coast. The Canadian Expeditionary Force (Siberia) was drawn from across the country and included 135 Russian-speaking members – former soldiers of the czar's army who were attached to Canadian units as interpreters. Major-General James H. Elmsley began organizing the force in London then sailed for New York aboard the ocean liner *Aquitania*, arriving on 27 September 1918, when he immediately boarded a train west.[1] From British Columbia to Quebec to Nova Scotia, the troops converged on Victoria's Willows Camp and camps at New Westminster and Coquitlam; 4,210 soldiers would ultimately deploy for Vladivostok while the remainder never left Canada. As General Sydney Mewburn, Canada's minister of militia and defence, had anticipated, 1,653 were conscripts.[2] In addition to small units of bakers, butchers, medics, artists, and other supporting troops – and Nursing Matron Grace Eldrida Potter, the lone woman in the force (and wife of Colonel Jacob Leslie Potter, head of the No. 11 Stationary Hospital) – the bulk of the CEFS consisted of the 16th Infantry Brigade (Canadian Rifles), a "mixed brigade" that included the 259th and 260th Battalions and Britain's 25th Battalion Middlesex Regiment and 1/9th Battalion Hampshire Regiment.[3] These infantry units were joined by a machine gun company and two artillery batteries, which began training at Petawawa. In Regina, "B" Squadron of the RNWMP Cavalry unit enlisted 181 horses and 215 men, all volunteers.[4]

The composition of the CEFS was outlined in the Privy Council order of early August (with slight amendments later that month and in September 1918) (Appendix A):

"B" Squadron, Royal North-West Mounted Police (Cavalry)
85th Battery, Canadian Field Artillery
16th Field Company, Canadian Engineers
6th Signal Company
259th Infantry Battalion
260th Infantry Battalion
20th Machine Gun Company

No. 1 Company Divisional Train
No. 16 Field Ambulance
No. 11 Stationary Hospital
No. 9 Ordnance Detachment[5]

The 16th Brigade was commanded by Brigadier-General H.C. Bickford, head of Military District 2, Toronto, during the veterans' riots of August 1918.[6] The main infantry units in the 16th Brigade drew from every Canadian province. The 260th Battalion, led by Lieutenant Frederick Charles Jamieson, was the more geographically diverse, consisting of 1,026 troops (including 520 conscripts) organized into four companies from the following military districts:

"A" Company, Nova Scotia and New Brunswick
"B" Company, Manitoba
"C" Company, Saskatchewan and Alberta
"D" Company, British Columbia

General Mewburn had suggested that the Siberian Expedition be publicized as a "most interesting service," appealing to the "public spirit of young Canadians." Among commissioned officers, interest exceeded the number of available spaces. However, three days after the Canadian government approved the formation of the force, Mewburn issued the following order: "if men are not coming forward voluntarily rapidly enough, fill ranks with men obtained under Military Service Act."[7]

The 259th Battalion – which emerged as the hotbed of dissent – was raised entirely from Ontario and Quebec. A much higher proportion of this battalion was drafted under the Military Service Act – 705 of 1,083 troops. "A" and "B" companies were raised from the military districts around London, Kingston, and Toronto, while "C" and "D" companies consisted mainly of French-speaking Québécois from the military districts around Montreal and Quebec City. Quebec City had experienced serious rioting in March and April 1918, with the registrar's office destroyed and five protesters killed, as the Borden government deployed one thousand troops to reinforce the local garrison and summoned an additional three thousand troops from the west.[8] Unrest continued throughout the summer of 1918. The registrar's office in Beauce County was ransacked and a farmer at Black Lake, while resisting the draft, shot a Dominion Police officer. In Montreal, the local branch of the Social Democratic Party called a protest meeting against Allied intervention in Russia, circulating leaflets in Yiddish and attracting seven hundred "Russian and Jewish socialists," thirty-nine of whom were arrested by Dominion Police.[9]

The 259th Battalion was led by Lieutenant-Colonel Albert E. "Dolly" Swift, a career soldier who had served in the 4th Infantry Brigade on the Western Front. On 20 September 1918, Swift established the battalion headquarters at Montreal. The troops mustered to camps in Ontario and Quebec to report for duty and await the trip west: "A" and "B" companies to Niagara Camp at Niagara-on-the-Lake; "C" Company to Montreal's Peel Street Barracks, and "D" Company to the Drill Hall at Quebec City.[10] The *Montreal Gazette* reported: "great activity has been shown by the Military Police during the past few days in rounding up men all over the city for military service." And, in late September, it suggested: "this time next month they will all be in Siberia."[11] Press censor Ernest Chambers warned the Canadian Press syndicate about the need for "absolute secrecy as to the composition of this Force."[12]

Problems plagued the 259th Battalion from the start. Mobilization coincided with the arrival of the Spanish flu in Canada, the worldwide influenza epidemic that took an estimated 50 million lives globally and spread rapidly through sundry military units. Critics later attributed the scale of the epidemic to wartime privation and the low level of nutrition that left military units and local populations susceptible to disease. "The mobilization of the Siberian Expeditionary Force (SEF) was the greatest single factor in the diffusion of the disease," a recent study found, "a direct consequence of the widening of Canada's commitment to the Great War." Troops travelling west infected towns "like an invading army ravaging a foreign country."[13] On 2 October, "D" Company relocated to Quebec City's Citadel and the following day the men were "placed in Quarantine owing to the epidemic of influenza in [the] City." "C" Company moved to the Guy Street Barracks at Montreal and was also quarantined. Despite these conditions, the "French-Canadian companies" (as the battalion war diary describes them) began preliminary training in squad drill. "C" Company left Montreal on 24 October, while "D" Company left Quebec City on 26 October after an inspection and address by Canada's governor general, the Duke of Devonshire. Battalion commander Lieutenant-Colonel Swift joined "D" Company aboard a special train to the West Coast, as Quebec's central health committee urged that "no transport of conscripts" proceed since they were "the cause of the dissemination of influenza" and "dangerous to the conscripts themselves."[14] The MP for Chambly-Verchères, Joseph Archambault, would later tell the House of Commons that "some of the men were forced to board a train for Victoria against their will."[15]

Dissent was not confined to the Quebec units of the CEFS. Dawn Fraser, a pharmacist from Saint John, New Brunswick, who voluntarily enlisted in "A" Company of the 260th Battalion, described conditions at the Aldershot Camp in Nova Scotia:

Oh! Aldershot, white-tented,
Cold, wet, and beastly grim,
Where my courage was first dented,
When someone screamed, "Fall In."[16]

Fraser's book of prose, *Songs of Siberia and Rhymes of the Road* (c. 1919), sheds light on the rank-and-file view of Canada's Siberian Expedition and offers a rare glimpse of working-class culture at this moment of labour unrest. "In every contest between labour and capital, I am with labour against capital, first, last, and all the time," Fraser declared, a view echoed in his poem "The Parasite":

The world is nicely arranged for them,
Who live by the efforts of other men;
Live by the sweat of the poor and the weak,
Then marvel that men turn Bolshevik.[17]

Among the Ontario troops in the 259th Battalion, dissent could also be detected. "A" and "B" companies had been quartered "under canvas" at the Niagara Camp since late September and had begun training in musketry. "It's getting pretty miserable," Rifleman Harold Steele wrote to his girlfriend Josie Libby in Cane Township, Ontario.[18] Like their Québécois counterparts, the companies were quarantined on 5 October as a result of the Spanish Flu. As soldiers began to die, the mayor of Toronto, Thomas Church, wrote to Canada's defence minister, saying that he feared "further casualties ... owing to heavy outbreak of this epidemic at Fort Niagara." He asked why the Siberian draft should be "singled out and kept there in tents" and suggested that they be moved to "good accommodation" at Toronto's exhibition grounds. General Mewburn consulted with military officials and rejected Church's proposal, but he expedited the troops' departure for British Columbia.[19] On 15 October, "A" and "B" companies left Niagara Camp for Toronto, where they boarded a train west. En route, seventy-five troops were dropped from the battalion due to influenza.[20] "That was in the middle of that awful influenza epidemic, which we brought with us from the East," recalled Captain Eric Elkington, a medical doctor attached to the CEFS.[21]

Siberian Commerce

As the Siberian Expedition mobilized to Victoria, the local press ramped up its campaign against Bolshevism, alluding to rumours of

the approaching downfall of the Bolshevist government, an event which has never been in doubt, the only question being, when? ... Whatever semblance of government exists is in the hands of Lenine and Trotzky, but the area throughout which their behests are obeyed is a constantly narrowing one ... Russia is gradually emerging from her wild dream. She is discovering Bolshevism is only a transitory force which thrives by revolution and that Lenine and Trotzky do not differ in their brutal impractical efforts at Government from Danton and Robespierre.[22]

While the press emphasized the defects of Bolshevism, a commercial motivation was evident from the outset. The Siberian Expedition was cast as a boon for the expansion of Canadian trade in the Russian Far East. "Siberia, in soil, climate, and agricultural capabilities, is remarkably like the prairie provinces of Canada," the *Colonist* reported in the article announcing the expedition: "There is sure to develop enormous trade, which will profoundly affect the commercial development of the Pacific ... Canada can look forward to a legitimate share in this future trade."[23]

This commercial motivation was again cited when Newton Rowell, president of the Privy Council, visited Victoria in late September as part of a national tour to boost support for the expedition. Addressing a luncheon of three hundred well-heeled members of the Canadian Club and Women's Canadian Club, including Premier John Oliver, in the regal Empress Hotel ballroom, Rowell suggested: "Canada may not be able to provide large sums of capital, but she can give Siberia the benefit of her experience along the lines of interior development ... As Canadians we must take every opportunity of establishing the closest connections with our great neighbour to the west. We may confidently expect that as a result of more intimate relations the greatest benefit may result both to Canada and Siberia."[24] Rowell said the Siberian Expedition was necessary "to support the elements and governments of the Russian people, which [were] battling against German armed force and intrigue" and "to reestablish the Eastern front."[25] The emphasis on German aggression coincided with heavy Allied losses on the Western Front – the most substantial of the war, with 2,849 Canadians killed in action in September 1918 and another 13,606 wounded, 967 of whom died from their wounds.[26] "I am still in the land of the living," stretcher-bearer Frederick Carne assured his mother in Victoria.[27] However, postal worker Christian Sivertz, secretary-treasurer of the Victoria Trades and Labor Council, was not so fortunate, receiving a telegram on 30 September stating that his twenty-four-year-old son Henry, a schoolteacher during peacetime, had been killed outside the French city of Cambrai.[28] Survivors described the engagement as the "cruelest fight of the war," with 2,089 Canadian casualties in a single day.[29] In October, nearly three thousand Canadians were killed in action as the Allies took Cambrai and pushed towards Germany.[30]

Newton Rowell warned his Canadian Club crowd that failure to intervene in Siberia would allow Vladivostok to fall into the hands of Germany, giving it a base of operations on the Pacific and threatening the security of Victoria: "You will have, therefore, an especial and peculiar interest in Canada's position as a Pacific power and in the Canadian Expeditionary Force which is now being mobilized at Victoria for service in Siberia." According to Rowell, Canada sought "no territorial or other advantage as a result of the war" but, rather, had only the interests of the Russian people in mind:

> When they finally threw off their corrupt and autocratic government because of its own inherent weakness and incapacity, we all hailed the Russian Revolution as the dawn of a new day for liberty and democracy and its consummation as one of the greatest triumphs of this war ... The Bolsheviki were pledged to secure peace and brought it at an awful price ... The disastrous terms of peace accepted by the Bolsheviki and Germany's method of enforcing them, together with the incapacity of the Bolsheviki to fulfill their pledges to the people are combining to undermine the Bolsheviki authority. Its power appears to be steadily waning ... The revelations recently made of the treachery and duplicity of Lenine and Trotzky should hasten the end of the Bolsheviki.

Rowell lauded the White Russians as the only party capable of restoring order and stability, citing Cossack governments in south and central Russia and the new "Government of the North" at Arkhangelsk. "A Russian government has also been established in Siberia with headquarters at Vladivostok," Rowell noted, "and the Allies are now able to co-operate with these various independent Russian governments, who are appealing to the Allies for help." Rowell concluded his talk with the hope that "an economic mission also may be sent to Siberia."[31]

In August, Canada had posted a trade commissioner to Vladivostok, Dana Wilgress, who had served in Omsk before the March Revolution and established an office in downtown Vladivostok.[32] On 21 October 1918, Canada's Privy Council passed order-in-council PC 2595, authorizing the formation of the Canadian Siberian Economic Commission. The commission was charged with the task of cooperating with the Allies to re-establish Siberia's productive industries, to reorganize its commercial activities, and to investigate local conditions of transport, agriculture, mining, forestry, fishing, and finance "with a view to the development of Canadian trade."[33] The commission consisted of Wilgress and Conradin F. Just, another former trade commissioner to czarist Russia; military liaison officer Colonel John S. Dennis, director of colonization for the CPR;

Ross Owen, the CPR's shipping agent at Vladivostok; A.D. Braithwaite, former assistant general manager of the Bank of Montreal; and Louis Kon, a Polish-Canadian who spoke fluent Russian and served as the commission's secretary.[34] In September, Dennis had written to Canada's minister of trade and commerce offering his services and those of Owen at "no expense."[35] Other Canadian businesses showed an interest. The Royal Bank of Canada sent officers and a fifty-seven-ton prefabricated building to Vladivostok to open a branch in early 1919.[36] At the bank's annual general meeting, Edson L. Pease, vice-president and managing director, described the emerging trade relationship. According to Pease, the commission had been formed: "to aid in supplying the pressing needs of Russia, and assist in stabilizing conditions there. The organization of a Siberian Supply Commission will follow, and through it goods will be purchased in Canada for shipment to Russia. Siberia needs commodities which Canada can supply."[37] In early October, before the commission was officially formed, Just and Owen sailed for Vladivostok with the first group of Canadians.

Advance Party to White Siberia

On 11 October 1918, the advance party of the CEFS, consisting of 680 troops, including Major-General Elmsley, the headquarters battalion, and eighteen members of the RNWMP, left Vancouver aboard the CPR liner *Empress of Japan*. The ship held two months' supplies for the entire force and three months' supplies for the advance party. The first day at sea, the weather was "fine but quite rough," according to the war diary: "about 30% of the troops are sea-sick."[38] Later at sea, the entire crew was vaccinated against typhoid and the weather improved, allowing for marching, physical exercise, sports, and musical concerts. The *Empress of Japan* crossed the International Date Line on 19 October, and the CEFS suffered its first casualty the following day: Private Edward Biddle, a steam engineer from Victoria who belonged to the BC Company ("D" Company) of the 260th Battalion, died of pneumonia brought on by the Spanish Flu. Biddle was buried at sea.[39] The ship passed through the Straits of Tsugaru (off Hakodate between the Japanese islands of Honshu and Hokkaido) on 24 October. Early on the morning of 26 October, two White Russian torpedo boats led the *Empress of Japan* into Golden Horn Bay. A Czech guard of honour and Allied commanders greeted the Canadians. The officers spent their first night in Russia aboard the ship, while the enlisted men slept "in the sheds on the quay."[40]

From the outset, the Canadian mission was mired in logistical problems. Unloading of cargo from the *Empress of Japan* was impeded by unmarked cases, inaccurate lists, and a labour shortage. "The advanced party for the Engineers should have been treble the number sent," the war diary records. Other units in the advance party were "insufficient" to supply guards and working parties.

Moreover, "warehouse space on the wharves [was] limited," as was "suitable accommodation" for force and base headquarters. The sixty-room Versailles Hotel had been claimed by the French mission, requiring the turfing of refugee inhabitants with "nowhere to go." The Canadian command lamented the "inequitable" distribution of accommodation, with the first Allied contingents claiming quarters that were "not occupied to their full capacity."[41] White Russian military commanders were powerless to requisition civilian buildings, and the White-sponsored Town Council was reluctant to supersede property rights. "There is no recognized law or force that can turn them out of their buildings," the Canadians complained.[42]

Three days after landing at Vladivostok, the Canadian command seized the Pushkinsky Theatre, a modern building in the centre of the city that housed the esteemed Vladivostok Cultural-Enlightenment Society. The society had operated in Vladivostok for thirty years, offering a city library, school, adult education courses, and musical and theatrical performances. The unilateral Canadian action angered local commercial leaders, who were staunchly anti-Bolshevik but resented foreign incursion into property rights and culture. At an emergency meeting on 1 November 1918, members of the Vladivostok Trade-Manufacturers' Assembly passed a protest resolution, with a scant five opposing votes, lambasting the "trampling" of the rights of Russian citizens and "interference" in Russia's "internal affairs": "It would seem that such a Society would have a just cause on inviolability, and meanwhile, our Allies, in the name of the Canadian command, have grasped the Society's premises," preventing its seven hundred members from continuing cultural-educational and "public work." The Vladivostok merchants and industrialists demanded "the clearing of the occupied premises" (see Appendix C).[43]

Elmsley refused this request, stating in an open letter, in Russian, in Vladivostok's *Dalekaya Okraina* newspaper that no other suitable premises were available and assuring the city's elite that the library and reading room would remain open. He reminded the industrialists that the "Allied armies ha[d] entered the country under the invitation of the Russian people who [had] repeatedly asked for help." While Europe had been ravaged by four years of war, and "all Russia ha[d] been devastated by the Bolshevist reign of terror," Vladivostok, on account if its unique geographical location, was fortunate to suffer only Allied occupation. The Canadians expressed "surprise" over opposition to "the temporary employment of a place of entertainment" for forces that had "come at the necessary hour to render assistance to their country."[44] The Canadian command posted guards at the Pushkinsky Theatre, which served as Force Headquarters and included billiard and card rooms. A concert was held there for the troops on 3 November.[45]

The Canadian soldiers, meanwhile, were quartered on the outskirts of Vladivostok, which, according to Trade Commissioner Dana Wilgress, "saved them from the criticism of uncivilized behaviour, which the Americans received."[46] The Canadians marched ten kilometres to the East Barracks, at the head of Golden Horn Bay. Elmsley and his staff slept in a nearby house, while officers were quartered in the cells of the Russian Naval Hospital military jail (see Map 4). Gunners from the 85th Field Battery, led by Lieutenant Raymond Massey, and sappers from the Canadian Engineering Corps began arranging permanent barracks for the two infantry battalions at Gornostai Bay, 15 kilometres east of Vladivostok.[47] On the afternoon of 28 October, Elmsley attended the semi-weekly Allied conference with British, American, French, Italian, Czech, Japanese, and Chinese representatives.[48] The sensitivity of Allied manoeuvres in Siberia was apparent in censorship orders that Elmsley issued to all officers and enlisted men under his command: "Officers and men are reminded that it is their duty to give no information of a military nature to anyone ... [including] relatives at home either personally, by letter or by telegram." This prohibition extended to the use of "code" to transmit information and explicitly forbade "all communications to the Press." Correspondence to Canada had to be directed through the Army Postal Service, and transgression of censorship orders would be "severely dealt with."[49]

The Canadians arrived in Vladivostok as Allied forces struggled to stabilize conditions in the Russian Far East. In August, a strike of Vladivostok freight handlers had impeded the unloading of Allied cargo. Troops were enlisted to handle goods and quash a "serious clash" between strikers and replacement workers at the local arsenal shops as railworkers threatened sympathetic action, imperilling the coal supply on the Suchan River, which fuelled the railroad and Vladivostok.[50] That month, General Horvath's dictatorship wavered after an aborted coup d'état, and the Allies were called upon to disarm White Russian troops.[51] Seeking to forge a new military cadre along British lines, the British Military Mission began preparations for a White Russian officers' training school on Russian Island, just south of Vladivostok at the mouth of Golden Horn Bay. Canadian intelligence officer James Mackintosh Bell was assigned to supervise the refurbishment of these czarist-era barracks, which had been ransacked during the revolution. Beginning in October, Mackintosh Bell marshalled the work of 150 German prisoners-of-war and Russian workers ("Bolsheviks ... but ... a jolly lot of fellows"). The school opened in late 1918, funded by the British government and administered by a White Russian commandant, General Sakharov, to fashion the leadership of a new Siberian army.[52]

Along the length of the Trans-Siberian Railroad – from Vladivostok to Samara on the Volga River – Czech, Cossack, Japanese, and British forces repelled

Bolshevik irregulars in autumn 1918, seizing the Soviet strongholds of Khabarovsk and Chita and opening telegraph and rail lines. "The capitals of the Entente powers are now in quick and certain communication with the situation throughout the length of the rail lines from Vladivostok to the Volga," an American general told the *New York Times*.[53] The Allies sought to connect the Czech forces on the Volga with British and American contingents at Arkhangelsk in the north. Meanwhile, in Moscow, Lenin survived an assassination attempt after addressing workers at the Mikhelson armaments factory, receiving two gunshot wounds from the disgruntled Socialist Revolutionary Fanya Kaplan.[54]

The Allies sought a strong, central government to consolidate White military efforts and to provide an alternative administration to the Moscow government – an objective complicated by competing authority claims among White Russian and Cossack generals. Horvath "has gone to Irkutsk and joined force with the Czechoslovaks," the *New York Times* reported with optimism in early September: "This removes the most troublesome factional differences among the anti-Bolshevist elements now virtually controlling Siberia and promises a quick solution of the governmental problem in that section of the world."[55] However, a new power base was emerging in the Russian Far East in autumn 1918, around Ataman general Grigori Semyonov, who commanded the Special Manchurian Detachment of Cossacks from his base at Chita and enjoyed the support of the Czech Legion and Japan.[56]

Political tension was also endemic among White Russians at Omsk, the capital and most important city of western Siberia. The Whites had seized Omsk from the Bolsheviks in June 1918, establishing a Western-Siberian Commissariat, which transferred power to a directory led by a cabinet of five. This new Provisional Siberian Government challenged the supremacy of the precarious Derber and Horvath governments in Vladivostok and Harbin and the Siberian Regional Duma based at Tomsk. In mid-July 1918, the Commercial-Industrial Congress at Omsk issued an ultimatum calling for the Tomsk Duma to disband. V.A. Zhardetskii, leader of the Kadet Party in Siberia, told attendees that, for the Whites to succeed "it is essential to bring in strong unipersonal authority."[57] Omsk newspapers carried favourable reports on General Kornilov and his failed 1917 coup, implying that a strong hand was necessary to quash Bolshevism. In mid-August, the Siberian Regional Duma held five days of meetings at Tomsk before disbanding on orders of the Omsk Directory. V.V. Kukilov, a member of the Omsk branch of the anti-Bolshevik Union of Regeneration, said: "at the present time it is impossible to establish parliamentarianism" and it is "essential to introduce state dictatorship and to dismiss the Duma."[58] Fifteen days of tense negotiations in September produced an all-Russian provisional government based in the city of Ufa and led by a five-member directory. Canada's Privy

Council president Rowell welcomed this development during his Empress Hotel speech on 27 September: "This morning we are in receipt of the welcome and cheering news that out of these various governments a central government for all Russia has been formed."[59]

Greater consolidation was on the agenda. On 21 September 1918, Admiral Aleksandr Kolchak, former commander of the czar's Black Sea Fleet, landed in Vladivostok from Japan. Kolchak had followed a circuitous path during the revolutionary upheavals of 1917. He travelled to Britain and the United States as an envoy of the Kerensky government and, after the Bolsheviks took power, assumed command of White Russian forces in Manchuria.[60] Kolchak served in the Horvath Cabinet in mid-1918 and developed close relations with Major-General Alfred Knox, head of Britain's Military Mission in Siberia.[61] He left Vladivostok for the interior in September 1918. As Kolchak travelled west along the Trans-Siberian Railroad, the White All-Russian Provisional Government moved from Ufa to Omsk, along with 651 million rubles of the Imperial Gold Reserve.[62] Kolchak arrived in Omsk four days later, on 14 October, and was appointed minister of war in the new Omsk government. Five days behind the admiral, Britain's eight hundred-strong 25th Battalion, Middlesex Regiment, reached the Siberian city.[63] As Lieutenant-Colonel John Ward, commander of the 25th Battalion, later wrote:

> It is certain that Admiral Koltchak would never have gone to Siberia, nor have become the head of the constitutional movement and government of Russia, if he had not been advised and even urged to do so by the Allies. He received the most categorical promises of whole-hearted support and early Allied recognition before he agreed to take up the dangerous duty of head of the Omsk Government.[64]

This point is reinforced by Kerensky, the deposed Russian premier who opposed Kolchak's autocratic ways: "I was in London and Paris myself while Admiral Kolchak's *coup* was being prepared, and had occasion therefore to look behind the scenes ... I sent a trusted messenger to Siberia with a letter, of which I still have a copy, in which I named all the participants in the conspiracy planned in the Allied capitals."[65]

The Allies had their point man in Russia, but victory was hardly certain. Problems of morale and logistics on both sides of the Pacific impeded the Canadian objective of White military supremacy in Siberia and the Russian Far East. White success depended on the free movement of troops and cargo along the 6,500-kilometre length of the Trans-Siberian Railroad from Vladivostok to the Urals, but this vital link remained vulnerable to sabotage, guerrilla attack, and discordant Allied interests – "most uncertain for both passenger and traffic services," Canadian general Elmsley warned.[66] Well-armed and well-organized Czech, Cossack, Japanese, and British units had overpowered irregular Bolshevik forces in eastern Russia, but trouble loomed. Growing domestic strains hindered the deployment of reinforcements once the Armistice ended fighting on the Western Front. Canada's Siberian Expedition mobilized against the backdrop of growing war weariness among the troops and mounting domestic opposition to interference in Russia's internal affairs. The Siberian Expedition began to unravel before it had gotten off the ground.

The Willows Camp

In autumn 1918, conscripts and volunteers from across Canada converged on Victoria's Willows Camp, a horse-racing track and exhibition ground on the edge of the city. They belonged to the CEFS. The advance party sailed for Vladivostok as the main body of the force gathered at the camp – influenced by the Spanish flu, a wet BC autumn, and two platoons of Russian soldiers attached to the CEFS. Poor camp conditions and the signing of the Armistice midway through their stay further sapped the morale of the troops, one-third of whom were conscripts, "MSA men" drafted under the Military Service Act. Labour radicals in Victoria actively encouraged dissent. At a series of mass meetings, trade unionists spoke directly to members of the CEFS, offering a critical perspective on Allied intervention and raising the slogan "Hands Off Russia." This dialogue between BC socialists and military conscripts laid the groundwork for mutiny.

The Willows Camp, located in the tony municipality of Oak Bay, had been selected as the assembly point for Canada's Siberian Expedition as a result of active lobbying by the local elite. "We see no reason why Macaulay Plains, or even the Willows Camp, should not be utilized," the *Colonist* had suggested in August at the time the expedition was announced, noting British Columbia's modest contribution of a company of 250 men. According to the *Colonist:* "City Council, the Board of Trade and our Island member of parliament [should] put forth their best efforts to induce Ottawa to establish a camp here."[67] Ottawa complied. In early October, part of Elmsley's advance party had been quartered under canvas at the Work Point camp in Esquimalt township, and the 85th Field Battery, RNWMP "B" Squadron, and other supporting units gathered at camps in New Westminster and Coquitlam.[68] However, the Willows was selected for the two infantry battalions, serving as the principal embarkation point for the Siberian Expedition.

The first troops arrived at the Willows Camp in early October, as the Spanish Flu reached Canada's Pacific coast aboard the troop trains of the 260th Battalion from Regina and the Maritimes.[69] On 7 October 1918, a "temperature parade" was held at the camp to identify the prevalence of the disease among the men. Thirty troops, while not actually diagnosed with influenza, were found to have "above normal" temperatures and were promptly quarantined by the CEFS's 16th Field Ambulance.[70] Throughout the city, 50 to 100 known cases of influenza were reported, the opening wedge of an epidemic that left 101 Victorians dead and another 2,800 ill.[71] The city's health committee banned all public gatherings on 7 October in an effort to contain the outbreak. Schools closed the morning of 8 October, as did "churches, theatres, pool-rooms, dance halls, and public meeting places."[72] The ban would not be lifted until the end of November, despite protests by Victoria's Anglican bishop and others.[73]

Such was the climate that greeted the soldiers of the Siberian Expedition as they gathered at the Willows Camp. The conscripts and volunteers from the 260th Battalion were followed by "A" and "B" companies of the 259th Battalion, who reached Victoria on the morning of 22 October aboard an overnight boat from Vancouver. The Ontario companies, consisting of 327 enlisted men and thirteen officers, marched through the city to the Willows Camp.[74] The soldiers of the 259th Battalion were quartered "under canvas" and in the stables used by racehorses during peacetime, vulnerable to the autumn winds, flooding, and driving rain.[75] Rifleman Harold Steele, a twenty-year-old railway worker from Cane Township, Ontario, who voluntarily enlisted in "B" Company of the 259th Battalion, described conditions at the Willows. "The weather is the worst," Steele wrote to his girlfriend Josie Libby. "It rains every day and sometimes two or three times a day."[76] As the *Times* later conceded, "It may not have been the best time of year for troops to have been quartered in Victoria ... The latter part of their stay has been marked by an unusual amount of rain with an attendant sea of mud at the Willows."[77] By the time the soldiers embarked for Russia, outdoor training was "impossible" and boardwalks were required to navigate over the flooded fields in the camp.[78]

The Spanish Flu and poor camp conditions provided a fertile climate for dissent, which extended throughout Canadian and British forces in the late stages of the war and demobilization.[79] Local conditions were compounded with the phenomenon of "war weariness," a public revulsion to warfare following "a long and severe bout of fighting."[80] One-half of all CEFS members had seen previous service in Europe, and their willingness to fight in Siberia diminished with the signing of the Armistice. These men were "veterans of the bloodiest fighting on the Western Front," according to historian John Skuce, and suffered serious wounds before returning to Canada for medical treatment.[81] While Harold Carne, the stretcher-bearer on the Western Front, wrote, "I'd sure hate like the devil to be in the shoes of those fellows who are still sporting around in 'civies,'" a growing number of Canadians were unwilling to serve overseas.[82]

Morale within the 259th Battalion was also influenced by the presence of 132 Russian soldiers and three officers, who were taken on strength at the Willows on 24 October to provide interpretive services in Siberia. Containing former members of the czar's army, the two Russian platoons had been attached to the Canadian Corps in France and then recalled for the Siberian force.[83] Evidence of Bolshevik sympathies soon arose.[84]

In the face of these conditions, the 259th Battalion continued its training regimen at the Willows Camp. On 25 October, Brigadier-General H.C. Bickford, commander of the 16th Infantry Brigade, inspected the troops during their first parade and rifle drill as a battalion. The troops "made a good appearance."[85] However, inclement weather led to the cancellation of a planned church parade on Sunday, 27 October and forced the cancellation of training the following day, prompting lectures, inoculations, and dental parades. On 31 October 1918, members of "D" Company arrived from Quebec City. Reflecting the mood of the period, the war diary records that the company "only lost one man on the way from Québec through illness."[86] In contrast, "C" Company arrived from Montreal a day later after losing six troops to influenza.[87] At the height of the influenza outbreak, the troops' sleeping quarters were transferred from tents to the stables and exhibition hall at the Willows Camp.[88]

At the Queen's Park Camp in New Westminster on the mainland, an RNWMP surgeon described the Mounties in "B" Squadron as "all very weak with severe coughs and poor appetites," "making a very slow recovery," and unfit for "an extended trip on the North Pacific ocean at this time of year." Five Mounties had already died from the flu. For this reason, the RNWMP commissioner thought it prudent "to postpone departure for one month, as [he did] not think that the Squadron [was] yet free from Spanish Influenza."[89] However, they were quickly pressed into service. On 17 November 1918, thirty officers and 395 other ranks, along with 287 horses, left Vancouver aboard the ship *Monteagle*, arriving in Vladivostok on 5 December. The party included 144 members of the RNWMP, 121 engineers, and Nursing Matron Grace Eldrida Potter, who had enlisted in the CEFS four days earlier and was attached to the Canadian Red Cross upon arrival in Vladivostok.[90]

Armistice?

At eleven o'clock on the morning of Monday, 11 November 1918 – two o'clock in the morning on Canada's Pacific coast – the last guns fell silent on the Western Front. German general Matthias Erzberger had signed the terms of surrender six hours earlier aboard a railcar near Compiègne, France, ending four years of bloody fighting in the trenches of France and Flanders. The last Canadian casualty, a conscript from Moose Jaw, Private George Price, was killed by a

German sniper at Havre, Belgium, two minutes before the ceasefire took effect.[91] "PEACE" declared the banner headline in the Victoria *Colonist*.

Ignoring the ban on public gatherings, Victorians responded with jubilant enthusiasm and wild partying: "By nine o'clock the streets were thronged with flag-waving crowds, who shook hands and fairly danced with joy. From the shipyards, from office desk and store counter, flocked the workers ... Broad Street from Yates to Fort was a seething mass of cheering, hand-shaking and flag-waving enthusiasts."[92] Firecrackers exploded through the centre as the mayor proclaimed a public holiday. That afternoon, a "monster parade" proceeded down Government Street and past the legislature to Beacon Hill Park, "a demonstration never before equaled in the history of the city." General Bickford, on horseback, led the Siberian force, three thousand strong, alongside other military contingents, British Columbia's lieutenant-governor, and marchers from the Canadian Red Cross, the Imperial Order of the Daughters of the Empire, and the Women's Auxiliary of the Great War Veterans' Association. Columns of shipyard workers, carpenters, machinists, and metal workers represented organized labour, while firefighters paraded with an effigy of the German kaiser. Prior to the march, a brief skirmish had erupted in front of the Labor Temple when a rebel worker attempted to hoist the Red Flag and unfurl a banner proclaiming the Marxist slogan "Workers of All Lands, Unite." He was accosted by more patriotic comrades.[93] The demonstration concluded with speeches and song as a huge bonfire roared atop Beacon Hill and another fire raged at the peak of Mount Tolmie, a promontory in neighbouring Saanich.[94]

Four days earlier, premature reports of the Armistice had provoked similar demonstrations in Victoria. On 7 November 1918, the one-year anniversary of the Bolshevik uprising in Petrograd, an inaccurate cable report from the United Press Association in Paris prompted Victoria's industrial workers to down tools:

> Shortly after 10 a.m. the report of peace circulated. Within a remarkably short space of time it had penetrated to the outskirts, the residents of which, aroused by the continuous whistles, ringing of bells and staccato blasts from boats in the harbour, kept the telephones busy ... The machinery in Victoria's industrial plants ceased to hum shortly after the news was announced ... Without waiting for orders the men quit work and threaded their way out of the shipyard gates and started for the downtown sector.[95]

The false report was triggered by the opening of talks between Germany and the Allies, after a train carrying German officials was permitted to cross Allied lines. The working-class response in Victoria and other cities reflected the burning desire for peace.

Fighting ended on the Western Front as rebellion erupted among German sailors, soldiers, and workers. At the end of October, German sailors in the port of Wilhelmshaven had refused to prepare for battle against the British navy. The unrest spread to Kiel and quickly enveloped ports and towns across Germany. Reminiscent of Russia a year earlier, mutinous sailors and workers demanded *Frieden und Brot* (Peace and Bread). On 6 November, the kaiser's government suspended diplomatic ties with Russia after Bolshevik pamphlets were discovered at the Soviet embassy in Berlin, pending a "guarantee from the Soviet government that in future no revolutionary propaganda against state institutions [would] be carried out in Germany."[96] On the first anniversary of the Bolshevik Revolution, the Victoria *Colonist* reported: "Mutinous German sailors in Kiel have seized the battleships *Kaiser* and *Schleswig-Holstein* and refused to return to work until a treaty of peace with the Allies is signed."[97] The next day's paper reported that German submarine crews had joined the revolution and that "a revolt had broken out in Hamburg":

> Kiel is governed by the Marines', Soldiers' and Workers' Council. All the workshops have been occupied by Red troops. The streetcar lines and railways are under the control of the Workmen's council ... The entire German navy and the greater part of Schleswig are in the hands of the revolutionists.[98]

German railworkers declared a general strike on 9 November as Hamburg was taken by the revolutionists, who hoisted red flags from every ship in the harbour. Soldiers joined the revolt in Bremen while a mass meeting of Bavarian workers proclaimed a republic.[99] On 10 November, Berlin workers formed a local Soviet. A bulletin from Copenhagen described the scene in the German capital: "The red banner has been hoisted over the royal palace and the red flag is waving from the Brandenburg gate." Armed workers and soldiers occupied a "majority of the public buildings and establishments."[100] Kaiser Wilhelm II abdicated the throne and fled to Holland.[101]

Peace was not on the agenda. White flags were raised over the Western Front as Allied troops streamed into Germany to suppress the nascent Soviets, seizing ships and disarming sailors and workers in accordance with the terms of the Armistice.[102] While historians have debated the extent and origins of the 1918 German naval mutinies, the unrest served to reinforce the fears of Allied leaders and to strengthen their resolve to intervene in Russia.[103] Bolshevism supplanted Kaiserism as the primary target of Allied military force. "Enough is obviously not being done in the matter of intervention in Russia," the Victoria *Colonist* argued on 8 November:

> The danger of Bolshevism, a doctrine which consists of killing all who do not espouse its tenets, is as great to civilization as Prussian autocracy has ever been ... If Middle Europe should become the prey of terrorist happenings the task of the Allies will take some months yet before it is finished. Allied occupation of all Middle Europe and Russia may be necessary before law and order can be established in the world.[104]

A day later, the *Colonist* outlined the philosophy driving the Siberian Expedition: "The Bolsheviki ... recognize no law but force, and like the Germans they must be opposed with force, 'without stint or limit.'"[105] Another report anticipated the "speedy collapse of the Bolsheviki regime."[106] In northwest Russia, Canadian troops marked Armistice Day on 11 November 1918 by joining British, American, and White Russian forces in a fresh offensive against Bolsheviks in the city of Tulgas on the Murmansk Front.[107] The military imperative was clear in a telegram sent to Ottawa by the Official Press Bureau: "All censorship restrictions withdrawn ... on mention of numbers and location of battalions in all theatres of war except Russia."[108]

News of the armistice reached Canadian prime minister Robert Borden aboard the ship *Mauretania* on the Atlantic crossing en route to peace talks in Europe. Writing in his diary, the prime minister reflected on the widening circle of unrest: "Revolt has spread all over Germany. The question is whether it will stop there. The world has drifted far from its old anchorage and no man can with certainty prophesy what the outcome will be."[109] In London, British prime minister David Lloyd George announced the dissolution of Parliament, stating: "At this moment the air of Europe is quivering with revolution. Two-thirds of Europe has been swept by its devastating deluge ... The institutions, even of this country, may follow those of many in the rest of Europe."[110]

In Vladivostok, the Canadian soldiers performed their first official duty in an Allied victory parade on 15 November 1918. Sixty-two members of the advance party marched down Svetlanskaya, the main street of the city. Shops and government offices closed while buildings were adorned with Russian and foreign flags. The *Dalekaya Okraina* described the event, which was inspected by Japanese general Kikuzo Otani, commander of Allied forces in the Russian Far East: "At the head of the column there were American armies, then the Chinese armies, the French sailors and *Annamites* (Vietnamese troops), English sailors, the Japanese armies, Canadians, Romanians, Russian sea company and the Siberian infantry. Serbs and Czecho-Slovaks brought up the rear."[111]

In the Siberian interior, the White Russians underwent a change of command. On 16 November, Admiral Aleksandr Kolchak and British Lieutenant-Colonel John Ward dined in a railcar outside Omsk, arriving in the Siberian capital the next evening at five-thirty in the afternoon. That night, 17-18 November 1918, with the men of the Middlesex Regiment asleep in their barracks, Cossack guards arrested the ministers of the Omsk Directory and Kolchak was proclaimed supreme ruler of Russia.[112] In his proclamation to the people, Kolchak declared: "I shall not go either on the road of reaction or on the fatal road of Party partisanship. I set as my main objectives the creation of an efficient army, victory over Bolshevism and the establishment of law and order."[113] Ward describes the events that followed:

> On the declaration of the Koltchak Government, General Denikin, General Dutoff, General Hovart, and the North Russian Governments made over their authority to Omsk. There was at once a clear issue – the Terrorist at Moscow, the Constitutionalist at Omsk. Had the Allies at this juncture translated their promises into acts, from what untold suffering Russia and Europe might have been saved![114]

The British government pledged "all possible help" to "organizations which tend toward stable government" – but ruled out "a general anti-Bolshevik crusade" and refused to deploy additional British troops, mindful of the impending election.[115] With tentative backing from the Allies, Kolchak offered an alternative to Bolshevism, the first semblance of a central White government. For the first time since November 1917, the prospects appeared bright that the Russian model of a new democracy would be short-lived. Fifty-five Canadians in Vladivostok prepared to embark "up country," to lay the groundwork for the anticipated arrival of Canada's Siberian Expeditionary Force at Omsk.[116]

Indecision in the Ranks

Back in Canada, the Armistice of November 1918 provoked misgivings over the Siberian Expedition – among a growing layer of workers and farmers, among the troops being mustered at the Willows Camp, and within Borden's Cabinet in Ottawa. On 13 November, the Privy Council had amended the notorious orders-in-council against working-class organizations, lifting the no-strike order and the ban on the Social Democratic Party while providing for the regulation of foreign-language publications. However, thirteen working-class organizations remained suppressed, and the Privy Council declared unlawful "for the duration of the war ... any association, organization, or corporation ... which teaches, advocates, or advises that any class should forcibly take possession of all property, or forcibly abolish all private ownership of property."[117] The *Semi-Weekly Tribune*, newspaper of the VTLC, lamented that "the dogs of war have still a work [sic] to do," dashing hopes that "peace meant a cessation of fighting." The paper urged Ottawa to "take organized labour into its confidence in regard to the proposed Siberian expedition" since workers would be the ones called upon to supply the "material resources" of war and "also ... much of the blood."[118]

Peace in Europe triggered a debate on whether Canadian troops should be deployed to Siberia. As Borden sailed aboard the *Mauritania* en route to peace talks in Europe, acting prime minister Sir Thomas White sent an urgent telegram from Ottawa:

> All our colleagues are of opinion that public opinion here will not sustain us in continuing to send troops, many of whom are draftees under the Military Service Act and Order in Council, now that the war is ended. We are all of opinion that no further troops should be sent and that Canadian forces in Siberia should, as soon as situation will permit, be returned to Canada. Consider matter of serious importance.[119]

Earlier that year, White had attempted to resign from Borden's Cabinet due to poor health but was persuaded to remain.[120] T.A. Crerar, a Winnipeg farmer and businessman who would soon defect from the Union Cabinet to lead the Progressive Party, was "absolutely opposed to sending any additional forces to Siberia." According to him: "The matter of how Russia shall settle her internal affairs is her concern – not ours." Borden rejected his ministers' advice, maintaining that troops should leave Victoria for Vladivostok: "In my judgment we shall stand in an unfortunate situation unless we proceed with [the] Siberian Expedition ... Canada's present position and prestige would be singularly impaired." Anticipating that Canadian troops would not be called upon to engage in active warfare, "beyond possible quelling of some local disturbances," he suggested they were needed to assist the new government of Admiral Kolchak, which sought to organize anti-Bolshevik forces into a professional army.[121] White reiterated his earlier opposition, pointing out that Canadian interests in Siberia differed from those of Britain and France because of Russia's indebtedness to those countries:

> Canada has no such economic or business interests as will justify the employment of a Canadian force composed of young men whose parents and friends desire should return at once to their ordinary occupations ... Canada should, now that the war is over and no necessity exists for the re-establishment of the Eastern front, discontinue further participation and expense. It seems clearly a task for

nations more immediately interested in the finances of Russia. There is an extra-ordinary sentiment in Canada in favour of getting all our men home and at work as soon as possible.[122]

Indicating that opposition was not confined to labour circles, the Toronto *Globe* weighed in on the debate: "Why should Canadians be forced into a service of which the purpose, if there is any definite aim, is hidden in the minds of public men? ... There has been no proposal to make Russia our enemy in any legal form. How can we say that our force in Siberia is being used for the defence of Canada?"[123] On 22 November, a scheduled troop sailing was postponed in-definitely by Mewburn, but this position was reversed days later when the Cabinet yielded to its prime minister and decided that the Siberian Expedition would proceed – with the proviso that any soldier who desired would be per-mitted to return to Canada within one year of the armistice. "We are advised that this will be satisfactory to the troops now in British Columbia," White as-sured Borden, prematurely, as events revealed.[124] Stuart Tompkins, an officer in the 260th Battalion, lamented the decision in a letter to his wife Edna in Ed-monton: "Well the worst has come. Instructions came through that all men were to be asked whether they wanted their discharge. Result about one third are quitting. So we are likely to be hung up here waiting for reinforcements for another month or so. It is discouraging."[125]

Morale among the troops at the Willows Camp waned in the face of vigorous propaganda by Victoria's labour movement, part of a national campaign against the Siberian Expedition. Socialists targeted their efforts at members of the CEFS. The VTLC met on 27 November after the lifting of the influenza ban and delegates voted to hold a mass meeting against censorship and the Siberian Expedition.[126] The council also sent a telegram to Ottawa expressing its "em-phatic disapproval" of the Siberian Expedition, calling on the government to "abandon" the mission and "immediately recall" all troops in Russia or at sea (see Appendix D).[127] The *BC Federationist* observed:

In Canada we are already seeing a great change in the attitude of the workers towards the actions of the government. While the workers have been satisfied to jog along and take all that has been handed out to them during the last four years with little protest, they are now taking a definite stand on the censorship, and the intervention of the Allies in Russia. Not only are the workers asking for some explanation as to the intentions of the Allied governments in the Siberian exped-ition, but some of the daily papers are asking questions, and from the information at hand, there is some little unrest amongst the men detailed for duty in that part of Russia.[128]

Another *BC Federationist* article quipped: "The Siberian invasion is not being looked forward to with a very charitable manner by the majority of the boys now located at the Willows Camp, and according to comments one can hear amongst them down town, they are wondering what the devil self-determination of nations really means."[129] Conditions at the Willows Camp were "not happy," a reporter with the *Colonist* confided to the local press censor.[130] However, the commanding officer, Brigadier-General Bickford, insisted there was "no truth whatever" to rumours that the Siberian troops were "getting out of hand."[131]

Seven hundred members of the Siberian Expedition attended the inaugural meeting of the Victoria branch of the Federated Labor Party, held at the Columbia Theatre on Sunday, 8 December, while "hundreds were turned away." Rifleman Joseph Guenard of the 259th Battalion's "D" Company recalled that the soldiers would "march down the streets together to go and attend."[132] Organizers had distributed leaflets on downtown street corners to troops on day leave from the Willows Camp. As the *BC Federationist* reported, "the way those boys applauded the Labor speakers showed in no uncertain manner where their sympathies lay." FLP organizer W.R. Trotter discussed the war, censorship, and intervention in Russia, describing Kolchak's coup at Omsk and the violent overthrow of the Vladivostok Soviet the previous June. "We know enough to distrust every reference to Russia in the capitalist press," Trotter told the crowd. The second speaker, FLP legislator Jim Hawthornthwaite, discussed postwar reconstruction and the Soviet form of government, where wealth was produced and distributed and owned communally by workers. "They should be left free to produce as they like, and when we are rid of tyranny and plunder here in Canada we will then be in a better position to judge others," Hawthornthwaite declared. When he suggested the soldiers were going to Russia to civilize the country, shouts such as "We aren't there yet!" arose throughout the theatre. Organizers took a collection of $46.75 and sold a number of publications, including the banned books of Kerr and Company.[133]

The *Daily Times*, considered the more liberal of Victoria's two dailies, railed against "certain elements of pronounced Socialistic tendencies" and claimed that the Siberian Expedition was needed to "maintain control of the trans-Siberian railroad along its whole length from the Pacific to the Urals."[134] Attempting to sway public opinion, the newspaper stated that Canadian troops would help establish "law and order in a land now terrorized by the Bolshevik ... part and parcel of the job foisted on them in 1914."[135] The *Times* quoted Canada's trade commissioner at Vladivostok, Dana Wilgress: "The population of Siberia is practically destitute of clothing, linen and shoes." The Canadian Siberian Economic Commission would restore Siberian industry and agriculture "and incidentally secure trade for Canada."[136]

Labour intensified its campaign against the Siberian Expedition, provoking a reaction from the military command. On 13 December, a second protest meeting was held, under the auspices of the VTLC. A group of CEFS officers attempted to disrupt the meeting, flooding onto the stage, singing "God Save the King," and accosting the speakers. One officer in the balcony was "repeatedly jumping up and down in his excitement, shaking his cane at the stage in a most ludicrous manner." Labour council president Eugene Woodward was the first speaker, reading a letter he had received asking trade unionists to "refrain from holding a meeting and expressing opinions on subjects of which they had little or no conception." Woodward claimed it was impossible to know if the Siberian Expedition was justified because the truth was suppressed. He described free speech as a safety valve and warned that if the government was not careful it would wake up with a revolution on its hands. The next speaker, socialist longshoreman Joe Taylor, said that Russian workers had overthrown the czar's regime and had taken the land from the barons; therefore he questioned why Canadian troops should be sent to the country. A sergeant offered an explanation:

We are going to Siberia as far as I know because Britain has loaned a great amount of money to Russia. I don't know how much, and the Bolsheviki has repudiated the loan money. This is as much ours as anybody's, and we are going there to get it.[137]

When a resolution against censorship was presented, officers flooded onto the stage. "Our fellows went down nearly in a body and broke it up and cleared the house," Lieutenant Stuart Tompkins of the 260th Battalion wrote to his wife Edna.[138] However, according to the *BC Federationist*, "the majority of their comrades in the body of the theatre watched their antics with undisguised disgust, which later developed into very heated debates, in which the remarks of the labour speakers were strongly defended."[139] Woodward was "roughly" handled during the melee and the police were called. The *BC Federationist* reported that "the majority of the soldiers present were with the labor speakers," while the *Semi-Weekly Tribune* claimed that "the whole house, composed mostly of the Siberian contingent, were unanimous in expressing their sentiments to the withdrawal of the troops."[140]

The prospect of soldier-labour unity created much apprehension in senior ranks, foreshadowing the heavy-handed response to veteran-labour unity in Winnipeg the following spring. The lieutenant-governor of British Columbia, shipping owner Frank S. Barnard, sent a secret letter to Borden on 4 December, requesting the prime minister to "urge upon the Imperial Government the importance of keeping a few large Cruisers upon this Coast, if for no other reason, than for that of having a force to quell, if necessary, any rising upon the part of the IWW." Barnard felt "the presence of a warship" would "do more than any local military force to settle any local trouble" since "the personnel of such force would not be subjected to the insidious socialistic propaganda which reaches the soldier – in other words, would be more amenable to discipline, and not affected by local influences ... In the event of labor strikes, with demonstrations leading to riots, a serious situation would arise if the soldiers were in sympathy with the strikers."[141]

From labour halls across the country, a flood of protest resolutions arrived in Ottawa. The Vancouver Trades and Labor Council placed itself "on record as being against intervention in Siberia or interfering in Russia's internal affairs." Ernest Winch, a Socialist Party member and president of the council, insisted that "if the government desired evolution, and not what was called revolution," it would halt its campaign of repression against radical labour.[142] In Winnipeg, the labour council entertained a proposal for a general strike to force the withdrawal of Allied troops from Russia. Toronto's labour council also declared against the Siberian Expedition, while a delegate by the name of Chalmers described the Bolsheviks as "the only movement that will emancipate the working class."[143] Victoria's *Semi-Weekly Tribune*, meanwhile, suggested: "Ottawa should at once be notified by the Military Authorities of the real state of affairs at the Willows. It is common knowledge that the vast majority of the men in camp are strongly averse to embarking for Siberia."[144]

Evidence of discontent at the Willows Camp abounds. In November, eighty-seven soldiers in the Russian platoons of the 259th Battalion were moved across the city to the Work Point Barracks, "these men not being anxious to proceed to Siberia."[145] Bolshevik sympathies had developed among the men, as did an aversion to fighting other Russians. A loyal soldier in the CEFS reported confidentially that the Russians at the Willows were "all Bolsheviki," that they intended to join the Red Army if deployed to Russia, and that they were "debating all the time the social question and predicting the downfall of the rich." He went on: "I am not afraid to fight the enemy ahead of me ... but I don't want to be shot from behind with our own machine guns."[146] Only eighteen of the Russian troops were deemed reliable for service in Siberia and permitted to leave Canada. Within the other units of the 259th, efforts were made to contain discontent: English-speaking troops were transferred out of "D" Company (which the War Diary describes as the "French-Canadian Company"), while French-Canadians were transferred from "C" Company to "D" Company. In the 20th Machine Gun Company, seven soldiers were declared "deserters" by a Court of Inquiry on 20 December 1918; every day, punishments were meted out for infractions ranging from "breaking out of camp" to "highly improper conduct in the ranks." As Skuce observed, "barrackroom lawyers fomented discord by pointing out the illegality of the government's intent," which was highlighted by a government order of 7 December authorizing MSA troops for service in Siberia.[147] A soldier wrote to his sister-in-law from the Willows Camp: "Well, things are beginning to look awful black over here. We are going to be railroaded to Siberia, and we cannot do a thing to help ourselves. They started to dish out our clothes to us the first day, and out of 78 of us 77 refused to take them."[148]

Unrest extended to both anglophone and francophone troops, sixty-three of whom were dismissed from the Siberian force for "Bolsheviki tendencies."[149] On 18 December, hundreds of dissidents in the 259th Battalion sent an urgent telegram to Montreal lawyer Sir Lomer Gouin: "Over 300 loyal French-Canadians in the 16th Brigade, S.E.F., who were willing to do their duty to annihilate the Hun menace, energetically protest against being sent today in Siberia, contrary to their will, in an expedition which is not justified and useless for our Country." The soldiers asked Gouin, a well-place Liberal, to intervene to prevent "injustice" (see Appendix E).[150] Canada's top military commander, chief of the general staff General Willoughby G. Gwatkin, admitted that "the Government is in a hole" and that "popular opinion is opposed" to the dispatch of Canadian troops for Vladivostok.[151]

Efforts to ameliorate the situation were unsuccessful. The YMCA provided regular recreation and entertainment for the troops, and the military organized a "sports day" and a mandatory lecture on the geography and political climate of Siberia, attempting to counter the influence of the labour meetings. George S. Conover, a rifleman in the 260th Battalion, wrote in the *Times*: "Some people have a mistaken idea concerning the Siberian Expeditionary Force ... [It] is not for the suppression of the working class in Russia, but to aid them to put a government of their own choice in power."[152] When gale-force winds and driving rain resulted in the cancellation of rifle practice at the Clover Point Range, brigade commander Bickford addressed all ranks in the CEFS "on discipline, complaints, etc. and propaganda against the Siberian Force." As the brigade war diary records, "So-called Socialistic meetings have been held in Victoria at which there were speeches made ... against the Siberian Force."[153] Acting Prime Minister Sir Thomas White wired Borden in London: "There is a good deal of feeling in labour and other quarters here against our continued participation and my personal view is that a serious political situation may arise later unless some definite statement can be made as to the return of the expedition within a reasonable time." Borden responded, insisting that Canada had made commitments that had to be honoured, regardless of the armistice in Europe.[154]

The stage was set for mutiny.

5
Departure Day

DEPARTURE DAY ARRIVED, Saturday, 21 December 1918. It was a cold, crisp day with the wind blowing from the north. A total of 856 enlisted men in the 259th Battalion and the 20th Machine Gun Company, along with Headquarters Detachment and several smaller units, left the Willows Camp for the six-kilometre march up Fort Street towards the outer wharves and the troopship SS *Teesta*. They were under the command of Lieutenant-Colonel Swift, along with forty-two other officers.[1] Canada's defence minister, Sydney Mewburn, had travelled to Victoria to personally inspect the troops before they embarked. The most detailed description of the events that followed appeared in a lieutenant's letter to his wife, mailed from Japan, which was published in the *BC Federationist* and is worth quoting at length:

> Yesterday morning (Saturday, December 21) we turned out at reveille, 5 a.m., and turned in all our camp equipment at quartermasters' stores. We breakfasted at 6 a.m., and marched out of camp at 7:30 a.m. for the wharf, a distance of four and a half miles. When we got half way the signal came from the rear to halt, so we stopped for about ten minutes. Then the commanding officer blew his whistle as a signal for everyone to resume his place in the column, and we jumped into our places waiting for the further signal to advance, which was an unusually long time coming.

> We could not see the rest of the column, as we had turned a corner of the road – and a few minutes later a shot rang out, but still we waited till eventually we received word to resume the march. In the meantime it appears that our gallant ... or a number of them, had absolutely refused to fall in again when the signal blew, or to go down to the boat at all. So then the colonel drew his revolver and fired a shot over their heads – in the main street of Victoria – when some more got into line, though there were still a large number who would not, so the other two companies from Ontario were ordered to take off their belts and whip the poor devils into line, and they did it with a will, and we proceeded.

> While all this was happening the general staff car was flying round with good effect, so that after marching another half mile we came to a "guard of honour"

(fifty men in close formation, with rifles and fixed bayonets on either side of the road) who presented arms in the approved fashion to us – scouts, bugle band, and the Toronto company – but as soon as the other company was just nicely between them the order was given to the guard to "Outwards turn," with the result that this company continued the march virtually at the point of the bayonet, they being far more closely guarded than any group of German prisoners I ever saw, and they were put under armed guard till we actually pulled out to sea, and even now a dozen of the ringleaders are in the cells – the two worst handcuffed together – awaiting trial.

We arrived at the wharf at 9 a.m., but found that the boat was not yet docked, so waited till she came in, exactly 13 hours later, and commenced to embark at 10:30 p.m. It was 3 a.m. before everything was on, and at about 5 a.m. we started off.[2]

"Mutiny and Wilful Disobedience"

Evidence to corroborate this story is sparse, the victim of military and press censorship and a historiography that failed to ask the right questions while the participants were still alive.[3] The accounts of Rodney, MacLaren, Swettenham, and Skuce consign the events of 21 December 1918 to the margins, providing only passing references that are neither explained nor interrogated for meaning.[4] These interpretations do not extend beyond a superficial reference to French-Canadian anti-militarism. Mirroring the weakness of the larger literature on conscription in Canada, these accounts ignore the complex interplay of class and national cleavages, and the dual role of soldiers as workers; they confine opposition to conscription to the province of Quebec.[5] In framing anti-conscription sentiment and mutinous activity as purely French-Canadian phenomena, these accounts distort the experience, and deny the agency, of British Columbia's working class and simplify the motivations of the Québécois troops themselves.

Research into the regimental records of the Siberian Expedition has produced sporadic evidence of the mutiny. According to the war diary of the 16th Infantry Brigade, "On the march from the camp to the dock some of the French-Canadians of the 259th Battn. created trouble and objected to embarking. The trouble was soon overcome, however, and the delinquents placed under arrest to be dealt with."[6] The diary of the 20th Machine Gun Company is even more vague: "Parade formed up at 7:00 A.M. to march to Rithet's wharf. Made several halts en route and arrived at wharf at 10:30 A.M."[7] A court martial later concluded that the trouble started "at the date when the men were asked whether they were willing to volunteer for service in Siberia." Brigadier-General Bickford admitted that only 40 percent of the troops agreed to go voluntarily. Due to a requirement of the Records Office, the troops marched in alphabetical order: "This completely changed the company organization so that the men were not under the command of their own Platoon officers and NCOs. There was one case of an officer who could not speak French being in charge of a platoon of men who could not understand English."[8] The commanding officer of the 259th, Lieutenant-Colonel Swift, described the troublemakers as "French-Canadians, farmers and recruits" with "very little education," who were "mislead [sic] by some civilians while stationed in Victoria, BC, in December 1918."[9] Ernest J. Chambers, chief press censor for Canada, reinforced this point in a letter to chief of defence staff Gwatkin: "the Socialistic organizations made particular efforts to create disaffection in the Siberian Force."[10]

Military censorship prevented contemporary reports from appearing in the press. The labour council's *Semi-Weekly Tribune* alluded to "recent happenings, the knowledge of which is common property in this community." But no details of these "happenings" are provided: "The *Tribune* has no desire to infringe the regulations by giving publicity to these happenings unless forced to do so in self defence."[11] It was later revealed that the local intelligence officer had visited the *Tribune*'s offices and extracted a signed pledge from the editor, a pledge the newspaper threatened to breach when Defence Minister Mewburn told the House of Commons that no men had been forced to embark against their will:

> If Gen. Mewburn does not know the truth concerning the circumstances under which some of the men now serving in the Siberian forces left the City of Victoria he should forthwith communicate with the local Intelligence Officer ... Not all Victorians were unfortunate enough to witness the scenes to which we refer ... The drama was enacted on the streets and wharves of Victoria in the full blaze of publicity ... Before many hours had passed the news had spread from mouth to mouth until the whole city was aware of the salient facts.[12]

A week passed before Victoria's mainstream newspapers even alluded to the *Teesta*'s departure, with a *Colonist* editorial accusing local "Hands Off Russia" campaigners of encouraging "anarchy and destruction" and "opposing the sending of food to Russia in the only possible way in which it could be sent."[13] In a letter dated 21 December, a correspondent suggested: "there are quite a few slackers who are making trouble about going to Siberia."[14] In the mainstream press, the Toronto *Globe* was one of the few voices calling for the withdrawal of the Canadian troops, citing protests "general throughout the country." While the *Globe* acknowledged "sixty to seventy per cent of the men despatched to Siberia went unwillingly," it dismissed reports of "something very like mutiny" aboard an unspecified troopship, commending the men for embarking "without serious disturbance."[15]

The commanding officer of Military District 11, Victoria, had wired Canada's chief press censor on 23 December, stating that there was "no truth" to reports of an "alleged mutiny of Siberian troops 21st December." He stated further: "The embarkation [was] carried out in perfect order" with "all men quite content. Two or three French-Canadians attempted to desert on the march to the steamer, but no trouble arose."[16] Chambers instructed all newspaper editors in the country to "suppress report regarding alleged mutiny of Siberian troops in British Columbia," suggesting that "publication [would] only cause unrest and bring discredit to our soldiers."[17] When the *Globe* and *Hamilton Herald* persisted in pursuing the story, Mewburn instructed Chambers to "take to task the Editors of the *Herald* and *Globe*" and discover "the identity of the egregious liars who ha[d] been in correspondence with them."[18] Chambers penned a strongly worded letter to the *Herald* editor – in Mewburn's Hamilton riding – lambasting the "scandalous story ... so basely reflecting on the honour and loyalty of Canadian soldiers."[19] Other publications, such as *Saturday Night* magazine, helped perpetuate this myth, describing the Siberian Expedition as "absolutely a voluntary force" and stating that "every member ... was willing and anxious to go."[20]

Correspondence from members of the CEFS also sheds light on censorship of the mutiny. Walter B. Ford, a soldier in the 259th Battalion who, "by military permission[,] had represented the Victoria *Colonist* in Siberia," later wrote to the Department of Militia and Defence offering to counter the view that the troops were ill-treated: "It seemed that our battalion especially was fated to be misunderstood. Even the mutiny of the French companies on the way to the boat in Victoria, in some way got past the censor in letter-writing and was published in garbled form in the East."[21] Stuart Tompkins, a lieutenant in the 260th Battalion, discussed the incident in a letter to his wife Edna, who lived in Edmonton:

> You may not know that we have had quite a lot of trouble here. This is strictly "sub rosa" and is not to be repeated. There has been a lot of socialistic agitation here and two weeks ago there was a meeting here largely attended by 259th men – French Canadians. At this meeting the Siberian Expedition was discussed and a strong resolution taken against it. Last Sunday night our fellows went down and broke up the meeting but the harm was done. When two companies of the 259th were marching down town yesterday to embark some of the men egged on by agitators refused to go on. They were escorted.[22]

Another letter posted from a Victoria mailbox, by Private Richard Garton Holmes of the 20th Machine Gun Company, illuminates the dynamics of the mutiny:

> They had some trouble at the camp and two companies (who are French Canadians) refused to get ready to march down, so they got another battalion and chased them out of their tents with bayonets. Then at one of the places where they let them rest along the way, they wouldn't fall in again to march the rest of the way, so the officer fired his revolver at their feet and made them walk or get hit ... It would have been the same, with the rest of us, only we didn't raise a row as there is no use doing that and getting it wrong like the Frenchmen have.[23]

For additional detail on the events that transpired in Victoria on 21 December 1918, one can turn to sources generated by the labour movement. "In Victoria, if street corner reports are true, some members of the Siberian Expeditionary Force refused to go, and were compelled to do so by the use of forceable [sic] methods, amongst which was the use of revolvers by the officers," the *BC Federationist* reported on 27 December, ignoring the censorship restrictions.[24] "Members of the working class" were being sent to Siberia "at the point of the bayonet," an editorial claimed, so that the "the avaricious dreams of the ruling class [could] be realized."[25] Two weeks later, the newspaper asked rhetorically:

> Why is the Canadian government so bent on sending troops to Russia that unwilling men were forced to embark for Siberia at Victoria ... after leading protestors were put under arrest? Surely the answer is not in the announcement of the birth of the Canadian Siberian Development Company, which we are told "has good ground for hoping to get valuable concessions." From whom? From Kolchak? And is it his party our troops are being sent to support? Kolchak is the Siberian Denikin, was an intimate of the Czar and is the present hope of the Romanoffs.[26]

J.S. Woodsworth addressed an FLP meeting in Vancouver, describing "some disgraceful scenes" that had taken place "when certain Canadian troops were only recently shipped at Victoria for Siberia." He went on: "We had grown accustomed to hear of German and in the past of Russian troops being driven by force to the fighting front, but it was something new for Canada, and ... for the British Empire itself, to have troops driven aboard ship by bayonet and revolver."[27] Having resigned from the Methodist Church, Woodsworth was working as a longshoreman in Vancouver, where, according to daughter Grace MacInnis, he "downed tools and gave up his day's work and pay" when he discovered he was loading munitions bound for Siberia.[28]

Further insight into the Victoria mutiny can be gleaned from the proceedings of the Western Labour Conference, which convened in Calgary in March 1919. Helen Armstrong, representing the Women's Labour League of Winnipeg, asked the BC delegates whether the troops aboard the *Teesta* had reached Vladivostok: "Some of our members have not been heard from since Christmas ... and we heard ... that it took half a regiment at Christmas to put the other half on the ship for Siberia." A Victoria delegate by the name of Flewin responded that as an organizer of the FLP meetings in the city, he had met personally with several soldiers, including some from Winnipeg: "When these boys were given notice they were to leave for Siberia there was a plan among them that they would refuse to go. There was one man chosen to lead them, but when he struck down one of the officers the rest didn't give him support. However, it took 23 hours to get those men aboard the ship."[29]

Out of these fragmentary pieces of evidence the general contours of the mutiny emerge. Influenced by labour agitation, their morale weakened by poor weather and the Spanish flu, two companies of Québécois conscripts in the CEFS refused to leave Victoria for Vladivostok, and the military authorities used force – revolvers, canvas belts, and bayonets – to ensure their deployment to Russia. "They didn't want to go to war," Captain Charles Hertzberg wrote in his diary after they reached Vladivostok.[30]

Court Martial

Testimony from the commanding officers of the 259th Battalion provides greater detail of the mutiny. "I arranged my company into two parties and went forward when I found a crowd of men on the side walk talking and muttering in French which I do not understand," Major A.G. Pourpore of "A" Company told a military investigator aboard the *Teesta:* "I ordered them to go on and one man standing directly in front of me said 'No, No.' I ordered my men to make them move and some of them took off their belts and struck one or two. We pushed them along for about six blocks when they started to move more quickly."[31] The soldiers in "D" Company continued to resist, prompting the "guard of honour" to hem them in on both sides and from the rear as they neared the outer wharves, marching them at bayonet point into a shed.[32] Forty soldiers were arrested and detained in the shed, then paraded before the 259th Battalion's commanding officer, Lieutenant-Colonel Swift. Thirty received summary sentences, ranging from seven to twenty-eight days Field Punishment No. II. A dozen others were remanded into custody, their charges held over for court martial "because the evidence pointed to their being more active in the affair."[33] Most faced the serious charge of: "While on Active Service Joining in a Mutiny in forces belonging to His Majesty's Auxiliary Forces."[34]

Conditions aboard the *Teesta* were "very poor," in the words of Lance-Corporal Erskine Ireland. Five days into the journey, the ship encountered a heavy storm, during which Rifleman Frank J. Kay fell down a coal chute and died. A Chinese crew member also died on the crossing. On New Year's Day, the troops received plum pudding, a bottle of beer, and an apple or orange.[35] Once the *Teesta* reached Vladivostok, the Canadian command convened a Field General Court Martial for the accused ringleaders of the mutiny. All had been conscripted under the authority of the Military Service Act and all held the rank of rifleman. They were: Onil Boisvert, a 22-year-old farmer from Drummond, Quebec; Sylvio Gilbert, a 20-year-old labourer from Jonquières; Joseph Guenard, a 19-year-old plumber from Quebec City; Edmond Leroux, a 22-year-old lumberjack from St-Apolline; Edgar Lebel, a 21-year-old farmer from St-Épiphane, Témiscouata County; Alfred Laplante, a 23-year-old mechanic from Richelieu; Edmond Pauze, a 30-year-old blacksmith from Joliette; Leonce Roy, a 22-year-old farmer, also from St-Épiphane; Arthur Roy, a 23-year-old saw-maker from Montreal who resided in St. Catharines at the time he was conscripted; and Adore Leroux, a 23-year-old mechanical engineer from Le Cèdres, Soulanges County, Quebec.[36] Guidelines adopted by the CEFS command stipulated: "In all cases in which a charge is serious and may entail the death penalty, a legal Officer should be procured to act as prisoner's friend."[37]

Over five days of hearings at Gornostai Barracks beginning on 25 January 1919, a committee comprised of Lieutenant-Colonel G.L. McDonnell, Major P.F. Sise, and Captain J. Hyde Bennett received evidence from witnesses and statements sworn by the accused and translated into English. "Although being kept under arrest since over 38 days, to date I have never been given permission to take a bath or supplied with a change of underwear," Alfred Laplante declared. He had been "used on all kinds of fatigues and works – being treated as a convicted prisoner instead of as a man awaiting trial." Laplante had attended the labour meetings in Victoria, where the soldiers "were advised that the Canadian Government could not force [them] to go to Siberia unless [they] were prepared to sign a written statement to that effect." A labour paper, "widely circulated in [the Willows] Camp," underscored this point, as did statements made by non-commissioned officers in "C" Company. On two occasions, Laplante was paraded with his platoon in front of the company officers and asked to sign a pledge stating his willingness to go: "On both occasions I refused to do so."[38]

Alfred Laplante insisted that he had "never joined in or caused a mutiny."[39] However, several witnesses identified him as the ringleader. Lieutenant Wallace Webb of "C" Company testified that Laplante was at the centre of a group of Québécois troops "bunched together in a doorway" at Fort and Quadra streets who refused repeated orders to "fall in." Rather than continue the march towards the wharf, Laplante defiantly shouted in English "About Turn, About Turn" – seeking to instigate a return to the Willows Camp. A corporal in the 259th Battalion, L.G. Bouillon, testified that Laplante told him to "mind his own business" when ordered to "fall in." [40] However, other officers testified to the motivations behind the mutiny – the broken promise that no soldier would be sent to Russia against his will. Platoon commander Lieutenant J.M. Pellerin described the "strong impression in [his] platoon, to which the accused belong[ed], that those who did not sign would be sent home." A non-commissioned officer, Sergeant E.M Tuffs, said that no attempt had been made to prevent soldiers from attending the labour meetings, and he testified that the *Semi-Weekly Tribune* was widely circulated in the Willows Camp. The final witness at Laplante's trial insisted that "the accused ... [did] not understand English." [41] In the face of this evidence, the military court found Laplante guilty of "joining in a mutiny in forces belonging to His Majesty's Auxiliary Forces" and sentenced him to two years' hard labour. [42]

The trials of the other accused followed the conviction of Laplante. Onil Boisvert (who had been hospitalized with influenza before leaving Montreal) was sentenced to two years' hard labour based, the conscript later wrote, on "the lies of others." [43] His trial heard evidence from Major Guy Boyer of "D" Company: "[Boisvert] kept on saying in French, 'We will not go to Siberia.' He was trying to persuade my men not to go." Sergeant J.A. Deguise of "C" Company said: "I noticed the accused on the side walk among the men of D. Company, saying 'Come on boys, C. Company is with you." [44] In a written statement, Boisvert insisted that he had refused to sign the consent form for Siberia because "as a farmer [he] was more useful at home." [45] Rifleman Arthur Roy received the harshest sentence – three years' penal servitude (later commuted to two years) on the charge of "Joining a Mutiny" – for conduct that Major Boyer described as "inciting the others not to comply" and threatening to strike the Catholic chaplain of the Battalion, Captain Jacques Olivier, who urged him to "Fall In": "He was surrounded by several men ... and acted as spokesman for this group ... He kept on shouting '*On y va pas à Siberia*' ... '*On y va pas*,' '*On y va pas*.'" On 20 December, the day before the mutiny, rumours had swirled around the Willows Camp. "There was likely to be trouble," Roy's platoon sergeant informed a senior officer, and "Rifleman Arthur Roy was one of the Ring Leaders." On a streetcar from the camp to downtown Victoria that evening, Roy was overheard announcing that Canada "had no right to fight against the Bolsheviki" and that it would "take a good man to put [him] on the boat." When he returned to the Willows that night, Lieutenant T.J. Morin informed

Roy of the grave consequences of "such a movement." Roy insisted at the time that there was no truth to the rumours.[46]

The other dissenters received lesser sentences. Edmond Leroux, who allegedly sat on a fence during the melee and refused a direct order from the battalion's commanding officer to fall in, was convicted of "wilful disobedience" and sentenced to one year's hard labour.[47] Joseph Guenard and Edmond Pauze – "one of the best soldiers in my company," according to Lieutenant E.J. Mantell – were found guilty of "Joining a Mutiny" and sentenced to six months' hard labour. Pauze had reportedly joked to a comrade, "On n'est pas assez pour faire un strike" (We are not enough to make a strike).[48] While serving his hard-labour sentence, Pauze strained his lumbar spine and spent ten days in hospital.[49] Sylvio Gilbert received ninety days Field Punishment No. 1, Leonce Roy received thirty days Field Punishment No. 1, and Egard Lebel received twenty-eight days Field Punishment No. 1, all of which were served at the Field Punishment Station at East Barracks, Vladivostok.[50] Adore Leroux was found not guilty on all charges.[51] The sentences imposed on these working-class Québécois youth were designed to have a deterrent effect within the CEFS. In April, however, as the Canadians prepared to evacuate Vladivostok and questions arose in Parliament over the legality of deploying conscripts, the judge advocate received an application to release, on suspended sentence, the "men convicted of mutiny at Victoria, BC" – a request that Elmsley authorized.[52]

The *Protesilaus*

With the *Teesta* at sea, another eighteen hundred Canadian troops prepared to depart from the Willows Camp. Fearing another disturbance, CEFS officers disrupted a labour meeting on 22 December, sparring with Labor MPP Jim Hawthornthwaite and summoning reinforcements waiting "at the corner of Yates and Government."[53] The scheduled departure of the troops was delayed until after Christmas, possibly to ease tensions among the men.[54] On 25 December 1918, the enlisted men in the Siberian force were fed a lavish Christmas banquet by their commanding officers and fifty women (members of the local chapter of the Imperial Order of the Daughters of the Empire). The dinner was arranged at the Willows Camp mess hall by C. Calza, manager of the Empress Hotel, who procured the donation of fifteen hundred pounds of turkey, while the Red Cross provided plum pudding and the Ontario government helped offset the cost. Following a toast to the king with pints of 2 percent "near beer," the men flooded into the Exhibition Building to dance to the music of the CEFS unit bands. They finished the night with a performance of "All-of-a-Sudden Peggy," presented by the Red Cross Stock Company in the Royal

Victoria Theatre.[55] The commanding officers, meanwhile, were wined and dined in the Empress Hotel ballroom where White Russian interpreter Lieutenant Aleksandr Ragosin entained the crowd with a traditional Russian dance.[56]

The next morning, 26 December 1918, the remaining infantry units of the Siberian Expeditionary Force broke camp at the Willows and marched to the outer wharves. Both the *Colonist* and the *Times* reported on the departure, suggesting it was a lavish, festive affair. "We had a great send off – all Victoria I think turned out," Lieutenant Stuart Tompkins wrote.[57] No evidence points to a disturbance along the lines of the 259th Battalion's departure. With bands from the local Foundation Company, the HMS *Lancaster*, and the Siberian force leading three columns of troops, the soldiers from the 260th Battalion and supporting units passed through the city, leaving Victoria for Vladivostok at 6:30 PM on the Blue Funnel liner *Protesilaus*.[58]

Aboard the *Protesilaus*, conditions were grim. The ship, which was heavily overloaded and battled rough weather all the way to Vladivostok, had been hastily equipped with makeshift sleeping quarters. "About half the men have bunks and half have hammocks," a lieutenant wrote.[59] Working-class poet Rifleman Dawn Fraser of the 260th Battalion commemorated the crossing in his poem "Boulion à la SS *Protesilaus*," lampooning the provisions and quarters aboard the ship:

> An over-loaded stomach, or may-be it was fear,
> My hammock tossing wildly, my head was feeling queer;
> The boat was tipping madly, the breakers fairly screamed;
> I have no idea what time it was, I fell asleep and dreamed.
> That the old *Protesilaus* dumped us out, along with all her crew,
> And we struggled vainly, vainly, in an Ocean made of Stew.[60]

On 30 December 1918, four days after leaving Victoria, the ship encountered a heavy storm. Private Harold Butler was killed and two other soldiers injured when a large case of ice and meat broke loose from its mountings and crushed them. "It was sickening," Lieutenant Tompkins recalled.[61] Two days later, a Chinese crew member went overboard during a storm and died. As the ship approached Russia, it encountered bad weather again, losing its port propeller on 7 January and becoming stuck in the ice fifty kilometres east of Vladivostok. The *Protesilaus* sent an SOS message by wireless. When word reached Vladivostok, two British cruisers were readied for departure, the HMS *Suffolk* and the HMS *Kent*. However, the *Protesilaus* sent a second wireless with its location and the message: "no assistance required." As Captain Eric Elkington recalled seven decades later: "We were rescued by a Japanese war ship." The *Protesilaus* limped towards Vladivostok on the power of a single propeller.[62]

No Turning Back

As Canada's Siberian contingent sailed for Vladivostok aboard the *Teesta* and the *Protesilaus*, uncertainty prevailed in the highest ranks regarding the future of the expedition. The Imperial War Cabinet had decided that British and Canadian troops would be restricted to a "defensive campaign" to help maintain the front in the Ural Mountains held by Czech and White Russian troops.[63] The day the *Teesta* left Victoria, 22 December 1918, the Privy Council withheld authorization for the CEFS's deployment "up country," citing hostile public opinion and unclear Allied policy.[64] The chief of defence staff in Ottawa wired Elmsley:

> Secret. Despatch of troops from Canada will for the present continue but they will all return next Spring. Meanwhile they will not engage in military operations nor, without concurrence of Canadian Government, move up country, and you yourself should not leave Base until Bickford reaches Vladivostok.[65]

As the *Protesilaus* left Victoria on 26 December, the *Daily Times* reported that Allied leaders meeting in Paris had decided against further intervention and that the troops would return home soon.[66] Japan announced that half its troops would be withdrawn from the Russian Far East.[67] In this climate, Ottawa cancelled a planned sailing of the troopship *Madras* from British Columbia on 5 January and demobilized the 85th Field Battery, citing "increasing popular opposition" and Japan's decision to pull troops from Russia.[68] Ottawa reiterated in a cable to the War Office that "the troops should not move inland."[69]

Amid growing misgivings over the Siberian Expedition, the British War Office considered recalling the main body of the Canadian contingent before the *Teesta* and the *Protesilaus* had even reached Vladivostok. Elmsley received a proposal from London on 8 January suggesting that "no more Canadians be sent and ... [that] the Canadian troops now en route might be recalled." The Canadian general reacted strongly, warning it could "prove disastrous at [the] present critical juncture" and asked that the "withdrawal of Canadians troops be held in abeyance."[70] Such a move would be interpreted as abandonment of the "anti-Bolshevik cause," Britain's high commissioner warned, creating "serious trouble" among the Czechs and inducing White Russian troops on the front "to join the Bolsheviks." Kolchak could be overthrown and anarchy would prevail in Omsk and other Siberian cities.[71] Faced with such prospects, the Imperial War Cabinet deemed that "the return of Canadian troops to Canada must await decision of associated Governments as to their general policy in Russia."[72] On 20 January, the lord of the admiralty, Sir Winston Churchill, assured Elmsley and Knox that the "general decisions" of the Paris Peace Conference regarding the Bolsheviks would be provided "in a few days."[73] The *Teesta* and the *Protesilaus* held course for Vladivostok.

Общій Видъ Г. Владивостокъ.
Birds Eye View of Vladivostock.
浦 塩 斯 德 全 景

1   Vladivostok's Golden Horn Bay, 1918. The picturesque harbour filled with foreign warships in the months following the November revolution. They lay at anchor until the Vladivostok Soviet was toppled by Allied forces in June 1918. *Sidney Rodger Collection, Beamsville, Ontario.*

2 International Workers' Day demonstration, Vladivostok, 1 May 1917. The social upheaval that had uprooted czarism spread rapidly from Petrograd to the Russian Far East over the course of 1917. *Boris I. Mukhachev Collection, Vladivostok, Russia.*

4 *Troops at Petawawa: Canadian Troops Marching Off to Siberia,* original drawing by C.W. Jefferys, 1918. *Library and Archives Canada, Imperial Oil Collection, 1972-026, IC-31.*

Facing page, bottom

3 The "Red Funeral" of Vladivostok, 4 July 1918. Coffins of longshore workers (*gruzshchiki*), killed during the Allied-Czech coup that toppled the local Soviet days earlier, are paraded through a crowd of twenty thousand citizens. *Albert Rhys Williams,* Through the Russian Revolution *(New York: Boni and Liveright, 1921), 256.*

5 "D" Company of the 259th Battalion (Canadian Rifles) at the Willows Camp, Victoria, before departing for Vladivostok, December 1918. This unit was mobilized from the Quebec City military district and emerged as the locus of dissent. Several soldiers were court martialled for their role in the Victoria mutiny of 21 December 1918. *Viateur Beaulieu Family Collection, Cacouna, Quebec.*

6 Major-General C.W. Leckie inspects soldiers of the 259th Battalion at the Willows Camp, Victoria, December 1918. As the *Daily Times* reported, "It may not have been the best time of year for troops to have been quartered in Victoria ... The latter part of their stay has been marked by an unusual amount of rain with an attendant sea of mud at the Willows." *Library and Archives Canada, Dorothy I. Perrin Collection, 1987-152 #17.*

7 Soldiers from the 259th Battalion on day leave in downtown Victoria, December 1918. Public gatherings had been banned by the city's health committee in an attempt to curb the influenza epidemic. Once the ban was lifted, soldiers made full use of their leisure time. *Sidney Rodger Collection, Beamsville, Ontario.*

8 French-Canadian conscripts of the 259th Battalion at a "Hands Off Russia" mass meeting, Columbia Theatre, Victoria, 13 December 1918. Organized by the Victoria Trades and Labor Council, this unique dialogue between Québécois soldiers and BC workers contributed to the mutiny of 21 December 1918. *Sidney Rodger Collection, Beamsville, Ontario.*

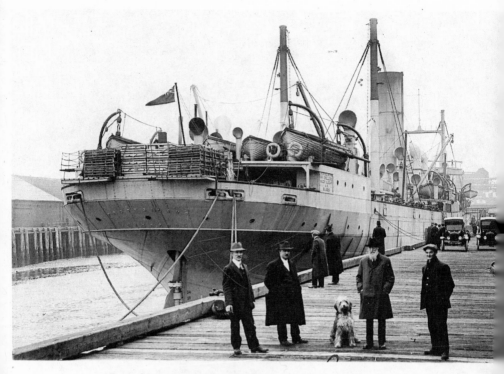

9 Troopship SS *Protesilaus* prepares to leave Victoria, 26 December 1918. There is no record of a disturbance along the lines of the *Teesta*'s departure days earlier. However, at sea, a soldier and a crewmember died in accidents, and the ship lost its port propeller after getting stuck in ice in the north Pacific. *British Columbia Archives, I-78247/HP018920.*

10   Soldiers marching towards the SS *Protesilaus* at Victoria's Rithet's Wharf, 26 December 1918. *British Columbia Archives, I-78248/HP018921.*

11   Canadian troopship at Egersheld Wharf, Vladivostok, 1919. A few kilometres south of the city centre, near the mouth of Golden Horn Bay, Egersheld was the main docking facility and the site of the Canadian ordnance shed. *Library and Archives Canada, Raymond Gibson Collection, 1977-157, C91765.*

12   Brigadier-General H.C. Bickford, second-in-command of the Siberian force, disembarks with members of the 259th Battalion at Egersheld, Vladivostok, 15 January 1919. *Library and Archives Canada, Raymond Gibson Collection, 1977-157, C91766.*

Facing page, bottom

14   *Canadians Outside the Depot – Siberia, Russia*, oil painting by Louis Keene, 1919. War artists Louis Keene and A.Y. Jackson were attached to the CEFS, a common practice of the day. Only Keene reached Vladivostok, as Jackson was awaiting transport in Vancouver when further sailings were cancelled by the Canadian government in February 1919. *Canadian War Museum, Beaverbrook Collection of War Art, 19710261-0316.*

13 *Unloading Ordnance Stores*, oil painting by Louis Keene, 1919. *Canadian War Museum, Beaverbrook Collection of War Art, 19710261-0325.*

15 Pushkinsky Theatre, Canadian force headquarters from 27 October 1918 to 5 June 1919. The eviction of the Vladivostok Cultural-Enlightenment Society, which had occupied the stately building, fuelled resentment among Vladivostok businesspeople, who organized a large protest meeting. The Canadians refused to vacate the premises. *Canadian War Museum, 19980027-020 #10.*

16 Gornostai Bay Barracks, east of Vladivostok, 1919. The main body of the Siberian force was quartered in these modern, czarist-era barracks, built less than a decade earlier in the wake of the Russo-Japanese War of 1904-5. *Sidney Rodger Collection, Beamsville, Ontario.*

17 Canadian barracks at Vtoraya Ryechka (Second River), north of Vladivostok, 1919. The officers of the RNWMP were quartered here, as were White Russian civilians displaced by the revolution in the Siberian interior. *Library and Archives Canada, Raymond Gibson Collection, 1977-157, C91757.*

18 A rare photograph of Nursing Matron Grace Eldrida Potter, the lone woman in Canada's Siberian Expeditionary Force, taken in Vladivostok, c. 1919. Potter sailed from Vancouver in November 1918 aboard the SS *Monteagle*, along with her husband, Colonel Jacob Leslie Potter. She served with the Canadian Red Cross Mission in the Russian Far East. *Canadian War Museum, Thomas Raymond Tubman Collection, Album.*

Facing page

19 Canadian soldiers at Gornostai Bay Barracks, 1919. According to one soldier, the modern czarist-era buildings were "better than anything we had in Canada." *Library and Archives Canada, Raymond Gibson Collection, 1977-157, C91717.*

20 Canadian and White Russian officers and civilians, Vladivostok, 1919. Major L.S.W. Cockburn, of the Base Training Depot, is seated second from right. *L.S.W. Cockburn Collection, Victoria, BC.*

21　Canadian ordnance officers moving stores at Gornostai, outside Vladivostok, in spring 1919. *Library and Archives Canada, Raymond Gibson Collection, 1977-157, C91749.*

22　Canadian soldiers and local fishers at Gornostai Bay, 1919. The Canadians seemed to interact more with Vladivostok's ethnically Chinese and Korean population (which totalled one-third of local inhabitants at the time) than with European Russians, who were suspected of Bolshevik sympathies. *Sidney Rodger Collection, Beamsville, Ontario.*

THE SIBERIAN SAPPER

Published by kind permission of the G. O. C., C. E. F. (S)., by 16th Field Co., Canadian Engineers.   Passed by Censor

Vol. 1—No. 4.   FEBRUARY 8, 1919.   PRICE—ONE ROUBLE

What Are We Doing Here?

(By an Amateur Guesser)

The Canadian in Vladivostok counts that day lost wherein he has not heard a rumour about going home. Some days he is informed that the transport will sail in two months; on other occasions a pessimist raises the bid to two years. At Egorscneldt you find a chap keeping his trunk ready packed against a sudden warning for Canada. At Gournastai there's a man who believes that some of us will get to Vancouver some day if we're not too old to stand the voyage. No harm being interested in the general subject of getting home again, but the bald fact appears to be that none of us know anything about it. We'll have to leave it "up to" the Peace Conference.

None of us are supposed to dabble in Russian politics. Which is mighty fortunate, on the whole, since only those of us who started life as Russians could make head or tail of this complicated maze of policital thought. Two or three parties are about all the average Canadian can digest. Twenty-seven are beyond comprehension. This is not a political treatise, for reasons just stated, but merely a contribution to the argument that goes on nightly in every barracks in this neck of the woods. The theme is: What are we doing here (except just staying,) and why did we come, and when will we go home?

It was simple enough at the beginning. Something had to be done to divert the attention of Germany on the east front so that Foch could mop them up on the west. The Russian Bolsheviks were, and are, a pro-German organization, so it was well within the provinces of the Allies to attack them. Britian was too much occupied to spare troops for

Siberia, so she turned to Canada in her hour of need,—and here we are, representing, with a few Imperial troops, the British Empire in the Russian Far East. And in the meantime the armistice came along, after the Hun had had enough of fighting, and the Russian situation took on an entirely new aspect. For there was no longer need of an eastern front against Germany. The Canadian force that started out to be an active fighting unit against the Bolsheviks and Germans remained to be a cog in a diplomatic wheel. And it is now the duty of the Peace Conference to decide what the next move is to be, withdrawal from

CONTENTS	Page
What Are We Doing Here? (The question of the hour)	1
Gossip	2
The Czecho-Slovaks (A Historical Sketch—2nd instalment)	3
Y. M. C. A. Notes	3
The Incurable Optimist (a poem)	4
Town Talks (I thank you)	4
Theatricals at Second River	5
Allied Rank Badges No. 3 (The Czecho-Slovak Army)	5
Correspondence (A la mode)	5
Ole Bill's Column	6
Letters to the Editor	6
Aunt Matilda	6
The Roadhouse Minstrels	7
Odds and Ends	7

the country, futher watchful waiting or a campaign in Russia.

Leaving aside all discussion of Russian political parties and political views, I cannot agree with the opinion so frequently expressed that the Canadians or British have no business in Russia to-day. So long as the Bolshevik armies hold European Russia terrorized it cannot be said that the German menace is at an end. The Bolshevik government, we are informed, has never been truly Russian. It has been composed largely of men of other than Russian blood, desperate fanatics in many cases. Bolshevik armies are led by Germans and Austrians who are not at all anxious to see peace and order restored in the world. Bolshevik missionaries are

spreading their doctrines in every country in the world, hoping for widespread anarchy. There is a mad dog running loose among the nations, and it would seem to be the duty of the nations to handle it as mad dogs usually are handled.

It is well to remember that in the early stages of the war Russia practically committed suicide to save the Allies on the west front. Her troops, many of them inadequately armed, were hurled against the Hun in immense numbers, and there was slaughter such as perhaps the world had never seen before. If later on her fighting power was paralysed by internal intrigue, the British must not forget Russia's generous martyrdom at the outset. Something must be done to save the remnant of Russia's best from the murdering, torturing hordes who showed their true character in the sack of Perm. That is one view of the question. Another, less altruistic, is that there can never be full peace in the world while Bolshevism rules in Russia.

Although they have done little or no actual fighting, the Brittish forces in Siberia have certainly accomplished something for the Russian cause. There has been a moral effect, at least. Well informed Russians admit that withdrawal of Allied troops would give the signal for a new outbreak of Bolshevism in Siberia. There would be another carnival of blood. No man with a collar and tie would be safe. The able, the educated, would be massacred. That is the Bolshevik way. Withdrawal would be regarded by the best of the Russians as a terrible calamity. The Bolsheviks, preparing at once to bring to light their hidden stores of rifles and machine guns, would welcome it.

Of course, it is difficult to see how the Russian problem will right itself for a long time to come. Actual crushing of the Bolshevik armies, disarmament, creation of a trustworthy army and navy—all these things would seem to be necessary before the Russian Parliament could safely carry on. That must be decided at the Peace Conference. It is unthinkable that the Allies should dictate to Russia what her future form of government is to be. Russians must work out the salvation of Russia. But there is need of a helping hand while the Bolshevik mad dog is abroad, and somehow or other, it seems very likely that the Allies will do their part.

This is one version of things, merely a contribution to that endless debate that makes up so large a part of Siberian Nights Entertainments. It does not answer one question: How long will we stay here? That matter is still on the knees of the gods.

---

23   The *Siberian Sapper* newspaper, published by the 16th Field Company (Canadian Engineers). One of two Canadian newspapers in Vladivostok in 1919. *Stephenson Family Collection, Burlington, Ontario.*

24 A *droshky* (horse-drawn cart) carries Allied officers along Svetlanskaya, Vladivostok's main street, 1919. Both officers and enlisted men travelled regularly from their barracks to the city centre. *Canadian War Museum, 19980027-012 #27.*

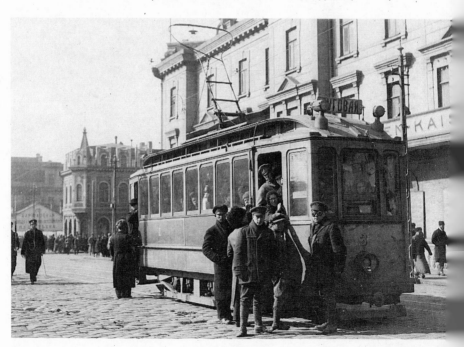

26 A sex trade worker at Kopek Hill, Vladivostok, 1919.
This seamy side of Vladivostok, a feature of all theatres of war,
contributed to one-quarter of all hospital cases among the
Canadians in 1918-19. *Canadian War Museum, 19980027-012 #25.*

Facing page, bottom

25 Canadian soldiers ride the tram into Vladivostok, 1919.
Lacking authorization to proceed into the Siberian interior, most
troops occupied themselves with routine drill, guard duty, athletic
pursuits, and day-leave in the city. *Canadian War Museum,
19980027-012 #28.*

27 Baseball team organized by the Canadians in Vladivostok, 1919. Other recreational pursuits included soccer, boxing, and hockey on frozen ponds. *Robert Patterson Aitchison McNay Collection, Katrine, Ontario.*

28 Gymkhana sports day, Vladivostok, 1 May 1919. Organized by the Canadians for the Allied contingents and White Russian dignitaries, the event concluded with a Bolshevik assassination attempt on General Horvath, while he was riding in his car. *Canadian War Museum, Tubman collection, Album.*

29 The Canadian garage at Egersheld, Vladivostok, lay in ruins after a fire in February 1919. Sixteen motor-lorries, shipped from Canada to Russia, were destroyed. *Canadian War Museum, Tubman collection, Album.*

30 The inter-Allied force deployed to the town of Shkotovo, April 1919. Two hundred Canadians joined Japanese, Czechoslovak, Italian, French, and Chinese troops to repel a partisan attack that threatened the coal supply for Vladivostok and the Trans-Siberian Railroad. When they reached the town, the partisans had retreated and the Canadians were recalled to Vladivostok. *Sidney Rodger Collection, Beamsville, Ontario.*

31 Canadian "Lewis Gun" team from "A" Company, 259th Battalion, at Shkotovo, April 1919. Rifleman Sidney Rodger is in the centre of the photograph holding the gun. *Sidney Rodger Collection, Beamsville, Ontario.*

32 Members of the Canadian Advance Party proceed "up country" to Omsk. The promised reinforcements never arrived as the Allies failed to secure their line of communication: the Trans-Siberian Railroad. *Stephenson Family Collection, Burlington, Ontario.*

33 Bridge destroyed by Bolsheviks in the Siberian interior. Dozens of attacks like this one in early 1919 paralyzed the Allies' line of communication and contributed to the evacuation of Siberia. This photograph was taken by Private Edwin Stephenson en route to Omsk. *Stephenson Family Collection, Burlington, Ontario.*

34 Private Edwin Stephenson at the Vladivostok Chinese market, prior to his death from smallpox. *Stephenson Family Collection, Burlington, Ontario.*

35 Private Edwin Stephenson's grave, Vladivostok Marine Cemetery, 1919. *Stephenson Family Collection, Burlington, Ontario.*

36 Chaplain Harold McCausland dedicates the Canadian memorial at Vladivostok Marine Cemetery, near the hilly Churkin peninsula outside the city, 1 June 1919. Fourteen Canadians are buried at the site. *Stephenson Family Collection, Burlington, Ontario.*

37 Canadian monument at Vladivostok Marine Cemetery, 2008. *Photograph by Benjamin Isitt.*

PART 2

To Vladivostok and Back

6
Vladivostok: 1919

The working classes of the Entente must force their governments to a peace negotiated with the mass of the Russian people. The Russian soviet will use its forces to oppose foreign capitalism.[1]

— V.I. LENIN, "LENINE'S VIEWS ARE PROCLAIMED," *COLONIST*, 29 DECEMBER 1918

As THE TEESTA and the *Protesilaus* plied the Pacific, the eleven hundred Canadians already in Vladivostok remained in a state of limbo. Conflicting Allied strategies and unstable supply lines prevented their deployment up country, to the active front against the Red Army in the Ural Mountains. A small force of fifty-five soldiers proceeded to Omsk, serving as headquarters staff for British troops in the Middlesex and Hampshire battalions. Most of the Canadians, however, never left Vladivostok, a city of 200,000, which an RNWMP officer described as "about ninety percent Bolshevik."[2] As the chief port in the Russian Far East and terminus of the Trans-Siberian Railroad, Vladivostok was flooded with refugees from the Siberian interior, "the backwash of revolution," people in desperate need of shelter, clothing, and food. Looting and murder were rife, along with attacks on Allied forces by irregular Bolshevik and partisan insurgents. The Allied presence in Vladivostok aggravated the situation, consuming scarce lodging and supplies, while the Canadians served as mere "spectators," making "the least contribution to the White cause" of all the anti-Bolshevik armies in Siberia.[3] "That was a tough place, Vladivostok," recalled Captain Eric Elkington, a doctor from Duncan, British Columbia, who served as a medical officer with the 16th Field Ambulance: "It was wintertime and there were always people getting killed or shot in the streets."[4]

Blurred Authority and Conflicting Strategy
The Canadians in Vladivostok, like all Allied forces in the Russian Far East, were under the supreme command of Japanese general Kikuzo Otani, a pattern established in 1918 when the first Allied contingents had landed in the city and

the ranking officer had been Japanese. Soon after the Canadian advance party arrived in autumn 1918, Otani invited two senior Canadian officers to dine and play bridge, but larger geopolitical manoeuvres generated tension among the Allies.[5] Otani led a force of seventy-three thousand Japanese troops – which dwarfed all other Allied contingents with the exception of the Czechs. From the outset, Britain, the United States, and other Allies were suspicious of Japan's motives, envisioning a power struggle for land and Siberian resources and resenting the size of the Japanese contingent and its refusal to deploy troops west of Lake Baikal. In mid-November, an American consular official at Tokyo had visited the Imperial Japanese Government to protest the size of the force and "monopoly" control in northern Manchuria and the Russian Far East. Japan's presence was considered hostile to American long-term interests in China, while the Japanese "merely asked for such mining rights in eastern Siberia as [would] render Japan independent of supplies from America."[6] Conflict between Japan and the United States contributed to a deterioration of railway operations, impeding the transport of troops and cargo from Vladivostok to the Ural Front and contributing to "extravagant prices" in western Siberia. This was "a potent cause of disorder."[7]

Japan's policy in Russia was predicated on establishing "peace and order as soon as possible" by supporting provisional governments in "distinct districts ... sustained by Russian troops." This meant propping up Dmitri Horvath at Harbin and Ataman general Grigori Semyonov at Chita, who refused to recognize Kolchak's authority and, as a British intelligence officer observed, "style[d] himself 'Commander-in-Chief of the Far Eastern Front.'"[8] In early December 1918, conflict between Czech and Cossack troops loyal to Semyonov and White Russians loyal to Kolchak threatened to erupt into bloodshed at the city of Irkutsk. Japan had provided "money, guns, rifles, [and] ammunition" to Semyonov while Kolchak sent troops to Irkutsk.[9] "This place will have to be abandoned until the arrival of reinforcements [from Omsk] owing to instability of locals," the British intelligence officer warned.[10] A flurry of diplomatic manoeuvring in Tokyo, London, and Siberia eased the crisis, with Japan's advising Semyonov to make peace with Kolchak, but tensions remained.[11] Canadian lieutenant Harold Ardagh of the 259th Battalion observed "the great amount of friction" between the Americans and the Japanese, who were "hated by all" and who "ha[d] their eyes on this country and mean[t] to fight to get it."[12] Nonetheless, a British military attaché at Tokyo said that Japan's presence was essential if Bolshevism were to be contained in the Russian Far East: "Mindful of the safety of the railway, if reduced there will be an immediate recurrence of Bolshevik activities."[13]

Reflecting concern over Japanese motives, Canadian general Elmsley was empowered to appeal any of Otani's orders to the British War Office, and he could not be overruled without the consent of the Canadian government (a decision resented by the head of Britain's Military Mission, Major-General Alfred Knox).[14] Canada's defence minister, Sydney Mewburn, also took precautions, appointing a special representative, Lieutenant-Colonel John F. Lash, to act as his eyes and ears on the ground.[15]

Britain pressed Canada to take a more active role in the Siberian interior. This policy was laid out in a letter from the Foreign Office to the high commissioner in Vladivostok, Sir Charles Eliot:

To remain for the present in occupation of Murmansk and Archangel.
To maintain present Siberian expedition and to proceed with such further arrangements connected with it as were contemplated prior to the Armistice.
To endeavour to induce the Czechs to remain in Western Siberia and to send out selected officers to that region.
To proceed with the occupation of the Baku-Batoum Railway.
To establish touch with Denikin at Novo Rossick and afford him all possible assistance in military material.
To supply the Baltic states with military material if and when they have Governments ready to receive and utilize such material.[16]

However, British aims in Siberia grew more opaque after the armistice. The original deployment had been intended "to prevent the transfer of German forces from Russia to the Western front," rather than "to carry out a campaign against Bolshevism and to secure by foreign intervention the restoration of peace and order," Foreign Minister Lord Balfour insisted. Britain was "neither able nor prepared" to pursue a more aggressive policy:

Public opinion in this country would not agree after more than four years of strenuous fighting to see British forces dissipated over [a] huge expanse of Russia in order to effect reforms in a country no longer a belligerent Ally ... [However], Anti-Bolshevik administrations have grown up under the shelter of Allied forces for whose existence H.M. Government are responsible and whom they must endeavour to support.[17]

Waning resolve in Britain reflected mounting strength for the Labour Party, which saw a surge of support in the December 1918 parliamentary elections on a platform that included withdrawing troops from Russia.[18] The British increasingly confined their activity to training White Russian forces at the officers' training school on Russian Island and similar facilities up country.[19]

Such were the circumstances that gave rise to the deployment of fifty-five Canadians to Omsk while the remainder of Canada's Siberian Expedition performed garrison duty at Vladivostok. According to Raymond Massey, a member of the advance party and lieutenant in the 85th Field Battery: "The point of the Canadian expedition was to establish a presence in Omsk as focal point of the White Russian effort against the Bolsheviks."[20] In November 1918, the British War Office had urged Borden to deploy troops to aid White armies in the Siberian interior: "Experience has shown ... that Russian troops will melt away if they have not the moral support and example of no matter how small an Allied contingent."[21] Britain asked that the RNWMP squadron proceed to Omsk, along with Elmsley, "to take command of the British and Canadian forces in Western Siberia."[22]

In his place, Elmsley sent Lieutenant-Colonel Thomas "Sid" Morrisey, a twenty-eight-year-old engineer from Montreal who led "a small party" of eight officers and forty-seven enlisted men to administer the 25th Battalion, Middlesex Regiment, and to arrange "supplies and billets for the main body of the force to follow."[23] The Canadian contingent consisted primarily of medical staff and Army Service Corps staff.[24] Elmsley instructed Morrisey to meet with French colonel Maurice Janin, commander-in-chief of Allied forces in western Siberia, to ascertain "his military programme," with the proviso that Canadian movements required British and Canadian authorization, that no operations "of a political nature" were permitted, and that the force was "not to proceed west of the Urals at present." The Canadians left Vladivostok with two months' supplies aboard British High Commissioner Sir Charles Eliot's train on 8 December 1918.[25] The train travelled through Harbin and stopped at the city of Chita, where Eliot met with Semyonov, hoping to reconcile the warring White factions. "Considerable quantities of goods are imported by Semenoff and sold in two stores which he has opened," Eliot noted, where they were bought by "speculators who retail at higher prices."[26]

Back in Vladivostok, Elmsley grappled with logistical problems and the limited abilities of the British troops under his command. The Middlesex and Hampshire battalions drew heavily from "C class" men, older troops relieved from service on other fronts. "About 240 O.R. [other ranks] of the Middlesex Battn. are being sent to Hong Kong, as they are unfit for service here," Elmsley notified Ottawa and London.[27] He recommended that two "weak" companies of the Middlesex Battalion should remain in Vladivostok, while another company should proceed to Krasnoyarsk and the fourth company should join the Hampshires at Omsk (435 soldiers in the Middlesex Battalion were taken off the strength of the CEFS in February and evacuated aboard the *Madras*).[28] A company of the 1/9th Battalion, Hampshire Regiment, left Vladivostok for Omsk a week behind Morrisey's Canadian party, with thirty-one officers and 831 other ranks, including four members of the Canadian YMCA.[29] While these troops were in transit, Elmsley authorized the redeployment of the second Hampshire company from Krasnoyarsk to Taiga, further in the interior, at the request of Janin.[30] He also deployed a Canadian captain, G.M. LeHain, to act as Canadian supply officer at Harbin, a key transit point on the route up country. "It should be bourne [sic] in mind that our present system of supplying troops at the front from our Base at Vladivostok is unsatisfactory in every respect," he lamented.[31] Elmsley expressed frustration over "the immediate and future employment of [his] Force," commenting: "It becomes increasingly difficult here to arrange for supplies and accommodation owing to the conditions here and lack of instructions from the War Office and Canada."[32] Alluding to chaos along the Trans-Siberian Railroad, Elmsley offered a keen prediction:

> Perhaps I am a false prophet – I hope so – but I feel certain that when the time comes for my troops to move west I shall find that the foundation of all military operations, viz., a secure L. of C. [line of communication], is wanting. However anxious we may be to assist a good cause, I would feel that I was breaking faith with my own Government if I moved a single unit from Vladivostok under these conditions.[33]

Vladivostok under Canadian Occupation

Battered by rough weather, the *Teesta* pulled into the northern Japanese port of Muroran for bunkering on 9 January. The officers were allowed ashore, while the lower ranks were not. Thirty-eight men were subsequently found guilty of being absent without leave and penalized fourteen days' forfeiture of pay. In contrast, the Canadian officers took a police boat into Muroran, touring the bustling city and then riding a train to a nearby village and *onsen* (hot springs), where they enjoyed an authentic Japanese feast of fish, chicken, and sake. They ate cross-legged on the floor, clad in kimonos with geisha girls at their sides. "We had a great experience in Japan," one officer recalled.[34]

The *Teesta* arrived in Vladivostok on 12 January, followed by the *Protesilaus* three days later. In these two ships, carrying 899 and 1,817 men, respectively, two-thirds of the Canadian force reached Russia.[35] When the *Teesta* docked at the Egerscheld wharves, ordnance personnel discovered "all blankets etc [were] infested with lice" and provided the troops, who lacked winter kit, with fur caps. According to the war diary of base headquarters, "All troops on board the S.S.

'TEESTA' had to be bathed on arrival owing to men [being] lousie." Midway through the bathing, the well ran dry. Determined to avoid a disturbance similar to the one at Victoria, officials had prepared a careful plan for the disembarkation of the men. Elmsley and other senior officers boarded the ship upon its arrival in Vladivostok, while fifty troops were detailed "to act as a guard" as the 259th unloaded in two stages – "C" Company and one platoon of "D" Company on 13 January and the remainder of "D" Company the following day. This strategy appears to have worked, but the unloading of cargo proceeded less smoothly: cranes, derricks, and other hydraulic equipment had frozen, so seventeen hundred tons of ammunition and 398 tons of other supplies were unloaded by hand, by Chinese labourers.[36]

The soldiers in the 259th Battalion made the arduous march from the Canadian Ordnance Dock near the mouth of the harbour to the East Barracks at the head of Golden Horn Bay, a distance of about ten kilometres through the centre of Vladivostok (see Map 4). The following day, they marched another eight kilometers to Gornostai Bay, where modern barracks sprawled along the slopes of a wooded valley near the sea. The czar's government had built the Gornostai barracks before the war, with accommodation for ten thousand troops and an elaborate network of coastal defences and underground tunnels.[37] A Canadian private described conditions at the camp:

> We marched to our new barracks this morning and are located in a big brick building which looks as though it is going to be quite comfortable ... There is a Y here and dozens of barracks, yes, hundreds of them, all over the country way up into the hills ... They are better than anything we had in Canada except for one thing – water. It's mighty scarce in this country and we haven't had a bath yet. The building is heated with stoves, and lighted with candles. We have iron bunks to sleep on.[38]

Three days behind the *Teesta*, the *Protesilaus* was towed into Golden Horn Bay. One group marched to the East Barracks while another endured a fifteen-kilometre train ride in sub-zero degree boxcars to the barracks at Second River (*Vtoraya Ryechka*).[39] "Our quarters here were formerly barracks occupied by Russian imperial troops built at great expense between 1905-14, but now abandoned to refugees and the allies," a Canadian officer wrote home. The Canadians were quartered alongside Japanese and Czecho-Slovak troops as well as well-healed Russian émigrés from the Bolshevik-held interior (Figures 16 and 17).[40] Elmsley appointed Brigadier-General Bickford as his general commander at Gornostai and Lieutenant-Colonel Frederick Charles Jamieson as commander at Second River.[41]

The *Teesta* and the *Protesilaus* reached Vladivostok as a typhus epidemic hit the city. The port town had a modern electricity grid and tramway system but no waterworks or sewers. Dead dogs and cats lay strewn across the roads. The lack of sanitation created a conducive climate for contagion, reflecting Vladivostok's "unfinished attempt at a flashy civilization" that had been "plunged into a sordid and dingy savagery."[42] To protect the Canadian troops, Elmsley issued an order forbidding "the unnecessary intermingling with the civilian population in trams, cinema houses, and other congested public places." When Ottawa sent an anxious telegram questioning whether the troops should be permitted to land at all, the Canadian commander assured the government that the spread of the illness among the troops was "negligible" and that among civilians it was "completely under control." The Canadian troops were "quite safe."[43] Earlier in January, Elmsley had authorized the opening of a fifty-bed hospital at Second River, to be staffed by personnel from the 16th Field Ambulance upon their arrival in Vladivostok, with smaller medical facilities opened at all Canadian barracks.[44] Despite these precautions, a case of cerebral-spinal meningitis was discovered at the East Barracks at the end of January.[45]

Difficulties unloading cargo from the *Teesta* and the *Protesilaus* constrained the operations of the Canadian command. A telegram from Elmsley to Omsk stated that the Canadians then in Vladivostok were "unable to move at once" as winter clothing had not yet been unloaded from the ships.[46] Poor communications had earlier resulted in a needless march of RNWMP "B" Squadron, from Gornostai to the commercial wharves and back, resulting in "several cases of frost bite." The troops had been deployed during a "blinding" blizzard to unload a ship that was not yet in port, but they failed to receive this information because of broken telephone lines.[47] The supply ship *War Charger* reached Egersheld on 26 January 1919.[48]

The situation in Vladivostok was far from pleasant. Rifleman Harold Steele of the 259th Battalion described the city as "one of the worst holes on the face of the earth," a "God foresaken hole."[49] Another Canadian called it "an end-of-the-road haven" for "scores of thousands of refugees – White Russians, Poles, Georgians, Mongolians, Chinese and Koreans; aristocracy, bourgeoisie, peasants and beggars ... It was said that one could have a man's throat cut for a rouble."[50] The refugees lived in abandoned boxcars and passenger cars that cluttered the sidings along the railroad, and they squatted in vacant buildings and the city's bullet-scarred rail station, a "foul place" that housed refugees "reeking with typhus."[51] Captain Eric Elkington, a doctor in the 16th Field Ambulance from the Vancouver Island town of Duncan, recalled the desperate state of affairs in an interview six decades later. "There was very little snow in Vladivostok, but it was damn cold, and very dusty":

The Trans-Siberian railway station in Vladivostok was full of thousands of starving refugees. Literally starving. They had a little area on the floor and they all had fled from the Bolsheviks. Well, we did what we could. We took some supplies, what we could. I can always remember having a loaf of bread, and a woman came rushing up, and I gave it to her, and she had the most starving looking baby you ever saw in your life.[52]

Elkington's recollections are blurred by the passage of time but provide a potent insight into conditions in Vladivostok:

A lot of these Russian refugees were of the aristocracy, a great many of them. There were an old general and his wife, living in this used railway carriage. And they were selling what things they'd managed to escape with their life, which was a tea and coffee service, all in gold. And they'd sell a cup, and then a plate. And I said to this old general, "What's going to happen when you've sold all that?" "We will just die." "We will just die." I suppose that was the most tragic scene. I've seen a great many tragic scenes in various parts of the world, but that – Vladivostok – was the worst. Awful.[53]

Elkington recalls walking down Svetlanskaya one evening and stumbling across a bank robbery in progress. The culprit ran into the street and was shot in the head by a gendarme: "He was piled up with the rest of the bodies, which was bigger than this room of dead bodies, frozen stiff. They couldn't bury them. Hundreds of dead bodies in this place."[54] Canadian troops found a morbid form of entertainment visiting "The Morgue," a dilapidated shed on a hill with "dead people just lying on the floor."[55] Vladivostok was "lawless," according to Elkington, and the Canadians tried to provide assistance: "We tried to supply these wretched people with what we could, but of course we hadn't got vast quantities at all."[56]

Doing Nothing

The Canadians in Vladivostok, numbering nearly four thousand soldiers by January 1919, saw little activity. Lacking authorization to proceed up country, and showing signs of ongoing dissent, the troops were occupied at the Second River and Gornostai Barracks and had secondary quarters at the East Barracks and Casino Barracks. "We saw or heard little of the Canadian troops, who were mostly quartered some distance outside the town," recalls Canada's trade commissioner in the city, Dana Wilgress: "They were kept out of mischief by being drilled intensively. The Russians saw little of them, which helped to maintain the good reputation they had."[57] On 3 and 18 February 1919, a handful of supporting troops arrived on the supply ships *Madras* and *Monteagle* from Vancouver. A final 311 troops arrived on the *Empress of Japan* on 27 February.[58] At the end of that month, all Canadian units except the RNWMP relocated from Second River to Gornostai, off the rail line to Vladivostok, apparently to discourage visits to the vice-filled port.[59]

Despite political tension, shortages of food and lodging, and the desperate refugee problem, Canadian recollections of "Vlady" (as they called the city) are not entirely negative. A social network developed among top Allied officers and ordinary rank-and-file troops. In December, Elmsley had assigned Lieutenant Raymond Massey (a future Hollywood actor) to produce a theatrical show, *The Roadhouse Minstrels*, which played twenty performances for Allied troops in the city.[60] In January, the Canadians organized an elaborate memorial service following the death of Prince John, British King George V's epileptic youngest son. The RNWMP "B" Squadron provided a mounted guard of honour for the ceremony, which was officiated by Canadian chaplain Major H. McCausland and attended by generals Horvath and Otani and other high-ranking White Russian and Allied officials.[61]

Among the Canadian officer corps, diaries and letters paint a picture of a vibrant social scene, with regular leave from the barracks to dine at restaurants and cafés, shop at the eclectic Chinese and Japanese markets and bazaars, bathe in authentic Russian bathhouses, and frequent theatres and private homes in the cosmopolitan port. The Canadians travelled on *droshky*, peculiar horse-driven carts, and trudged the long cobblestone and dirt roads between the city and the camps.[62] At their mess halls, they feasted on duck and geese. Many took lessons in the Russian language. Some developed strong camaraderie with the loyal Russian officers attached to the CEFS, such as Lieutenant Aleksandr Ragosin, a former officer in the czar's army who worked with the Canadian force headquarters. The small coterie of foreign women in Vladivostok, such as Nursing Matron Grace Eldrida Potter and Olive Beatrice Owen, wife of the CPR envoy Ross Owen, provided entertainment for the troops and offered civilian relief.[63]

Life was more mundane for the Canadian enlisted men, but an array of recreational activities took shape during their short stay in Vladivostok. The YMCA and Knights of Columbus, which had assigned representatives to the Siberian Expedition, organized canteen huts, readings rooms, and movie theatres at the Canadian barracks, and they held concerts, lectures, dances, boxing matches, baseball and soccer games, and church services.[64] In early February, the Illusion Idyllion Theatre on Svetlanskaya was leased for four months and transformed into the Maple Leaf Cinema and Café, a facility intended to be "as nearly Canadian in all its services as possible."[65] At the Second River Barracks, the Knights of Columbus opened a cinema called the British Columbia Hall. An eight-team hockey league was established, as were two brigade newspapers, the *Siberian Bugle* and the *Siberian Sapper*. On occasion, the men marched to a central bathhouse at Gornostai for a hot shower.[66]

The days were often mild, prompting one Canadian officer to comment: "Weather and everything considered, we are much more comfortable than we were in Victoria."[67] Lieutenant Stuart Tompkins described ice-skating on a frozen bay near Second River, while Captain Elkington recalled "one of the streams outside Vladivostok, [where] you'd pick up little bits of gold."[68] In May 1919, shortly before the last troops departed, the Canadians organized a "gymkhana," a sporting event at a racetrack outside the city, attended by several thousand Allied troops and civilians as well as White Russian dignitaries such as Horvath (who narrowly escaped a partisan ambush on his return to the city). The RNWMP performed their famous Musical Ride, while the 260th Battalion won the inter-Allied tug-of-war, which excited the spectators to the point that they "broke most of the fences." During the bucking competition, three children were injured when a Canadian horse charged into the stands; however, the event was generally viewed as "a huge success." "It pleased the spectators, in spite of some rather unnecessary roughness which to the Russians seemed too much like school-boy antics," Wilgress recalls.[69] The soldiers' unruliness extended to Vladivostok's tram system, with the force command's issuing instructions against spitting, "singing, whistling, etc." and "entering or leaving cars through the windows."[70]

Vladivostok had less innocent diversions as well. Venereal disease was prevalent among the Canadians, despite an official ban on visits to the red-light district known as "Kopek Hill."[71] Before the main body of the CEFS arrived, the quartermaster general had issued an order to all ranks stating that sexual intercourse with a woman, which was seen as equivalent to a self-inflicted wound, was an offence punishable by court martial: "The percentage of Venereal Disease in our Force is very high and unless there is some improvement ... in the near future, it will be necessary ... to modify or cancel the privilege of passes in the City." Between one-quarter and one-half of all Canadian hospital beds were occupied by patients with venereal disease, prompting the force command to threaten to ship afflicted troops back to Canada and to inform family members of the cause.[72] The CEFS's standing orders mandated that any soldier who contracted a venereal disease would "report to a Medical Inspection Room within five hours of such exposure for early treatment;" failure to comply was a "serious offence," and soldiers requiring hospitalization were docked pay. All commanding officers were instructed to arrange regular lectures for their units, involving the chaplain, on the prevention of venereal disease through "moral suasion from the standpoints of efficiency, patriotism, morality, and health."[73]

In contrast with this Canadian policy of abstinence, Japanese troops received ration cards for "comfort visits" to regulated Japanese-run brothels in the city.[74] Captain Elkington describes the situation on the ground:

> There was an awful place, known as the "bucket of blood" ... where the troops would go in and there were just these sort of cubicles, and you could see the action which you liked best. Oh, that was the devil, trying to keep these lads away from that place. You could buy condoms in the streets. Syphilis ... Asiatic syphilis is a dreadful thing. When we came back from Vladivostok, two lads were sent home, and they both died from syphilis, despite 606 [a pharmaceutical drug] and everything else.[75]

The most graphic incident of prostitution in Vladivostok is recorded in the proceedings of a military court of inquiry. Lance-Corporal Peter Marchik, an interpreter with the force headquarters battalion, was "shot in the penis" by a Russian woman at a Vladivostok brothel. The hearing, held on 5 February 1919, found that Marchik suffered a "flesh wound" that was not fatal.[76]

As a doctor with the 16th Field Ambulance and an officer monitoring the conduct of the Canadians in Vladivostok, Captain Elkington saw the underbelly of the port city at first hand. One day he stumbled across two troops lying in the snow after having annihilated themselves on vodka at a "house of ill fame": "We had to carry them about two miles home to save them."[77] Elkington also recalls the prevalence of smallpox and typhus among the force. Guidelines issued through the *Siberian Sapper* in February urged men to "bathe frequently," "change [their] underwear," and "keep out of congested buildings, picture shows and street cars."[78] The soldiers exchanged dirty clothing for a clean set each time they bathed. As the typhus epidemic spread through Vladivostok – infecting 142 people in a single February day – the Canadian command declared the central rail station, East Barracks, and other facilities "out of bounds." The ban soon spread to streetcars and to "mixing with native crowds": "There is war to the death on the 'cootie,' through whose wanderings typhus spreads," CEFS correspondent Captain Wilfred Playfair wrote in the Toronto *Globe*.[79] However, in a medical war that paralleled the larger Canadian debacle, a proposed Canadian-led anti-typhus hospital in Vladivostok never got off the ground.[80]

The Canadian Red Cross was embedded in the CEFS, as it was in other theatres of war, offering medical and social services for the troops stationed in Vladivostok and limited relief for Russian civilians in need. According to historian

Jennifer Polk, the organization was "an important part of the Canadian war establishment," walking "hand-in-hand with the Department of Militia and Defence and the army's medical services."[81] The Red Cross Mission was headed by Colonel John S. Dennis, transportation agent for the CEFS and chair of the economic commission (as well as director of colonization for the CPR and assistant to the president). The commission's interim report underscored the connection between economics and humanitarian relief: "It is certain that unless large quantities of food and clothing are forwarded at once, serious suffering and starvation will be experienced during 1919 ... A quantity of food and clothing ... distributed through the Canadian Red Cross ... will have the effect of laying a strong foundation upon which to develop Canadian trade later on."[82]

Nursing Matron Grace Eldrida Potter, who, as mentioned, was the lone woman in the Canadian force and a member of the Red Cross Mission, had embarked on a high-profile shopping trip through Vancouver's wholesale district prior to her departure for Vladivostok. With a reporter in tow and armed with $5,000 in Red Cross funds, Potter purchased underwear, sewing hooks, clocks, oil-cloth, and wool needles for "the unfortunate individuals" in the Russian Far East. Earlier, at a Red Cross meeting, she urged "that assistance be given to the women and children of Russia."[83] However, in Vladivostok, the Canadian Red Cross Mission's work among civilians was limited. Potter and her colleagues focused primarily on tending to injured troops and arranging banquets and social activities for the force. Interaction with refugees and other Russians in need was restricted to the provision of British Red Cross supplies and incidental exchanges aboard the Inter-Allied Anti-Typhus Train, which plied the Trans-Siberian Railroad between December 1918 and May 1919. The train's purpose, according to instructions for its inaugural journey into the "danger zone," was to "first clear up Soldiers, then civilians who were endangering soldiers."[84]

The Canadian Siberian Economic Commission was another civilian wing of Canada's Siberian Expedition that failed to achieve its stated aims. It had been formed by order-in-council in October 1918 and was chaired by Colonel Dennis, a well-placed member of the Canadian elite whose father had served as the Dominion's first surveyor general.[85] While the six-member commission had been formed with a view towards strengthening Canadian trade in Siberia – an "enormous market for Canadian manufacturers" – Dennis later warned of the "unwisdom of shipping goods to this port."[86] Preliminary steps had been taken to arrange for the shipment of Canadian seed and agricultural implements to Siberia, in preparation for the 1919 growing season (financed with a 3.6-million ruble loan authorized by Kolchak), and many Canadian firms expressed strong interest.[87] However, trade was impeded by serious problems of logistics and finance. One Calgary businessman learned a hard lesson when he sailed to

Vladivostok on the *Empress of Japan* with a quantity of boots and shoes and was unable to dispose of his goods.[88] Insufficient wharf space in Vladivostok and poor transportation along the Trans-Siberian Railroad prevented the movement of goods, thwarting the primary objective of the commission. In early March, as the security situation deteriorated, the commission decided to disband and return to Canada.[89]

The idea of expanded trade with Siberia was stymied by the general financial picture of post-revolutionary Russia. As A.D. Braithwaite, assistant director of the Bank of Montreal, reported after a trip up country to Omsk, there was no capacity to raise credit as there was no constitutional government capable of raising revenue or securing loans or currency. The Bolsheviks had repudiated all debts to foreign banks and nationalized foreign-owned property, creating a repulsive climate for outside capitalists. While Kolchak claimed to have the remnants of the czar's gold in his possession, no gold standard existed to back currency. Vladivostok and other Far Eastern and Siberian centres lacked a common or stable currency since the motley White administrations issued a dozen variations of scrip. This saw the value of scrip plummet in 1918-19 as it circulated alongside Romanov, Kerensky, and Bolshevik notes (as well as American dollars, Japanese yen, and Chinese yuan).[90] The Horvath government's kopek is a case in point. Canadian soldiers were paid at the rate of 9.25 rubles to the dollar when they landed in January 1919. Within two months, the rate was 11.55 rubles to the dollar, and, by the time the last troops departed, it had dropped to more than 30 rubles to the dollar.[91] The Kerensky government had ordered paper currency from the United States after the March 1917 revolution, but the Allies withheld shipment on account of the unstable political situation and then forbade the exchange of rubles outside Russia, China, and Japan.[92] This "may have been in accordance with the principles of high finance but from our point of view it was disastrous," Major-General Alfred Knox, head of the British Military Mission, confided to his Vladivostok deputy: "The machinery here is inadequate to print in sufficient quantities."[93] After the Royal Bank of Canada opened its Vladivostok branch on Svetlanskaya in February 1919 (with a guard of five provided by the Canadian force), transactions were confined to Allied troops stationed in the city.[94]

A half-century later, Canada's trade commissioner at Vladivostok, twenty-six-year-old Dana Wilgress, commented: "Looking back, I am amazed how little consultation took place with the Russians on the spot and whom we were supposed to be assisting. The general philosophy seemed to be that the Russians had made such a bad mess that it was necessary for foreigners to take over and try to restore order."[95] One of the greatest achievements of the commission involved arranging an overseas trip by a Russian businessman to Vancouver to meet with local timber barons and to "study the saw-mill industry ... and [the] Canadian system of work in British Columbia and elsewhere."[96] Seeking to dampen the appearance of imperialist aims, the Canadians in Vladivostok met with representatives of the powerful consumer and financial cooperatives – which counted about half of Siberia's 13 million inhabitants among their membership – "encouraging communications between Canadian co-operative societies and their counterparts in Siberia."[97]

Captain Elkington suggests that the citizens of Vladivostok were hostile to the presence of the Allied troops in the city: "It wasn't a pleasant life, I can tell you ... They were not at all hospitable ... the majority."[98] The Canadian command had inflamed the local population when it seized the Pushkinsky Theatre, headquarters of the Cultural-Enlightenment Society, days after landing in Vladivostok.[99] Relations did not improve. Discontent was widespread but rarely erupted into open confrontation. As Elkington recalls: "There were no pitched battles. There were just odd casualties here and there, because the Bolsheviks were not there in force. It was more or less held by the White Russians. But the whole of Vladivostok was infiltrated with Bolsheviks." He remembers walking back to Gornostai one night with Lieutenant Aleksandr Ragosin, the former czarist officer who was attached to the Canadian force headquarters as an interpreter. They encountered three Bolsheviks. Ragosin shot one of them, and Elkington says he shot another: "'Bang!' he got one of them. I went 'bang!' and I helped get one." While the Allies' stated aims in Siberia shifted like the tide, Elkington's purpose in Russia was clear: "to try to defeat the Bolsheviks."[100]

Bolsheviks and Partisans

Resentment towards Allied intervention in Vladivostok fuelled a robust partisan movement not only among Bolsheviks who had led the short-lived Soviet but also among peasants outraged over the exercise of White power in the Far East. Partisan bands had formed spontaneously, with little coordination, but over time coalesced into an effective army under the direction of the Russian Communist Party. To curb resistance, the Allied forces conducted surveillance of dissidents and established an international military police force in Vladivostok, with headquarters in Svetlanskaya, led by American Major Samuel I. Johnson with staff from all Allied contingents, including six non-commissioned officers of Canada's advance party.[101] The two Canadian infantry battalions alternated to provide weekly guards for Allied positions and the central railway station, the Royal Bank of Canada branch, and abundant war matériel along the wharves, which reached 900,000 tons by 1919.[102] These forces were ill-suited for the irregular guerrilla campaign waged by partisans in Vladivostok and the surrounding taiga.

While the official history of Canada's war effort claims that "the mass of the Siberian people, who were generally content with their ordered existence under the old regime, had little leaning towards the Bolshevik system," the head of the RNWMP "B" Squadron, Major George Stanley Worsley, suggested otherwise, estimating in 1919 that, in Vladivostok, "the inhabitants [were] about ninety percent Bolshevik."[103] Canadian Press correspondent Captain Wilfred Playfair offered a more nuanced perspective to *Daily Times* (Victoria) readers: "[While] there is undoubtedly a Bolshevik element in Siberia, the leading problem at present is not Bolshevism but the conflict between various types of reactionaries and the democratic element."[104] British and Japanese forces courted the animosity of the local population by aligning themselves with monarchists, while the Americans, who refused operations of a political nature, rose in public esteem. The commander of the American Expeditionary Force, William S. Graves, explained how the term "Bolshevik" broadened in tandem with the partisan insurgency of the winter of 1918-19: "In Siberia, the word Bolshevik meant a human being who did not, by act or word, give encouragement to the restoration to power of representatives of Autocracy in Russia."[105] A Canadian officer offered a similar view: "The people of Siberia resent the presence of the Allied troops ... They regard us as intruders ... They are all Bolshevists in the meaning of the word as it is used here. A Bolshevist, with them, is one who wants a change."[106]

With the violent overthrow of the Vladivostok Soviet in June 1918, the local Bolshevik Party organization had gone underground. American journalist Albert Rhys Williams, who counted Bolshevik leaders among his friends, spent his final night in Vladivostok in July 1918 with *tovarische* (comrades) "in a hiding place in the hills" above the city: "The Soviet had not been destroyed. It had gone underground. In the secret retreat the leaders yet uncaptured, gathered to plan and organize."[107] The Vladivostok party was the "most important and largest Communist group" in the Russian Far East, historian Canfield Smith wrote, led by "very able young men and women in their 20s and 30s."[108] These Bolshevik leaders included Konstantin Sukhanov, the twenty-four-year-old student who had led the Vladivostok Soviet and was killed in captivity in November 1918; thirty-year-old I.G. Kushnarev, who had joined the party during the 1905 revolution; and 25-year-old Sergei Lazo, who joined in 1917 but rose rapidly through party ranks to become an astute, sometimes ruthless, military commander (Lazo would die at the hands of the Japanese in 1920). The Bolsheviks distributed the newspaper *Krasnoe Znamya* (*Red Banner*) in Vladivostok and throughout the Russian Far East. They formed the nucleus of a far-flung party organization of between three thousand and four thousand members that was battered but not destroyed by White and Allied occupation.[109]

The Allied advance north from Vladivostok along the Trans-Siberian Railroad had pushed the Bolsheviks into the wooded hills between the Pacific and the Manchurian border, and into the taiga north of the Amur River (see Map 5).[110] Three principal bases of partisan strength took root near Vladivostok, in the town of Anuchino (in a valley 150 kilometres north of the city), at the port of Olga (three hundred kilometres distant but accessible by boat), and around the Suchan mines (today called Partizansk, one hundred kilometres east of Vladivostok).[111] The Suchan miners were "generally sympathetic to the partisans and provided them with mine explosives for destroying bridges, railway tracks, and other strategic targets."[112] Partisan strength in the Suchan Valley meant control over the coal supply for the railroad and Vladivostok. In December 1918, a key partisan meeting at the village of Frolovka, on the Suchan River, brought together organizers from the surrounding area. These organizers made common cause with the underground Bolshevik organization based in Vladivostok.

Bolshevik partisans also enjoyed growing support among the peasantry in Primorsky Krai. While the British high commissioner believed the peasantry were "probably anti-Bolshevik as a whole," he conceded that "they like[d] to cut wood in Government forests and distil spirits as they cho[se]." Those with grievances "listened to the Bolsheviks" and joined partisan bands, which came into their villages in the cold months and launched attacks on White-held towns. When Kolchak imposed a draft in December 1918 to raise troops for his new Siberian army – a force staffed by officers for the British and Canadian-built Russian Island school – peasant youths fled to the taiga.[113] The ruthlessness of White Russian generals drove the peasants into sympathy with the Bolsheviks. These generals "were brutal in seeking recruits, ferreting out Communists, and administering cruel punishments including death, to those who aided revolutionary forces or who illegally possessed weapons," Canfield Smith writes: "There was no way for peasants to protect themselves from these White activities except to organize partisan units and strike back."[114] The partisans sunk roots in villages along the length of the Trans-Siberian Railroad, while Bolshevik organization deepened in Vladivostok and other Far Eastern cities. In Nikolsk-Ussuriisk, one hundred kilometres to the north, railworkers formed the nucleus of the underground, alongside former prisoners from Kolchak's notorious "death train," which had transported captured Bolsheviks on a gory journey from the Urals to the Pacific.[115] At Khabarovsk, workers at the local arsenal and sailors in the Amur River Fleet spearheaded partisan groups.[116]

The Vladivostok underground grew as the civilian population struggled to obtain basic foodstuffs and to sustain meagre social services, turning to the Bolsheviks in the face of White terror and corruption. While General Horvath had nominal authority as Kolchak's plenipotentiary in Eastern Siberia, a ruthless commander named General Pavel Ivanov-Rinov ruled the port city with a free hand. Ivanov-Rinov had arrived in Vladivostok two days ahead of the Canadians in October 1918. He proceeded to implement a reign of terror against all shades of dissent. When socialist members of the Omsk Town Duma fled to Vladivostok in the wake of Kolchak's coup, Ivanov-Rinov ordered their arrest and detention without trial. Some were killed. These dissidents were not Bolshevik, but they sought to establish Vladivostok as an "All-Russian Socialist Center."[117] Foreshadowing later events, in January Japanese general Otani warned Horvath and Ivanov-Rinov: "Such action may easily inflame the citizens of Vladivostok [so] as to cause them to make resistance to what appears to them illegal and arbitrary arrests."[118] Canadian intelligence officer James Mackintosh Bell confirms this view: "The moderate socialists instead of standing with [Kolchak] at first wavered and then sided with the Bolsheviks, more as a *modus operandi* than from any actual sympathy. Anything was better than a return to Czarism, which they read clearly in the tactics of Kolchak's followers."[119]

The main body of the Canadian force reached Vladivostok in the wake of the political arrests as Bolshevik feeling and partisan activity flourished in the city and surrounding countryside. A lieutenant in the 260th Battalion recalled that the civic administration "changed twice at least during [his] stay."[120] Bolshevik candidates had won "an overwhelming majority" in elections to the Vladivostok municipal Duma in late 1918, and, when subsequent elections were held in the spring, a victory for pro-monarchist candidates was "backed up by Allied bayonets."[121] Demonstrating developments on the ground, the parents' committee at the Vladivostok Ladies High School sent an appeal to the Canadian command in February, inviting officers to a "charity concert ball" to raise funds for the "poorer pupils."[122] In April, as the Canadians prepared to evacuate Vladivostok, a Russian print shop expelled Canadian soldier Roderick Rogers, halting publication of the *Siberian Sapper*. The Russians claimed that the Canadian was a drunk, while Rogers insisted that "the Russian press men [were] Bolsheviks."[123]

Against this backdrop, the Vladivostok Bolsheviks took steps to formalize their underground organization. They formed the Maritime Oblast Committee (Obkom) of the Communist Party and extended their organization across the Russian Far East. Rioting in the village of Mazanovo, north of the Amur River near Manchuria, alerted the Allies to mounting partisan strength amid rumours of "a gathering of Bolsheviks in the neighbourhood of Blagoveshchensk and a possibility of a rising of brigands."[124] In February, a force of over three thousand Bolsheviks clashed with Japanese troops east of Blagoveshchensk on the Amur River, killing three hundred Japanese, including two battalion commanders, and seizing two field guns.[125]

Closer to Vladivostok, in the strategic Suchan Valley and the port of Olga up the coast, the partisans launched a major offensive in February and March 1919. They took the village of Vladimiro-Aleksandrovskoye at the mouth of the Suchan River on 15 February, disarming the local White Russian militia and seizing the town weapons arsenal. An appeal from the rebels conveyed the political mood: "We rose because with all our heart we want to help our Soviet country to get rid of the executioner Kolchak, to reinstall Soviet power in Siberia and the Far East, and to get rid of the interventionists."[126] Five days later, on the night of 20-21 February, partisans attacked White positions at Olga and at the Tetyukhe mines, seizing control of the Tetyukhe post and telegraph office and arresting the local militia. The military-revolutionary committee of the Tetyukhe mines sent reinforcements on horseback to Olga, which fell to the partisans on 4 March. An estimated fifteen hundred guerrilla fighters repulsed White attempts to reclaim Vladimiro-Aleksandrovskoye, establishing sentry posts around the small White garrison in the town, as rebellion spread throughout the Suchan Valley. Five hundred American troops rushed from Vladivostok to guard the mine works.[127] However, when the Whites asked Japan to send a force to Olga, Japanese commanders refused, citing "an insufficient number of troops."[128] Attempts to land troopships at Amerika (now Nakhodka) Bay, at the mouth of the Suchan River, failed, as partisans "opened fire from the hills," killing White Russian sailors capable of navigating the first ship and then repulsing a second boat. The British warship HMS *Kent* killed four partisan fighters in the melee.[129] According to historian Boris Mukhachev, "The whole seashore from Nakhodka Bay to Emperor's Harbour was controlled by guerillas."[130]

A Canadian intelligence officer attributed the disturbances at Suchan and Olga to "the government order for the conscription of men of military age" and to a second order for the surrender of arms: "The peasants say they do not like the Kolchak government or believe its democratic professions and hence do not want to fight for it." They objected to the second order since arms were "vital to their welfare against tigers, bears and robbers": "As the Kolchak men approach a village the young men clear off into the hills with their rifles and large bands are reported to have collected in outlying hill villages."[131] The Allies were reluctant to aid counter-insurgency operations as reports surfaced of atrocities committed by Kolchak's troops. On the morning of 8 March 1919, three hundred White Russian and Chinese soldiers entered the village of Brovnichi in the Suchan Valley. The youths fled to the hills, while the man who had warned them was tied to the rafters of a house and beaten for four hours. The next day, the Kolchak troops entered the nearby village of Gordyevka and ordered all men to relinquish their arms. One man was taken to a house, "where he was stretched by his neck to a pin in the rafter, his hands tied, and terribly beaten about the body and head until the blood splashed even on the walls of the rooms ... He was later stood in a row at 2 o'clock p.m. and shot to death with eight others." The White troops took another man, who was an invalid, and "broke one of his arms," "cut out his finger nails," and beat him "with a rifle knocking out all his front teeth," before shooting him with the rest. As the Kolchak soldiers retreated from Gordyevka, partisans armed the villagers with rifles and "plenty of ammunition" and posted sentries on the hilltops approaching the town, vowing to slaughter any Japanese or Kolchak soldiers who returned.[132]

Such was the climate as Vladivostok Bolsheviks met again with Suchan miners and other partisans at Frolovka in March 1919. At this meeting, conducted under the nose of the occupying Allied troops, the delegates elected the Provisional Military-Revolutionary Staff of Partisan Detachments, commanded by the Bolshevik Sergei Lazo, with a view to re-establishing local Soviets.[133] The radicalization of the peasantry in Primorsky Krai was directly tied to the authoritarian character of the Kolchak regime. Attempts to resolve grievances through official channels only produced further repression. When a delegation of peasants sailed from Olga to Vladivostok to meet with Allied commanders and to lodge an appeal against Kolchak's conscription law, they were arrested by White authorities.[134] An American intelligence report estimated the presence of ten thousand partisan fighters between the town of Shkotovo and Suchan. It said that these fighters were "not really Bolsheviki" but, rather, "entirely a peasant uprising, resulting from atrocities of the Kolchak troops."[135] The Far Eastern District Committee of the Communist Party (Dalkom) issued an appeal to "Comrades, Workmen and Peasants," condemning the "mutilation and shooting of peaceful inhabitants, the burning down of cottages and villages." The Bolsheviks called on the local population to not give "a single soldier" to Kolchak's White forces.[136]

Under the yoke of foreign occupation, the Bolshevik partisans wreaked havoc on the Allied forces in Vladivostok and sabotaged rail operations to Suchan and points up country (see Chapter 7).[137] "Quite often the lights went out and someone would say casually: 'They are trying to seize the power station,'" British observer Bernard Pares recalled.[138] Insurgents also cut telegraph wires and stole copper cable used by the 6th Signal Company to relay messages between the Pushkinsky Theatre and outlying Canadian barracks.[139] While no proof of sabotage has been found, the Canadian force's garage and sixteen military vehicles were "completed destroyed by fire" in February 1919.[140] Bolsheviks ambushed White Russian and Allied officers along the roads connecting Vladivostok with Gornostai Barracks and Second River, employing torture and mutilation to good effect. In mid-March 1919, two White Russians were found crucified on the road near First River, their noses, eyes, ears, and tongues cut off and their hands "nailed to their shoulder blades with six inch spikes to serve in lieu of epaulettes."[141] According to Canadian officer Raymond Massey: "We continually found the bodies of these men, bearing obscene evidence of torture before death. Many times through the winter, we were alerted to take action stations according to prearranged anti-riot plans, but nothing happened 'above-ground.'"[142]

By March 1919, the situation had grown desperate, as White repression fuelled partisan resistance in and around Vladivostok and the Allies lost any semblance of unity. On 2 March, Kolchak's military commander in the district, General Ivanov-Rinov, had ordered the arrest without trial of Vladivostok's mayor and five other dissidents, "not Bolsheviks but plain radicals," four of whom were spirited away to a prison on the Manchurian border, inflaming the local population. "The Bolsheviki have placarded the city calling on the working men to gather to-morrow and protest against the action," Captain Charles Hertzberg wrote in his diary on 9 March. Three days later, a huge demonstration celebrated the second anniversary of the Romanovs' fall.[143] Japanese general Otani warned Elmsley of a "considerable amount of unrest among the Russians in Vladivostok," suggesting "an uprising [was] not improbable," while consular officials – citing "political reasons" – closed the port of Vladivostok to "all Russians returning to Siberia from America."[144] Demonstrating deep divisions among the foreign armies, the Americans refused to cooperate with Otani, on grounds of the political arrests, while the Canadians pledged to support operations of a "non-political" nature.[145] "The Bolsheviks are making Vladivostok sort of a city of refuge," Hugh Robertson, a sapper in the 6th Signal Company, wrote to his mother in the midst of the crisis: "They know that the Allies are here to stop any trouble that may arise, and so they come to Vladivostok in order to get to safety. There are a lot of them there now, but as long as they keep quiet they will be left alone."[146]

The Canadian command issued instructions for the anticipated uprising in Vladivostok. The RNWMP squadron would occupy the head of land above the Pushkinsky Theatre, while other units were to converge on the East Barracks under Bickford's command, in "assault kit," with twenty-four hours' rations of bully beef, biscuits, and bread. All Canadian infantry troops received training with live bombs, as Canadian eighteen-pound guns and ammunition were transported from Second River to guard the officers' training school on Russian Island.[147] In the harbour, a landing party of 120 British marines and two machine guns were placed on alert aboard the cruiser HMS *Kent*, which was ready to land on a half hour's notice.[148] Elmsley feared that "the chief danger of an uprising [would be] that the Allies, acting independently, [would] come into armed conflict with each other," as there was "no unity of policy or command," and "strong Allied guards [were] intermingled throughout Vladivostok and feeling between Americans, Japanese and Russians [was] far from friendly." Seeking to mediate a solution, he proposed that counter-insurgency operations be undertaken by the International Police alone and that the arrested dissidents be returned to Vladivostok to stand trial.[149]

Instructions were issued to all ranks of the CEFS against travelling alone at night, and the men were advised to carry arms at all times.[150] The sense of apprehension was apparent when a belligerent Russian civilian appeared at the Canadian Ordnance shed at Egersheld, demanding gasoline on the grounds that "the czar was dead ... and everything was public property." The local sentry panicked and stabbed the man in the groin with his bayonet.[151] On 19 April 1919, the Vladivostok Bolsheviks organized a secret meeting in the port city, in contempt of the occupying Allied armies. This was the third Far Eastern regional conference of the Russian Communist Party, with delegates of partisan forces from Suchan, Khabarovsk, Chita, Harbin, and other points.[152] Two weeks later, the partisans ambushed General Horvath's car as he returned to Vladivostok from the Canadians' gymkhana sporting event outside the city, throwing two bombs and injuring several civilians. The attack occurred near Elmsley's apartment at No. 5 Svetlanskaya, and Canadian guards scrambled to apprehend the attackers.[153] An "Operation Plan for Evacuation of Vladivostok," while couched in hypothetical terms, betrayed the fears of the Canadian command: "The whole country has risen in revolt and large Bolsheviki irregular forces, indifferently armed, are preparing to attack this detachment."[154]

Dissent among the Troops

Opposition to the Siberian Expedition was not confined to Bolshevik and partisan insurgents, with evidence pointing to ongoing discontent among the Canadians in Vladivostok. In late December, Private James McNeill had been court martialled for "striking his superior officer" and sentenced to fourteen days' field punishment.[155] In January 1919, shortly after the *Teesta* and the *Protesilaus* landed at Vladivostok, the Canadian command prohibited the distribution of private mail to Canada, citing "limited personnel available for duty as despatch riders," but ulterior motives may also have been at play.[156] "Letters sent by men show discontent," one of the force's mail censors noted in his unit's war diary.[157] While military regulations prohibited enlisted men from keeping personal diaries, signs of dissent appeared in letters home, particularly after censorship restrictions were loosened in the middle of February. "I am about fed up

with this hole," Rifleman Harold Steele of the 259th Battalion wrote to his girlfriend Josie Libby in Ontario.[158]

Restlessness could be detected among both officers and enlisted men. "No
one seems to know what is to become of us – whether we stay here indefinitely
or return to Canada or go Up Country," Lieutenant Harold Ardagh wrote, coin-
ing the acronym "Comical Expeditionary Force – CEF."[159] With their mission
increasingly uncertain, the Canadians had "nothing to do," performing little
training and occupying themselves instead with mundane tasks such as fetching
water from Gornostai's well or assisting Chinese "coolie" labourers who hauled
coal and wood for the stoves in the camp.[160] "The monotony of the life is, to say
the least, irksome ... very dreary and drab," a captain in the force headquarters
battalion wrote in *Maclean's* magazine: "If the war were still on the troops would
accept their monotonous lot ... The homesickness is quite as prevalent as the
seasickness on the voyage out."[161]

Inaction bred boredom and criticism of their purpose in Russia. In March,
the Canadians attended two lectures delivered in Vladivostok's Casino Theatre
by Bernard Pares, the British historian, who said: "We are here for the building
up of democratic Russia."[162] This prompted Lance-Corporal Erskine Ireland, a
future Toronto lawyer who belonged to the 259th Battalion, to conclude:

> It should rest with the Russians to settle their own internal affairs ... If it has been
> decided that the outside Powers should intervene, then intervention should be
> on a large scale ... But such an effort to suppress Bolshevism and establish stable
> government in Russia would involve tremendous casualties for the Allies, and
> sacrifices which I cannot conscientiously feel that we should bear. Therefore, I
> maintain that our policy should be one of non-intervention. The colossal popula-
> tion of Russia, consisting of people of diverse nationalities, cannot be moulded
> into a sane and democratic nation in a day. It is something that must be created
> by the inhabitants of Russia by themselves.[163]

The *Siberian Sapper* newspaper ran a front-page story attempting to counter
the widespread view that "the Canadians [and] British have no business in
Russia to-day."[164] Disciplinary infractions were frequent, from allegations of
"Bolshevik activities" on the part of a private in the 259th Battalion to the more
benign conduct of Private James Payton of the 260th Battalion, who pawned
his army-issue sweater-coat for a can of vodka.[165] When another private,
Russian-born John Kovalchuk of the 260th Battalion, volunteered to remain
in Siberia with the British Military Mission, he was declined on the grounds
of his having "Bolshevik tendencies." "Private Kovalchuk ... is suspected of

knowing some of the Bolshevik Leaders in the District of Vladivostok, and about their movements," a British officer warned: "Kovalchuk is a supporter of the Bolsheviks."[166]

The Canadian command downplayed unrest in the ranks. While American general Graves recalls a "serious situation" in the Canadian force when several officers refused orders from the British high commissioner and were "sent back to Canada," no evidence of this exists in the records of the CEFS.[167] When the War Office wired Elmsley in February regarding "serious discontent amongst Canadian troops at Vladivostok," the Canadian general responded that there was "no discontent, and troops [were] quite happy."[168] The chief of general staff, Gwatkin, offered a similar response, saying that "some incidences of compulsion" had been "necessary to induce the troops to embark" but that there had been "no discontent among Canadian troops at Vladivostok."[169] However, the diary of British Lieutenant-Colonel John Ward, commander of the 25th Battalion, Middlesex Regiment, paints a different picture. As Ward wrote on 3 February 1919:

I heard news of general insubordination among the Canadian troops that had just arrived at Vladivostok. If all the information received could be relied upon, the sooner they were shipped back to Canada the better. There is enough anarchy here now without the British government dumping more on us.[170]

Ward believed it was a "great mistake to mix Canadians and British troops in one Brigade," suggesting: "Nothing but the wonderful sense of order in the make-up of the average Englishman has prevented us from becoming an Anglo-Canadian rabble, dangerous to Bolshevik and Russian alike."[171] When a call was issued for Canadian volunteers to help the British operate their section of the Siberian railroad, Rifleman Harold Steele of the 260th Battalion lamented: "I guess they will do the same as they did at Victoria. If they can't get volunteers they will just keep the whole works. I hope they don't for I am about fed up with this hole."[172]

The strain on the Canadian forces in Vladivostok was graphically illustrated with the untimely death of Lieutenant Alfred Thring, a forty-year-old insurance clerk from Saskatoon who had suffered a head wound and shell shock on the Western Front before joining the 260th Battalion of the Siberian force. On 18 March 1919, Thring's body was discovered in a ditch beside Gornostai Road, between Gornostai Barracks and Vladivostok, with a bullet hole in the temple. Thring held his service revolver in his right hand. Torn photos and letters from his wife lay scattered on the ground. While a court of inquiry concluded that

Thring had taken his own life while suffering "an attack of epileptic insanity," his service records stated that he had been "accidentally killed" – "a gentle whitewash," according to Skuce. Witnesses at the Vladivostok inquiry testified that Thring was depressed, fearing nightmares and asserting that he hoped to clash with the Bolsheviki so he could "go out clean."[173]

Decades later, Captain Eric Elkington conceded that the troops in Vladivostok had grown restless: "We realized it was a hopeless state of affairs really ... The Bolsheviks had taken over all the rest of the country ... We realized we weren't going to do any good unless they had a huge force there and rushed right through Siberia and into Russia."[174]

"Up Country" and Evacuation

FEW CANADIANS VENTURED "up country," to the Siberian interior, where Czech and White Russian troops engaged the Red Army in active warfare on the Ural Front. The original intention to move the main body of the Canadian force to Omsk – 5,350 *versts*[1] (5,700 kilometres) inland from Vladivostok, a journey of two to five weeks – dissolved in the face of ambivalent Allied strategy and growing supply problems along the Trans-Siberian Railroad. Elmsley's "secure line of communication" grew increasingly unstable, subject to sabotage and labour strikes, imperilling the small Canadian force at Omsk, which served as headquarters staff for the British Middlesex and Hampshire battalions.[2] Canadian resolve evaporated before the majority of soldiers had even reached Russian soil, though the final decision was not taken until after they had landed. Beyond policing duties in Vladivostok and routine camp life, a few hundred Canadians ventured to the town of Shkotovo, on a key rail line northeast of Vladivostok, to repel a Bolshevik advance and to secure the Allies' coal supply. They arrived to find that the enemy had dispersed, which was symptomatic of the irregular guerrilla tactics in the Russian Far East. Up country was an elusive place for most Canadians – a site of danger and action that evaded the problem-plagued Siberian Expedition.

Omsk and the Ural Front

Lieutenant-Colonel Thomas "Sid" Morrisey and fifty-four Canadians rode the Trans-Siberian Railroad to Omsk, the capital of Admiral Kolchak's White government, arriving on the afternoon of 27 December 1918.[3] They arrived at a moment of tension, in the wake of a Bolshevik uprising on 22 December that had been suppressed by "unnecessarily harsh measures" - the summary court martial and execution of several hundred insurgents, which inflamed the local population and created a "dangerous situation."[4] The Bolsheviks, armed with forged documents, had launched an early-morning raid on the local prison, liberating and arming the inmates, including former members of the Constituent Assembly. They seized the Kulomsino rail station and Kolokolnikov Mill south of the city, and blew up part of a bridge over the Irtysh River. Czech and British troops intervened on behalf of Kolchak, and the uprising was "entirely liquidated by the afternoon," with many arrests and executions. As the *BC Federationist* reported in British Columbia:

> Twelve men were shot by courtmartial orders after an armed uprising by Bolsheviki at Omsk on the night of December 22 ... The Bolsheviki succeeded in freeing prisoners in the Omsk prison, but a detachment of government soldiers quickly arrested twelve men who had participated in the outbreak. They were promptly tried and executed.[5]

The repression did not end there. White officers executed several members of the Constituent Assembly who surrendered themselves at the prison.[6] In the most gory display of retribution, several hundred insurgents were marched across the frozen Irtysh River and shot en masse.[7] "It cost nearly a thousand lives to restore order, but the lawless elements, top and bottom, were taught a lesson they [were] not likely to forget," recalled British colonel John Ward.[8] While a British intelligence officer suggested that "Kolchak's power [was] stronger than ever," the high commissioner warned that "the murders perpetrated during the recent rising at Omsk ha[d] produced a deplorable effect."[9]

The arrival of the Canadians at Omsk created conflict between Morrisey, a young officer at age twenty-eight, and Ward. The British commander had grown accustomed to operating autonomously and resented his subordinate position within Elmsley's Canadian brigade. As Ward recalls:

> Revolutionary plans in connection with the distribution of my battalion, and other matters, were instantly proposed. Some of them were actually carried out, with the result that a strained feeling became manifest in the British camp at Omsk, which caused me to propose to Brigadier-General Elmsley that my headquarters should be transferred to Vladivostok.[10]

Elmsley refused, insisting that Ward remain in Omsk "until future policy [was] decided."[11] The situation eased after the British high commissioner intervened and the 1/9th (Hants) Battalion, Hampshire Regiment, arrived in the city. "All well," Morrisey informed Elmsley.[12] However, all was not well. Canadian and British troops at Omsk remained in a state of limbo as the Allies vacillated over the future of the Siberian Expedition and White Russians grew restless. The Hants Regiment evicted refugees in order to secure their sleeping quarters, and the Canadians opened a small hospital and supply depot at the local yacht club. Kolchak's minister of the interior had urged the Omsk Town Council to adapt a local theological school for barracks space, anticipating the arrival of the Canadian army in a "short time." According to Morrisey, it was "manifestly unfair" to reserve barrack space at Omsk when it remained unclear whether the main body of the CEFS would ever reach the city. Elmsley capitulated, instructing Morrisey to "cancel [the] order regarding the reservation of barrack accommodation at Omsk ... until ... future policy ha[d] been definitely decided."[13]

In January 1919, the Canadian command still believed that the main body of the CEFS would proceed to Omsk.[14] The Bolsheviks in Siberia were "not a formidable adversary for even a small well-organized force," Britain's high commissioner insisted. Canadian troops could perform garrison duty in the towns between Irkutsk and Omsk without "running much more risk than if they remained in Vladivostok."[15] However, the fifty-five Canadians and fifteen hundred British troops under Elmsley's command up country were hamstrung by divisions among the Allies and White Russians as well as by an increasingly ambivalent British strategy.[16] Intelligence reports pointed to animosity between White Russian and Allied officers. When British warplanes reached Siberia, Elmsley asked that they give priority to Canadian and British, rather than to White Russian, forces.[17] The commander-in-chief of Allied troops in western Siberia was French general Maurice Janin, a career soldier fluent in Russian who arrived at Omsk after the civil war was in full swing. Kolchak refused to recognize Janin as commander-in-chief, believing it would "weaken his authority."[18] Britain, meanwhile, recognized Janin but not Kolchak.

"Until the Kolchak government has been recognized by England you should avoid any action which might tend to convey prematurely the impression that is has been recognized," Elmsley instructed the commander of the Hampshire Battalion.[19] The delicate political situation was highlighted when rumours surfaced of British troops escorting a jailed former member of the Kolchak Cabinet to China. Elmsley wired Morrisey in Omsk demanding an explanation.[20] "Past experience ... shows that Russian Political Prisoners are not safe," Morrisey replied, explaining that the prisoners had asked British guards to "accompany them [the] whole way and not leave them at the Chinese frontier."[21] Elmsley's instructions to the Hampshire Battalion reflected ambivalence in Canadian strategy: he ordered that no troops move west of the Urals, that no operations "of a political nature" be undertaken, and that the troops "not move from Omsk without consulting [him]."[22] At the end of January, Elmsley's planned departure up country was cancelled. The British War Office issued definitive orders "not to go to Omsk, until the Allied policy ha[d] been decided upon at Paris."[23]

January 1919 saw a heavy concentration of White Russian and Allied troops along the Ural Front – a line that extended from the mountains north of Yekaterinburg to the shores of the Caspian Sea. The Whites had suppressed Bolshevik uprisings at Omsk and rail lines near Krasnoyarsk but had surrendered the city of Ufa to the revolutionaries. The Canadian command attributed this defeat to

Troop disposition on the Ural Front on 24 December 1918

Front/Group	Enemy strength	Enemy unit	White/Allied strength
Yekaterinburg	27,600	Second & Third Soviet Armies	38,000
Kama	22,000	Fifth Soviet Army	16,000
Samara	25,500	First Soviet Army	10,000
South-West/Orenburg	41,000	Fourth Soviet Army	12,000

Source: "Military Situation, December 31st, 1918," War Diary of Force Headquarters CEF (S), December 1919, app. 42.

"the numerical superiority of the enemy and shortages of ammunition." It also pointed out that "want of clothing caused many losses by frost bite."[24] The loss of Ufa was offset by victory over the Third Soviet Army on the Yekaterinburg line, with the capture of 31,000 prisoners, 120 guns, 100 machine guns, 180 troop trains, 9 armoured trains, 30 automobiles, several thousand horses and "all the Reds' supplies."[25] However, as the above table reveals, Yekaterinburg was the only section of the Ural Front where Whites outnumbered Reds. A Red Army offensive near Orenburg, in southern Russia, prompted an urgent request to Elmsley for seven Canadian soldiers and a company of British troops; the British War Office denied this request, refusing to agree "to any further dispersal of the small British Force in Siberia."[26] Orenburg fell to the Red Army in late January 1919 as Major-General Knox warned: "Everything here may collapse."[27] Reports also surfaced that the Reds had begun training for the use of poison gas.[28] Demonstrating the vulnerability of Allied forces up country, a Canadian censorship order forbade any mention of the location of Allied units east of Lake Baikal.[29]

The political climate in western Siberia was unstable, reflecting shortages of supplies, disease, and divisions among White Russian and Allied forces. "The Siberian troops can perform creditably in action but they appear to become affected by contact with Social Revolutionary and Bolshevik ideas when quartered in the towns," a Canadian intelligence report noted. Railway lines were not secure unless guarded by Allied troops, and, with the exception of basic foodstuffs, there were shortages of all supplies. Typhus was prevalent amid fears of a general epidemic with the coming of warmer weather.[30] While the Kolchak government enjoyed the support of military officials and "propertied classes," it did not meet with the same acceptance from more liberal political groups who opposed its "reactionary and monarchist tendencies." Kolchak's influence was particularly weak east of Lake Baikal, in the Transbaikal, Amur, and Ussuri regions, where Cossack troops and some Czechs recognized Semyonov rather than Kolchak.[31] These fissures in the White camp were exposed in late January when several hundred Ussuri Cossacks mutinied near Khabarovsk. "It is rumoured that they have been influenced by Bolshevik agitators who without doubt are to be found among American troops here," a secret telegram noted, citing the deserters' grievances over "bad feeding, non receipt of wages and inhuman treatment."[32]

In early 1919, Allied commanders in western Siberia worked with Kolchak to train his 100,000-strong New Siberian Army and to launch a renewed offensive on the Ural Front. "British officers were making desperate efforts to organise and equip forces capable of dealing a death-blow to the Bolsheviks in early spring," Ward recalled.[33] Knox, head of the British Military Mission, "travelled from 'Vlady' to Omsk, from Omsk to 'Vlady,' as though the 5,000-mile journey was just a run from London to Birmingham ... preparing an army with the sole objective of fighting the Bolsheviks."[34] However, reports indicated that the Allies were "very unpopular" on the Ural Front and that Janin "ha[d] absolutely no power." Kolchak was eager to command front-line operations but was ill and remained in Omsk.[35] Intelligence from the front at the end of February showed the Whites seriously overpowered, with 66,087 rifles to 114,461 for the Red Army.[36] Serious obstacles undermined the Allied and White Russian war effort. A frigid winter saw the temperature hover between minus 40 and minus 70 degrees Fahrenheit, leading to rampant frostbite. Siberian towns were flooded with refugees ("five to six times [their] normal population"), creating a scarcity of accommodation. Significantly, the bastion of anti-Bolshevik military strength in Siberia, the Czecho-Slovak Legion, became paralyzed by internal dissention – conflict between military officers and members of the Czech National Council, who were ordered deported in January 1919. "Till this organization is completely wiped out and the officers given a chance there can be little hope," Knox observed: "It is very doubtful if any of the Czech units will fight again."[37] Czech dissidents were evacuated to Vladivostok, while Czech leaders considered a deal with the Bolsheviks for safe overland passage to Bohemia.[38] "The fighting value of the Czechs is gone," the Canadian commander at Omsk observed as two Czech divisions were recalled from the Ural Front.[39]

The small Canadian contingent at Omsk faced similar problems to those confronting the main body of the CEFS at Vladivostok, including poor logistics and mounting civilian unrest. A Canadian officer described the city of 500,000 as "very spread out," with some "very fine buildings" but "little or no sewage or sanitary conditions": "They don't go in for those sort of things in this country." Thousands of refugees had occupied about six hundred passenger railcars and "thousands" of boxcars, choking the railway sidings and inhibiting traffic along the line. Sporadic shooting erupted every evening after dusk. "We never go out at night without arms," the Canadian lieutenant noted.[40] On 31 January 1919, five White Russian officers were killed during a "small mutiny" in Omsk, when an armed band of soldiers stormed the barracks of the 1st Cadet Regiment, leading to the arrest of thirty rebels.[41] Tension also spiked after the Kolchak government reintroduced vodka, which had been prohibited by the czar during the war and which Bolsheviks in other towns dumped in the streets.[42] Britain's high commissioner at Omsk warned that Canadian and British soldiers would be in a "distinctly dangerous position" if the Red Army advanced on the city.[43] However, Canadian commander Morrisey assured Elmsley that his forces were "not in unreasonable danger" thanks to the Czech presence at Omsk and along the railroad.[44] To occupy the "tedium of their days," the Canadians played sports, organized amateur concerts, and ice-skated on the Irtysh River. According to a White émigré in Omsk, they "lived their own lives, apart from the rest."[45]

At the beginning of March, Sid Morrisey fell ill with typhus and was rushed back to Vladivostok, then evacuated to Canada as he was "unfit for further service in Siberia." The commander's illness revived discussion of deploying a special Canadian "anti-typhus train" across Siberia.[46] Elmsley appointed Major George Morrison of Hamilton as interim commander, while British-born Lieutenant-Colonel Reginald Brook proceeded to Omsk.[47] On 12 March 1919, "all Canadian details" were ordered to leave Omsk for Vladivostok, with the exception of twenty-one medical staff, three soldiers of the YMCA, and a member of the Postal Corps. A Canadian medical officer and artillery Major Lestock Cockburn of Victoria remained stationed with British troops at Krasnoyarsk.[48] A week later, the Canadians relinquished vacant barrack space in Harbin, China, which had been intended as a transit stop for troop movements to the Siberian interior.[49] Despite pleas from Elmsley and others, Ottawa refused to allow the small Canadian contingent to remain up country.[50] The Canadians evacuated Omsk between 28 March and mid-April 1919, transferring supplies to British units as the Canadian supply officer left Harbin.[51] In the volatile climate of civil war and intervention, Bolsheviks, partisans, and railworkers laid siege to the communication lifeline of Allied and White Russian forces in Siberia: the Trans-Siberian Railroad.[52]

The Trans-Siberian Railroad under Allied Occupation

Attempts to move reinforcements up country in 1919 were impeded by a raft of problems along the Trans-Siberian Railroad. In December 1918, British high commissioner Sir Charles Eliot had deplored the "scandalous conditions" of the railroad, a link "of vital importance as the only communication between the Omsk Government, Eastern Siberia and foreign countries." Eliot attributed the situation to: (1) the division of the railroad into separate administrations, which refused to cooperate with each other; (2) non-payment of wages to rail-workers; (3) the absence of spare parts, which prevented the repair of loco-motives; and (4) detention of rolling stock by Semyonov and others. The situation grew worse in 1919, severing Allied communications and dealing a death-blow to Canada's Siberian Expedition.[53]

Britain, the United States, and Japan had each sent railway officials to admin-ister sections of the Siberian track, after the Czechs seized the railroad from the Bolsheviks in mid-1918. The British commission was headed by Colonel Archi-bald Jack, a New Zealand-born engineer who had worked in South Africa, China, and Latin America.[54] According to Canada's trade commissioner in Vladivostok, Colonel Jack "found it impossible to do anything" because of the Japanese-American rivalry. Shipments of military supplies, merchandise, and Red Cross relief were "almost all suspended."[55] "It can now be said that transportation has completely broken down, no goods trains having left Vladivostok for [the] last ten days," Colonel Jack informed Knox at the beginning of January: "Under existing conditions I am compelled to advise you that no further British troops should be sent west from Vladivostok until allied control is reestablished."[56] Later that month, British soldiers in the Hampshire Battalion were interrupted en route to Omsk when Japanese troops prevented their train from proceeding west, fearing they had been sent to attack Semyonov's forces.[57] Attempting to resolve the impasse, the Americans and Japanese agreed to form a special inter-allied committee to supervise the railroad, headed by a White Russian with technical experts drawn from the Allied forces.[58] Britain arranged for the ship-ment of fifty-one steam locomotives and thirty-one thousand tons of railway parts from Canada, but other problems loomed.[59]

In the first months of 1919, Bolsheviks and partisans laid siege to the Trans-Siberian Railroad, debilitating the Allies' line of communication between the Pacific and the Ural Front. The epicentre of unrest was the "Yenisei edge," the area of central Siberia around Krasnoyarsk, where "new settlers prevailed." Estonian and Latvian immigrants were particularly hostile to the Whites. Cooperative societies also served as a locus of guerrilla activity, owing to a large number of political exiles, particularly in the area around Taishet station. Winter conditions thwarted White Russian and Allied operations against Bolshevik guerillas, who enlisted peasants and villagers and employed knowledge of local terrain.[60] As historian Sergey Nikolaevich Shishkin explains:

The interventionists hardly had time to repair one bridge and pass to the next before the first was again destroyed. The Japanese armored trains, specially al-located for protection of the railroad, did not help to save bridges because they often got ambushed, cut off by destroyed sections of track. To destroy a railway for a greater distance, groups chose sites with high embankments, then moved several links of rails to the edge, together with the ties, then put them over the edge. Gravity caused the rails to fall down, pulling down adjacent sections of track.[61]

Partisan attacks on the railroad in January 1919 forced the Allied command to redeploy Czech units from active service on the Ural Front to Irkutsk "for the purpose of protecting the railway."[62] A few days later, partisans seized the town of Bodaibo.[63]

On 10 February 1919, word reached the Canadians in Vladivostok that five hundred Bolsheviks had taken Yeniseisk and were "attacking villages and outposts on railway bridges."[64] Skirmishes erupted between White troops and partisan bands north of Krasnoyarsk, prompting the Allied command to deploy additional troops to guard the track.[65] Reflecting a shift in policy, Ottawa empowered Elmsley to "move Canadian troops inland" if he deemed it necessary to protect "the lives of Canadian and British troops west of Vladivostok." The RNWMP squadron was detailed to patrol the railroad for "some distance out of the city."[66] By March, the guerrilla fighters outnumbered White Russians and Allied soldiers in the Taishet district, seizing towns along the railroad and then cutting telegraph wires and "firing at trains." In the first four months of 1919, eight military trains were wrecked near Taishet. A Canadian who travelled to Omsk in March 1919 – A.D. Braithwaite, former assistant manager of the Bank of Montreal, who met with Kolchak – counted nine bridges destroyed by the Bolsheviks.[67]

According to historian Pavel Novikov, these were not spontaneous actions but, rather, well-orchestrated military operations executed in concert with the Red Army.[68] At Omsk, the Russian Communist Party organized an underground Siberian regional congress on 21 March 1919 – in the seat of Kolchak's power – to lend cohesion to these guerrilla efforts. Delegates from as far away as Vladivostok attended the gathering.[69] One-hundred and fifty Bolshevik organizers, under the direct supervision of Trotsky, fanned out across Siberia "to agitate against Czecho-Slovaks and Allies, to murder them and provoke scandals on the streets and in public localities."[70]

White Russian generals responded ruthlessly to the escalating partisan attacks on the Trans-Siberian Railroad, exhibiting tactics that further alienated local civilians and undermined Czech and Allied support. General Horvath's forces stormed the village of Zinkovka in February, flogging residents for refusing to hand over clothing and cutting firewood on government reserves. One man had his ear burned with a hot iron.[71] Further up country, Kolchak's military governor for eastern Siberia, General Sergei Rozanov, issued an order at Krasnoyarsk in spring 1919, which indicated that,

> for every attack on the railroad line by the Bolsheviks[,] he would take a certain number of the Bolshevik and suspected Bolshevik prisoners in his jails and hang them on the line at the spot where the rails had been damaged. Their corpses were left on the gallows to be eaten by the birds. For every one of his men killed, he murdered ten hostages. For every house burned, he burned ten houses.[72]

Bolshevik leader Aleksandr Krasnoshchekov, former commissar of the Far Eastern Soviet and a front-line commander of the Red Army in the Amur region, was captured and detained at Irkutsk prison in April 1919, under the nom de guerre Mikhail Semönovich Gotkovskii.[73] Later that month, at the nearby village of Birjusinsky, White forces deployed poison gas after a failed attack on Bolshevik guerrillas.[74] In this climate, the Czechs mutinied against Rozanov in May.[75]

Finally, Allied troop movements up country were impeded by deteriorating labour relations. As the head of the British Military Mission at Omsk had observed in late January 1919: "The lack of paper money to pay the men is to a great extent the cause of the discontent on the railway."[76] Railworkers were a traditional locus of militancy in Siberia and the Russian Far East, heart of the 1905 revolution, with control over the vital link between the Pacific and European Russia. During the civil war, railworkers went for months without pay and grew increasingly sympathetic to Bolsheviks and partisans who were disrupting operations along the track. In autumn 1918, the British Middlesex Battalion had been halted at Zema, between Irkutsk and Omsk, by a strike of Russian railworkers shortly after Bolshevik organizers entered the town. Colonel John Ward used force to disarm the strikers, arrested the leaders, and declared martial law so that his unit could proceed.[77] Other rail strikes erupted in Siberia, from the Krasnoyarsk depot to stations along the line to Chita, gaining the support of coal miners in the Grishin and Kemerovo districts.[78] Worker militancy mounted through the winter of 1918-19. In February 1919, Kolchak sent Ward – a Labour MP in Britain – "to undertake a mission along the Trans-Siberian Railway to pacify striking railwaymen."[79] Another British officer, Brigadier-General Blair, who commanded the officers' training school near Vladivostok, proposed sending "a Canadian detachment to guard the workmen in the Chita shops."[80]

Canadians completed two dozen return journeys along the Trans-Siberian Railroad in 1918-19, as small numbers of soldiers plied the 5,700 kilometres of track to relieve Canadian units at Omsk and to transport munitions for Kolchak's White Russian forces on the Ural Front. "The real importance of the Allied role in the Russian Civil War was in the vast quantities of military supplies the Allies – and principally the United Kingdom – made available to the White forces," Steuart Beattie argues.[81] Sporadic accounts of these journeys can be found in the records of the force and in the personal memoirs of the Canadians who served in Siberia and the Russian Far East. One such journey is illuminated by the recollections of Captain Eric Elkington of Duncan, British Columbia.[82] As Elkington's train approached Lake Baikal, "the deepest lake in the world," as he described it, they were halted by a strike of Russian railworkers:

> We had hoped to go as far as Lake Baikal. But we had a Russian train, and Russian drivers. And eventually they refused to go any further. Despite being prodded in the backside with bayonets. So we never got any further. Which was probably a good thing, because we wouldn't have soon come back again, I don't think ... The White Russians weren't doing very well ... So we went back to Vladivostok after staying out for about two or three weeks. They wouldn't drive the train any more.[83]

In the wilds of Trans-Baikal, the lawless province where Bolshevik guerillas clashed with Japanese troops and Ataman Semyonov's Cossack force, the Canadians were turned back. On 15 April 1919, the Canadian command sent orders "to Omsk for final clearing of all Canadian troops west of Vladivostok."[84]

As the Canadians evacuated positions up country, another train sped towards Omsk. The thirty-two-car train code-named *Echelon 2051* was loaded with shells, grenades, railway parts, and clothing for White Russians in the Siberian interior. It was under the command of Lieutenant Harold Ardagh of the 259th Battalion and eleven other Canadians. The train had left Vladivostok in late March, confronting myriad delays and obstacles: a fire in one of the boxcars loaded with shells and fuses, the disappearance of the locomotive outside Harbin, and an accident in which a Canadian sergeant was run over by a railcar and lost both legs. As the train proceeded west from Irkutsk in the middle of April, the Canadians halted when the track was "destroyed by Bolsheviks." No trains moved west for five days, and coal trains then took priority due to "a great scarcity of coal up the line." Further inland, one hundred kilometres beyond Nizhneudinsk, another section of track was destroyed. "I am advised it is a dangerous part of the line from here to Krasnoyarsk," Ardagh wrote: "I will post sentries on the various platforms of our train from now on." As they passed the volatile section of track near Taishet, Ardagh observed "a number of wrecks," "burnt railway stations," and severed telegraph lines. The Canadians reached Omsk on 25 April, a month after leaving Vladivostok, and relinquished the shells, grenades, and supplies. They remained in the Kolchak capital for two weeks, attending a concert in the city's modern opera house and church services at its large cathedral. The mood of the British Military Mission was "optimistic," Ardagh observed, with Kolchak preparing to take command at the front and move his headquarters to Yekaterinburg: "The impression is that the Allies will be in Moscow by the 1st of August, and that it will be 'all over' before the winter. I have my doubts, but *nous verons* [we shall see]."[85]

Harold Ardagh's journey back to the Pacific was equally hazardous. With thirty-two Canadian and British soldiers, he left Omsk the second week in May aboard a passenger train and travelled as far as Krasnoyarsk. There the train halted, "owing to trouble on the lines." The Canadians' *teplushkas* (railcars) were transferred to a special armoured Czech train but were halted again near Taishet, where a section of track was "blown up" and another "destroyed for two versts" (about two kilometres). On 19 May, after leaving Taishet, the Canadian train was fired upon by partisans: "Four Bolsheviks were seen in the woods, armed. We returned their fire." The Canadians suffered no casualties. They continued east, reaching Vladivostok on 1 June 1919.[86]

Shkotovo

The lone military operation involving the Canadians occurred in mid-April 1919. The town of Shkotovo, located on a key rail line fifty kilometres northeast of Vladivostok at the head of Ussuriski Bay, was attacked by partisan forces on 11 April, who aimed to free 700 Bolshevik prisoners held by the local White garrison. The insurgents had earlier seized a quantity of arms and arrested White Russian police at their base in the nearby village of Novorossiskaya.[87] The partisans threatened to sever the Allies from their coal supply on the Suchan River, isolate American and Japanese troops in that partisan stronghold, and endanger the main rail line up country. The Allied command in Vladivostok acted swiftly. Japanese general Otani called for detachments to defend the town.[88] Elmsley deployed 192 troops from the 259th Battalion's "B" Company, under the command of Major M.M. Hart, who reached Shkotovo by train on 13 April, along with two Japanese infantry companies of 700 troops and 87 French, 21 Italian, 16 Czechoslovak, and 7 Chinese troops – an Allied force of more than 1,000 soldiers alongside 150 White Russians. However, by the time the Allied troops attacked Novorossiskaya on 19 April 1919, the Bolsheviks had evacuated the area.[89]

"We marched about 14 miles to the village and when we got there, there was one old man and a couple of women there. So all we could do was come back," wrote Rifleman Harold Steele, who participated in the operation: "It was no cinch with 50 pounds on one's back."[90] Captain Elkington offers further detail:

We were going forth to attack some villages, which were being held by the Bolsheviks. We got into a train, and off we went ... We went to attack this village. The force marching towards this village was led by a little Italian officer on horseback, who I don't think knew anything about horses. He ran away and attacked the village! Far ahead of anybody else, because he couldn't stop his horse. And when we got to the village it had been evacuated.[91]

The only casualties were two soldiers, a Japanese and a Canadian, who suffered minor wounds when they were accidentally shot by a Frenchman testing his revolver.[92] The Canadians returned to Shkotovo, where they were rewarded by General Otani with ninety-six bottles of wine, eighteen bottles of whisky, and three casks of sake; the Canadian officers attended a banquet hosted by the Japanese command. On 21 April, the Canadian company returned to Vladivostok.[93] In a letter to Defence Minister Mewburn, Elmsley noted: "It is really rather remarkable that, at this stage of the proceedings, there should be an insurgent force 30 miles ... this side of Vladivostok."[94] The Americans had stayed out of the affair, believing the unrest was "not of Bolshevik organization or tendency, but the natural result of people forced to gather in self-defence."[95] An eye-witness attributed the disturbance to the shooting of a peasant by the Shkotovo garrison.[96]

In the midst of the Shkotovo campaign, the Japanese command had sent emissaries, including Canadian lieutenant-colonel Ernest James, to the headquarters of the local partisan detachment, urging the insurgents to lay down their arms and to guarantee free passage along the railroad. However, the partisan commander-in-chief, Gavrila Shevchenko, declared "a war to the death" on the Allied armies: "We will not give you one inch of the railway which we have built with our very blood ... Our aim is not only Shkotovo, but also as you may know, Vladivostok ... Just as the Allied troops left Odessa and Archangel, so also you will be forced to leave Vladivostok. Until that time we will never lay down our arms" [see Appendix H].[97]

The Canadians returned from Shkotovo as White strength crested in Siberia. Japan and the United States were already withdrawing troops, while Cossack soldiers mutinied against General Kalmykov in Khabarovsk, and the Czecho-Slovaks mutinied against Rozanov, Kolchak's military governor in eastern Siberia. "We are unwilling to send our troops alone in the Interior," acting prime minister Sir Thomas White had earlier informed Borden.[98] Allied intervention faltered as the Bolsheviks gained in strength. In an interview with a Canadian captain in April, Kolchak warned that, despite White successes on the Ural Front, this was only "an introductory stage of the fighting" and that "great battles would come in the summer and autumn."[99] In a prescient remark, the supreme ruler of White Russia told the Canadian he was prepared to die fighting. Trotsky, architect of the Red Army and Soviet commissar of war, observed at the time: "The line of Kolchak's advance has wavered ... Kolchak reached the apogee of his success in mid-April 1919."[100]

Unrest on the Home Front

Unrest mounted on both sides of the Pacific as the campaign against the Siberian Expedition heightened labour and farmer discontent in Canada and provoked general opposition in the province of Quebec. The agitation of trade unionists and socialists had contributed to the Victoria mutiny of 21 December 1918, and this agitation only intensified after the main body of the CEFS departed for Russia. With the *Teesta* and the *Protesilaus* at sea, labour held another protest meeting in Victoria's Columbia Theatre. "There was a marked difference in the personnel of the audience," the *BC Federationist* reported, "as the khaki clad boys of the Siberian Expeditionary Force were absent, most of them having departed on the expedition."[101] Federated Labor Party organizer Charles Lestor told the crowd that "Allied guns or bayonets could never resuscitate capitalism in Russia."[102] Unrest mounted among labour and farm organizations. The labour councils in Canada's four largest cities – Vancouver, Winnipeg, Toronto, and Montreal – declared against the Siberian Expedition, as did the labour federations of British Columbia and Alberta and union locals of AFL-affiliated machinists and railway workers. A mass meeting in Winnipeg's Walker Theatre – described as the "penultimate event" to the Winnipeg General Strike – called for the immediate withdrawal of the troops.[103] Reflecting agrarian discontent, the United Farmers of Ontario sent a letter of protest to Mewburn, demanding that conscripts be "returned at once" from Siberia, while the Wentworth County Council and Mount Hope Grain Growers Association in Saskatchewan demanded that all troops be "immediately recalled.[104]

Business-aligned newspapers sharpened the attack. In Defence Minister Mewburn's Hamilton riding, the *Herald* lambasted the commercial motivation behind the mission and declared that "outsiders really ha[d] no right to interfere" in Russia's civil war; the *Spectator* said that the Canadian expedition was becoming "more and more unsatisfactory."[105] Labour and farmer outrage against the Siberian Expedition reached the pages of *The Nation* magazine, published in New York, which declared in February 1919: "Canada's participation in military expeditions in Russia is meeting with criticism in every province of the Dominion."[106]

British Columbia remained a locus of labour protest. The province's militant working-class traditions clashed with the embarkation of troops and cargo for Vladivostok. At their first meeting in 1919, Victoria Trades and Labor Council delegates planned a mass meeting against censorship, the jailing of workers under the Military Service Act, and the Siberian Expedition.[107] Longshore worker Joe Taylor asked delegates to take leaflets for distribution in Victoria's shops and yards, while labour's *Semi-Weekly Tribune* predicted that protests against the "whole deplorable venture" would echo "from one end of the country to the other."[108] On 12 January, Victoria workers packed the Columbia Theatre again, this time to hear William Pritchard, the socialist longshoreman from Vancouver who would be jailed five months later during the Winnipeg General Strike. Pritchard invoked the demand "Hands Off Russia," saying the Soviet government was defending itself against the "intrigue of diplomats from France and Britain and the few rich land barons" struggling to "re-organize broken industry": "No matter how many millions of gallons of Allied blood were to be spilt in combating the Soviet regime, and no matter how successful it might be in subduing it, nothing could overthrow the conditions which had brought the Soviets into existence."[109] Exposing the financial impetus behind the Allied intervention, Pritchard said that Canadian workers were more concerned about postwar conditions "than in the collection of French debts through the Siberian expedition." He raised the Bolshevik slogan "All power to the Workingmen's and Soldiers' Councils": "This is where Democracy is in the making, and when you see the same thing in this country you will know that democracy is in the making here."[110] Attendees gave three cheers for the Bolsheviks and German Spartacists, and socialists sold over four hundred copies of the newspaper *Red Flag*.[111] That night in Vancouver, J.S. Woodsworth addressed a capacity crowd in the Rex Theatre, discussing the Victoria mutiny and calling for the "complete overthrow of the present system of production in Canada."[112]

Vested interests tried in vain to curb the growing labour unrest. When the management of the Columbia Theatre refused to rent the hall to the FLP, organizers booked the Labor Temple on North Park Street.[113] Five hundred workers attended a 2 February meeting, which began when a veteran of the Western Front hobbled into the hall on crutches and in full uniform, demanding that the Red Flag replace the Union Jack on the speaker's pedestal. He had gone to France to fight for the Union Jack, he said, but conditions in Canada had convinced him that there was only one flag today: the Red Flag.[114] The main speaker was Thomas Barnard, a leader of the Great War Veterans' Association from New Westminster, who railed against wartime profiteering and ridiculed local alderman Joseph Patrick's comments on "red" meetings in Victoria. Barnard attacked the "capitalistic financially saturated press," suggesting all news reports about Russia were "conceived" or "doctored." "If it were Bolshevism to talk this way, then he was a Bolshevik," Barnard declared.[115]

February 1919 was marked by intense labour disputes in several industries. Seattle was paralyzed by a general strike in support of striking shipyard workers, prompting elite fears of "an attempted revolution" and sympathetic action in Victoria.[116] In Vancouver, protracted disputes of shipyard workers and laundry workers demonstrated the divide between workers and employers and amplified calls for a general strike. In Victoria, 178 school teachers waged a strike of historic proportions, demanding higher wages and indexation to inflation – one of the first teachers' strikes in the British Empire.[117]

It was in this climate that Victoria's labour movement declared its open sympathy with the Bolsheviks in Russia. On 24 February 1919, VTLC delegates debated a resolution from the Alberta Federation of Labour, protesting Allied intervention and threatening a general strike to force a withdrawal of the troops (see Appendix F). After what the minutes describe as a "protracted and interesting discussion," the council voted seventeen to two to endorse "the aims and purposes of the Russian Revolution and Germany also giving the executive authority to call general strikes, should the Allies continue to oppose same or oppose a Soviet government that may be formed elsewhere."[118] Secretary-Treasurer Christian Sivertz, who had served as a mail censor during the war and had "made no secret of his conviction that this World War called for total mobilization," attempted to water down the motion but failed.[119] Canada's Siberian Expedition had sharpened the divide between workers, employers, and the state, driving a section of workers into open sympathy with the Russian Bolsheviks. The general strike tactic – which would erupt from Victoria to Winnipeg to Amherst months later – was endorsed as the means for forcing Canadian troops from Siberia. The VTLC instructed its delegates to support any similar resolutions that arose at the upcoming BC Federation of Labor convention, and it ordered 350 copies of the pamphlet *The Soviet at Work*.[120]

Western Canadian workers inaugurated a new chapter in Canadian labour history when they met in Calgary in March 1919 and formed the One Big Union (OBU). At the BCFL convention, held immediately prior to the Western Labor Conference in Calgary, delegates heartily endorsed the formation of the OBU, an initiative approved at the Alberta federation's convention in January.[121] When the Western Labor Conference opened the next day, 234 delegates from Victoria to Port Arthur approved "the principle of 'Proletariat Dictatorship,'" called for "the abolition of the present system of production for profit," and sent fraternal greetings to Russia's Soviet government and the German Spartacists. They endorsed the OBU, along with resolutions demanding withdrawal of Allied troops from Russia, the release of political prisoners, the six-hour work day, the five-day week, and a general strike beginning 1 June to enforce these demands.[122]

Canadian workers embraced revolutionary industrial unionism as the Russian Communist Party invited the world's workers to cement their allegiances with organizational ties. At a Moscow conference in March 1919, Bolsheviks formed the Third International (Comintern).[123]

The militant turn of the Canadian working class coincided with deteriorating economic conditions on the Home Front. Demobilization of hundreds of thousands of soldiers from Europe coincided with the slowdown of wartime production, driving up unemployment. Seeking to strengthen their influence in the political field, a group of Victoria veterans formed the Ex-Servicemen, Dependents and Relatives of Sailors and Soldiers, an organization whose platform called for the nationalization of railways, mines, sawmills, electrical plants, water power, cold storage, grain elevators, flour mills, and the fishing industry.[124] J.S. Woodsworth, the former Methodist preacher and Vancouver dockworker, called on BC workers to back up their words with deeds, pointing to the hypocrisy of dockworkers' supporting pro-Bolshevik resolutions while at the same time loading arms for Russia: "If we're not prepared to stand by them, don't let us pass any more pious resolutions of sympathy with the Bolsheviki. We're accusing the church people of sending guns and Bibles to the heathen, don't let us send guns and resolutions to Siberia! Cut out the one or the other." According to Woodsworth: "Many soldiers have refused to go to Siberia."[125]

Capital and the state responded to this growing labour radicalism with a vengeance, extending the jurisdiction of the RNWMP into British Columbia and strengthening its surveillance of working-class organizations and leaders. RNWMP detachments were opened at Esquimalt and Vancouver as the number of officers doubled from twenty-five hundred to five thousand men.[126] Security service reports from spring 1919 reflect the heightened alarm. A BC agent warned the RNWMP comptroller in Ottawa of a "projected revolution movement about June 1st," while another agent warned that "arms, ammunition and explosives" in the Victoria district were "insufficiently guarded."[127] The Russian Workers' Union came under surveillance amid reports of "a considerable clandestine trade in Russian [ruble] notes, linked in an undesirable manner with the revolutionary movement."[128] From Vancouver, the RNWMP command received word of the "theft of high explosives" and the "pilfering of grenades bound for Siberia."[129] Sir Thomas White, Borden's acting prime minister, reiterated the lieutenant-governor's earlier request for British warships to help maintain order on the West Coast. Borden refused, claiming: "As far back as 1885 we attended to our own rebellions."[130]

By spring 1919, a growing number of inquiries flowed from the families of CEFS troops to the authorities in Ottawa. Josefine Savarie of St. Charles, Ontario, asked that Defence Minister Mewburn "return my son back to me once more now that god has been good enough to settle up this cruel war." Rifleman Felix Savarie had not been heard from since Christmas, and his family needed the conscript's wages, with the father being sick at home after the winter of the Spanish flu.[131] W.G. Millson of Munro, Ontario, asked Mewburn if her husband at Omsk might have been "overlooked in the arrangements for returning the men."[132] This discussion reached the chambers of the House of Commons. Responding to a question from Marie-Joseph Demers, MP for St. Johns-Iberville, Quebec, Mewburn's department said that the troops would be brought home on the "first available" transport ships. An internal department memo recommended providing this information "personally" to Demers so that he could "withdraw the question from the Order Paper" and avoid debate in the House of Commons.[133] The tone of discussion sharpened as the lag since the Armistice grew. At a public meeting on 11 March 1919, Dr. Hermas Deslauriers, MP for the Montreal riding of St-Mary, declared that the Siberian Expedition "should ... be considered a crime."[134]

In April, the government came under fire for deploying conscripts to Russia. On 8 April 1919, another Quebec MP, Edmund William Tobin of Richmond-Wolfe, asked in the House of Commons "how many men enlisted under the provisions of the Military Service Act, 1917, were dispatched for Siberia" before and after the Armistice and under "what law, Order in Council or other authority said men were sent to Siberia."[135] Ottawa wired Elmsley in anticipation of the question, asking whether "any draftees objected to doing Military Service in Siberia." Elmsley replied: "No objection on part draftees to doing military service in Siberia brought to notice." However, the commanding officer of the 16th Infantry Bridge, H.C. Bickford, wrote: "At Victoria, BC, the men were asked if they would volunteer for service in Siberia. Approximately 40 per cent did so." On 14 April, as the Department of Militia and Defence prepared its response to Tobin's inquiry, Elmsley suspended the sentences of the Québécois conscripts in the 259th Battalion who had been "convicted of mutiny at Victoria."[136] The department informed Tobin that 166 conscripts had been deployed to Siberia prior to 11 November 1918 and an additional 1,048 after that date, under the authority of PC 1983 of 14 August 1918, which designated the Siberian troops as "members of the Canadian Expeditionary Force."[137]

Reports from Siberia and the Russian Far East grew increasingly grim. The Socialist Party of Canada's *Red Flag* newspaper ran an "Appeal for Help of Vladivostok Unions." Twelve hundred Khabarovsk workers had been "shot and slain" by Japanese and Cossack troops, with "thousands" more killed in Krasnoyarsk; unions were banned in Vladivostok under Kolchak and unemployment soared as factories closed.[138] From Paris, former Russian premier Aleksandr Kerensky and other exiled members of the Constituent Assembly came out publicly against armed intervention – at the same time that Allied leaders at the Versailles Peace Conference gave de facto recognition to the Kolchak government.[139] Kolchak's repressive regime attracted hostile attention in British Columbia's labour press, which carried reports on the notorious "train of death," the summary execution of draft resisters, the treatment of Jews and other minority groups, and White losses on the Ural Front.[140] "The Allies will have many crimes to answer at the bar of public opinion," declared Victoria's *Semi-Weekly Tribune:* "All lovers of liberty and right will welcome the news that Kolchak's reign of terror and despotism in Siberia is nearing its end."[141]

Evacuation

The tide turned against the Allies in Siberia in spring 1919, exposing a clash of interests and competing strategies that had plagued the mission from the start. Japan's presence – it had the largest foreign army, with seventy-three thousand men – created misgivings among the other Allied powers. According to Canada's trade commissioner in Vladivostok, Dana Wilgress, the main American motive was "thwarting the Japanese from gaining a foothold in Siberia."[142] American resolve waned as President Woodrow Wilson's support for national self-determination clashed with the image of American troops in Russia.[143] Britain remained the most determined partisan in Siberia, as naval secretary Winston Churchill and other hawks in the Lloyd George Cabinet vowed to recoup British loans and defeat Bolshevism. However, even in Britain, the emboldened Labour caucus in the House of Commons and growing working-class protests in the streets amplified the demand "Hands Off Russia."[144] The Soviet government was saved "not by a proletarian revolution across Europe, but by the British and French if not Canadian voters," a 1957 graduate thesis observed.[145] In January 1919, with the Bolsheviks' position precarious and eleven hundred Canadian troops awaiting deployment to Vladivostok, the British admiralty cancelled planned troop sailings from British Columbia aboard the *Monteagle* and the *Empress of Japan.*[146]

Canada wavered between these conflicting strategies, seeking an exit from the Russian Far East yet wary of disappointing the British government. On 24 December 1918, the Imperial War Cabinet (then in London preparing for peace talks with Germany) discussed the situation in Russia and agreed to enter into formal negotiations with the Bolsheviks.[147] A Bolshevik emissary approached the Allies on 27 December regarding terms of peace, but "the proposals met with no response, as they emanate[d] from a government which is not recognized," the Victoria *Daily Colonist* reported.[148] The topic was again discussed in London on 30 December. Lloyd George told the assembled heads of government that President Wilson was opposed to "armed intervention in Russia" and was "not favourable to the Siberian expedition."[149] Canadian prime minister Borden responded, suggesting that, "in lieu of forcible intervention," a peace conference should be held with representatives of "the Governments of the various States of Russia."[150]

This idea coalesced into the Prinkipo initiative, a conference scheduled for 14 February 1919 on Princes' Island in the Sea of Marmara off Istanbul, Turkey. On 4 January, the British Foreign Office wired the Canadian command in Vladivostok, proposing that "the various governments in Russia refrain from further aggression" and send representatives to discuss "a permanent settlement."[151] Later that month, the British Empire delegation to the Paris Peace Conference reaffirmed the "policy of non-intervention." Lloyd George asked Borden to serve as chief British delegate at Prinkipo.[152]

Prinkipo never took place. The Allies sent an invitation to warring Red and White factions, issued through the Moscow press and radio since no Allied power had recognized the Bolshevik government. Upon receipt of the invitation, Soviet foreign commissar Chicherin sent a reply on 4 February, offering concessions on resources, territory, and debt payments to the Allies in exchange for peace and expressing his government's willingness "to enter into immediate negotiations on Princes Island or in any other place." Chicherin asked the Allies to inform Russia "without delay" of the place to which it should send its representatives as well as the time and route. However, White leaders were outraged by the Allied proposal to make peace with the Reds. The White general at the helm of the Government of the North had photographs of Woodrow Wilson removed from shop windows in Arkhangelsk. General Denikin, commander-in-chief on the south Russian Front, sent a personal message of protest to the Allies.[153] In Omsk, Admiral Kolchak was "nervous and depressed," the British high commissioner noted, arguing that "the invitation to meet the Bolsheviki at Princes Island had undermined his authority and that his Government was in danger." Kolchak's government rejected the invitation almost as soon as it was received, insisting: "A wave of public opinion including all parties except the left wing of the Social Revolutionaries absolutely condemns any agreement whatever with the Bolsheviks."[154] The outrage extended to the Allied diplomatic and military corps in Paris, London, Washington, and Russia. American diplomats in Omsk and Arkhangelsk threatened to resign, and British general Knox wired a protest to London. Despite the efforts of Canada's prime minister, White generals, Allied diplomats, and military officers vetoed a negotiated peace with the Bolsheviks.[155] Demonstrating the tenor of international relations, Australia placed the Soviet ambassador in Melbourne under arrest.[156]

Borden's failed attempt to organize the Prinkipo peace conference contributed to the decision to withdraw the CEFS from Russia. On 1 February, the Canadian command in Vladivostok had received word from the prime minister that the troops in British Columbia would be demobilized "immediately" and that those in Vladivostok "should not be sent forward pending further developments, which [he believed would] decide that they be recalled to Canada at an early date."[157] On February 13, Borden wrote Lloyd George from Paris informing him that Canadian troops would be withdrawn from eastern Russia. He wired Mewburn in Ottawa the same day, instructing him to withdraw the troops in early spring. On 17 February, the British Empire Delegation to the peace talks again debated intervention in Russia; however, as Borden wrote: "I adhered absolutely to my determination to withdraw our troops from Siberia in April."[158] An army had been mobilized to the Russian Far East, but, in a strange irony, it was never given authorization to fight.

With Canadian forces dispersed over Europe, the British Isles, Mesopotamia, and the several fronts encircling Bolshevik Russia, the Dominion government scrambled for ships to bring the troops home. Alarming reports of unrest from Vladivostok prompted Ottawa to requisition steamers from the Canadian Pacific Ocean Services (CPOS) fleet – at a handsome price. "The cables we have from Vladivostok are very disturbing," A.K. MacLean, acting minister of naval affairs, wrote in March: "It is absolutely essential that these troops should be returned early in April." The CPOS demanded $100 to $125 per enlisted man and $250 for every officer travelling first class, a price the government paid. "You will understand that the ships could only be requisitioned either at the price agreed to by the CPOS or else at the cost of litigation," an internal memo noted.[159] A telegram from the chief of general staff in Ottawa to the War Office, London conveyed the sense of urgency: "Dominion Government insists on withdrawing Canadian troops from Siberia soon as possible .... In spite of cost, 'Monteagle,' 'Empress of Asia' and 'Empress of Russia' must be utilized."[160]

The Canadian decision to withdraw from Siberia and the Russian Far East provoked a stern response from British political and military leaders, particularly Winston Churchill, who had been appointed secretary of state for war in January.[161] British officials in Siberia, including Knox and High Commissioner Sir Charles Eliot, were "very discouraged" over the Canadian decision to withdraw.[162] However, on 17 March, as the Bolshevik insurgency around Vladivostok intensified, Churchill relented: "In view of the very decided attitude taken up by Canada, the War Office have no option but to acquiesce, as they have felt it impossible to continue to urge the Dominion Government to share, against its will, in a task of much difficulty and anxiety."[163] Churchill made a final appeal in May for a "small contingent" consisting of a "few hundred Canadian volunteers" to relieve Allied units in North Russia and to participate "in our mission to Admiral Koltchak": "I no longer feel that I am asking you to share in a failure. The hopes of success are sufficient to justify me in appealing to you to participate in a hopeful and prosperous policy ... If Canada takes the lead, Australia will be bound to follow." Churchill's optimistic tone failed to move the prime minister, and the Canadian evacuation proceeded.[164]

The Journey Home

On 21 April 1919, 1,076 Canadians boarded the CPR steamer *Monteagle* in Vladivostok for the journey across the Pacific. Most belonged to the restive 259th Battalion, conscripts who took precedence over volunteers in priority for evacuation.[165] En route, 165 fell ill, a situation worsened by the requirement that the soldiers remain below deck as civilian passengers "had the promenade deck of the steamer all to themselves."[166] On 9 May, an additional 638 troops from the 260th Battalion sailed for Canada's west coast aboard the *Empress of Japan*. According to the British embarkation officer, some of the departing troops, belonging to the Headquarters and Signalling companies, had stashed Bolshevik propaganda, in English, in their kit bags for distribution upon their return home.[167] The Canadian evacuation of Vladivostok coincided with an outbreak of scarlet fever in the CEFS's No. 11 Stationary Hospital, delaying the departure of several RNWMP members and taking the life of medic and Anglican priest Private Edwin Stephenson.[168] On 19 May 1919, 1,490 troops – including the bulk of the 259th Battalion – boarded the *Empress of Russia*. "The hillsides were covered with little low-growing rhododendrons, and they were just coming out when we left," Eric Elkington remembered. While he claimed to have spent "very nearly a year" in Russia and to have left individually, there is evidence tying him to the sailing of the *Empress of Russia*: smallpox. "When we came back we had smallpox on the ship," Elkington said.[169] While at sea, the disease spread like wildfire, and the troops were quarantined for a fortnight when they reached British Columbia.[170]

On 5 June 1919, Major-General Elmsley and 747 Canadian soldiers boarded the *Monteagle* during a heavy downpour, to the music of American, British, and White Russian bands. Force headquarters was transferred from the Pushkinsky Theatre to the ship, where General Horvath and other dignitaries enjoyed refreshments. At noon, the *Monteagle* was towed by tugboat out of Golden Horn Bay, leaving Vladivostok for Victoria.[171] In his final report before leaving Russia, Elmsley conceded that Kolchak's government represented "autocracy and militarism and every undesirable factor that [the Allies] ha[d] been fighting in Europe during the last four and a half years." He went on: "Nevertheless, the recognition of Kolchak's Government is now the only alternative if peace in

Russia is to be secured."[172] With the conclusion of peace talks at Versailles later that month, Germany abrogated the Brest-Litovsk Treaty, signalling the rejection of diplomacy between Russia and the West.[173]

A small number of Canadians remained in Russia, some attached to the British Military Mission and the British Railway Mission and others attached to a rear party that returned to Canada in August.[174] Lieutenant-Colonel John Warden stayed behind to supervise British trainers at the White Russian officers' training school on Russian Island.[175] The situation continued to deteriorate. The day before Elmsley and the CEFS left Vladivostok, a train carrying six Canadians from the RNWMP was ambushed up country by Bolshevik guerillas. They were travelling west from Irkutsk aboard the transport train *Echelon 2209*, destined for Yekaterinburg on the Ural Front, carrying 154 RNWMP horses, fourteen mules, and a number of White Russian, Czecho-Slovak, and British troops. Between Zamzor and Alzama stations, Bolsheviks fired on the train, causing it to derail, and nineteen boxcars were "smashed to atoms." Two White Russian soldiers and eighteen Canadian horses were killed. Evidence pointed to the disappearance of pins connecting the railcars. The Canadians gathered the surviving horses and eventually continued west on another train, passing eleven wrecks near Taishet, where they learned that Czecho-Slovaks had "captured and hung 26 of the Bolsheviks that [had] wrecked [their] train, including the chief wrecker." At Yekaterinburg, the Canadian Mounties handed over the horses and mules to Kolchak's White Russian forces; however, on 8 July 1919, the Canadians were forced "to evacuate Ekatinburg to the Bolsheviks."[176]

The Canadian Siberian Economic Commission was wound up along with the military expedition. Its operations were transferred to a new company, the Siberian Supply Company, formed with the assistance of the British government and headed by Leslie Urquhart, a London mining magnate who had controlled lead and zinc mines in western Siberia prior to the Russian Revolution. Urquhart's appearance in Russia was resented by British merchants in Vladivostok who had invested time and money to expand Siberian trade.[177] One of the final functions of the Canadian economic commission involved arranging the shipment of a quantity of agricultural seed from Canada to Siberia, which was "urgently required for the spring sowing." Other commercial ventures – in timber, fishing, mining, agriculture, and manufacturing – envisioned at the commission's inception were abandoned in the face of unreliable supply lines along the Trans-Siberian Railroad and Russia's financial collapse. Four of the six members of the Canadian Siberian Economic Commission left Vladivostok with the troops, holding a final meeting in Ottawa with Canadian trade and commerce minister Sir George Foster.[178] Ross Owen remained in the city to "look after the interests" of the CPR, while Trade Commissioner Dana Wilgress married a Russian woman and returned to Canada in the fall, later serving as Canada's first ambassador to the Soviet Union. The Royal Bank of Canada "temporarily" closed its Vladivostok branch in October 1919 after six months of operation.[179] A number of horses, mules, motorcycles, and lorries were transferred from the Canadian force to the British Military Mission, while munitions were given to the White Russian officers' training school on Russian Island.[180]

Nineteen members of the CEFS did not return home. Two died in accidents; sixteen died of diseases such as influenza, smallpox, pneumonia, and spinal meningitis; and one soldier, Lieutenant Alfred Thring from the 260th Battalion, took his own life. Fourteen of the Canadian dead were buried at Vladivostok's Marine Cemetery, near the hilly Churkin Peninsula southeast of the city, alongside fourteen British graves. Before leaving Vladivostok, the Canadian command dedicated a stone monument at the site on 1 June 1919.[181] Four other Canadians – Private Edward Biddle, riflemen Frank J. Kay and Harold Butler, and Lance-Corporal George Buckwalter – were buried at sea. Private Wilfred C. Lane, a soldier in the headquarters battalion who contracted pneumonia and died at sea after leaving Vladivostok in March, was buried in Hong Kong.[182] Two additional soldiers, Private Richard Massey and Rifleman Peter McMillan, fell ill with smallpox on the return crossing and died at the William Head Quarantine Station, outside Victoria, in May and June 1919 (see Appendix J). Five Russian-born members of the Canadian force – Sergeant Samuel Braun and riflemen Frofin Nosovez, John Petrovitch, Peter Guidasmachuk, and Cyril Shumski – deserted in Russia.[183]

8
Afterword

There can be no peace in the world until Bolshevism is no more.[1]

— MAJOR-GENERAL SIR JOCELYN PERCY,
18 FEBRUARY 1921, SPEECH TO THE CANADIAN CLUB
IN VICTORIA'S EMPRESS HOTEL

THE CANADIANS LEFT the Russian Far East as working-class unrest mounted on both sides of the Pacific. General strikes erupted from Victoria to Winnipeg to Amherst, Nova Scotia, as Canadian workers embraced industrial methods in what they viewed as an international movement to usher in the New Democracy. Reflecting a rising "Red Scare" across the industrialized world, the Canadian state responded with an iron fist, doubling the size of the militia to ten thousand troops, deploying force to reclaim the city of Winnipeg, and authorizing an RNWMP crackdown on labour militants and socialists across the country.[2] The Criminal Code and the Immigration Act were hastily amended by Parliament to broaden police powers against sedition and to allow the deportation of dissidents without trial. Reflecting ruling-class fears, Borden described the general strikes as a "deliberate attempt to overthrow the existing organization of the Government and to supersede it by crude, fantastic methods founded upon the absurd conceptions of what had been accomplished in Russia."[3] The Canadian evacuation from Vladivostok coincided with the collapse of the White Russian war effort in the face of waning Allied resolve and growing Bolshevik strength. Omsk fell to the Red Army and Admiral Kolchak was summarily tried and executed at Irkutsk. In Vladivostok, Bolsheviks took power in a bloodless January 1920 coup. Following several skirmishes with the Whites and the retreat of Japanese forces, the Red Army occupied the port city in 1922. Bolshevism asserted its authority over the Russian Far East at the same time as it came under siege in North America.

The Canadian Labour Revolt

Canada's Siberian troops returned to a country divided along the lines of social class. Elmsley and the *Monteagle* arrived in Victoria on 19 June 1919, along with eight Russian stowaways who had disguised themselves as Canadian soldiers and boarded the ship in Vladivostok – "Bolshevik emissaries sent out to this country with the object of spreading Bolshevik propaganda," the Victoria *Times* speculated.[4] Hours before the *Monteagle* reached Victoria's outer wharves, local longshore workers refused to unload five hundred tons of cargo from the ship *Africa Maru* because it was bound for strike-riddled Vancouver, and they refused to handle mail from the mainland.[5] Meeting that night, the longshore workers voted to strike in sympathy with coastal seamen and Vancouver longshore workers, to protest the arrest of the Winnipeg General Strike leaders, and to defend the principle of collective bargaining.[6] At a special meeting the following day, Victoria boilermakers and ships' caulkers voted sixty-one to thirty-six to strike in sympathy with Winnipeg, beginning "at noon Saturday at the latest if the different shop committees [did] not call it before."[7] The Metal Trades Council, representing three-quarters of Victoria's seven thousand union workers, primarily in the shipyards, voted to join the strike.[8] "Indignant over the recent arrest of the Winnipeg leaders," rank-and-file shipyard workers had directed their shop stewards to call a strike. "The men were beyond control," Metal Trades Council president James Dakers told the press: "We are out until the Winnipeg strike committee says everything is satisfactory there."[9] A *Times* report emphasized the importance of shipbuilding in Victoria's economy: "even should no outside unions join in the walkout, the strike will be almost general in character."[10]

The wave of industrial unrest extended from the Pacific to distant Nova Scotia, where workers at the Canadian Car and Foundry Company and other plants in Amherst struck for the OBU.[11] The *Monteagle* reached Vancouver on 22 June with the remnants of Canada's Siberian Expeditionary Force. One hundred and fifty Mounties from RNWMP "B" Squadron disembarked to a barrage of bricks and stones from angry longshoremen and were promptly ordered to serve strike duty.[12] "There appears to be no definite reason for [the strike] except [the] desire of alien agents, apparently in control of unions, to provoke class war throughout America and get control of all production in their own hands," Lieutenant Colonel Geoffrey McDonnell observed.[13]

A day earlier – 21 June 1919, remembered as "Bloody Saturday" in the annals of Manitoba labour – their counterparts in RNWMP "A" Squadron and four regiments of the Canadian army broke the back of the Winnipeg General Strike. A "silent parade" of war veterans and strikers was suppressed by three charges of Mounties on horseback, who fired revolvers into the crowd, killing two and injuring fifty. Machine guns rolled into the streets as the prairie capital fell under military occupation.[14] Under the banner of the OBU, a substantial layer of Canadian workers employed industrial methods in what they viewed as an international movement to usher in the New Democracy. The *BC Federationist* had discussed the relationship between domestic unrest and international events two years earlier:

> The Russian revolution has everywhere heartened the foes of present-day society. It has given them a territorial focus, a base of operations, and if the "Reds" overthrow the provisional government of Russia and replace the liberal leaders, Miliukov, Lvov, etc. by chiefs of really crimson hue, we shall see a wave of syndicalist unrest sweep over the whole earth.[15]

The Russian Revolution had provided Canadian workers with an interpretive framework, and an example of agency, to challenge the authority of employers and the legitimacy of the state.

In the aftermath of the Winnipeg General Strike and 1919 sympathy strikes, the Canadian state targeted militant working-class leaders in every city. This was part of the "Red Scare" that set in across the Western world. On 30 June, six plainclothes officers raided the Victoria homes of BCFL vice-president Joe Taylor and VTLC president Eugene Woodward, and targeted the local headquarters of the Socialist Party, the striking longshoremen's union, and labour's *Semi-Weekly Tribune*, seizing a quantity of paperwork. No arrests were made, but Woodward accused police of abusing their powers and considered initiating legal action, declaring that he was "not a Socialist and not a member of the party."[16] The Victoria raids were part of a national dragnet that enveloped labour radicals from Vancouver to Montreal, with the *BC Federationist* accusing the Dominion government of conspiring, through the RNWMP, "to establish a reign of terror so far as organized labor [was] concerned."[17] J.S. Woodsworth, released on charges of seditious libel, went further in a speech to an FLP meeting in Esquimalt in which he anticipated that there would be "a lot of unemployment and unrest this winter and because of this the government [was] rushing in Royal North West Mounted Police." "They must be coming over the mountains to shoot down the workers of this country," Woodsworth opined.[18]

The war against Bolshevism did not end with the collapse of the Siberian Expedition and the suppression of the postwar strikes. The RNWMP was rebranded as the Royal Canadian Mounted Police (RCMP) in 1920, confirming the national dimensions of radicalism and repression. The agency opened security files on 4,806 Canadians in its first decade of operations.[19] Tom Barnard, a leader of the Great War Veterans' Association and FLP candidate who lost an October 1919 Victoria federal by-election amid allegations of vote-rigging, expressed the radical mood. "Until we revolt we will not get our freedom," Barnard told an OBU meeting in Nanaimo, predicting "revolution and bloodshed."[20] A worker in Cumberland, British Columbia's, Vendome bar told an undercover RCMP agent that "the present system of Government should be overthrown and a Soviet Government established, for this form of Government was the only kind for the working man and he was ready anytime to do all in his power to assist in this movement."[21] The capitalist class was forcing Canadian workers towards bloody revolution, George Palmer of Calgary claimed: "I would take up arms tomorrow under the Red Flag."[22] Rather than silence and moderate working-class demands, intervention in Siberia and repression at home had amplified the divide between workers, employers, and the state.

Canadian workers responded in different ways to the consolidation of capitalism in the wake of 1919. A layer gravitated closer to the Russian orbit, concluding that Canadian capitalism could only be transcended by armed force and the extra-parliamentary methods of the Bolsheviks. This debate split the Socialist Party of Canada, a locus of labour radicalism since the turn the century and the leading element behind the OBU and postwar strikes. Majorities of SPC members in Victoria, Calgary, Edmonton, and Winnipeg favoured affiliating with the Soviet-led Third International. "This is no time to split hairs. Let me urge you, comrades, to strive for an affirmative vote in the name of the Revolution," Fred Caplan of Winnipeg wrote in the *Western Clarion*.[23] These revolutionary Canadian workers joined the clandestine Communist Party of Canada, founded in a barn outside Guelph in May 1921, and rallied behind its public face, the Workers' Party of Canada, a development noted in the Russian Communist organ *Bednota (The Poor)*.[24] In the 1930s, these Communist workers spearheaded militant organizations of the unemployed and industrial unions of miners, loggers, and manufacturing workers.[25] Like comrades in sister parties around the globe, they maintained an organizational link with the Soviet Union, which provided a unifying symbol in a chaotic geopolitical space but which also fomented crises at key moments in Soviet history – such as Trotsky's expulsion from Russia in the late 1920s, Stalin's alliance with Hitler in 1939, and Khrushchev's infamous 1956 revelations of Stalinist brutality followed by Soviet military incursions in Hungary and Czechoslovakia.[26]

Other Canadian workers responded to the events of 1919 by strengthening their commitment to parliamentary change. State power had been exercised to the detriment of workers during the 1919 strikes, they concluded, urging workers to "strike at the ballot box" and to elect labour representatives to write better laws. In provincial elections in Ontario in 1919 – and in Manitoba, British Columbia, and Alberta in 1920 – workers disrupted partisan alignments, vying for power with farmer parties. In Manitoba, three leaders of the Winnipeg General Strike were elected to the legislature while serving prison terms for seditious conspiracy.[27] In 1921, another martyr of the Winnipeg strike, J.S. Woodsworth was elected MP for Winnipeg Centre, one of only two labour representatives in the 235-seat House of Commons. Along with Calgary journalist William Irvine and a handful of radical farmer members from the west, Woodsworth nurtured the seeds of Canada's socialist political current.[28] Meighen's Conservative government, successor to the Borden Unionists responsible for the Siberian Expedition, "was one of the most unpopular governments in Canadian history when it collapsed at the first postwar test at the polls in 1921."[29]

The Collapse of White Siberia

Back in Siberia, the White Russian military effort collapsed over the course of 1919. The Canadian retreat foreshadowed the evacuation of British forces, with the Middlesex and Hampshire battalions retreating from Omsk to Vladivostok and sailing home by November.[30] The once-reliable Czecho-Slovak Legion grew increasingly restless, its members unwilling to prolong their return to the new homeland. As the Victoria *Daily Times* reported in June, some Czech regiments had become "infected with Bolshevism and a general spread of Red ideas [was] feared if the men [were] kept from their homes another winter."[31] The threat of a general mutiny was palpable by September, as Czech units clashed with Japanese and White Russian forces.[32] However, when the Allied command authorized the Czechs' retreat to Vladivostok, Kolchak threatened to blow up the rail bridges along Lake Baikal to prevent their evacuation. In November 1919, the White capital of Omsk fell to the Red Army. Kolchak fled eastward, with the remnants of the Imperial Gold Reserve in a sealed railcar, arriving in Irkutsk, where he hoped to re-establish a power base. However, French general Maurice Janin broke an agreement between Kolchak and the Allies and handed the admiral over to the Czechs, who in turn surrendered him to the Bolshevik-controlled Irkutsk Political Centre, which by then controlled the town.[33] On 7 February 1920, the former "Supreme Dictator" of White Russia and close ally of Canada was summarily tried, shot, and dumped into the Angara River.[34] The remnant of the gold reserve – 5,143 boxes and 1,678 bags of gold coins, ingots, and bars worth 409 million gold rubles – was loaded onto a train for Moscow bearing the banner: "To Dear Vladimir Ilyich, from the city of Irkutsk."[35]

The Red Army rolled into Irkutsk in March 1920 as the armies of Colonel Denikin collapsed in southern Russia and General Wrangel's forces retreated into the Crimea.[36] On 1 April 1920, the last Americans left the Russian Far East, and, a month later, the Czecho-Slovaks were finally permitted to evacuate Vladivostok. They sailed to Vancouver, arriving on three ships in June 1920, and marched through the city, fully armed, before travelling across Canada by train for the voyage home.[37] "Yes, they wanted us to lay down our arms in Siberia

before we came here, but we refused," a Czech soldier told a reporter from the
BC Federationist: "So long as I have my rifle and equipment, I am a free man;
when I part with them, I am a slave."[38] The Czechs celebrated Dominion Day,
1 July 1920, in Valcartier, Quebec, then boarded trains to Halifax and sailed
across the Atlantic to their new homeland.[39] Japan alone retained a presence in
the Russian Far East, hoping for territorial gain and "giving breathing space and
some protection to the Whites."[40]

In Vladivostok, Bolshevik partisans had overthrown Kolchak's administrator,
General Sergei Rozanov, in a bloodless coup on 31 January 1920. Rozanov was
"typical" of White generals, who were "noted for their cruelty, self-interest, lack
of scruples, unpopularity, and pro-Japanese sympathies."[41] His military authority
evaporated with Kolchak's capture, as two columns of partisans marched into
Vladivostok amid a general strike by trade unions, supported by the local garrison. A provisional *zemstvo* government took power, a coalition of Bolsheviks
and Social Revolutionaries that governed with a moderate hand to avoid inflaming Allied forces still in the city. Rozanov escaped to Japan, disguised as a Japanese
officer aboard the steamer *Orel.*[42] For two years, a power struggle ensued between
Reds and Whites, as the Bolshevik-sponsored Far Eastern Republic, based in
Chita, served as a buffer state between Moscow and the remnants of White
power. A small Canadian Red Cross mission continued to administer aid to
White Russian troops and civilian refugees until January 1921.[43] The Ataman
general Grigori Semyonov – accused of thirty thousand executions in a single
year – fled to Vancouver in March 1922, where he was "entertained by business-
men at the best clubs in the city" en route to the United States (where he faced
Senate deportation hearings).[44] Finally, on 25 October 1922, the last Japanese
forces withdrew and Red Army troops marched into Vladivostok. While Japan
lingered on Sakhalin Island until January 1925, Siberia and the Russian Far East
were undeniably Red.[45]

The scale of terror committed by both White and Red forces during the Russian Civil War left wounds that never fully healed – an all-too-common occur-
rence in national struggles that pit rival sections of a people in a bloody and
headstrong fight. British colonel John Ward, commander of the Middlesex
Battalion and a Labour MP, condemned international support for the Moscow
regime, saying that "a section of people at home" viewed the Bolsheviks as "a
party of political and democratic idealists," but that when one was brought face
to face with their work, they were "proved to be a disgusting gang of cut-
throats."[46] However, another observer, American general William S. Graves,
claimed that "the anti-Bolsheviks killed one hundred people in Eastern Siberia
to every one killed by the Bolsheviks."[47] The press correspondent attached to

Canada's Siberian Expeditionary Force, Captain Wilfred Playfair, recalled the sight of "the Bolsheviks hanging from trees," while intelligence officer James Mackintosh Bell viewed the atrocities committed by both Whites and Reds as "symptomatic of the general condition of brutalization produced by the war, the wild delirium of the revolution, and the intense political antagonisms, which developed therefrom."[48]

In a post-mortem on the Siberian campaign, British colonel Ward lambasted the Allies' failure to fulfill their promises to Kolchak: "Had these urgings and promises been ungrudgingly performed a Constituent Assembly would be now sitting at Moscow hammering out the details of a Federal Constitution for a mighty Russian Republic or a parliamentary system similar to our own." Ward cited the Allies' failure to recognize the Omsk government as well as "positive wilful obstruction":

> The Japanese, by bolstering up Semianoff and Kalmakoff, and the Americans, by protecting and organising enemies, made it practically impossible for the Omsk Government to maintain its authority or existence. The most that could be expected was that both would see the danger of their policy in time to avert disaster. One did; the other left when the evils created had got beyond control. Koltchak has not been destroyed so much by the acts of his enemies as by the stupidity and neglect of his Allied friends.[49]

Ward described Bolshevism as "a disease which, if we cannot attack, we can isolate until convalescence sets in" – understating the strategy the West would follow as the twentieth century unfolded.[50]

In Russia, the Bolsheviks developed repressive apparatus to win the civil war and consolidate power. As historian Pavel Novikov writes, the civil war was bound up with "the establishment of a totalitarian system" in Russia.[51] Notorious agencies such as the Cheka, the NKVD, and the OGPU became permanent institutions in Soviet Russia, undermining the egalitarian rhetoric of Lenin, Trotsky, and the Bolsheviks. Mutinous sailors in the port of Kronstadt – at one time valiant defenders of the Bolshevik revolution – were slaughtered by government forces as the Red victory was consolidated in the spring of 1921. Anarchist movements in the Ukraine, led by Nestor Makhno, were ruthlessly suppressed.[52] Peasant risings challenged Bolshevik power in Siberia for years to come as the Moscow government drew heavily on the region's grain to feed the cities and industrial centres of European Russia, provoking famine.[53] In 1928, Aleksei Karvop of Olga village northeast of Vladivostok wrote to the editors of *Pravda*, warning of a "protracted and severe crisis": "Here in the provinces ... everything is given to the collective farms ... and all resources are being poured into heavy industry."[54] In the 1930s, the Russian Far East emerged as the infamous centre of Stalin's dreaded *Gulag*, with Vladivostok serving as a key transit point for political prisoners bound for Magadan and "corrective labour camps" in the frozen tundra.[55]

"Cowboy Capitalism" in Vladivostok

Canadian capitalism had failed to penetrate Vladivostok in 1919 as the Bolshevik ethos of social ownership permeated Primorsky Krai and barred profit-making by Russians and foreigners for the next seven decades. The Royal Bank of Canada closed its Vladivostok branch and the Canadian trade commissioner fled the city for more hospitable climes. The lofty hopes of the Canadian Siberian Economic Commission – a brisk trade in agricultural implements and the rapid development by Canadian firms of Siberia's untapped timber, fish, and mineral resources – came to nothing. Indeed, relations between Russia and the West tightened with the advent of the Cold War in the 1940s. Soviet leaders declared Vladivostok a "closed city," denying access to foreigners and closely guarding its Pacific Naval Fleet. And yet, in a sign of détente, they hosted a 1974 Vladivostok summit between American and Soviet presidents Gerald Ford and Leonid Brezhnev, respectively. In the 1980s, the Soviet Union bristled with the winds of reform. Mikhail Gorbachev introduced *perestroika* (restructuring) and *glasnost* (openness), aspiring to transform Russia into "a socialist beacon" along Scandinavian lines. However, a coterie of Kremlin insiders led by Boris Yeltsin tapped public discontent with the problems of a planned economy. They dissolved the Soviet Union and then the post-Soviet Parliament and embarked on a blitzkrieg of "Chicago School" capitalism. A new class of billionaire *oligarki* tycoons rose with the fire sale of state assets, while half Russia's population descended into poverty and life expectancy fell from seventy to sixty-five years.[56]

As the *New York Times* Moscow bureau chief observed in 1993, in Vladivostok "the muscle of the old empire blend[ed] with the hustle of a newly free market."[57] With Communism's collapse, Japanese, Chinese, South Korean, Italian, American, and Canadian investors descended on Primorsky Krai. The United States opened a consulate in 1992, while South Koreans opened a casino and Italians built an airport. Two Canadians from Fort St. John, British Columbia, purchased the Vlad Motor Inn, located in a secluded forest outside the city, complete with tennis courts, colour television, and a menu that catered to Western palates: cheeseburgers, chili, and steak.[58] Vladivostok's economy remained based in the extractive-resource sectors: fishing accounted for four-fifths of commercial production in 1995, alongside timber products, metals, and ships.[59] The phenomenon of "cowboy capitalism" that unfolded across Russia in the 1990s replaced Communism's drab egalitarianism with gangsterism, pollution, and a sharp class divide. Reminiscent of the 1918-19 era, "people talk of two or three murders a night," *New York Times* bureau chief Serge Schemann noted, imbuing Vladivostok with "the unruliness of Dodge City and the landscape of San Francisco."[60]

Vladivostok's streets were flooded with sleek Japanese sedans and beefy sport utility vehicles, its air choked with dioxins, and its coastal waters contaminated with noxious pollutants.[61] The city's once-pristine waters – residents swam in Amurski Bay until the 1950s – were devastated by the dumping of raw sewage and the elimination of environmental controls following the privatization of ships, ports, and cargo companies in the 1990s.[62] Vessels designed to remove surface oil and floating garbage were sold, deemed unprofitable by their new owners, while air quality in two-thirds of Vladivostok's neighbourhoods was designated a health hazard.[63] Housing costs soared, as condominium towers sprouted on the hills surrounding Golden Horn Bay, with rents exceeding a school-teacher's monthly pay. "We predict it will soon become impossible to live here," said Gennady Nesov, former head of the Primorsky Krai Department of Transportation and founder of the Marine Ecological Foundation.[64] Capitalism's belated arrival in Vladivostok – seventy-five years after the Russian Revolution and the landing of Canadian troops – presented fresh opportunities for affluence, but it also exposed old exploitations and risks.

Conclusion

*When the true history of the machinations of the Allied countries in
their efforts to overthrow the Soviet regime is written, it will disclose
such an amazing story of intrigue and duplicity as to make honest people
shudder ... Not half of the story has been told, and never will be told if
the ruling class of the Allied nations can prevent it. But they will not be
able to cover up the tracks; the workers of the world are moving forward,
and it will be the function of that class to uncover how secret diplomacy
has functioned against the new democracy.*[1]

– "Lessons to Be Learned," *BC Federationist*, 17 October 1919

In the early 1930s, staff at the Canadian Department of Militia and Defence's
Historical Section began compiling the official history of the Siberian Expedition. It was a delicate and unsavoury topic, a world away from the image of
valour being constructed around the Canadian Corps on the Western Front.[2]
Records had been loaned to Major-General Elmsley in the mid-1920s for an
article in the *Canadian Defence Quarterly*, which "Gentleman Jim" never completed.[3] In 1931, Archer Fortescue Duguid, director of the historical section,
received a request from Colonel Charles H. Morrow, a former commander of
American forces in Russia and then commandant at Fort Niagara, New York,
for information on the CEFS. Duguid admitted: "In our work on the Official
History we have not quite reached Siberia yet."[4] In a letter to a colleague, he
lamented having received the request: "Sometimes I wish that fewer people were
interested in what happened in 1914-1919, or rather that they could possess their
souls in patience yet a while; then we could go straight ahead with the work of
the official History which will contain replies to all questions in proper order."[5]
However, Duguid was a stickler for detail, and the official history languished
and was then superseded by the Second World War, which was tackled as the
first priority of the new Army Historical Section.[6] When Canada's official history of the First World War finally appeared in 1962, a scant six pages were
devoted to Siberia.[7] The Imperial War Graves Commission, the body responsible
for the fourteen Canadian graves at Vladivostok's Marine Cemetery, evasively

attributed the loss to "the period of confusion in Siberia which followed the Treaty of Brest Litovsk."[8]

On the surface, Canada's Siberian Expedition was a complete failure. It had been "conceived as part of a concerted plan to overthrow the Communist regime that had seized power in Russia," according to Dana Wilgress, Canada's trade commissioner to Vladivostok and first ambassador to the Soviet Union.[9] Hopes for commercial gain went nowhere. From the outset, Canadian military commanders alienated would-be supporters, such as Vladivostok businesspeople who had been outraged over the seizure of the Pushkinsky Theatre. Though naturally anti-Bolshevik and eager for outside help, the manufacturers and traders resented the Canadians' incursion into property and culture, and they sent a loud protest to Elmsley (which was ignored). Relations failed to improve. The ruthless exercise of White power in Allied-protected areas aggravated tensions between the foreign armies, while mobilizing peasant youth to take up arms in concert with local Bolsheviks. Stubbornly, the Reds defeated the White Russian armies of Kolchak, Semyonov, Kalmykov, Denikin, Dieterichs, and Wrangel and repulsed the thirteen Allied armies that invaded Russia on four fronts. "A million-bayonetted ring of steel closed in upon the Revolution," American journalist Albert Rhys Williams noted at the time, but "one after another the armies of the Counter-Revolution crumpled up or melted away like snow in a Russian spring."[10] The Soviet regime survived this White-Allied onslaught to hold power for seven decades. Canada, meanwhile, hastily evacuated its troops from Vladivostok in the face of the robust partisan insurgency and worker, farmer, and Québécois opposition on the Home Front, abandoning any ambitions in the region.

However, the Red victory was ambiguous. While the Allies failed to replace Bolshevism with a more traditional class system, the civil war inflicted deep wounds on Russia and shaped the course of its revolution. As the official history of Canada's war effort records, "it is possible to claim certain far-reaching indirect results. Preoccupation with the internal struggle prevented the diversion of men and munitions to foment political, social and economic disorders in countries outside Russia."[11] Allied intervention contained the spread of Russia's revolution abroad while debilitating it at its source. Communism survived in name, but its form and substance were irrevocably altered, stripped of hope and compassion and maintained through terror and fear. "What this regime seeks is to make the Socialists of the entire world its associates in its policy of persecution, something which Czarism, for obvious reasons, never aimed at," wrote the German socialist Karl Kautsky in 1922: "Socialists who resort in this struggle against the opinions of other Socialists to guns, bayonets, Cheka organizations and jails are committing an act of violence against the proletariat and the idea of the class struggle."[12] Historians and idealists continue to debate the nature and development of Russian Bolshevism, with some claiming that terror was bound up in Bolshevism from the start, that an ideology that sought to take power by force was compelled to use force to maintain its hold on power. Others emphasize the trajectory of Russian history in the wake of 1917, insisting that the civil war impelled the Bolsheviks towards repressive tactics and imposed the bureaucratic apparatus that led to Stalin's rise. The preceding study has not attempted to resolve this debate, but it seems reasonable to suggest – as Nicholson does in Canada's official history – that Allied intervention had an impact on events.

From the strictly military standpoint, however, Canada's Siberian Expedition – the first military campaign spearheaded by the Dominion and its inaugural adventure in the Far East – can be described as a fiasco.[13] "This expedition was a political error, a military mistake, and a wanton extravagance," Dr. Henri Sévérin Béland, MP for Beauce, told the House of Commons on 10 June 1919, a year after his release from a German prisoner-of-war camp.[14] This outcome was anticipated by Canada's top military commander in a telegram to Prime Minister Robert Borden before the main body of the Siberian force left Victoria. The December 1918 message, drafted by chief of general staff General Willoughby Gwatkin, and cabled under Defence Minister Sydney Mewburn's signature, summarized the key points of an intelligence report from Canada's political officer in Vladivostok: "that arrangements in Siberia lack co-ordination and control, that the railway system is in a condition seriously disorganized, that among Allies there is no general agreement, that Americans are inactive, that the Japanese, bent on commercial penetration, are subsidizing insurgent elements." This combination of factors placed Elmsley and his 4,200-strong Canadian force "in a difficult position ... an undertaking which may terminate in disaster." The Canadian prime minister, citing obligations made to certain "well disposed persons in Russia," ordered that the mission proceed.[15]

Borden's decision to ignore the advice of his Cabinet and military commanders and to persist with the Siberian Expedition revealed a fundamental streak of subservience in Canadian foreign policy. This contradicts the dominant historiographic narrative of the period. In contrast with the image of a country that had grown assertive and had become independent from Britain during the First World War, we see a subordinate dominion that kowtowed to Winston Churchill and other British "hawks" by engaging in an unpopular and dangerous intervention, an ill-fated plan to use force against Russia's revolution and to prop up a decaying imperial order. Canada earned a seat at Versailles and the League of Nations, but this role was established as a result of loyalty to (rather than independence from) the Empire – the attrition of sixty-six thousand

Canadians in France and Flanders, followed by the deployment of men and arms to Vladivostok, Murmansk, Arkhangelsk, and Baku. Rather than emerging from the First World War as an autonomous "free agent" in an egalitarian world system of states, Canada bowed to the most powerful imperialist and its initiative of the day – demonstrating an enduring pattern in Canadian foreign policy.

The Siberian Expedition demonstrates linkages between military history and working-class history and between domestic and international events. The Canadian government's determination to deploy troops to Vladivostok strained class and linguistic antagonisms – within the CEFS and the broader country – provoking mutiny in the streets of Victoria in December 1918 that resulted in violence and imprisonment for those who proclaimed *"On y va pas à Siberia!"* Canadian commanders seemed more willing to use force against their own soldiers to ensure their deployment to Russia than to engage the Bolshevik enemy overseas; during Canada's seven-month sojourn in Siberia and the Russian Far East, soldiers participated in only one military engagement, the Shkotovo mission of April 1919. Within the broader Canadian society, the Siberian Expedition brought about censorship of major newspapers such as the *Toronto Globe* and intensified the repression of working-class and socialist parties. The widening labour and farmer revolt in postwar Canada was bound up with the government's decision to deploy troops to Russia, which contributed to the general strikes that erupted from Victoria to Winnipeg to Amherst in spring 1919. As an unpublished 1957 graduate thesis concludes, the Siberian Expedition "helped to provoke the worst labour troubles in Canadian history."[16] Among workers, farmers, and the general population of Quebec, seething anger over conscription and profiteering was inflamed by the Canadian government's insistence on sending troops to Russia long after the armistice. These social cleavages in postwar Canada endured. While the nine Québécois conscripts convicted of mutiny at Victoria were spared the fate of twenty-five other Canadian soldiers, who were executed by firing squad on the Western Front, they suffered distinct forms of degradation.[17] The expedition cost Canada $2,823,960 in 1919 currency - covering soldiers' pay and clothing as all other costs were borne by the British government (see Appendix I) - money otherwise available to train and house hundreds of thousands of veterans demobilized from Europe.[18] There is also an enduring testament to Borden's Siberian adventure: the tombs of fourteen Canadians on a hillside outside Vladivostok, casualties in a muddled geopolitical fight.

The original wooden crosses at Vladivostok's Marine Cemetery rotted through time and neglect as Red scares and cold wars severed Vladivostok from the wider world.[19] Canada and its Allies waged new adventures from Dieppe to Korea to Kandahar – as time and diplomacy laid the groundwork for "normal" relations between Canada and the Soviet Union.[20] Commemorations of the First World War either ignored the Siberian Expedition or treated it as a curious footnote to the real battles waged on the Western Front.[21] The expedition became "only a memory for old soldiers."[22] The CEFS, born out of the chaotic social pressures of the First World War and the Russian Revolution, was too complex a story to be told in tandem with the image of valour being constructed around the Canadian Corps at Vimy Ridge. From Victoria to Vladivostok, the Canadian government had engaged in a battle against labour radicalism – Bolshevism, in the lexicon of the day – a failed attempt to alter the outcome of the Russian Revolution and to install a more sympathetic government in Russia. In the unstable climate following the war in Europe, geopolitical patterns were contested in Siberia and in the streets of Victoria. Decades before the Cold War, the battle lines were drawn. The seething tensions and ambitions surrounding the Siberian Expedition – among anglophone and francophone workers and farmers, Siberian peasants and partisans, White Russian soldiers and motley foreign troops, and Canadian financiers and the state – exposed the class basis of Canadian foreign policy. Canada lost in Siberia, its first foray as a world power, and then quietly ignored this history.[23]

Appendices

APPENDIX A
Composition of Canadian Expeditionary Force (Siberia)

	Officers	Enlisted men	Total sailing strength
Force Headquarters	34	79	113
Base Headquarters	33	90	123
Base Guard	3	113	116
No. 1 Company CASC	16	125	141
No. 17 Supply Depot CASC	1	17	18
Field Bakery CASC	1	25	26
Remount Squadron	1	22	23
No. 9 Detachment COC	9	74	83
No. 11 Stationary Hospital CAMC	20	175	195
No. 4 Advance Medical Stores CAMC	1	9	10
No. 10 Sanitation Section CAMC	1	25	26
"B" Squadron RNWMP	6	179	185
No. 16 Field Company CE	5	133	138
No. 6 Company Signal Section CE	8	192	200
Military Mounted Police	–	6	6
Base Records	4	8	12
Canadian Army Postal Corps	5	13	18
85th Battery CFA	4	79	83
Ammunition Column CFA	4	85	89
No. 20 Company CMGC	27	194	221
16th Field Ambulance CAMC	24	168	192
Field Butchery CASC	–	5	5
Red Cross	6	–	6
No. 16 Supply Depot CASC	1	13	14
259th Battalion, Canadian Rifles	41	1,042	1,083
YMCA	3	–	3
Catholic huts	1	–	1
260th Battalion, Canadian Rifles	42	984	1,026
Base training depot	10	20	30
No. 6 Mobile Section CAVC	1	23	24
Total	302	3,908	4,210

Abbreviations:

CASC	Canadian Army Service Corps	CFA	Canadian Field Artillery
COC	Canadian Ordnance Corps	CMGC	Canadian Machine Gun Corps
CAMC	Canadian Army Medical Corps	CAVC	Canadian Army Veterinary Corps
CE	Canadian Engineers		

Source: J.E. Skuce, *CSEF: Canada's Soldiers in Siberia, 1918-1919* (Ottawa: Access to History Publications, 1990), 54.

APPENDIX B
Troop and cargo movements to and from Vladivostok, 1918-19

From Canada	Departure from Canada	Arrival at Vladivostok
SS *Empress of Japan*	11 October 1918 (Victoria)	26 October 1918
SS *Monteagle*	17 November 1918 (Vancouver)	5 December 1918
SS *Ningchow*	11 December 1918 (Vancouver)	29 December 1918
SS *Teesta*	22 December 1918 (Victoria)	12 January 1919
SS *Protesilaus*	26 December 1918 (Victoria)	15 January 1919
SS *War Charger*	30 December 1918 (Vancouver)	26 January 1919
SS *Madras*	10 January 1919 (Vancouver)	3 February 1919
SS *Monteagle*	31 January 1919 (Vancouver)	18 February 1919
SS *Empress of Japan*	12 February 1919 (Victoria)	1 March 1919
SS *Cyclops*	28 March 1919 (Vancouver)	14 April 1919

From Russia	Departure from Vladivostok	Arrival in Canada
SS *Monteagle*	21 April 1919	5 May 1919 (Victoria)
SS *Empress of Japan*	9 May 1919	21 May 1919 (Vancouver)
SS *Empress of Russia*	19 May 1919	30 May 1919 (Vancouver)
SS *Monteagle*	5 June 1919	19 June 1919 (Victoria)

Sources: Naval Service, Ottawa to Divisional Transports, Vancouver, LAC, RG 24, vol. 3969, file NSC 1047-14-24 (vol.1) "Telegraphic Communications Concerning Contingents for Siberia"; "CEF (Siberia)" (Disposition of Units by Troopship), n.d, LAC, RG 24, ser. C-1-a, vol. 1992, file HQ-762-11-25, "Returns of Strength CEF (Siberia)"; J.E. Skuce, *CSEF: Canada's Soldiers in Siberia, 1918-1919* (Ottawa: Access to History Publications, 1990), 54.

APPENDIX C

Protest resolution by Vladivostok Trade-Manufacturers' Assembly against Canadian seizure of Pushkinsky Theatre, Vladivostok

1 November 1918

[from *Dalekaya Okraina* newspaper]

The protest Resolution accepted at the emergency general meeting of members of the Vladivostok Trade-Manufacturers' Assembly, 1 November 1918, the majority of all against five:

All allied commands, entering into Russia, assured before the people of all the world full non-interference with internal Russian affairs. But now we see the exact opposite phenomenon: interests of Russian citizens are continually trampled. Namely: the Allies with one hand build theatres, clubs and meeting halls for their soldiers, and with the other grasp premises of the Cultural-Enlightenment Society which has existed in Vladivostok for more than 30 years. The Trade-Manufacturers' Assembly owns the best library, school, courses, and theatre in the city and spends almost all income on enlightenment and charity. It would seem that such a Society has a right to inviolability, however, our Allies, namely the Canadian command, have grasped the Society's premises and have deprived its members and their families, numbering 700 persons, and all trade and manufacturing classes, from continuing cultural-enlightenment and public work.

Because there are many empty premises in the city and its vicinity, this general meeting of members of the Society protests against the capture of the Society's premises and charges the selected delegation to draw the attention of the Canadian command to the inadmissibility of the requisition and insist on the clearing of the occupied premises. The same delegation is instructed to ask for assistance from the stock exchange committee of the Trade-Manufacturers' Assembly and the unions: trade and manufacturers, teachers and threatrical workers.

(signed)

Oilanov
Denisov
Shcherbinsky
Malko
Sherstnyov

Delegates of the Trade-Manufacturers' Assembly

Source: "K rekvizitsii Pushkinskogo Teatra" [On the Requisition of Pushkinsky Theatre], *Dalekaya Okraina* [Far Suburb] (Vladivostok), 4 November 1918, Vladivostok State Historical Archive.

APPENDIX D
Protest letter from Victoria & District Trades and Labor Council to Gen. Sydney C. Mewburn, Minister of Militia and Defence, Ottawa, 6 December 1918

6 December 1918

The Honourable
The Minister of Militia and Defence,
Ottawa

Sir,

I have the honour, by directions of the Victoria and District Trades and Labor Council, to express the emphatic disapproval of that Body of the Government's apparent purpose in sending an expeditionary force to Siberia. Now that the war is won and ended, the members of the various workmens' organizations and the common people in general, fail to see any justification for a military enterprise being pursued in that direction. More particularly as we as a country and a nation are not at war, nor have been at war, with the Russian people.

I am therefore to recommend to you and the Government the advisability of immediately abandoning the Siberian Expeditionary effort and at once recall all Canadian forces that may be in that country now or on the way there.

I have the honour to be,

Sincerely yours,

Christian Sivertz,
Secretary-Treasurer

Source: Sivertz to Mewburn, 6 December 1918, LAC, RG 24, ser. C-1-a, vol. 1992, file 762-11-24, "Queries Relating to CEF (Siberia)." For the government's response, see Deputy Minister of Militia and Defence to Christian Sivertz, 19 December 1918, LAC, RG 24, ser. C-1-a, vol. 1992, file 762-11-24, "Queries Relating to CEF (Siberia)."

APPENDIX E
Resolution from French-Canadian members of the 16th Infantry Brigade, CEF (Siberia), 18 December 1918

Telegram sent by Sir Lomer Gouin (Montreal), to General S.C. Mewburn, Minister of Militia and Defence, and Sir Thomas White, Acting Prime Minister (Ottawa), 20 December 1918

Victoria, BC
Dec. 18, 1918

Sir Lomer Gouin:

Plus de 300 loyaux Canadiens francaise de la 16eme brigade SEF qui etai ent prets faire leure devoir lorsquil sagissait daneantir le menace tudesque protestent energiquement detre envoye aujourdhui en Siberie contre leur gre dans une expedition qui n'est pas justifie par des interets et inutile pour notre pays. Premier citoyen de notre province digne representant de votre race et maintenant nous vous demandons intervenir pour qu une telle injustice ne soit pas commis.

Signe,
259th battalion

PS. I believe it is my duty to send this telegram to yourself and Sir Thomas White, acting premier of Canada.
Lomer Gouin

[More than 300 loyal French-Canadians in the 16th Brigade, SEF, who were willing to do their duty to annihilate the Hun menace, energetically protest against being sent today in Siberia, contrary to their will, in an expedition which is not justified and useless for our Country. As first citizen of our province and worthy representative of our race, we beg that your influence may be used to prevent such an injustice.]

Source: LAC, RG 24, ser. C-1-a, vol. 1992, file 762-11-24, "Queries relating to CEF (Siberia)."

APPENDIX F
Resolution adopted by Alberta Federation of Labor, January 1919

RESOLVED, that this body places itself on record as being in full accord with the aims and purposes of the Russian and German socialist revolutions, and be it further

RESOLVED, that this body gives the executive full power to call a general strike should the Allied powers persist in their attempt to overthrow the Soviet administration in Russia or Germany or in any other country in which a Soviet form of government is or may be established.

Source: Tim Buck, *Canada and the Russian Revolution: The Impact of the World's First Socialist Revolution on Labour and Politics in Canada* (Toronto: Progress Books, 1967), 45-46.

Administrators of Vladivostok and the Russian Far East, 1917-22

Name	Position	Time period
Nikolay L. Gondatti	Governor-General of Priamur, for Czar Nicholas II	1911–March 1917
Aleksandr N. Rusanov	Commissar of the Far East, for Provisional Gov't	April 1917–May 1917
L.E. Gerasimov	Chairman of Dalsovnarkom (Prov Gov't)*	May 1917–Aug 1917
Nikolay S. Vakulin	Chairman of Dalsovnarkom (Prov Gov't)	Aug 1917–Dec 1917
Aleksandr Krasnoshchekov	Chairman of Dalsovnarkom (Soviet)	Dec 1917–Aug 1918
Konstantin A. Sukhanov	Chairman of Vladivostok Soviet	Nov 1917–June 1918
Pyotr Y. Derber	Head of Provisional Gov't of Autonomous Siberia	July 1918–Sep 1918
Gen. Dmitri L. Horvath	Self-proclaimed "Temporary Ruler of Russia"	Sept 1918–Nov 1918
Gen. Dmitri L. Horvath	Far Eastern High Plenopotentiary for Kolchak	Nov 1918–Jan 1920
Gen. Pavel Ivanov-Rinov	Military governor for Kolchak	Nov 1918–Sept 1919
Gen. Sergei N. Rozanov	Military governor for Kolchak	Sept 1919–Jan 1920
Aleksandr S. Medvedev	Chairman of Provisional Zemstovo Gov't of Vlad.	Jan 1920–mid 1920
Vasily G. Antonov	Chairman of Provisional Zemstovo Gov't of Vlad.	mid-1920–May 1921
Aleksandr Krasnoshchekov	Chairman of Prov. Govn't of Pribaikalia	Mar 1920–Apr 1920
Aleksandr Krasnoshchekov	President of Far Eastern Republic	Apr 1920–Nov 1920
Nikolay M. Matveyev	President of Far Eastern Republic	Nov 1920–Nov 1922
Spiridon D. Merkulov	Head of Provisional Priamur Government	May 1921–June 1922
Mikhail Dieterichs	Voevoda of Vladivostok Estates–General	June 1922–Oct 1922
Pyotr A. Kobozev	Chairman of Dalrevkom, USSR†	Nov 1922–

* *Dalsovnarkom:* People's Commissariat for the Russian Far East. Formed by the provisional government, May 1917. Transformed by the Bolsheviks into the People's Commissariat of Far Eastern Soviets, December 1917.

† *Dalrevkom:* Far Eastern Revolutionary Committee of the Russian Soviet Federated Socialist Republic.

Sources: John J. Stephan, *The Russian Far East: A History* (Stanford: Stanford University Press, 1994), 110–54; B.I. Mukhachev, ed., *Dal' nii Vostok Rossii v period revoliutsii 1917 goda i grazhdanskoi voi ny* (Vladivostok: Dal'nauka, 2003).

APPENDIX H
Proclamation to Allied forces at Shkotovo issued by Gavrila Shevchenko, commander-in-chief of partisan detachments, 15 April 1919

We farmers, who aim to affect the revolution of farmers and workmen issue the following proclamation:

1. We do not recognize any Allied command because the Japanese, French, English, Italian and American governments are endeavoring to bring pressure against the Great Russian Revolution which marks the beginning of liberty for the working classes of the whole world. Profiting by the state of chaos in Russia, the Allied countries with false promises of not interfering in the internal affairs of the country have invaded Siberia with their troops. In reality they desire only to satisfy their ambitions and to seize the railway, mines and riches of Siberia.

2. The capitalist is temporarily in power, thanks to the Allied forces and capitalists and have begun the extermination of the workmen and farmers. It is in vain that these foreigners seize railways and the wealth of Siberia, in conjunction with the so-called government at Omsk, because the workmen and farmers do not recognize it.

3. According to your proclamation, you are placing troops here for the purpose of maintaining order but on behalf of the workmen and farmers, we ask you the following questions:

   Who has asked you to re-establish order in our country?
   Who has given you the right to do it?
   How is it the Allied troops take upon themselves the task of maintaining order in our country?

   Is it for the purpose of maintaining order that they establish themselves throughout Siberia, lending a strong hand to the Koltchak troops, knocking down the peaceable people and shooting them. Perhaps you excuse the burning of villages in the maritime province by Japanese troops by saying it is for the purpose of maintaining order. The workmen and peasants of Russia who have a real Soviet Government have been neither injured nor mutilated as they have been by your troops and those of Koltchak.

4. It is no longer Bolsheviks and the Red Guard which oppose you. It is also the farmers and workmen. You ask us to give you full control of the Suchan railway and the main Siberia line in order to be able to move freely your troops and Koltchak's troops who wish to wipe us out. This is not only childish but insolent. Orders should come from us and not from you. We demand that you evacuate our territory and go back from whence you came. If you will not submit to this order we will not give you one inch of

the railway which we have built with our very blood. We declare war upon you to the death. Remember that in this we are not alone but the working classes of the whole world are with us. No matter how great our sacrifices may be, victory finally remains in our hands. We accept your challenge to engage in battle. Our aim is not only Shkotovo, but also as you may know, Vladivostok, which is your main base of operations. Just as the Allied troops left Odessa and Archangel, so also you will be forced to leave Vladivostok. Until that time we will never lay down our arms.

Signed   Shevchenko
             Commander-in-Chief of the Army of Volunteers of Farmers
             and Workmen of the Province of Priamur, in the name of the
             Federal Soviet Republic of All Russia

Sources: Communique No. 5, 18 April 1919, LAC, War Diary, 16th Infantry Brigade CEF(S), April 1919, app. 15. See also Response of Schevatchenko [sic.], 17 April 1919, LAC, War Diary, General Staff CEF(S), April 1919, app. O(13).

APPENDIX I

Expenses incurred by Britain in the Russian Civil War (thousand pounds sterling), 11 November 1918 - 31 October 1919

	British naval and military operations				Assistance to White Russians				
	North Russia	Caucasus	Baltic and Black Seas	Total British forces	Baltic states	Admiral Kolchak	General Denikin	Total White forces	Total Anti-Bolshevik forces
Expense of British military contingents	9,477,000	3,051,000	6,370,000	18,868,000	177,000	1,430,000	194,000	1,890,000	20,758,000
Sea transport	3,160,000	410,000	–	3,570,000	338,000	1,523,000	2,295,000	4,156,000	7,726,000
Money to provisional government	1,350,000	–	–	1,350,000	–	–	–	–	1,350,000
Food and supplies for Russian troops	2,500,000	–	–	2,500,000	200,000	30,000	850,000	1,080,000	3,580,000
Munitions and stores for Russians (marketable)	1,762,000	–	–	1,762,000	735,000	5,000,000	5,856,000	11,591,000	13,353,000
Total cash and marketable stores	18,219,000	3,461,000	6,370,000	28,050,000	1,450,000	7,983,000	9,915,000	18,628,000	46,678,000
Munitions and stores for Russians (non-marketable)	244,000	–	–	244,000	391,000	523,500	1,794,000	2,760,000	3,004,000
Grand total (cash and marketable and non-marketable)	18,463,000	3,461,000	6,370,000	28,294,000	1,841,000	8,506,500	11,709,000	21,388,000	49,682,000

Source: "Statement of Expenditure on Naval and Military Operations in Russia, from the Date of the Armistice to the 31st October 1919," 1920, LAC, Defence, ser. C-1-A, vol. 2013, file HQ-11-762-36.

APPENDIX J

Deaths among officers and other ranks in the CEF (Siberia)

Name	Unit	Date of death	Cause
Lieut. Alfred H. Thring	260th Btn	18 March 1919	Suicide
Pte. Edward Biddle	Base Guard	22 October 1918	Influenza
Pte. Walter Boston	16th Field Ambulance	16 April 1919	Endocarditis
L/Cpl. George H. Buckwalter	20th Machine Gun Co.	25 April 1919	Pneumonia
Rfn. Harold Leo Butler	259th Btn	31 December 1918	Accident
Rfn. William Edward Dodd	260th Btn	5 April 1919	Toxaemia
Rfn. Earl Gillespie	260th Btn	14 March 1919	Meningitis
Tpr. William John Henderson	RNWMP	30 December 1918	Meningitis
Rfn. David Higgins	260th Btn	6 March 1919	Pericarditis
Rfn. Frank Joseph Kay	259th Btn	28 December 1918	Accident
Pte. Wilfred Charles Lane	Force H.Q.	10 March 1919	Pneumonia
Rfn. Romeo Lariviere	259th Btn	11 March 1919	Pneumonia
Rfn. James Florence Manion	260th Btn	22 February 1919	Pneumonia
Rfn. Joseph Emmett McDonald	259th Btn	28 February 1919	Pneumonia
Rfn. Roy Sothern	260th Btn	4 March 1919	Pneumonia
Pte. Edwin Howard Stephenson	11th Stationary Hospital	23 May 1919	Small pox
Gunner Frederic Eaton Ward	20th Machine Gun Co.	3 March 1919	Pneumonia
A/QMS Ernest Worthington	Base H.Q.	6 March 1919	Pneumonia
Sgt. John Shirley Murray Wynn	16th Field Co. (Engineers)	14 January 1919	Exposure
Pte. Richard Leonard Massey	No. 9 Detachment COC	30 May 1919	Small pox
Rfn. Peter Roy McMillan	259th Btn	6 June 1919	Small pox

Sources: "Officers and Others Ranks, CEF (Siberia) Who Have Died," LAC, RG 24, ser. C-1-a, vol. 1992, file 762-11-25 "Returns of Strength CEF (Siberia)"; "Casualty Form – Active Service," LAC, RG 150, acc. 92-93/166, vol. 6020, file "Massey Richard Leonard"; "Casualty Form – Active Service," LAC, RG 150, acc. 1992-93/166, vol. 7119, file "Macmillan Peter R."

Notes

Preface

1 For the naming of the CEFS, see Major to Adjutant-General, 19 September 1918, Library and Archives Canada (hereafter cited as LAC), Department of National Defence Fonds, Record Group (hereafter cited as RG) 24, ser. C-1-A, vol. 1992, file H-Q-762-11-8 (Nomenclature CEF Siberia).

2 "Draft of Interview by Captain Playfair with Admiral Kolchak, Omsk, April 27th, 1919," LAC, Department of Militia and Defence Fonds (Militia and Defence), RG 9, ser. III-A-S, vol. 362, file A3, SEF (file 118), "Report – Russian Military and Political Situation, by Canadian Expeditionary Force (Siberia) Vladivostok, June, 1919, Maj-Gen. J.H. Elmsley," 57.

Introduction

I wish to acknowledge P. Whitney Lackenbauer for providing inspiration for this chapter title. See P. Whitney Lackenbauer, "Why Siberia? Canadian Foreign Policy and the Siberian Intervention, 1918-1919," *Canadian Military Heritage Project*, 1998, http://www/rootsweb. com/~canmil/siberia/siberia1.html (viewed 21 January 2009).

1 Dawn Fraser, "The Mud-Red Volunteers," *Songs of Siberia and Rhymes of the Road* (Glace Bay, NS: Eastern Publishing, c. 1919), 13.

2 Minutes, 4 December 1918 and 18 December 1918, University of Victoria Archives and Special Collections (hereafter cited as UVASC), Victoria Labour Council Fonds (hereafter cited as VLC Fonds), acc. 80-59, box 3; "Federated Labor Party Launched at Victoria," *British Columbia Federationist* (hereafter cited as *BC Federationist*), 13 December 1918; "Organized Attempt to Wreck Mass Meeting," *BC Federationist*, 20 December 1918.

3 "There Can Be No Peace," *BC Federationist*, 20 December 1918.

4 Report of Field General Court Martial, Vladivostok, 2 February 1919, LAC, RG 9, ser. III-A-3, vol. 378, file A3, SEF Courts Martial.

5 Of 1083 troops in the Battalion (some of whom departed after the *Teesta*), only 378 had enlisted voluntarily. See "Disposition by Unit of MSA Personnel in the CSEF," 9 April 1919, War Diary of Base Headquarters CEF(S), LAC, RG 9, ser. III-D-3, vol. 5057; J.E. Skuce, *CSEF: Canada's Soldiers in Siberia, 1918-1919* (Ottawa: Access to History Publications, 1990), 23; Defensor to Elmsley, 1 April 1919: Bickford to Headquarters CEF(S), 5 April 1919; Elmsley to Defensor, 10 April 1919 (all in LAC, RG 9, ser. III-A-3, vol. 373, file A3, SEF Force HQ MSA); Swift to Brigade Headquarters, 8 April 1919; Barclay to Elmsley, 11 April 1918; Barclay to Elmsley, 12 April 1919; "Suspension of Sentence," 14 April 1919 (all in LAC, RG 9, ser. III-A-3, vol. 371, file A3, SEF Force HQ 23); Canada, *The Military Service Act, 1917* (Ottawa: J. de Labroquerie Taché, 1917).

6 Report of Field General Court Martial, Vladivostok, 2 February 1919, LAC, RG 9, ser. III-A-3, vol. 378, file A3, SEF Courts Martial.

7 "Verbatim Report of the Calgary Conference, 1919," *One Big Union Bulletin* (Winnipeg), 10 March 1927.

8 "What a Muddle," *BC Federationist*, 28 February 1919.

9 "Trial of No. 3312133 Rifleman Arthur Roy," 28 January 1919, LAC, RG 24, ser. C-1-A, vol. 1992, file H-Q-762-11-10, "Courts Martial in CEF (Siberia)."

10 "What a Muddle," *BC Federationist*, 28 February 1919; War Diary of 259th Battalion CEF(S), December 1918, LAC, RG 9, ser. III-D-3, vol. 5057.

11 As quoted in Roy MacLaren, *Canadians in Russia, 1918-19* (Toronto: Macmillan, 1976), 175-77.

12 "What a Muddle," *BC Federationist*, 28 February 1919. For military records pertaining to troops and cargo aboard the *Teesta*, see Divisional Transports, Vancouver, to Naval Service, Ottawa, 23 December 1918, LAC, RG 24, vol. 3969, file NSC 1047-14-27 (vol. 1). For details of the YMCA mission in Siberia, see Charles W. Bishop, *The Canadian YMCA in the Great War: The Official Record of the Activities of the Canadian YMCA in Connection with the Great War of 1914-1918* (Toronto: National Council of Young Men's Christian Associations of Canada, 1924), 304-10.

13 "The Siberian Expedition," *Victoria Semi-Weekly Tribune* (hereafter cited as *Tribune*), 19 December 1918.

14 The Canadian experience on the Western Front is explored in Desmond Morton and J.L. Granatstein, *Marching to Armageddon: Canadians and the Great War, 1914-1919* (Toronto: Lester and Orpen Dennys, 1989). See also Granatstein and Morton, *Canada and the Two World Wars* (Toronto: Key Porter Books, 2003); Morton, *When Your Number's Up: The Canadian Soldier in the First World War* (Toronto: Random House of Canada, 1993); and Morton, *Canada and War: A Military and Political History* (Scarborough: Butterworths, 1981). See also Andrew Iarocci, *Shoestring Soldiers: The 1st Canadian Division at War, 1914-1915* (Toronto: University of Toronto Press, 2008); Gerald W.L. Nicholson, *Official History of the Canadian Army in the First World War: Canadian Expeditionary Force, 1914-1919* (Ottawa: Queen's Printer and Controller of Stationery, 1962); and Robert Craig Brown and Ramsay Cook, *Canada, 1896-1921: A Nation Transformed* (Toronto: McClelland and Stewart, 1974). The impact of stress and exhaustion on the morale of troops, particularly in the Second World War, is the subject of Terry Copp and Bill McAndrew's *Battle Exhaustion: Soldiers and Psychiatrists in the Canadian Army, 1939-1945* (Montreal and Kingston: McGill-Queen's University Press, 1990). Copp points towards a more "bottom-up" method of military history in *The Brigade: The Fifth Canadian Infantry Brigade* (Stoney Creek: Fortress, 1992).

15 Studies of the Siberian Expedition include Gaddis Smith, "Canada and the Siberian Intervention, 1918-1919," *American Historical Review* 64 (July 1959): 866-77; J.A. Swettenham, "Allied Intervention in Siberia, 1918-1919," Report No. 83, Historical Section (GS) Army Headquarters, 20 October 1959, http://www.forces.ca/dhh/ downloads/ahq/ahq083.pdf; J.A. Swettenham, *Allied Intervention in Russia, 1918-19: And the Part Played by Canada* (Toronto: Ryerson, 1967); Robert N. Murby, "Canadian Economic Commission to Siberia, 1918-1919," *Canadian Slavonic Papers* 11, 3 (1969): 374-93; James Eayrs, *In Defence of Canada*, vol. 1, *From the Great War to the Great Depression* (Toronto: University of Toronto Press, 1964), 27-40; Aloysius Balawyder, *Canadian-Soviet Relations between the Wars* (Toronto: University of Toronto Press, 1972), 3-21; MacLaren, *Canadians in Russia*; Skuce, *CSEF*; Timothy C. Winegard, "The Canadian Siberian Expeditionary Force, 1918-1919, and the Complications of Coalition Warfare," *Journal of Slavic Military Studies* 20, 2 (2007): 283-328; William Rodney, review of J.A. Swettenham's *Allied Intervention in Russia*, in *Canadian Historical Review* 49, 2 (1968): 184-86; and William Rodney, review of Roy MacLaren's *Canadians in Russia* in *Canadian Historical Review* 58, 4 (1977): 515-17. Several graduate theses have also examined the topic, including Steuart Beattie, "Canadian Intervention in Russia, 1918-1919" (MA thesis, McGill University, 1957); Robert Neil Murby,

"Canada's Siberian Policy, 1918-1919" (MA thesis, University of British Columbia, 1969); Jean-Guy Lalande, "'Russia and the Soviets as Seen in Canada': Une analyse de l'opinion politique de la presse canadienne, de 1914 à 1921" (PhD diss., McGill University, 1981); Mary Ann Van Meenan, "The Canadian Intervention in Siberia, 1918-1919" (MA thesis, Dalhousie University, 1989); Jennifer Ann Polk, "The Canadian Red Cross and Relief in Siberia, 1918-1921" (MA thesis, Carleton University, 2004). Gerald W.L. Nicholson provides only a brief mention of the expedition. See Nicholson, *Official History of the Canadian Army*, 517-23. For a detailed account of the Russian experience in Siberia, see N.G.O. Pereira, *White Siberia: The Politics of Civil War* (Montreal and Kingston: McGill-Queen's University Press, 1996). A one-hour CBC radio documentary on the subject, compiled by Rodney and narrated by Leigh Taylor, can be found at William Rodney, *Canada and the Siberian Intervention, 1918-1919*, tape reel, n.d. (ca. 1970), UVASC, range 43, ID no. 416, 006.

16 Studies of labour and the left in British Columbia during this period include David Bercuson, *Fools and Wise Men: The Rise and Fall of the One Big Union* (Toronto: McGraw-Hill Ryerson, 1978); Gerald Friesen, "'Yours in Revolt: Regionalism, Socialism, and the Western Canadian Labour Movement," *Labour/Le Travailleur* 1 (1976): 139-57; Ronald Grantham, "Some Aspects of the Socialist Movement in British Columbia" (MA thesis, University of British Columbia, 1942); Ross Alfred Johnson, "No Compromise – No Political Trading: The Marxian Socialist Tradition in British Columbia" (PhD diss., University of British Columbia, 1975); Mark Leier, *Where the Fraser River Flows: The Industrial Workers of the World in British Columbia* (Vancouver: New Star Books, 1990); and A. Ross McCormack, *Reformers, Rebels, and Revolutionaries: The Western Canadian Radical Movement, 1899-1919* (Toronto and Buffalo: University of Toronto Press, 1977).

17 Rodney, review of A. Swettenham's *Allied Intervention in Russia*, 186.

18 Raymond Massey, *When I Was Young* (Toronto: McClelland and Stewart, 1976), 200; "Canadian 'Syren' Party, Northern Russian Expeditionary Force (The Murman Front)," and "Canadian 'Elope' Party, Northern Russian Expeditionary Force (Archangel Front)," LAC, RG 24, vol. 1872, file 15. See also H.F. Wood, "Adventure in North Russia," *Canadian Army Journal* 11, 4 (1957): 112-24; L.I. Strakhovsky, "The Canadian Artillery Brigade in North Russia, 1918-1919," *Canadian Historical Review* 39, 2 (1958): 125-46; John Bradley, *Allied Intervention in Russia* (Lantham, New York, and London: University Press of America, 1968); George A. Brinkley, *The Volunteer Army and Allied Intervention in South Russia, 1917-1921: A Study in the Politics and Diplomacy of the Russian Civil War* (Notre Dame: University of Notre Dame Press, 1966); Peter Kenez, *The Defeat of the Whites: Civil War in South Russia, 1919-1920* (Berkeley: University of California Press, 1977); MacLaren, *Canadians in Russia*, 9-124; Leonid I. Strakhovsky, *Intervention at Archangel: The Story of Allied Intervention and Russian Counter-Revolution in North Russia, 1918-1920* (New York: Princeton University Press, 1944); and Swettenham, *Allied Intervention in Russia*, 187-274. The Canadian intervention in Russia has received significantly less attention than have the activities of American and British forces. See R.M. Connaughton, *The Republic of the Ushakovko: Admiral Kolchak and the Allied Intervention in Siberia, 1918-20* (London and New York: Routledge, 1990); Christopher Dobson and John Miller, *The Day They Almost Bombed Moscow: The Allied Intervention in Russia, 1918-1920* (New York: Atheneum, 1986); David S. Foglesong, *America's Secret War against Bolshevism: US Intervention in the Russian Civil War, 1917-1920* (Chapel Hill and London: University of North Carolina Press, 1995); Michael Kettle, *The Road to Intervention: March–November 1918* (London and New York: Routledge, 1988); Robert J. Maddox, *The Unknown War with Russia: Wilson's Siberian Intervention* (San Rafael, CA: Presidio, 1977); Clarence A. Manning, *The Siberian Fiasco*

(New York: Library Publishers, 1952); Betty Miller Unterberger, *America's Siberian Exped-
ition, 1918-1920: A Study of National Policy* (Durham, NC: Duke University Press, 1956);
Carl J. Richard, "'The Shadow of a Plan': The Rationale behind Wilson's 1918 Siberian
Intervention," *Historian* 49 (November 1986): 64–84; and John Silverlight, *The Victors'
Dilemma: Allied Intervention in the Russian Civil War* (London: Barrie and Jenkins, 1970).
For the Australian role in Siberia, see Bruce Muirden, *The Diggers Who Signed on for More:
Australia's Part in the Russian Wars of Intervention, 1918-1919* (Kent Town, Australia: Wake-
field, 1990). The Japanese contribution is explored in John Albert White, *The Siberian
Intervention* (New York: Princeton University Press, 1950). The French role is examined
in Michael J. Carley, "The Origins of the French Intervention in the Russian Civil War,
January-May 1918: A Reappraisal," *Journal of Modern History* 48, 3 (September 1976): 413-
39; and Michael J. Carley, *Revolution and Intervention: The French Government and the
Russian Civil War, 1917-1919* (Montreal and Kingston: McGill-Queen's University Press,
1983). See also Jonathan Smele, ed., *The Russian Revolution and Civil War, 1917-1921: An
Annotated Bibliography* (Continuum: London and New York, 2003); U.A. Poliakov et al.,
eds., *Antisovetskaia interventsiia i ee krakh, 1917-1922* [The Anti-Soviet Intervention and
Its Break-Up, 1917-1922] (Moscow: Izd-vo polit. lit-ry, 1987).
19 "The Soviet's Reply to Allied Gov'ts," *BC Federationist*, 20 December 1918.
20 Commemoration of the Great War is the subject of Jonathan F.W. Vance's *Death So Noble:
Memory, Meaning, and the First World War* (Vancouver: UBC Press, 1997).
21 The propensity of troops to engage in collective crowd action is examined in P. Whitney
Lackenbauer, "Soldiers Behaving Badly: CEF Soldier 'Rioting' in Canada during the First
World War," and other essays in Craig Leslie Mantle, ed., *The Apathetic and the Defiant:
Case Studies of Canadian Mutiny and Disobedience, 1812 to 1919* (Kingston: Canadian
Defence Academy Press/Dundurn, 2007), 195-260; Desmond Morton, "'Kicking and
Complaining': Demobilization Riots in the Canadian Expeditionary Force, 1918-19," *Can-
adian Historical Review* 61, 3 (September 1980): 334-60; P. Whitney Lackenbauer, "The
Military and 'Mob Rule': The CEF Riots in Calgary, February 1916," *Canadian Military
History* 1, 10 (2001): 31-43; P. Whitney Lackenbauer, "Under Siege: The CEF Attack on the
RNWMP Barracks in Calgary, October 1916," *Alberta History* 49, 3 (2001): 2-12; P. Whitney
Lackenbauer and Nikolas Gardner, "Soldiers as Liminaries: The CEF Soldier Riots of 1916
Reassessed," in *Canadian Military History since the 17th Century*, ed. Yves Tremblay, 164-74
(Ottawa: National Defence, 2001); Lawrence James, *Mutiny in the British and Common-
wealth Forces, 1797-1956* (London: Buchan and Enright, 1987); Julian Putkowski, *British
Army Mutineers, 1914-1922* (London: Francis Boutle, 1998); Julian Putkowski, "The Kinmel
Park Camp Riots 1919," *Flintshire Historical Society Journal* 32 (1989): 55-107; Chris Madsen,
Another Kind of Justice: Canadian Military Law from Confederation to Somalia (Vancouver:
UBC Press, 1999); and Jeffrey Ricard, "Bringing Boys Home: A Study of the Canadian
De-Mobilization Policy after the First and Second World Wars" (MA thesis: University of
New Brunswick, 1999). The historiography of collective crowd action was inaugurated in
George Rudé, *The Crowd in History: A Study of Popular Disturbances in France and England,
1730-1848* (New York: Wiley, 1964). For opposition to conscription in Quebec during the
First World War, see Elizabeth H. Armstrong, *Le Québec et la crise de la conscription, 1917-
1918* (Montréal: VLB Éditeur, 1998); Bernard Dansereau, *Le mouvement ouvrier montréalais
et la crise de la conscription, 1916-1918* (Montréal: Université du Québec à Montréal, 1994);
Gaston Dugas, "Le Québec et la crise de la conscription, 1917-1918," *L'Action nationale* 9
(November 1999): 139-41; Gérard Filteau, *Le Québec, le Canada et la guerre, 1914-1918*
(Montréal: L'Aurore, 1977); J.L. Granatstein and J.M. Hitsman, *Broken Promises: A History*

of Conscription in Canada (Toronto: Copp Clark Pitman, 1985), 24-99; and Ferdinand Roy, *L'appel aux armes et la réponse canadiennne-française: Étude sur le conflit des races* (Québec: Garneau, 1917).

22 "The Swedish Portent," *BC Federationist*, 8 June 1917.

23 "In Fear of Russia," *Victoria Daily Colonist* (hereafter cited as *Colonist*), 9 March 1917; "Russians Are Fighting with Allied Forces in the West," *Colonist*, 11 March 1917; "Russian Hospitality," *Colonist*, 11 March 1917. See also Alfred W.F. Knox, *With the Russian Army, 1914-1917* (New York: Arno, 1971), 532-52.

24 See Nicholson, *Official History of the Canadian Army*, 510 and 518; Swettenham, "Allied Intervention in Siberia," 4-5; Skuce, *CSEF*, 4-6.

25 "Siberia Offers Vast Opportunity," *Colonist*, 28 September 1918.

26 Alexandra Kollontai, *The Autobiography of a Sexually Emancipated Communist Woman*, trans. Salvator Attanasio (New York: Herder and Herder, 1971 [1927]), 38. Kollontai, people's commissar of social welfare in the new Soviet government, describes the controversy: "My efforts to nationalize maternity and infant care set off a new wave of insane attacks against me. All kinds of lies were related about the 'nationalization of women,' about my legislative proposals which assertedly ordained that little girls of twelve were to become mothers." An example of Allied allegations of the mistreatment of women in Russia appears in "Women in Soviet Russia" in one of the CEFS newspapers, the *Siberian Bugle* (Vladivostok), 6 March 1919, in War Diary of 259th Battalion Canadian Rifles CEF(S), LAC, RG 9, ser. III-D-3, vol. 5057. See also "Anarchist Proclamation," War Diary of Force Headquarters CEF(S), January 1919, app. XC-IV, p. 70, LAC, RG 9, ser. III-D-3, vol. 5056, reel T-10950. The article claimed: "Nationalization of women has been attempted in various parts of Bolshevik Russia. One instance of this occurred in the town of Saratov, where a decree declaring all women to be property of the nation was promulgated by the Free Love Association of the Anarchists' Club, and later given force of law by the Soviet of the district." See also Deputy Minister of Militia and Defence to Christian Sivertz (draft), 18 December 1918, LAC, RG 24, ser. C-1-a, vol. 1993, file 762-11-24, "Queries Relating to CEF (Siberia)"; "Nationalization of Women," *Tribune*, 24 April 1919; Beatrice Brodsky Farnsworth, "Bolshevism, the Woman Question, and Aleksandra Kollontai," *American Historical Review* 81, 2 (April 1976): 292-317. For the story of Lenin's passage through Germany in 1917, see Michael Pearson, *The Sealed Train* (New York: Putnam, 1975). For a proposal by BC labour organizations to send their own correspondent to Russia to determine the extent of "Bolshevik atrocities," see "Bolshevik Atrocities," *Tribune*, 10 March 1919. See also "Acts of Brutality" and "Official Report – International Commission of Physicians," 15 December 1918, War Diary of General Staff CEF(S), March 1919, app. 36, LAC, RG 9, ser. III-D-3, vol. 5057, reel T-10950.

27 The Czecho-Slovak Legion consisted of prisoners-of-war and deserters from the Austrian army who joined the czar's forces to bolster their nationalist cause and who won recognition as an official Allied army following the March Revolution. Beyond their military value on the ground, the Czecho-Slovaks provided propaganda fodder for the Allies. As Rowell told the Canadian Club, a primary motivation of the Canadian mission in Siberia was "to aid the brave Czecho-Slovak army." See "Siberia Offers Vast Opportunity," *Colonist*, 28 September 1918. For more detailed information on the Czecho-Slovak Legion, see John F.N. Bradley, *The Czechoslovak Legion in Russia, 1914-1920* (Boulder: East European Monographs, 1991); Connaughton, *Republic of the Ushakovko*, 36-40; Edwin P. Hoyt, *The Army without a Country* (New York: Macmillan, 1967); Victor M. Fic, *The Bolsheviks and the Czechoslovak Legion: The Origin of Their Armed Conflict, March-May 1918* (New Delhi:

Abhinav Publications, 1978); and Betty Miller Unterberger, *The United States, Revolutionary Russia, and the Rise of Czechoslovakia* (Chapel Hill: University of North Carolina Press, 1989).

28 F. Seymour Cocks, ed., *The Secret Treaties and Understandings* (London: Union of Democratic Control, n.d. [c. 1918]).

29 See N.W. Rowell's speech to the Canadian Club, "Siberia Offers Vast Opportunity," *Colonist*, 28 September 1918; Rowell speech in Canada, *House of Commons Debates* (1 April 1919), 1063; J. Castell Hopkins, *Canadian Annual Review of Public Affairs* (Toronto: Canadian Annual Review, 1918-19), 53, 419; George M. Wrong, "Canada and the Imperial War Cabinet," *Canadian Historical Review* 1, 1 (1920): 19; Henry Laird Borden and Heath MacQuarrie, eds., *Robert Laird Borden: His Memoirs* (Toronto: McClelland and Stewart, 1969), 2:146. For the larger picture of Rowell's influence in shaping Canadian foreign policy in the years between 1917 and 1921, see Margaret Prang, *N.W. Rowell: Ontario Nationalist* (Toronto: University of Toronto Press, 1975). Borden's tenure as prime minister during the war is discussed in Robert Craig Brown, *Robert Laird Borden: A Biography*, vol. 2, *1914-1937* (Toronto: Macmillan, 1980). The Versailles peace talks, where Canada had its first experience formulating a foreign policy independent of Britain, is explored in Margaret MacMillan, *Paris, 1919: Six Months that Changed the World* (New York: Random House, 2002). See also "Will Sit at League Table," *Globe* (Toronto), 24 January 1919; "Treaty of Peace between the Allies and Associated Powers and Germany, Signed at Versailles, June 28, 1919," in Canada, *Sessional Papers* 55, 1 (1919): 5-171; "The League of Nations," *Tribune*, 26 May 1919.

30 M.I. Svetachev, *Imperialisticheskai'a' intervent's'ii'a' v Sibiri i na Dal'nem Vostoke* [The Imperialistic Intervention in Siberia and the Far East] (Novosibirsk: Nauka, Siberian Division, 1983), 75.

31 Smith, "Canada and the Siberian Expedition," 866. See also Gaddis G. Smith, *Nation and Empire: Canadian Diplomacy during the First World War* (New Haven, CT: Yale University Press, 1969).

32 See Murby, "Canadian Economic Commission to Siberia." See also MacLaren, *Canadians in Russia*, 224; Lothar Deeg, *Kunst & Albers Wladiwostok: Die Geschichte eines deutschen Handelshauses im russischen Fernen Osten 1864-1924* (Essen: Klartext-Verlagsges, 1996). Murby provides the comparison between Kunst and Albers and the Hudson's Bay Company. The report proposing Canadian acquisition of the Kunst and Albers interests in Siberia was provided by Major James Mackintosh-Bell, a Canadian who was attached to the British Intelligence Mission in Russia. See James Mackintosh Bell, *Side Lights on the Siberian Campaign* (Toronto: Ryerson, n.d. [c. 1922]); Beattie, "Canadian Intervention in Russia," 76-77.

33 "What Russia Will Do after the War Is Over," *BC Federationist*, 29 June 1917.

34 "Siberia Offers Vast Opportunity," *Colonist*, 28 September 1918.

35 See Borden to White, 8 August 1918, LAC, Robert Borden Papers (hereafter cited as Borden Papers), Manuscript Group (hereafter cited as MG) 26, H1(a), vol. 103: "Confidential. United States and Great Britain are sending economic commission to Siberia in connection with military expedition. I consider it essential that Canada should take like action"; Mewburn to Borden, 12 July 1918, LAC, MG 26, H1(a), vol. 103: "It has been suggested that trade conditions in this territory, will be a vital factor, looking to the future, and it might be advisable to have some Canadian representative accompany this force, as far as Trade and Commerce goes." See also Privy Council Order (hereafter cited as PC) 2595, 21 October 1918, Canada, Department of External Affairs, *Documents on Canadian External Relations*, vol. 1, *1909-1918* (Ottawa: Department of External Affairs, 1967), 211-13; Murby, "Canadian

Economic Commission to Siberia"; Hopkins, *Canadian Annual Review of Public Affairs* (1918), 432; Edson L. Pease, vice-president and managing director, Royal Bank of Canada, as quoted in Hopkins, *Canadian Annual Review of Public Affairs* (1919), 801; Dana Wilgress, "From Siberia to Kuibyshev: Reflections on Russia, 1919-1943," *International Journal* 22, 3 (Summer 1967): 364-75.

36 The repudiation of the czar's war loans was announced by the Bolshevik government on 28 January 1918. The total value of these loans appears in G.G. Shvittau, *Revolutsiya i Narodnoe Khoziaistvo v Rossii, 1917-1921* [The Revolution and National Economy in Russia] (Leipzig: Tsentral'noe kooperativnoe izdatel'stvo, 1922), 337, as quoted in Richard Pipes, *The Russian Revolution* (New York: Vintage Books, 1990), 578. A contemporary discussion appeared in Henry Hazlitt, "Repudiation," *Nation* (New York), 21 February 1918, 220.

37 "The Alarming Spectre of Repudiation," *BC Federationist*, 8 March 1918.

38 Jonathan D. Smele, "White Gold: The Imperial Russian Gold Reserve in the Anti-Bolshevik East, 1918-? (An Unconcluded Chapter in the History of the Russian Civil War)," *Europe-Asia Studies* 46, 8 (1994): 1317-47. In comparison, in 1914 the gold reserve of Britain amounted to 800 million gold rubles, while that of France was valued at 1.5 billion gold rubles.

39 "Organized Attempt to Wreck Mass Meeting," *BC Federationist*, 20 December 1918.

40 "Bolsheviki Infection Spreading," *BC Federationist*, 25 January 1918.

41 *Siberian Sapper* (Vladivostok), 8 February 1919, LAC, RG 9, ser. III, vol. 363, file 119, as reproduced in Skuce, *CSEF*, 142.

42 "Lenine's Doctrine Scares Ruling Class," *BC Federationist*, 14 December 1917.

43 Minutes, 8 January 1919, UVASC, VLC Fonds, acc. 80-59, box 3. For the original letter and long draft that was never sent, see Deputy Minister of Militia and Defence to Christian Sivertz, 19 December 1918. See also Draft, 18 December 1918, LAC, RG 24, ser. C-1-a, vol. 1993, file 762-11-24, "Queries Relating to CEF (Siberia)."

Chapter 1: 1917

1 "The Trifling Cost of Three Years of War," *BC Federationist*, 19 October 1917.

2 "Munitions Workers Go Out on Strike," *Colonist*, 11 March 1917; "The Munition Workers," *Colonist*, 28 December 1918; Ronald A. Lacroix, "Problems of Plant Closures and Worker Relocation: A Case Study of James Island, BC" (MA thesis, University of Victoria, 1981), 14. See also Walter Sidwell, *The Island I Can't Forget* (Deroche, BC: Sidwell, 2002).

3 "Strike Settlement Is Not in Sight," *Colonist*, 13 March 1917; "Both Parties Hold Firm Attitude," *Colonist*, 14 March 1917; "Matters Now Rest with Striking Party," *Colonist*, 15 March 1917. On 15 March, the *Colonist* reported that the provincial government had appointed a special representative to investigate the sanitary conditions and that the company had submitted an offer to the strikers, who were expected to return to the island for work the following day. The strike was settled on 24 March 1919. See Canada, *Labour Gazette* 17, 4 (April 1917): 279-80.

4 Minutes, 16 and 29 November 1916, UVASC, VLC Fonds, acc. 80-59, box 3.

5 Minutes, 21 February 1917, UVASC, VLC fonds, acc. 80-59, box 3.

6 "Justice of Labor's Claim Is Being Admitted," *BC Federationist*, 26 January 1917. Throughout the war, the *BC Federationist* was socialist in its orientation and was edited by Parmeter Pettipiece, a Vancouver trades unionist and member of the Socialist Party of Canada. However, this did not translate into a uniformly anti-war position, reflecting the diversity of socialist thought on war and militarism. While a radical layer of Canadian workers had opposed the war since August 1914, the dominant perspective in Canadian labour viewed the German kaiser as the epitome of reaction and, therefore, embraced the war effort.

The *BC Federationist* published few anti-war tracts in the early war years, instead echoing other labour papers and the mainstream press in condemning "the autocracy of Mid-Europe" and "Teutonic Aggression." However, by 1917, as the war dragged on, and inflation, profiteering, and conscription fuelled a radicalization in working-class ranks, the tone of the *BC Federationist* changed. Though subject to censorship regulations from 1914 to 1919, the newspaper increasingly defied restrictions against coverage "prejudicial to Canada's war effort" and became openly anti-militarist. See *BC Federationist*, August 1914-June 1919. See also Jeff Keshen, "All the News That Was Fit to Print: Ernest J. Chambers and Information Control in Canada, 1914-19," *Canadian Historical Review* 73, 3 (1992): 315-43.

7 "Cuban Rebels Defeated," *Colonist*, 9 March 1917.

8 "Swedish Cabinet Crisis," *Colonist*, 7 March 1917.

9 "No Conference," *Colonist*, 11 March 1917.

10 "Food or Revolution," *Colonist*, 11 March 1917. In January, Frederick Carne, a stretcher-bearer with the 8th Field Ambulance, wrote: "I have a hunch that when the biggest push of all starts in the early spring, Bill [Kaiser Wilhelm II] will find that he'll have an internal revolution to contend with as well as the Allies." See Carne to Mother, 10 January 1917, UVASC, Frederick Carne Fonds (hereafter cited as Carne Fonds), acc. 97-051, "Letters."

11 Nicholson, *Official History of the Canadian Army*, 198-99.

12 Carne to Mother, 25 September 1916 and 19 November 1916, UVASC, Carne Fonds, acc. 97-051, "Letters." Carne's letters, like those of all enlisted men, were subject to censorship. As he wrote in February 1917: "Seems to me that I have done wonderfully well in the letter writing line, considering the censorship to which we are subjected to. And if, as you say, I write an interesting letter under such conditions, what couldn't I do were we given free rein. No use conjecturing, is there, for that won't help matters any, so will just have to carry on with material that isn't of any military value." See Carne to Mother, 22 February 1917, UVASC, Carne Fonds, "Letters."

13 Carne to Mother, 1 December 1916, UVASC, Carne Fonds, "Letters"; "Happenings in Brief – Must Do Base Duty," *Colonist*, 14 March 1917.

14 H.A.C. Machin, *Report of the Director of the Military Service Branch to the Honourable Minister of Justice on the Operation of the Military Service Act, 1917* (Ottawa: J. de Labroquerie Taché, 1919), 90.

15 Granatstein and Hitsman, *Broken Promises*, 49-50.

16 Minutes, 6 December 1916, UVASC, VLC Fonds, acc. 80-59, box 3.

17 Martin Robin, "Registration, Conscription, and Independent Labour Politics, 1916-1917," in *Conscription 1917*, ed. Ramsay Cook, 60-77 (Toronto: University of Toronto Press, 1969).

18 Studies of class formation on British Columbia's industrial frontier include Martin Robin, "British Columbia: The Company Province," in *Canadian Provincial Politics: The Party Systems in the Ten Provinces*, 2nd ed., ed. Martin Robin, 28-60 (Scarborough: Prentice-Hall, 1978); Ross Alfred Johnson, "No Compromise – No Political Trading: The Marxian Socialist Tradition in British Columbia" (PhD diss., University of British Columbia, 1975); and Leier, *Where the Fraser River Flows*.

19 George Hardy, *Those Stormy Years: Memories of the Fight for Freedom on Five Continents* (London: Lawrence and Wishart, 1956), 55. See also J. Kavanagh, *The Vancouver Island Strike* (Vancouver: BC Miners Liberation League, 1913); William Bennett, *Builders of British Columbia* (Vancouver: Broadway Printers, 1937), 65-76.

20 "Ends in Fiasco," *Daily Times*, 5 August 1914; Minutes, 5 August 1914, UVASC, VLC Fonds, acc. 80-59, box 3; Hardy, *Those Stormy Years*, 55. At the next meeting of the Victoria Trades and Labor Council, delegate J.L. Martin of the Labourers' Protective Association took responsibility for having organized the meeting.

21 Robin, "Registration, Conscription, and Independent Labour Politics."
22 "President's Report," *BC Federationist*, 2 February 1917. Borden was joined by future prime minister R.B. Bennett, MP for Calgary and director-general of the National Registration Commission. The BCFL delegation consisted of outgoing president James McVety, secretary Victor Midgley, and vice-presidents Morrison and Yates.
23 Ibid.
24 Minutes, 20 December 1916, UVASC, VLC Fonds, acc. 80-59, box 3; President's Report, *BCFL Proceedings* (1917), as quoted in *BC Federationist*, 2 February 1917. Delegates rejected a resolution from the Victoria Trades and Labor Council secretary, postal worker Christian Sivertz, that emphasized "the difficulty of making any effective opposition to the registration scheme."
25 "Justice of Labor's Claim Is Being Admitted," *BC Federationist*, 26 January 1917.
26 "Forces of Provincial Labor Meet at Revelstoke," *BC Federationist*, 2 February 1917.
27 "Resolutions Considered," *BC Federationist*, 2 February 1917.
28 The referendum question read: "Are you prepared to place in the hands of the executive of the British Columbia Federation of Labor the power to call a general strike in the event of conscription, either military or industrial, being made effective by the Dominion government?" Circulars were sent to two hundred labour bodies, forty of which responded. See "BC Federation of Labor Issues Referendum," *BC Federationist*, 8 June 1917; "First Unwilling Conscript to Be Signal for 'Down Tools,'" *BC Federationist*, 7 September 1917.
29 "Russian Hospitality," *Colonist*, 13 March 1917.
30 "Russians Are Fighting with Allied Forces in West," *Colonist*, 11 March 1917; Knox, *With the Russian Army*, 532-52.
31 "In Fear of Russia," *Colonist*, 9 March 1917. See also "Casualties in European War," *Colonist*, 13 March 1917.
32 "The War" and "British Forces Now Occupy Baghdad," *Colonist*, 13 March 1917; "The War," 14 March 1917; "Mesopotamia," *Colonist*, 18 March 1917.
33 "On the Russian Front," *Colonist*, 7 March 1917; "Russians Are Fighting with Allied Forces in West," *Colonist*, 11 March 1917.
34 S.A. Smith, *Red Petrograd: Revolution in the Factories, 1917-1918* (Cambridge: Cambridge University Press: 1983), 51; David Mandel, *The Petrograd Workers and the Fall of the Old Regime* (London: Macmillan, 1983), 44.
35 Isabel A. Tirado, "The Socialist Youth Movement in Revolutionary Petrograd," *Russian Review* 46, 2 (April 1987): 135-56; Diane Koekner and William G. Rosenberg, "Skilled Workers and the Strike Movement in Revolutionary Russia," *Journal of Social History* 19, 4 (Summer 1986): 605-29.
36 Oskar Anweiler, *The Soviets: The Russian Workers, Peasants, and Soldiers Councils, 1905-1921* (New York: Pantheon, 1974).
37 "Briefs," *BC Federationist*, 16 February 1917.
38 For the purpose of clarity, I use the Gregorian calendar, which the Bolshevik government adopted in February 1918. At the time of the 1917 revolutions, however, Russia used the Julian calendar, which was fourteen days behind that of the West. Hence, 23 February in Petrograd was 8 March in Victoria, and the Bolshevik seizure of power on 25 October occurred on 7 November in the West. The terms "February Revolution" and "October Revolution" reflect the earlier calendar.
39 "Shortage of Bread," *Colonist*, 14 March 1917; "Emperor Has Abdicated and Duma Now Controls," *Colonist*, 16 March 1917; "Russia to Be Republic Is Present Probability," *Colonist*, 17 March 1917; "Tracing Course of Revolution" and "Not Commenced by Any Faction," *Colonist*, 18 March 1917; Knox, *With the Russian Army*, 553-54; Mandel, *Petrograd Workers*

and the Fall of the Old Regime, 64-65, 164. The Putilov metalworkers had gone on strike on 3 March.

40 "Emperor Has Abdicated and Duma Now Controls" and "Russian Socialists," *Colonist,* 16 March 1917; "New Russian Minister of Justice Insists on Absolute Freedom of Speech and the Press Hereafter," *Daily Times,* 16 March 1917.

41 "Fighting in Petrograd," *Colonist,* 17 March 1917.

42 "Settling Down in Petrograd," *Colonist,* 18 March 1917.

43 "Guards Acclaim Duma President," *Colonist,* 17 March 1917.

44 "Not Commenced by Any Faction," *Colonist,* 18 March 1917.

45 "Russia to Be Republic Is Present Probability," *Colonist,* 17 March 1917.

46 Ibid., "Famous Citadel Now in Hands of Revolutionists," "French Approve Change in Russia," and "Prince Kropotkin," *Colonist,* 17 March 1917; "Settling Down in Petrograd," "Provinces Give Their Approval," and "Exiled Socialists Return to Russia," *Colonist,* 18 March 1917; Mandel, *Petrograd Workers and the Fall of the Old Regime,* 66; Knox, *With the Russian Army,* 553-92.

47 "Shortage of Bread – Crowds in Petrograd Engage in Mild Demonstrations Because of Scarcity," *Colonist,* 14 March 1917.

48 "Russian Revolt Was Expected," *Colonist,* 16 March 1916; "More Vigorous War Measures," *Colonist,* 17 March 1917. See also "Russian Revolution Is the Final Blow in Shattering Germany's Cherished Dreams of Domination," *Daily Times,* 17 March 1917.

49 "The Russian Revolution," *Colonist,* 16 March 1917.

50 "Revolution in Russia," *Colonist,* 17 March 1917.

51 William Rodney, "Broken Journey: Trotsky in Canada, 1917," *Queen's Quarterly* 74, 4 (Winter 1967): 649-65; Leon Trotsky, *My Life: An Attempt at an Autobiography* (New York: Charles Scribner's Sons, 1930), 279-85.

52 Trotsky to Miliukoff (Minister of Foreign Affairs), n.d. [1917], in Leon Trotsky, *V Plenu u Anglichan* [In British Captivity] (Petrograd, n.d.), reprinted as "In British Captivity," *The Class Struggle* (New York) 2, 4 (December 1918): 542-47; Trotsky, *My Life,* 280.

53 "Recollections of Captain F.C. Whiteman, RCE," *Ottawa Citizen,* 22 August 1940.

54 Trotsky, *V Plenu u Anglichan.*

55 Ibid.

56 "MI5 Detained Trotsky on Way to Revolution," *The Guardian* (Manchester), 5 July 2001.

57 "Russian Revolutionist Trotzky and Family Were in Nova Scotia for Several Weeks," *Halifax Herald,* 12 November 1917.

58 Trotsky, *My Life,* 284-85; Knox, *With the Russian Army,* 728.

59 Anweiler, *The Soviets,* 150; "Aprel'skiye tezisy" [April Theses], *Pravda* (Petrograd), 4 April 1917; Michael Pearson, *The Sealed Train* (New York: Putnam, 1975).

60 Mandel, *Petrograd Workers and the Fall of the Old Regime,* 112; William G. Rosenberg and Diane P. Koekner, "The Limits of Formal Protest: Worker's Activism and the Social Polarization in Petrograd and Moscow, March to October, 1917," *American Historical Review* 92, 2 (April 1987): 303.

61 Rosenberg and Koekner, "Limits of Formal Protest", 309.

62 Mandel, *Petrograd Workers and the Fall of the Old Regime,* 115-17.

63 "Russian Crisis Passes Safely," *BC Federationist,* 18 May 1917.

64 "The Oncoming Tread of the Proletariat Is Now Heard," *BC Federationist,* 4 May 1917.

65 "Briefs," *BC Federationist,* 4 May 1917.

66 Mandel, *Petrograd Workers and the Fall of the Old Regime,* 127-28.

67 Ibid.; Rosenberg and Koekner, "Limits of Formal Protest," 316; Alexander Kerensky, *The Crucifixion of Liberty* (New York: John Day, 1972), 364-69. For an eye-witness account of

the July Days, which is "mild compared with the description one read later in the foreign press," see Mackintosh Bell, *Side Lights on the Siberian Campaign*, 14-16.

68 Rosenberg and Koekner, "Limits of Formal Protest," 315; Mandel, *The Petrograd Workers and the Soviet Seizure of Power* (London: Macmillan, 1984), 213; Alexander Kerensky, *The Catastrophe: Kerensky's Own Story of the Russian Revolution* (New York: D. Appleton and Co., 1927), 271-76. During the April Crisis, Kornilov had ordered his garrison to fire on demonstrating workers and soldiers. A massacre was averted only because gunners refused to fire without the Soviet first counter-signing the order.

69 G. Pedroncini, *Les mutineries de 1917* (Paris: Presses universitaires de France, 1967); L.V. Smith, *Between Mutiny and Obedience: The Case of the French Fifth Infantry Division during World War I* (Princeton: Princeton University Press, 1994). A month earlier, on 14 March, France's minister of war, General Louis Lyautey, resigned in the face of parliamentary opposition to legislation calling for the re-examination of men rejected for service on grounds of poor health and "providing for the incorporation of priests into the fighting units." However, a *London Times* correspondent failed to anticipate the upheaval, noting "the universal look of confidence" on the face of French troops. See "Deputies Snub Gen. Lyautey," *Colonist*, 16 March 1917; "Leave Days of French Soldiers," *Colonist*, 18 March 1917.

70 Borden, *Memoirs*, 698. See also Speech to Parliament, 18 May 1917, Borden, *Canada at War: A Speech Delivered in Parliament by Rt. Hon. Sir Robert Borden* (Ottawa 1917), 30, Canadian Institute for Historical Microreproductions (hereafter cited as CIHM) no. 76128: "The unsettled political conditions in Russia undoubtedly have handicapped the effort on the eastern front, and thus enable Germany to make a greater effort on the western front."

71 Michael Kettle, *The Allies and the Russian Collapse, March 1917-March 1918* (London: Deutsch, 1981), 60-63.

72 Mandel, *Petrograd Workers and the Soviet Seizure of Power*, 244-47.

73 "Briefs," *BC Federationist*, 12 October 1917.

74 Koekner and Rosenberg, "Skilled Workers and the Strike Movement," 611.

75 Rosenberg and Koekner, "Limits of Formal Protest," 326.

76 Tirado, "Socialist Youth Movement in Revolutionary Petrograd," 154.

77 Mandel, *Petrograd Workers and the Soviet Seizure of Power*, 297 and 309.

78 "Trouble Looms in Petrograd," *Colonist*, 7 November 1917.

79 The *Colonist* took several days to straighten out the Bolshevik leader's first initial. Across North America, from 1917 to 1919, the labour and daily press used the phonetic spelling "Lenine."

80 "Another Russian Crisis," *Colonist*, 8 November 1917.

81 Ibid.

82 "Russian Radicals Upset Government and Assume Power," *Colonist*, 9 November 1917; Kerensky, *The Catastrophe*, 324-70.

83 "Russian Radicals Upset Government and Assume Power," *Colonist*, 9 November 1917.

84 Ibid.

85 "M. Lenine's Coup d'Etat," *Colonist*, 9 November 1917.

86 "No Change of Heart," *Tribune*, 6 February 1919.

87 Studies of the relationship between Bolshevism and Canada's working class include Balawyder, *Canadian-Soviet Relations between the Wars*, 22-34; Tim Buck, *Canada and the Russian Revolution: The Impact of the World's First Socialist Revolution on Labour and Politics in Canada* (Toronto: Progress Books, 1967).

88 "The Russian Revolution," *BC Federationist*, 23 March 1917.

89 "Sidelight on the Situation in Russia," *BC Federationist*, 22 June 1917.

90   "The Russian Revolution," *BC Federationist*, 23 March 1917.
91   Ibid.
92   "Suggestion for Labor's Programme throughout Canada," *BC Federationist*, 27 April 1917. See also "Soldier's Part in Revolution," *Colonist*, 17 March 1917.
93   "Coal Miners Sound Rallying Cry to Labor," *BC Federationist*, 11 May 1917.
94   "The Oncoming Tread of the Proletariat Is Now Heard," *BC Federationist*, 4 May 1917.
95   Ibid.
96   "Briefs," *BC Federationist*, 4 May 1917.
97   "Russian Crisis Safely Passes," *BC Federationist*, 18 May 1917.
98   "The Swedish Portent," *BC Federationist*, 8 June 1917.
99   Canada, *The Military Service Act, 1917* (Ottawa: J. de Labroquerie Taché, 1917); Machin, *Report of the Director of the Military Service Branch*, 147-48; Martin F. Auger, "On the Brink of Civil War: The Canadian Government and the Suppression of the 1918 Quebec Easter Riots," *Canadian Historical Review* 89, 4 (December 2008): 503-40.
100 "Action of Delegate to Montreal Endorsed," *BC Federationist*, 22 June 1917; "Briefs," *BC Federationist*, 15 June 1917.
101 The referendum ballot asked affiliated members: "Are you prepared to place in the hands of the executive of the British Columbia Federation of Labor the power to call a general strike in the event of conscription?" See "BC Federation of Labor Issues Referendum," *BC Federationist*, 8 June 1917; "Action of Delegate to Montreal Endorsed," *BC Federationist*, 22 June 1917; "First Unwilling Conscript to Be Signal for 'Down Tools,'" *BC Federationist*, 7 September 1917.
102 "Empress Theatre Meeting of June 13," *BC Federationist*, 15 June 1917.
103 "Israel Zangwill Scores Smug Pharisees," *BC Federationist*, 31 August 1917.
104 "Socialist Group of Japan Double Greeting," *BC Federationist*, 10 August 1917.
105 "Sidelight on the Situation in Russia," *BC Federationist*, 22 June 1917.
106 "New SDP Organizer Named," *BC Federationist*, 14 September 1917.
107 "First Unwilling Conscript to Be Signal for 'Down Tools,'" *BC Federationist*, 7 September 1917.
108 "Trades and Labor Council Favors Down Tools," *BC Federationist*, 21 September 1917.
109 "First Unwilling Conscript to Be Signal for 'Down Tools,'" *BC Federationist*, 7 September 1917.
110 "'Ginger' Goodwin's Size-Up," *BC Federationist*, 2 November 1917.
111 Canada, *Labour Gazette* 17, 12 (December 1917): 976, 984, 986; Susan Mayse, *Ginger: The Life and Death of Albert Goodwin* (Madeira Park, BC: Harbour, 1990), 124.
112 Mayse, *Ginger*, 103.
113 "Warning to Workers: Strike on at Trail," *BC Federationist*, 16 November 1917.
114 "Labor Council Does Not Endorse Appeal," *BC Federationist*, 22 March 1918; Roger Stonebanks, *Fighting for Dignity: The Ginger Goodwin Story* (St. John's: Canadian Committee on Labour History, 2004); Mayse, *Ginger*, 119-48.
115 "Trades and Labor Council Favors Down Tools," *BC Federationist*, 21 September 1917.
116 Borden, *Memoirs*, 715-16; Martin Robin, *Radical Politics and Canadian Labour, 1888-1930* (Kingston: Queen's University Industrial Relations Centre, 1968), 136-37. See also Borden, *Extension of the Term of Parliament*, 17 July 1917, CIHM reel 76107.
117 Borden, *Memoirs*, 708-9; Robin, "Registration, Conscription, and Independent Labour Politics," 60-77. See also Tarah Brookfield, "Divided by the Ballot Box: The Montreal Council of Women and the 1917 Election," *Canadian Historical Review* 89, 4 (December 2008): 473-501.
118 "Labor's Statement to the Electorate," *BC Federationist*, 9 November 1917.

119 Ernest J. Chambers, ed., *Canadian Parliamentary Guide* (Ottawa: Mortimer, 1918), 194-240.
120 "Everybody!" *BC Federationist*, 16 November 1917.
121 "Bolsheviki Infection Spreads," *BC Federationist*, 25 January 1918.
122 "Political Parties in Russia," *BC Federationist*, 15 February 1918; Canada, *Canada Gazette* (1918) (Ottawa: J. de Labroquerie Taché, 1917-19), 1295.
123 "Lenin's Doctrine Scares Ruling Class," *BC Federationist*, 14 December 1917.
124 "The Plute Press and the Russian Revolution," *BC Federationist*, 14 December 1917.
125 Ibid.
126 Mary Ellen Smith contested the constituency of Vancouver City, which had been vacated due to the death of her husband Ralph Smith, a former Nanaimo coal miner, Independent Labour MP, and one-time leader of the Trades and Labor Congress of Canada. Following her election, Mary Ellen Smith sat in the Liberal caucus and later served as the first female Cabinet minister in the British Empire. See Elizabeth Norcross, "Mary Ellen Smith: The Right Woman in the Right Place at the Right Time," in *Not Just Pin Money: Selected Essays on the History of Women's Work in British Columbia,* ed. Barbara K. Lantham and Roberta J. Pazdro, 357-64 (Victoria: Camosun College, 1984).
127 "A Bird's Eye View of the Situation and a Prophesy of What Is to Follow," *BC Federationist*, 11 January 1918.
128 "Hawthornthwaite Elected by Two to One," *BC Federationist*, 25 January 1919. Hawthornthwaite took 931 votes to 448 for Liberal candidate George Cavin.
129 "Sensational Speech at Columbia," *Tribune*, 20 January 1919; "Hawthornthwaite's Speech," *Tribune*, 23 January 1919; "Federated Labor Party Repudiate Statement," *Tribune*, 27 January 1919; "Mme. Breshkovskaya on Way to America," *Colonist*, 13 November 1918.
130 "Labor Convention Decides to Form United Working Class Political Party," *BC Federationist*, 1 February 1918.
131 "Working Men of British Columbia Need Only to Stand Fast to Have Control of the Government," *BC Federationist*, 1 March 1918.
132 "Federated Labor Party Alive On the Island," *BC Federationist*, 8 March 1918.
133 Ibid.
134 Borden to Cahan, 19 May 1918, LAC, Borden Papers, as quoted in Balawyder, *Canadian-Soviet Relations between the Wars*, 23-24; Beattie, "Canadian Intervention in Russia," 14.

Chapter 2: Vladivostok, 1917

1 The Muraviev-Amurski Peninsula, the landmass on which Vladivostok is situated, is located between Amurski Bay and Ussuriski Bay, in the body of water known as Peter the Great Bay on the northwestern coast of the Sea of Japan. Golden Horn Bay (*Zolotoi Rog* in Russian), named for its resemblance to Istanbul's Golden Horn, is a protected natural harbour on the peninsula and a hub of shipping and naval traffic. Vladivostok is also known in Chinese as *Haishenwai* [Sea Cucumber Cliffs]. See John J. Stephan, *The Russian Far East: A History* (Stanford: Stanford University Press, 1994), 8-16, 349-54; Amir Khisamutdinov, "Vladivostok: Window or Fortress?" in *The Russian Far East: Historical Essays* (Honolulu: Center for Russia in Asia, 1993), 131-50.
2 Judith Thornton and Charles E. Ziegler, eds., *Russia's Far East: A Region at Risk* (Seattle and London: National Association for Asiatic Research and University of Washington Press, 2002).
3 The Treaty of Peking (1860) confirmed Russia's claim, redrawing the Chinese-Russian border along modern lines. See Stephan, *Russian Far East*, 49.
4 Stephan, *Russian Far East*, 14-80; Erwin Lessner, *Cradle of Conquerors: Siberia* (Garden

City, NY: Doubleday and Company, 1955); David J. Nordlander, *For God and Tsar: A Brief History of Russian America, 1741-1867* (Anchorage: Alaska Natural History Association, 1994); Orcutt Frost, *Bering: The Russian Discovery of America* (New Haven, CT: Yale University Press, 2003). For the Treaty of Nerchinsk, 1689, which saw Russia recognize Chinese sovereignty and establish trade ties with the Qing dynasty, see V.S. Frank, "The Territorial Terms of the Sino-Russian Treaty of Nerchinsk, 1689," *Pacific Historical Review* 1, 3 (August 1947): 265-70. See also Vincent Chen, *Sino Russian Relations in the Seventeenth Century* (The Hague: Martinus Nijhoff, 1966). For Siberia's early history as a czarist penal colony, see George Kennan, *Siberia and the Exile System* (New York: Century Company, 1891). For British fears that Russia "had gone to enormous expense at Vladivostock [sic], in the hope of one day pouncing upon Australia or Vancouver Island," see Glynn Barratt, *Russian Shadows on the British Northwest Coast of North America, 1810-1890* (Vancouver: UBC Press, 1983), 134.

5 On the same trip, Nicholas II survived an assassination attempt in Nagasaki, suffering minor head wounds when a renegade police constable attacked him with a sword. See George Alexander Lensen, "The Attempt on the Life of Nicholas II in Japan," *Russian Review* 20, 3 (July 1961): 232-53.

6 For a contemporary account of the railroad's construction, see James Young Simpson, *Side-Lights on Siberia: Some Account of the Great Siberian Railroad, the Prisons and Exile System* (Edinburgh and London: William Blackwood and Sons, 1897), 16-60. See also Steven G. Marks, *Road to Power: The Trans-Siberian Railroad and the Colonization of Asian Russia, 1850–1917* (London: Taurus, 1991). For a description of the Trans-Siberian journey, see Mackintosh Bell, *Side Lights on the Siberian Campaign*, 18-33.

7 In 1900, Russia had sent troops into Manchuria as part of the international force to suppress the Boxer Rebellion. See Lanxin Xiang, *The Origins of the Boxer War* (New York: Routledge, 2003), 155-59. See also Alena N. Eskridge-Kosmach, "Russia in the Boxer Rebellion," *Journal of Slavic Military Studies* 21, 1 (January 2008): 38-52; Diana Preston, *The Boxer Rebellion: The Dramatic Story of China's War on Foreigners That Shook the World in the Summer of 1900* (New York: Berkley Books, 2001).

8 Michael Florinsky, "Twilight of Absolutism: 1905," *Russian Review* 8, 4 (October 1949): 329; Alexis R. Wiren, "The Lessons of Port Arthur," *Russian Review* 1, 2 (April 1942): 40-43; H.M.E. Brunker, *Story of the Russo-Japanese War, 1904-05* (London: Forster Groom, 1909); Christopher Martin, *The Russo-Japanese War* (London: Abelard-Schuman, 1967). Russia was forced to recognize Japanese influence over Korea, withdraw troops from Manchuria, and cede Port Arthur and half of Sakhalin Island to Japan.

9 Henry Reichman, "The 1905 Revolution on the Siberian Railroad," *Russian Review* 47, 1 (January 1988): 25.

10 Reichman, "The 1905 Revolution," 25-31. Between 1895 and 1904, 1,105,800 European Russians migrated to Siberia, a trend that intensified following the outbreak of war with Japan. Revolutionary pamphlets moved eastward to be consumed by railworkers, who were better educated and more literate than the general Siberian population: fully 82 percent of the workforce on the Trans-Baikal line could read, compared with 18 percent of Siberians generally.

11 Reichman, "The 1905 Revolution," 33-34.

12 Ibid., 34-36, 38.

13 "Vladivostok in Ruins," *International Herald Tribune*, 16 November 1905.

14 "Mutiny at Vladivostok," *New York Times*, 16 November 1905; "Ex-Prisoners Mutinous," and "Wouldn't Go to Vladivostok," *New York Times*, 21 November 1905; "Half Vladivostok

Burned," *New York Times*, 20 November 1905. See also Michael Florinsky, "Twilight of Absolutism: 1905," *Russian Review* 8, 4 (October 1949): 330; Reichman, "The 1905 Revolution," 42.

15 Reichman, "The 1905 Revolution," 43.

16 Bushnell, *Mutiny amid Repression*, 86; as quoted in Reichman, "The 1905 Revolution," 43.

17 Reichman, "The 1905 Revolution," 38-47.

18 Stephan, *Russian Far East*, 102-3.

19 "A Naval Battle at Vladivostok," *New York Times*, 31 October 1907; "Kumeric Arrives from the Orient," *Colonist*, 24 November 1907.

20 "Girls Instigated Mutiny: Curious Report Reaches Victoria about Vladivostok Troubles," *New York Times*, 25 November 1907; "A Naval Battle at Vladivostok," *New York Times*, 31 October 1907.

21 "More Anti-Jewish Riots," *New York Times*, 29 October 1907; "Murder for Revenge," *New York Times*, 20 January 1908; "Find Headquarters of the Terrorists," *New York Times*, 23 February 1907; "Duma to Czar," *Colonist*, 26 November 1907; Amy Knight, "Female Terrorists in the Russian Socialist Revolutionary Party," *Russian Review* 38, 2 (April 1979): 139-59; Stephan, *Russian Far East*, 101-7.

22 "That Expedition to Siberia," *Colonist*, 31 September 1900; "To Seek Gold in Siberia," *New York Times*, 14 May 1900.

23 "Big Russian Concession," *New York Times*, 5 April 1902; "To Mine Gold in Siberia," *New York Times*, 28 July 1902; Stephan, *Russian Far East*, 88; Thomas C. Owen, "Chukchi Gold: American Enterprise and Russian Xenophobia in the Northeastern Siberia Company," *Pacific Historical Review* 77, 1 (February 2008): 49-85.

24 Murby, "Canadian Economic Commission to Siberia," 382. Migration figures for 1895 to 1904 are provided in Reichman, "The 1905 Revolution," 28. Even following the outbreak of hostilities between Russia and Germany, and the chaotic conditions of war, Kunst and Albers maintained sales worth 40 million rubles in 1918.

25 C.F. Just report to Sir George Foster, 29 August 1918, "The Case of Kunst and Albers," 1, as quoted in Murby, "Canadian Economic Commission to Siberia," 383; Stephan, *Russian Far East*, 81-91.

26 MacLaren, *Canadians in Russia*, 225. See also "Development of Trade between Canada and Siberia," c. 1900, LAC, Department of Trade and Commerce Fonds, RG 20, ser. A-1, vol. 1215; "Clive Phillips-Wolley. Application for the Position as Commissioner to Siberia," 1895, LAC, RG 20, ser. A-1, vol. 1112, file 2249; Memorandum, Foreign Office, 24 July 1912, in Canada, *Documents on Canadian External Relations*, 1:15-16; David Davies, "The Pre-1917 Roots of Canadian-Soviet Relations," *Canadian Historical Review* 70, 2 (June 1989): 180-205.

27 "Desire of British Columbia Board of Trade that a Commissioner Be Sent to Siberia to Investigate Trade Prospects," c. 1901, LAC, RG 20, ser. A-1, vol. 1222.

28 Whyte to T.G. Shaughnessy, President CPR, 30 August 1901; Whyte to Shaughnessy, 5 September 1901, CPR Archives, copy in Centre for Research on Canadian-Russian Relations (hereafter cited as CRCR), ser. 1, sec. 1, pt. C, "Canadian Pacific Railway and Russia"; John Murray Gibbon, *Steel of Empire: The Romantic History of the Canadian Pacific, the Northwest Passage of Today* (Toronto: McClelland and Stewart, 1935), 355; "American Trade Helped by Siberian Railroad," *New York Times*, 19 November 1900.

29 Eva S. Balough, "Hesitant Encounter: Episodes from Early Russo-Canadian Trade Relations," *Canadian Slavonic Papers* 8 (1966): 216-30; Murby, "Canadian Economic Commission to Siberia," 375. In 1915, a shipment of piles for Siberia was halted at the Port of Vladivostok

because the ship, SS *Saxonia*, was operated by the German-owned Hamburg-American Line. See Thomas Mulvey (Under Secretary of State, Ottawa) to Deputy Minister of Justice (Ottawa), 8 March 1915, LAC, RG 13, Department of Justice Fonds, ser. A-2, vol. 192, file 475-1915, "Consignment of Piles on SS 'Saxonia' to Siberia Held at Vancouver."

30 W. Kaye Lamb, "Building Submarines for Russia in Burrard Inlet," *BC Studies* 7 (Autumn 1986): 3-26.

31 Cahan to Borden, 17 April 1915, LAC, Borden Papers, as quoted in Beattie, "Canadian Intervention in Russia," 14.

32 Balawyder, *Canadian-Soviet Relations between the Wars*, 3-4; Murby, "Canadian Economic Commission to Siberia," 375.

33 See Murby, "Canadian Economic Commission to Siberia." See also MacLaren, *Canadians in Russia*, 225; O. Mary Hill, *Canada's Salesman to the World: The Department of Trade and Commerce, 1892-1939* (Toronto and Montreal: Institute of Public Administration and McGill-Queen's University Press, 1977), 210-20.

34 Stephan, *Russian Far East*, 109; Marks, *Road to Power*, 174-205.

35 Canfield F. Smith, *Vladivostok under Red and White Rule: Revolution and Counterrevolution in the Russian Far East, 1920-1922* (Seattle: University of Washington Press, 1975), 4; Stephan, *Russian Far East*, 71-80.

36 Smele, "White Gold," 1317-47; "Loan of Allies," *Colonist*, 14 March 1917.

37 Smele, "White Gold," 1319.

38 "Cannot Get Labor to Discharge Cargo," *Colonist*, 15 March 1917.

39 B.I. Mukhachev, ed., *Dal' nii Vostok Rossii v period revoliutsii 1917 goda i grazhdanskoi voi ny* [The Far East of Russia in the Period of the Revolutions of 1917 and Civil War] (Vladivostok: Dal'nauka, 2003), 89. See also Mukhachev et al., eds., *Podgotovka i nachalo interventsii na Dal'nem Vostoke Rossii, oktiabr 1917-oktiabr 1918: Dokumenty i materialy* [Preparation and Beginning of the Intervention in the Far East of Russia, October 1917 to October 1918: Documents and Materials] (Vladivostok: Institute of History, Archeology and Ethnography of the Far Eastern Peoples, Russia Academy of Sciences, 1997).

40 Mukhachev, *Dal' nii Vostok Rossii*, 89 and 91; Stephan, *Russian Far East*, 111-12.

41 Stephan, *Russian Far East*, 111.

42 Ibid., 110.

43 Ibid., 110-13; Mukhachev, *Dal' nii Vostok Rossii*, 107. See also L.I. Belikova and S.A. Ivanov, eds., *Bor ba za vlast Sovetov v Primor e (1917-1922): Sbornik dokumentov* [The Struggle for Control of the Soviets in the Primor'ye (1917-1922): A Collection of Documents] (Vladivostok: Primorskoe knizhnoe izd-vo, 1955).

44 Mukhachev, *Dal' nii Vostok Rossii*, 90 and 114-15; Albert Rhys Williams, *Through the Russian Revolution* (New York: Boni and Liveright, 1921), 222-23.

45 Mukhachev, *Dal' nii Vostok Rossii*, 89-91.

46 Ibid., 91.

47 Mackintosh Bell, *Side Lights on the Siberian Campaign*, 38.

48 White, *Siberian Intervention*, 97-98; Bernard Pares, *My Russian Memoirs* (London: Jonathan Cape, 1931), 503; Bell, *Side Lights on the Siberian Campaign*, 57.

49 Murby, "Canadian Economic Commission to Siberia," 382.

50 "What Russia Will Do after the War Is Over," *BC Federationist*, 29 June 1917.

51 James Mackintosh Bell, a Harvard-trained geologist, worked in Siberia as a mining engineer prior to the war and was then attached to the British Intelligence Mission in Russia. See Mackintosh Bell, *Side Lights on the Siberian Campaign*, 27; "Obituary: James Mackintosh Bell," *Geographical Review* 24, 3 (July 1934): 535; "Sir George Bury," *Canadian Railway and Marine World* (November 1918), 492, Canadian Pacific Archives (copy in CRCR, ser. 1, sec.

1, pt. C, "Canadian Pacific Railway and Russia"); "Russia Through Eyes of Canadians," *Montreal Gazette*, 29 January 1918; "The Bolshevik Echo" and "Fourteen More Aliens Caught," *Montreal Star*, 29 July 1919.

52 Beattie, "Canadian Intervention in Russia," 76-77.

53 Lamb, "Building Submarines for Russia in Burrard Inlet," 20-21.

54 Mukhachev, *Dal' nii Vostok Rossii*, 93.

55 William Rodney, "Russian Revolutionaries in the Port of Vancouver, 1917," *BC Studies* 16 (Winter 1972/73): 25-31. See also Vadim Kukushkin, "Protectors and Watchdogs: Tsarist Consular Supervision of Russian-Subject Immigrants in Canada, 1900-1922," *Canadian Slavonic Papers* 44, 3-4 (September/December 2002): 209-32.

56 Mackintosh Bell, *Side Lights on the Siberian Campaign*, 39-43; MacLaren, *Canadians in Russia*, 178-79.

57 Mukhachev, *Dal' nii Vostok Rossii*, 119.

58 Ibid., 119-22.

59 Ibid., 96-103, 109, 122-24.

60 Ibid., 93.

61 Mukhachev, *Dal' nii Vostok Rossii*, 94-95 and 119; Minutes, 10-11 March 1917, Socialist Party of America National Executive Committee Minutes, *Socialist Party Bulletin* (Chicago), 1, 3 (March 1917): 10-12.

62 Mukhachev, *Dal' nii Vostok Rossii*, 96.

63 "Briefs," *BC Federationist*, 24 August 1917.

64 Kerensky, *The Catastrophe*, 271-76.

65 Mukhachev, *Dal' nii Vostok Rossii*, 92-93.

66 Stephan, *The Russian Far East*, 112-13.

67 Mackintosh Bell, *Side Lights on the Siberian Campaign*, 38.

68 On 10 June 1917, Menshevik D.F. Orzheshko succeeded Goldbreikh as chair of the Vladivostok Soviet. See Mukhachev, *Dal' nii Vostok Rossii*, 91.

69 Stephan, *Russian Far East*, 113.

70 Mackintosh Bell, *Side Lights on the Siberian Campaign*, 38.

71 Stephan, *Russian Far East*, 112. According to Mukhachev, Bolsheviks gained "a dominant position" in Vladivostok's unified Social Democratic Party, a process mirrored in nearby Nikolsk-Ussuriisk, while Mensheviks continued to hold sway in Khabarovsk, Blagoveshchensk, and Nikolayevsk-on-Amur. See Mukhachev, *Dal' nii Vostok Rossii*, 106.

72 Stephan, *Russian Far East*, 113; B.I. Mukhachev, *Aleksandr Krasnoshchekov: Istoriko-biograficheskii ocherk* [Aleksandr Krasnoshchekov: A Historico-Biographic Study] (Vladivostok: Far Eastern Division of the Russian Academy Sciences, 1999), 36.

73 Mukhachev, *Dal' nii Vostok Rossii*, 128-32.

74 Stephan, *Russian Far East*, 113.

75 Mukhachev, *Dal' nii Vostok Rossii*, 128-32; Mukhachev, *Aleksandr Krasnoshchekov*, 38; Stephan, *Russian Far East*, 342.

76 Mukhachev, *Dal' nii Vostok Rossii*, 133-37.

77 Ibid., 110.

78 Ibid., 125-27. A *desyatina* was equal to 1.09254 kilograms, while a *pood* was equal to 16.38 kilograms. Both units of measurement were abolished in 1924 when the Soviet Union adopted the metric system.

79 Evidence suggests that a majority of Siberia's 13 million inhabitants belonged to cooperatives in the wake of the 1917 revolutions and, in the city of Chita, the membership in cooperatives was "one hundred percent." See Pares, *My Russian Memoirs*, 505, 519-21; Canada, Department of Trade and Commerce, *Report of the Canadian Economic Commission*

(Siberia) (Ottawa: J. de Labroquerie Taché, 1919), app. D, "Report of the Joint Meeting Held with the Representatives of the Co-operatives at Vladivostok on Wednesday, March 5, 1919."

80 Mukhachev, *Dal' nii Vostok Rossii,* 127.
81 Ibid., 113-19. See also Mackintosh Bell, *Side Lights on the Siberian Campaign,* 37-38.
82 Mukhachev, *Dal' nii Vostok Rossii,* 117-19.
83 Mackintosh Bell, *Side Lights on the Siberian Campaign,* 43-46, 50-54. On 28 November 1917, Mackintosh Bell received a message from the 9th Company of the 4th Artillery Regiment in the Fortress of Vladivostok, stating that the "government in power after Nicholas II did not fulfill their promises or carry out the demands of the newly-awakened nation."
84 Carl W. Ackerman, *Trailing the Bolsheviki: Twelve Thousand Miles with the Allies in Siberia* (New York: Scribner, 1919), 42; Beattie, "Canadian Intervention in Russia," 352-53.
85 As quoted in Mukhachev, *Dal' nii Vostok Rossii,* 135.
86 Mukhachev, *Dal' nii Vostok Rossii,* 135-36.
87 Ibid., 135-36.
88 Ibid., 138-39.
89 Stephan, *Russian Far East,* 114.
90 Mukhachev, *Aleksandr Krasnoshchekov,* 49-50.
91 White, *Siberian Intervention,* 97.
92 Pavel Aleksandrovich Novikov, *Grazhdanskaya voina v Vostochnoi Sibiri* [The Civil War in Eastern Siberia] (Moscow: Tsentrpoligraf, 2005), 21-39; James Morley, *The Japanese Thrust into Siberia, 1918* (New York: Columbia University Press, 1957), 75.
93 Mukhachev, *Aleksandr Krasnoshchekov,* 55; Stephan, *Russian Far East,* 114-15 and 121-22; Morley, *Japanese Thrust into Siberia,* 74; Novikov, *Grazhdanskaya voina v Vostochnoi Sibiri.*
94 Stephan, *Russian Far East,* 114; Pereira, *White Siberia,* 45.
95 Balawyder, *Canadian-Soviet Relations between the Wars,* 4-5; Pereira, *White Siberia,* 45; "Briefs," *BC Federationist,* 1 February 1918; Beattie, "Canadian Intervention in Russia," 352; MacLaren, *Canadians in Russia,* 127; Kettle, *Allies and the Russian Collapse,* 200-1.

Chapter 3: The Road to Intervention
For the inspiration for this chapter title, see Kettle, *Road to Intervention.*
1 "Kerensky Goes to England," *Colonist,* 7 November 1917.
2 "Canadian 'Syren' Party, Northern Russian Expeditionary Force (The Murman Front)," and "Canadian 'Elope' Party, Northern Russian Expeditionary Force (Archangel Front)" (both in LAC, RG 24, vol. 1872, file 15); Silverlight, *Victors' Dilemma.*
3 Massey, *When I Was Young,* 200.
4 "What Causes Revolution?" *Tribune,* 27 January 1919. See also "An Open Letter to Catherine Breshkovska," *Tribune,* 10 February 1919.
5 "Empire War Council Meets Tomorrow," *Colonist,* 18 March 1917; George M. Wrong, "Canada and the Imperial War Cabinet," *Canadian Historical Review* 1, 1 (1920): 3-25. On 19 June 1918, Lord Curzon said that, in the past 474 days, the Cabinet had held 555 meetings, guided by the principal "to postpone nothing until to-morrow which could be decided to-day." For the difficulties involved in managing the quantity of paperwork at these meetings, see Borden to Lloyd George, 16 August 1918, Canada, *Documents on Canadian External Relations,* 1:358.
6 Kerensky, *The Catastrophe,* 324-70. Several Cossack units under the command of General Krasnov were easily defeated at Pulkovskiye Heights by Red Guards under the direction of Lenin.

7 Robert Laird Borden, *Memoirs* (Toronto: Macmillan, 1938), 692-93; Kettle, *Allies and the Russian Collapse*, 200-209. See also Silverlight, *Victors' Dilemma*, 12-16; Evan Mawdsley, *The Russian Civil War* (Boston: Allen and Unwin, 1987). On 16 January 1918, British prime minister David Lloyd George asked a meeting of Allied leaders: "Who can overthrow the Bolsheviks?" See Kerensky, *Crucifixion of Liberty*, 353.

8 "Official Proceedings of the Eight Annual Convention of the BCF of L," *BC Federationist*, 1 February 1918.

9 Silverlight, *Victors' Dilemma*, 23. In February 1918, as the Allied expatriates in Petrograd grew increasingly afraid, Canadian trade commissioner Constantin Just fled to Finland aboard a special train, making his way via Scandinavia and Britain to Canada before joining the Canadian Siberian Economic Commission in Vladivostok in autumn that year. See Hill, *Canada's Salesman to the World*, 216-17.

10 Kettle, *Allies and the Russian Collapse*, 213-15.

11 Morley, *Japanese Thrust into Siberia*, 60-61, 63.

12 The Japanese arrived first, when the ship *Iwami* reached the ice-clogged harbour of Vladivostok on the morning of 12 January 1919. Two days later, the HMS *Suffolk* landed from Hong Kong. A second Japanese ship, the *Asahi*, reached the city on 18 January and became the rear admiral's fleetship. See Morley, *Japanese Thrust into Siberia*, 60-63; Silverlight, *Victors' Dilemma*, 17-18; MacLaren, *Canadians in Russia*, 126.

13 White, *Siberian Intervention*, 97. According to a labour report, the Allies occupied Harbin "because the Bolsheviki closed the Red Light district. It was owned by Japanese capitalists. So the Northern Government of China, which is completely subject to the will of the Allies, sent troops to Harbin. Now the Red Light district is open as ever." See "Sidelights on the Invasion of Russia," *Tribune*, 13 March 1919.

14 Silverlight, *Victors' Dilemma*, 17-23; Morley, *Japanese Thrust into Siberia*, 60-61.

15 John Ward, *With the "Die-Hards" in Siberia* (London: Cassell, 1920), 1. See also Bernard Pares, "John Ward: Obituary," *Slavonic and East European Review* 13, 39 (April 1935): 680-83.

16 Ward, *With the "Die-Hards" in Siberia*, 8.

17 *The New Europe*, 20 December 1917, reprinted in F. Seymour Cocks, ed., *The Secret Treaties and Understandings* (London: Union of Democratic Control, n.d. [c. 1918]), 10. See also Leon Trotsky, *Socheneniya* [Collected Works], 3, no. 2 (Moscow: State Publishing House, 1924), 64.

18 Sir John Wheeler-Bennett, *Brest-Litovsk: The Forgotten Peace, March 1918* (London: Macmillan, 1938). Knox, *With the Russian Army*, 723-40; Kettle, *Allies and the Russian Collapse*, 250-69; "Address of Russian Workers Stating the Case," *BC Federationist*, 19 April 1918.

19 MacLaren, *Canadians in Russia*, 127.

20 Novikov, *Grazhdanskaya voina v Vostochnoi Sibiri*, 53-63; Stephan, *Russian Far East*, 120-22; Williams, *Through the Russian Revolution*, 234-39; Jamie Bisher, *White Terror: Cossack Warlords of the Trans-Siberian* (London: Routledge, 2005).

21 Skuce, *CSEF*, 34.

22 Williams, *Through the Russian Revolution*, 220.

23 Ibid., 228-33, 237-38.

24 "Tokio Points Out Danger in Siberia," *New York Times*, 19 March 1918.

25 Morley, *Japanese Thrust into Siberia*, 74.

26 "Tokio Points Out Danger in Siberia," *New York Times*, 19 March 1918.

7 The repudiation of the czar's war loans was announced by the Bolshevik government on 10 February 1918. The total value of these loans appears in G.G. Shvittau, *Revolutsiya i Narodnoe Khoziaistvo v Rossii, 1917-1921* [The Revolution and National Economy in

Russia] (Leipzig: Tsentral'noe kooperativnoe izdatel'stvo, 1922), 337, as quoted in Richard Pipes, *The Russian Revolution* (New York: Vintage Books, 1990), 578; Kettle, *Allies and the Russian Collapse*, 228. A contemporary discussion appeared in Henry Hazlitt, "Repudiation," *Nation*, 21 February 1918, 220.

28 Kettle, *Allies and the Russian Collapse*, 228. See also N. Nordman, "The Finances of Russia," *Echo* (Vladivostok), 13 April 1919, reprinted in Canada, *Report of the Canadian Economic Commission (Siberia)*, app. F, "Report on Financial Conditions in Siberia," 61.

29 "The Alarming Spectre of Repudiation," *BC Federationist*, 8 March 1918.

30 "Why They Fear the Bolsheviki," *BC Federationist*, 15 March 1918.

31 Kettle, *Road to Intervention*, 30.

32 Kettle, *Allies and the Russian Collapse*, 176-219; Kettle, *Road to Intervention*, 30-31.

33 Kettle, *Road to Intervention*, 35.

34 "The Consul at Vladivostok to the Secretary of State," 5 April 1918, United States of America, *Foreign Relations of the United States*, vol. 2, *1918 Russia* (Washington: United States Government Printing Office: 1932), 100; David R. Woodward, "The British Government and Japanese Intervention in Russia during World War I," *Journal of Modern History*, 46 (December 1974): 663-85.

35 Connaughton, *Republic of the Ushakovko*, 36-40; Pereira, *White Siberia*, 53; Kettle, *Road to Intervention*, 35.

36 "Directives to the Vladivostok Soviet," 7 April 1918, in V.I. Lenin, *Collected Works*. vol. 27, 3rd English ed. (Moscow: Progress Publishers, 1965), 226.

37 James Mackintosh Bell, discussion with Stuart Tompkins, 22 April 1918, in Stuart Ramsey Tompkins, *A Canadian's Road to Russia: Letters from the Great War Decade*, ed. Doris H. Pieroth (Edmonton: University of Alberta Press, 1989), 331.

38 "Briefs," *BC Federationist*, 19 April 1918.

39 "Jap Ambassador Roasts Jingoists," *BC Federationist*, 26 April 1918.

40 A. Denikine, *The White Army*, trans. Catherine Zvegintzov (Gulf Breeze, FL: Academic International, 1973); Viktor G. Bortnevski, "White Administration and White Terror (The Denekin Period)," *Russian Review* 52 (July 1993): 354-66; Connaughton, *Republic of the Ushakovko*, 70, 79, 88, and 98.

41 "150,000 Finn Reds Resisting Germany," *New York Times*, 19 March 1918.

42 Richard Luckett, *The White Generals: An Account of the White Movement and the Russian Civil War* (Edinburgh: Longman, 1971), 196-208.

43 "Tokio Points Out Danger in Siberia," *New York Times*, 19 March 1918.

44 Mackintosh Bell, *Side Lights on the Siberian Campaign*, 84-86.

45 "Britain States Aims in Russia," *Colonist*, 30 July 1918; "Ask Horvath to Yield Dictatorship Claims," *New York Times*, 16 July 1918; "Menace to Czechs Lifted – Pro-Ally Forces Control Railways from Vladivostok to Point on Volga," *New York Times*, 8 September 1918; "Tokio Points Out Danger in Siberia," *New York Times*, 19 March 1918; Mukhachev, *Aleksandr Krasnoshchekov*, 85; MacLaren, *Canadians in Russia*, 134; Pereira, *White Siberia*, 54, 73; Pares, *My Russian Memoirs*, 503.

46 "Ask Horvath to Yield Dictatorship Claims," *New York Times*, 16 July 1918.

47 See Pares, *My Russian Memoirs*, 502-504; "Elect Mazaryk First President," *Colonist*, 13 November 1918. Masaryk escaped from Vladivostok under the pseudonym Thomas Marsden.

48 Hoyt, *Army without a Country*, 88-92; Leon Trotsky, *The Military Writings and Speeches of Leon Trotsky*, vol. 1, *1918: How the Revolution Armed* (London: New Park, 1979), 275-305.

49 Novikov, *Grazhdanskaya voina v Vostochnoi Sibiri*, 63-73; John F.N. Bradley, *The Czecho-slovak Legion in Russia, 1914-1920* (Boulder: East European Monographs, 1991); Con-naughton, *Republic of the Ushakovko*, 36-40; Hoyt, *Army without a Country*; Victor M. Fic, *The Bolsheviks and the Czechoslovak Legion: The Origin of Their Armed Conflict, March–May 1918* (New Delhi: Abhinav Publications, 1978); Betty Miller Unterberger, *The United States, Revolutionary Russia, and the Rise of Czechoslovakia* (Chapel Hill: University of North Carolina Press, 1989); John Swettenham, *Allied Intervention in Russia, 1918-19* (Toronto: Ryerson Press, 1967), 88-94; MacLaren, *Canadians in Russia*, 134; "Threaten Russia over Czech Troops," *New York Times*, 13 July 1918.

50 Kettle, *Road to Intervention*, 222.

51 MacLaren, *Canadians in Russia*, 134.

52 Williams, *Through the Russian Revolution*, 247.

53 "The Red Funeral of Vladivostok," *BC Federationist*, 13 December 1918 (reprinted from the *New Republic*). For another account, by Dorothy Findlay, wife of British trade repre-sentative John Findlay, see Dorothy Findlay letter, 1 July 1918, in "Letters from Vladivostok, 1918-1923," *Slavonic and East European Review* 45, 105 (July 1967): 497-502.

54 Mukhachev, *Aleksandr Krasnoshchekov*, 85-86; Stephan, *Russian Far East*, 123-25.

55 "Acts of Brutality" and "Official Report – International Commission of Physicians," 15 December 1918, War Diary of General Staff CEF(S), March 1919, app. 36; Mackintosh Bell, *Side Lights on the Siberian Campaign*, 72-73.

56 "The Red Funeral of Vladivostok," *BC Federationist*, 13 December 1918; Mackintosh Bell, *Side Lights on the Siberian Campaign*, 75.

57 MacLaren, *Canadians in Russia*, 134.

58 "Siberian War Cabinet Chosen by Horvath," *New York Times*, 15 July 1918; "Ask Horvath to Yield Dictatorship Claims," *New York Times*, 16 July 1918; "Britain States Aims in Russia," *Colonist*, 30 July 1918; Mackintosh Bell, *Side Lights on the Siberian Campaign*, 87-90, 97-102; MacLaren, *Canadians in Russia*, 134; Pereira, *White Siberia*, 54, 73; B.I. Mukhachev et al., eds., *Kolchak i interventsiia na Dal'nem Vostoke: Dokumenty i materialy* [Kolchak and the Inter-vention in the Far East: Documents and Materials] (Vladivostok: Institute of History, Ar-cheology and Ethnography of the Far Eastern People, Russian Academy of Sciences, 1995).

59 Beattie, "Canadian Intervention in Russia," 67.

60 Kettle, *Road to Intervention*, 220-21.

61 Ibid., 222. See also Wrong, "Canada and the Imperial War Cabinet," 19.

62 Nicholson, *Official History of the Canadian Army*, 362-76; Ward, *With the "Die-Hards" in Siberia*, 8; "Allied Intervention in Siberia and Russia," 2 July 1918, LAC, RG 9, ser. III-A-3, vol. 362, file A3, SEF (file 115); Betty Miller Unterberger, "The Russian Revolution and Wilson's Far-Eastern Policy," *Russian Review* 16, 2 (April 1957): 35-46; Nicholson, *Official History of the Canadian Army*, 519; Stephan, *Russian Far East*, 127-29; "US and Japan Give Plan to Aid Russia," *Washington Post*, 4 August 1918.

63 MacLaren, *Canadians in Russia*, 138.

64 On 9 July, Privy Council president Newton Rowell received a request from the War Office, London, regarding Canadian participation in Siberia. General Sydney Mewburn, minister of militia and defence, wrote to Borden on 12 July, discussing the Canadian contingent and "trade conditions" in Siberia, and he attached a letter from London proposing the composition of the Canadian force. See Redcliffe to Rowell, 9 July 1919, Mewburn to Borden, 12 July 1919, Redcliffe to Mewburn, 12 July 1919, Mewburn to Militia (Ottawa), 12 July 1919 (all in LAC, Borden Papers, MG 26, H1[a], vol. 103); LAC, RG 9, ser. III-A-S, vol. 362, file A3, SEF (file 117); Mewburn to Gwatkin, 13 July 1918, Gwatkin to Mewburn, 16 July

1918 (both in LAC, RG 24, ser. C-1-A, vol. 2557, file HQC-2514 [vol. 1]); MacLaren, *Canadians in Russia*, 139 and 144. See also Canada, *Documents on Canadian External Relations*, 1:206-15.

65 MacLaren, *Canadians in Russia*, 140.

66 "Ex-Csar of Russia Killed by Order of Ural Soviet," *New York Times*, 20 July 1918; Hopkins, *Canadian Annual Review of Public Affairs* (1918), 50; Paul Bulygin, *Murder of the Romanovs: The Authentic Account* (London: Hutchinson, 1935). Yekaterinburg fell to the Czechs in August 1918. By December, reports surfaced from London suggesting that the execution of the Romanovs was a lie created by the Bolsheviks for propaganda purposes and that the czar and his family were living safely in a location known to Allied authorities. See "Claim Now Is Made Russian Ex-Czar and Family Are Alive," *Daily Times,* 27 December 1918; "Czar Reported Still Alive," *Nanaimo Free Press*, 27 December 1918.

67 Doherty to Borden, 28 July 1919, LAC, Borden Papers, MG 26, H1(a), vol. 103, reel 4333; Borden and MacQuarrie, *Robert Laird Borden*, 2:146; MacLaren, *Canadians in Russia*, 140. The authorization and administration of the Canadian contingent are discussed in Ian C.D. Moffat, "Forgotten Battlefields: Canadians in Siberia, 1918-1919," *Canadian Military Journal* 8, 3 (Autumn 2007): 73-86. In late July, the British government had irritated Borden when it sent a telegram regarding expenses for the Siberian force directly to Canada's governor general, Lord Cavendish, without communicating first with Borden or his Cabinet. See Borden to White, 25 July 1919, LAC, RG 24, ser. C-1-A, vol. 2557, file HQC-2514 (vol. 1).

68 "Briefs," *BC Federationist*, 26 July 1918.

69 "Britain States Aims in Russia," *Colonist*, 30 July 1918.

70 Order of the People's Commissar of Military and Naval Affairs, 15 July 1918, no. 561, in Trotsky, *Military Writings and Speeches*, 1:407; Smele, "White Gold," 1319-21. After Kazan was taken, White forces bickered over control of the gold, which was transferred from Kazan, to Ufa, to Chelyabinsk, finally ending up in Omsk in late September 1918. Prior to the fall of Kazan, the Bolsheviks had planned to transport the gold up the Volga to Moscow.

71 Ward, *With the "Die-Hards" in Siberia*, 4-52; Mukhachev, *Aleksandr Krasnoshchekov*, 94; Mackintosh Bell, *Side Lights on the Siberian Campaign*, 76-83; "British Troops Land at Vladivostok," *New York Times*, 8 August 1918; "Allies' Forces Move in Siberia," *Colonist*, 22 August 1918; "Inflict Defeat on Bolsheviki," *Colonist*, 27 August 1918. In the wake of this Allied victory, two battalions of Chinese troops were deployed as a permanent guard along the Ussuri Railway. See Knox to Chief of General Staff (hereafter cited as CGS) (Ottawa), 12 December 1918, LAC, RG 24, ser. C-1-A, vol. 2557, file HQC-2514 (vol. 2). In the midst of the Ussuri battles, the War Office sent an "urgent appeal" to Mewburn "to dispatch troops in advance to Siberia owing to the critical position of the Czechs about Lake Baikal." See Elmsley to Mewburn, 31 August 1918, LAC, RG 24, ser. C-1-A, vol. 2557, file HQC-2514 [vol. 1]). See also Mewburn to Burrell, 10 August 1918, Gwatkin to Mewburn, 13 August 1918, Kemp to Elmsley, 28 August 1918 (all in LAC, RG 24, ser. C-1-A, vol. 2557, file HQC-2514 [vol. 1]); "Czecho-Slovaks Are Forced Back," *Colonist*, 20 August 1918.

72 "Allied Forces Control in North," *Colonist*, 6 August 1918; "Strikes Blow at Bolsheviki," *Colonist*, 9 August 1918.

73 "Soviets Arrest British Consul," *Colonist*, 10 August 1918; "Trotzky Ready to Declare War," *New York Times*, 9 August 1918.

74 "The Week," *The Nation* (New York), 31 August 1918, 213.

75 The one thousand troops in Britain's 25th Middlesex Regiment left garrison duty in Hong Kong for Vladivostok; they were later joined by the nine hundred-strong 1/9 Hampshire

Regiment and served under Elmsley and the Canadian command. Japan's presence in eastern Siberia represented the largest foreign contingent in Russia, with General Kikuzo Otani's providing overall leadership to Allied forces in the region. The Allied campaign in western Siberia, on the active front against the Red Army in the Ural Mountains, was led by French general Maurice Janin and was composed heavily of Czecho-Slovak and White Russian troops. The American force, originally pegged at seven thousand, rose to twelve thousand. In Siberia, the Czecho-Slovak Legion numbered fifty-five thousand, joining over 200,000 White Russian troops. See Hopkins, *Canadian Annual Review of Public Affairs* (1919), 53; "Bolsheviki Lose Hold on Russia," *Colonist*, 16 August 1918; "Siberia Force to Be Composite," *Colonist*, 25 August 1918; Kettle, *Road to Intervention*, 301; MacLaren, *Canadians in Russia*, 137, 181; Skuce, *CSEF*, 6-7; Swettenham, *Allied Intervention in Russia*, 126-27.

76 See Canada, *Documents on Canadian External Relations*, 1:207-09; PC 1983 and PC 2073, LAC, RG 24, ser. C-1-A, vol. 2557, file HQC-2514 (vol. 1). Subsequent orders of 23 August 1918 (PC 2073) and 5 September 1918 (PC 2151) augmented the original force. In early August, at the request of the chief cable censor in Washington, Canadian censors at Bamfield, Montreal, Halifax, Canso, and North Sydney had suppressed wireless reports of the Japanese-American decision to intervene in Siberia. See Director of Cable Censorship (Ottawa) to Censor, 4 August 1918 and Director of Cable Censorship (Ottawa) to Chambers, 5 August 1918, LAC, RG 24, ser. C-1-A, vol. 2566, file HQC-2698. See also Censor (North Sydney) to Director of Cable Censorship (Ottawa), 6 August 1918, Censor (Halifax) to Director of Cable Censorship (Ottawa), 7 August 1918, ZCC to Ben Deacon (Deputy Chief Censor), 8 August 1918, Director of Cable Censorship (Ottawa) to Censor, 9 August 1918 (all in LAC, RG 24, ser. C-1-A, vol. 2566, file HQC-2698); MacLaren, *Canadians in Russia*, 141; "Plan for Siberia Is Almost Ready," *Colonist*, 6 August 1918; "Draws Up Plans for Russian Aid," *Colonist*, 8 August 1918.

77 "Canada to Send Force 4,000 Strong to Help Russia in Siberia," *Colonist*, 13 August 1918; Hopkins, *Canadian Annual Review of Public Affairs* (1918), 419; Skuce, *CSEF*, 7-8; Massey, *When I Was Young*, 202. For details on the shipment of ammunition, see Major-General for Military Secretary to Naval Secretary, 16 August 1918, LAC, RG 24, vol. 3969, file NSC 1047-14-26 (vol. 1). The military also arranged for the shipment of "articles of clothing as [were] issued for winter wear in Canada." See Deputy Minister of Militia and Defence to Under Secretary of State for External Affairs, 13 August 1918, LAC, RG 24, ser. C-1-A, vol. 2557, file HQC-2514 (vol. 1).

78 Hopkins, *Canadian Annual Review of Public Affairs* (1918), 419.

79 Mewburn to Borden, 13 August 1918, LAC, Borden Papers, MG 26, H1(a), vol. 103, reel 4333. Uncertainty was also clear in a letter from Elmsley to Mewburn, which asked for permission to proceed to Vladivostok before any troops: "Here [in London], or in Canada, it is difficult or well nigh impossible to pick up the knowledge of facts and factors, which I should be thoroughly au fait with, before Canadian troops are committed to any action." See Elmsley to Mewburn, 31 August 1918, LAC, RG 24, ser. C-1-A, vol. 2557, file HQC-2514 (vol. 1).

80 "Albert Goodwin Shot and Killed by Police Officer Near Comox Lake," *BC Federationist*, 2 August 1918; Mayse, *Ginger*, 160-70; Stonebanks, *Fighting for Dignity*.

81 "German or British – Which?" *Sun*, 2 August 1918.

82 "Albert Goodwin Shot and Killed by Police Constable Near Comox Lake" and "Trades and Labor Council Endorse 24-Hr. Protest," *BC Federationist*, 2 August 1918; "Labor Temple Scene of Trouble and Rioting" and "A Statement to the Public by the Executive of the Trades and Labor Council," *BC Federationist*, 9 August 1918; Paul A. Phillips, *No Power*

Greater: A Century of Labour in British Columbia (Vancouver: BC Federation of Labour and the Boag Foundation, 1967), 72-74.

83 "Goodwin Buried at Cumberland," *BC Federationist*, 9 August 1918; Mayse, *Ginger*, 181-85.

84 "Labor Convention Decides to Form United Working Class Political Party," *BC Federationist*, 1 February 1918; "Working Class Conference Organizes Political Party," *BC Federationist*, 8 February 1918; "Federated Labor Party Alive on the Island," *BC Federationist*, 8 March 1918.

85 For organizational gains in various industries, see Minutes, June–August 1918, UVASC, VLC Fonds, acc. 80-59, box 3; *BC Federationist*, June to August 1918. See also "The Labour Situation in Canada," *The Nation* (New York), 7 September 1918, 253-54.

86 "Will Sit on Capital Steps until They Are Heard," *BC Federationist*, 15 February 1918.

87 Minutes, 7 August 1918, UVASC, VLC Fonds, 80-59, box 3; "The Week under Ban," *Colonist*, 21 July 1918; "Intervention in Russia," *Week* (Victoria), 20 July 1918, and "Here We Are Again!" *Week*, 1 May 1920; "Labour Militant," *Tribune*, 13 January 1919; F. Seymour Cocks, ed., *The Secret Treaties and Understandings* (London: Union of Democratic Control, n.d. [c. 1918]).

88 "Editorial," *BC Federationist*, 9 August 1918; "BC Federationist Will Change Tune," *Colonist*, 7 August 1918.

89 PC 146, 17 January 1917, Consolidated Orders Respecting Censorship, *Supplement to the Canada Gazette* (3 February 1919); Gregory S. Kealey, "State Repression of Labour and the Left in Canada, 1914-20: The Impact of the First World War," *Canadian Historical Review* 73, 3 (1992): 281-314.

90 "Arrest of Naylor at Cumberland," *BC Federationist*, 16 August 1918; "Naylor Is Found Not Guilty at Nanaimo," *BC Federationist*, 11 October 1918; "Naylor Found 'Not Guilty,'" *Tribune*, 14 October 1918. The grand jury at the Nanaimo Assizes threw out the charges against Naylor on the grounds of insufficient evidence.

91 Minutes, 17 January 1917, UVASC, VLC Fonds, acc. 80-58, box 3.

92 "Returned Soldier Defeats All Comers," *BC Federationist*, 5 July 1918; Elections British Columbia, *An Electoral History of British Columbia, 1871-1986* (Victoria: Elections British Columbia, 1988), 136. Giolma took 3,624 votes to 1,359 for Langley, 1,001 for Conservative candidate Richard Perry, and 71 for Independent Socialist candidate John "Jack" McDonald.

93 Minutes, 17 July 1918, UVASC, VLC Fonds, acc. 80-58, box 3.

94 Minutes, 17 July 1918, 14 August 1918, 16 September 1918, 8 January 1919, UVASC, VLC Fonds.

95 Minutes, 7 September 1918, UVASC, VLC Fonds, acc. 80-58, box 3.

96 "Mobs in Toronto Demolish Cafes," *Colonist*, 4 August 1918; "Toronto Mobs Give Trouble," *Colonist*, 7 August 1918.

97 Gerald Friesen, "Yours in Revolt: Regionalism, Socialism, and the Western Canadian Labour Movement," *Labour/Le Travail* 1 (1976): 141.

98 See "Trades and Labor Congress Expresses Fear of the Masses – Demagogic Talk," *The Worker* (Toronto), 30 September 1933.

99 "Delegates to Trade Congress Make Report to Central Body," *BC Federationist*, 4 October 1918.

100 Ibid.

101 "To Extirpate Bolshevism," *Toronto Globe*, 11 October 1918.

102 C.H. Cahan to C.J. Doherty, 14 September 1918, Cahan to Doherty, 20 July 1918, Borden to Cahan, 17 September 1918 (all in LAC, MG 28, Borden Papers, vol. 104, as cited in

Balawyder, *Canadian-Soviet Relations between the Wars*, 24); C.H. Cahan, *Socialistic Propaganda in Canada: Its Purposes, Results and Remedies*, Address delivered to St. James Literary Society, Montreal, 12 December 1918 (Montreal: n.d. [c. 1918]); Joshua Bennet, "Canadian National Security: Legislations vs. Practices 1919-1946," paper presented to the Conference of Defence Associations 6th Annual Graduate Defence Symposium, October 2003.

103 Canada, *Canada Gazette* (1918), 1278.
104 Ibid., 1278.
105 Ibid.
106 Ibid., 1295.
107 "Political Parties in Russia," *BC Federationist*, 15 February 1918.
108 Canada, *Canada Gazette* (1918), 1461.
109 Ibid., 1294-96, 1379, 1391, 1525, and 1626.
110 Ibid., 5 October 1918 and 26 October 1918, 1295 and 1525.
111 Ibid., 1444; "Anti-Strike Order Passed," *Toronto Globe*, 12 October 1918; "May Draft Men Who Stop Work," *Colonist*, 22 October 1918.
112 "The Suppression of the Social Democratic Party," *Tribune*, 17 October 1918; "Social Democratic and Social Labor Parties Dissolved" and "The Strike at Calgary," *Tribune*, 14 October 1918. For Woodward's political views, see "The Good and Bad of Bolshevism," *Tribune*, 13 February 1919 and 3 March 1919, University of British Columbia Special Collections, Eugene S. Woodward Fonds.

Chapter 4: Mobilization

1 "Major-Gen. Elmsley to Be Here Wednesday," *Tribune*, 7 October 1918; MacLaren, *Canadians in Russia*, 146; LAC, Department of Employment and Immigration Fonds, RG 76, ser. C-1-E, Ships' Passenger Manifests, reel T-4731. In New York, the head of the British-Canadian Recruiting Mission held a dinner for departing CEFS officers at the Hotel Vanderbilt, followed by a theatre party at the New Amsterdam Theater. See "Dinner to Canada's Siberia Force," *New York Times*, 18 September 1918.
2 Elmsley to Defensor, 9 April 1919, War Diary of General Staff CEF(S), April 1919, app. 8.
3 For details on the composition of the force, see "The Force Dispatched to Siberia," n.d., LAC, RG 24, vol. 1741, file DHS 4-20; "Disposition of Officers, NCO's and Other Ranks of the Canadian Expeditionary Force in Siberia, Friday, January 31st, 1919," LAC, RG 24, vol. 1872, file 15; "Memorandum Respecting the Organization and Status of the Proposed Canadian Siberian Expeditionary Force," n.d. [c. 9 November 1918], LAC, RG 24, ser. C-1-A, vol. 2557, file HQC-2514 (vol. 1); Skuce, *CSEF*, 23–24; Massey, *When I Was Young*, 199-200. War artists Louis Keene and A.Y. Jackson were attached to the CEFS (though Jackson never left Canada since the expedition was cancelled prior to his deployment). Additional war art, such as the charcoal drawing *Troops at Petawawa: Canadian Troops Marching Off to Siberia*, by C.W. Jefferys, was completed in Canada prior to the embarkation of the main body of the force. See Skuce, *CSEF*, 15.
4 S.W. Horrall, "The Force's Siberian Patrol," *RCMP Quarterly* 36, 5 (July 1971): 3-8; "Siberian Expeditionary Force Mobilization of Ammunition Column," LAC, RG 24, ser. C-1-A, vol. 1994, file 762-12-1; "Total Strength of Squadron," 14 November 1918, LAC, Royal Canadian Mounted Police Fonds, RG 18, vol. 1929, file "RCMP 1918 – Siberian Draft Pt. 1" (see also vol. 1936, file "RCMP 1919 No. 14"). The initial call for recruits stipulated that members of the RNWMP Siberian Squadron "should be robust, [of] cheerful temperament, expert horsemen and good shots." See Letter to Officer Commanding RNWMP Prince Albert Detachment, 18 August 1918, LAC, RG 18, vol. 1930, file "Siberian Draft 3-6." Data on the

horses can be found in Memorandum to the Officer Commanding RNWMP, Depot Division, Regina, 20 August 1919, LAC, RG 18, vol. 1930, file "RCMP 1918 – Siberian Draft 3-6," "Instructions Issued to All Divs. and OC Squadron." The RNWMP spent a total of $33,305 on horses for Siberia. See "RE Siberian Remount Purchasing Board," no. 29a, RG 18, vol. 1929, file "RCMP 1918 Siberian Draft Pt. 1."

5 Order-in-Council 2073, 23 August 1919, LAC, RG 9, ser. III-A-1, vol. 98, file 10-14-19 (pts. 2, 3, and 4) "Lists of Orders in Council"; Swettenham, *Allied Intervention in Russia,* 128.

6 "Mobs in Toronto Demolish Cafes," *Colonist,* 4 August 1918; "Toronto Mobs Give Trouble," *Colonist,* 7 August 1918.

7 Mewburn to Burrill, 7 August 1918, Mewburn to Gwatkin, 15 August 1918 (both in LAC, RG 24, ser. C-1-A, vol. 2557, file HQC-2514 [vol. 1]); Deputy Minister Militia and Defence to RNWMP Comptroller, 7 September 1918, LAC, RCMP Fonds, RG 18, vol. 3179, file G989-3-24 (vol. 1); "Siberia Holds Immense Opportunity to Members of Canadian Contingent," *Daily Times,* 17 December 1918.

8 Borden, *Memoirs,* 786-88; Machin, *Report of the Director of the Military Service Branch,* 147-48; Auger, "On the Brink of Civil War," 503-40; Granatstein and Hitsman, *Broken Promises,* 86-89; Morton, *When Your Number's Up,* 67-68.

9 "Draft Evaders Make Trouble," *Colonist,* 15 August 1918; "Bolsheviki Rally Upset by Police," *Montreal Gazette,* 29 July 1918; Beattie, "Canadian Intervention in Russia," 180.

10 War Diary of 259th Battalion CEF(S), September 1918; Director for Record to J.K. Laflamme (Director of Personal Services), 1 August 1923, LAC, RG 24, ser. C-1-a, vol. 1993, file 762-11-24, Queries Relating to CEF (Siberia).

11 "Will Shortly Be on Their Way to Siberia," and "Siberian Force Men Despatched," *Montreal Gazette,* 30 September 1918.

12 Chambers to Editors, 2 October 1918; Mewburn to Chambers, 22 September 1918, LAC, RG 24, ser. C-1-A, vol. 2566, file HQ-2758 (Suppression of Information with Reference to the Siberian Expeditionary Force).

13 Mark Osborne Humphries, "The Horror at Home: The Canadian Military and the 'Great' Influenza Pandemic of 1918," *Journal of the Canadian Historical Association* 16, 1 (2005): 235-60; Janice P. Dickin McGinnis, "The Impact of Epidemic Influenza: Canada, 1918-1919," *Historical Papers of the Canadian Historical Association* 12, 1 (1977): 120-40; Howard Phillips and David Killingray, eds., *The Spanish Flu Pandemic of 1918: New Perspectives* (London and New York: Routledge, 2003); LAC, RG 24, ser. C-1-a, vol. 1992, file 762-11-15 (Infectious Diseases, Siberian Expeditionary Force CEF).

14 Deputy Minister of Militia and Defence to Deputy Minister of Justice, 31 October 1918, LAC, RG 13, vol. 1939, file 2362-1918, as quoted in Humphries, "Horror at Home," 258; War Diary of 259th Battalion CEF(S), October 1918.

15 Canada, *Report of Debates of the House of Commons* (Ottawa: J. de Labroquerie Taché, 1919-26), 25 June 1919, 4001.

16 Fraser, "The Mud-Red Volunteers," 11.

17 Dawn Fraser, "The Parasites," in *Songs of Siberia and Rhymes of the Road* (Glace Bay, NS: Eastern Publishing, c. 1919), 178.

18 Harold to Josie, 1 October 1918, LAC, Harold Steele Fonds, MG 30, E564, file "Correspondence, 1 August 1918-23 November 1918."

19 Church to Mewburn, 8 October 1918, Captain to Church, 15 October 1918 (both in LAC, RG 24, ser. C-1-a, vol. 1992, file 762-11-15 [Infectious Diseases, Siberian Expeditionary Force CEF]). See also various files in LAC, RG 9, ser. II-F-9, vol. 474; Ian Hugh Maclean Miller, *Our Glory and Our Grief: Torontonians and the Great War* (Toronto: University of Toronto Press, 2002).

20 War Diary of 259th Battalion CEF(S), October 1918.

21 Eric Henry William Elkington interview, 16 June 1980, UVASC, Military Oral History Collection, SC 141, 169.

22 "Reaction in Russia," *Colonist*, 14 August 1918.

23 "Canada to Send Force 4,000 Strong to Help Russia in Siberia," *Colonist*, 13 August 1918.

24 "Siberia Offers Vast Opportunity," *Colonist*, 28 September 1918.

25 Ibid.

26 Machin, *Report of the Director of the Military Service Branch*, 125.

27 Carne to Mother, 6 October 1918, UVASC, Carne Fonds, "Letters."

28 Bent Gestur Sivertz, *The Sivertz Family*, book 2, *Elinborg* (Canby, OR: Copy-Rite, 1982), 6 and app.; "Was Leading His Men in Rush for Hun Machine Gun," *Daily Times*, 12 November 1918.

29 Desmond Morton and J.L. Granatstein, *Marching to Armageddon: Canadians and the Great War, 1914-1919* (Toronto: Lester and Orpen Dennys, 1989), 227.

30 Machin, *Report of the Director of the Military Service Branch*, 125.

31 "Siberia Offers Vast Opportunity," *Colonist*, 28 September 1918.

32 Leolyn Dana Wilgress, *Memoirs* (Toronto: Ryerson 1967), 50; Wilgress, "From Siberia to Kuibyshev: Reflections on Russia, 1919-1943," *International Journal* 22, 3 (Summer 1967): 364-75.

33 PC 2595, 21 October 1918, LAC, Department of Trade and Commerce, RG 20, vol. 1369, file 21916 (vol. 1) (Canadian Economic Commission in Siberia); Hopkins, *Canadian Annual Review of Public Affairs* (1918), 432; PC 2596, 23 October 1918, LAC, RG 24, ser. C-1-A, vol. 1992, file 762-11-7 (Economic Mission, CEF Siberia); Canada, *Documents on Canadian External Relations*, 1:211-17; "Commission Will Work in Siberia," *Colonist*, 23 October 1918; Hill, *Canada's Salesman to the World*, 210-20.

34 Hopkins, *Canadian Annual Review of Public Affairs* (1918), 432; Wilgress, *Memoirs*, 52.

35 Dennis to Sir George Foster, 24 September 1918; Mewburn to Foster, 18 September 1918, LAC, RG 24, ser. C-1-a, vol. 1992, file H-Q-762-11-7 (Economic Mission, CEF Siberia). For a biographical sketch of Dennis, see Polk, "Canadian Red Cross and Relief in Siberia," 78-81.

36 According to Captain Charles Hertzberg, head of the Canadian Engineers in Vladivostok, the building was a "rotten affair" brought over at a "ridiculous" price. It was never used for the bank branch and was instead assembled by the Canadian forces as an outbuilding for the No. 11 Stationary Hospital at Second River. See Hertzberg Diary, 21 March 1919, LAC, Hertzberg Fonds, vol. 1, file 1-18, diary no. 9; D.C. Rea, "Vladivostok, Siberia-in-Russia, Branch" (draft), n.d., Royal Bank of Canada Archives (copy in CRCR, ser. 1, sec. 1, pt. B, "Royal Bank of Canada"); "War Diary: Pages from the Chronicle of the Bank's Adventures in Troubled Times," *Royal Bank Magazine* (March 1945), 12-14; Duncan McDowall, *Quick to the Frontier: Canada's Royal Bank* (Toronto: McClelland and Stewart, 1993), 194-95; Hopkins, *Canadian Annual Review* (1918), 801; Wilgress, *Memoirs*, 52;

37 Hopkins, *Canadian Annual Review* (1918), 801.

38 War Diary of Force Headquarters CEF(S), 11 October 1918; Charles Hertzberg, *Military Engineering with the Canadian Brigade in Siberia 1919*, 2, LAC, Hertzberg Fonds, file 1-4; Hertzberg Diary, 11 October-26 October 1918, LAC, Hertzberg Fonds, vol. 1, file 1-18, diary no. 8 (10 May 1918-15 Nov. 1918). For the organization of the Advance Party, see Elmsley to Mewburn, 31 August 1918, Troopers to CGS (Ottawa), 10 September 1918 (both in LAC, RG 24, ser. C-1-A, vol. 2557, file HQC-2514 [vol. 1]).

39 Elmsley to CGS (Ottawa), 26 October 1918, appended to War Diary of Force Headquarters CEF(S); Massey, *When I Was Young*, 202.

40 War Diary of Force Headquarters CEF(S), 11 October 1918; "Marching in State," 26 October 1918, appended to War Diary of Force Headquarters CEF(S); "Canadians in Siberia," *Toronto Globe*, 3 December 1918.

41 War Diary of Force Headquarters CEF(S), 27 October 1918; Correspondence of Major George Addison McHaffie, Deputy Assistant Director of Supplies and Transport, Canadian Army Service Corps, Vladivostok, in LAC, George Addison McHaffie Fonds, MG 30, E22. Earlier inquiries for Canadian office space had been made by Knox, head of the British Military Mission, and CPR representative Ross Owen. See Knox to CGS (Ottawa), 29 September 1918, LAC, RG 24, ser. C-1-A, vol. 2557, file HQC-2514 [vol. 1]).

42 "Situation at Vladivostok under Allied occupation," n.d. [c. 27 October 1918], War Diary of Force Headquarters CEF(S), October 1918, app. G.

43 Resolution passed by Vladivostok Trade-Manufacturers' Assembly, 1 November 1918, "K rekvizitsii Pushkinskogo Teatra" [On the Requisition of Pushkinsky Theatre], *Dalekaya Okraina* [Far Suburb] (Vladivostok), 4 November 1918, Vladivostok State Historical Archive.

44 "Raz'yasneniee po povodu rekvizitsii Pushkinskogo teatra" [Explanation Concerning Requisition of Pushkinsky Theatre], *Dalekaya Okraina* (Vladivostok), 6 November 1918, Vladivostok State Historical Archive; "Otvet Kanadksogo Komandovaniya na rezolyutsiyu protesta bynesennogo na obschem sobranii torgovo-Promyshlennogo Obschestva" [The answer of the Canadian Command to the Resolution of Protest of General Meeting of the Commercial and Industrial Society], *Primorskaya Zhizn'* (Vladivostok), 7 November 1918, Vladivostok State Historical Archive.

45 The program for the concert – which included a Czechoslovak quartet, a pipe band from the Canadian Army Medical Corps, and violin, trumpet, and viola performances by other members of the Siberian force – was recorded in "Program – Theatre," 3 November 1918, Edwin Stephenson Diary, Stephenson Family Collection (private collection); War Diary of Force Headquarters CEF(S), 29 October 1918 and 31 October 1918; War Diary of Advance Party, 6th Signal Company CEF(S), 3 November 1918, CRCR Special Collections, ser. 1, sec. 1 (Archival Materials); Hertzberg Diary, 3 November 1918, LAC, Hertzberg Fonds, vol. 1, file 1-18, diary no. 8; MacLaren, *Canadians in Russia*, 151.

46 Wilgress, *Memoirs*, 52.

47 "Diagram of Quarters Occupied by Advance Party, CEF Siberia," n.d., War Diary of Force Headquarters CEF(S), October 1918, app. F, p. 31; Massey, *When I Was Young*, 204-7; Hertzberg, *Military Engineering with the Canadian Brigade*, 10-13, LAC, Hertzberg Fonds, file 1-4; Hertzberg Diary, 28 October 1918, LAC, Hertzberg Fonds, vol. 1, file 1-18, diary no. 8; G.S. Worsley Report on "B" Squadron RNWMP, 11 October 1919, LAC, RCMP Fonds, RG 18, vol. 3179, file G 989-3-24 (vol. 2). At the end of November, Elmsley acquired an apartment at No. 5 Svetlanskaya, the main road in Vladivostok. See Hertzberg Diary, 29 November 1918, LAC, Hertzberg Fonds, vol. 1, file 1-18, diary no. 9.

48 War Diary of Force Headquarters CEF(S), 28 October 1918; War Diary of Advance Party, 6th Signal Company CEF(S), 27 October 1918.

49 "Censorship Orders for Troops in the Field," 23 October 1918, War Diary of Force Headquarters CEF(S). For the postal history of the CEFS, see Edith M. Faulstich, "Mail from the Canadian Siberian Expeditionary Force," *Postal History Journal* 12, 1 (January 1968): 3-33; Robert C. Smith, "Markings of the Canadian Expeditionary Force (Siberia)," *Postal History Society of Canada Journal* 36 (December 1983): 4-10; Robert C. Smith, *A Canadian in Siberia, 1918-1921: BNAPS Exhibits Series No. 12* (Saskatoon: British North American Philatelic Society, 1999); C.R. McGuire and R.F. Narbonne, "A Siberian Expeditionary Force Discovery," *BNA Topics* 58, 2 (April-June 2001): 42-49.

50 "Germans at Work in Vladivostok," *Colonist*, 23 August 1918; "Inflict Defeat on Bolsheviki," *Colonist*, 27 August 1918; Dorothy Findlay to Family, 18 November 1919, and Dorothy Findlay to Mother, 16 August 1918, in "Letters from Vladivostok, 506.

51 "Inflicts Defeat on Bolsheviki," *Colonist*, 29 August 1918; "Horvath Seizes Power in Siberia by Coup d'Etat," *New York Times*, 28 August 1918; "Menace to Czechs Lifted: Pro-Ally Forces Control Railways from Vladivostok to Point on Volga," *New York Times*, 8 September 1918; Mackintosh Bell, *Side Lights on the Siberian Campaign*, 97-102.

52 In spring, Sakharov was replaced by General Rodzianko, a former officer on the czar's staff who was serving in Italy at the time of the revolution. He joined the British army, married an Englishwoman, and then returned to Siberia on a trip arranged by the British government. See Hertzberg Diary, 27 May 1919, LAC, Hertzberg Fonds, vol. 1, file 1-18, diary no. 9; Mackintosh Bell, *Side Lights on the Siberian Campaign*, 104-23; "Russian Army Is Growing in Siberia," *Daily Times*, 24 October 1918; Clifford Kinvig, *Churchill's Crusade: The British Invasion of Russia, 1918-1920* (London: Continuum, 2006), 301; Pares, *My Russian Memoirs*, 501; Skuce, *CSEF*, 31; MacLaren, *Canadians in Russia*, 154-57 and 179-81; Blair (Vladivostok) to Troopers (London), 4 February 1919, High Commissioner (Irkutsk) to High Commissioner (Vladivostok), 12 February 1919, War Diary of General Staff CEF(S), February 1919, apps. 27 and 29. For a list of Canadians attached to the Russian Island training school, see "No. 224, Appointments," 15 March 1919, War Diary of General Staff CEF(S), Daily Routine Orders, March 1919, app. 41, p. 16.

53 "Menace to Czechs Lifted – Pro-Ally Forces Control Railways from Vladivostok to Point on Volga," *New York Times*, 8 September 1918; Wilgress, *Memoirs*, 51.

54 Semion Lyandres, "The 1918 Attempt on the Life of Lenin: A New Look at the Evidence," *Slavic Review* 48, 3 (Autumn 1989): 432-48.

55 "Menace to Czechs Lifted – Pro-Ally Forces Control Railways from Vladivostok to Point on Volga," *New York Times*, 8 September 1918.

56 "Military Situation, December 31st, 1918," War Diary of Force Headquarters CEF(S).

57 Pereira, *White Siberia*, 68-80.

58 Ibid., 75, 80.

59 "Siberia Offers Vast Opportunity," *Colonist*, 28 September 1918; Pereira, *White Siberia*, 96.

60 Connaughton, *Republic of the Ushakovko*, 70.

61 For Knox's appointment, see War Office to Knox, 26 July 1918, LAC, RG 24, ser. C-1-A, vol. 2557, file HQC-2514 (vol. 1).

62 Smele, "White Gold," 1319-21.

63 Connaughton, *Republic of the Ushakovko*, 79, 88; Ward, *With the "Die-Hards" in Siberia*, 106-14.

64 Ward, *With the "Die-Hards" in Siberia*, x.

65 Kerensky, *Crucifixion of Liberty*, 352; Mackintosh Bell, *Side Lights on the Siberian Campaign*, 102-03.

66 Elmsley to Mewburn, 2 November 1918, LAC, RG 24, ser. C-1-A, vol. 2566, file HG-2738, "Diary GOC Canadians Siberia."

67 "Victoria Should Act," *Colonist*, 17 August 1918.

68 War Diary of 16th Infantry Brigade Headquarters CEF(S), 23 October 1918, LAC, RG 9, ser. III-D-3, vol. 5057, reel T-11119; War Diary of 85th Battery Canadian Field Artillery CEF(S), September-October 1918, LAC, RG 9, ser. III-D-3, vol. 5057, reel T-11119. The troops in the 85th Battery, all volunteers from existing artillery units of the CEF, had been enlisted at the beginning of September and left Petawawa for New Westminster on 2 October 1918. The units of the Advance Party, including the Canadian Engineering Corps, left the Willows on 7 October for Vancouver. The enlisted men were quartered in the drill hall, while

the officers stayed at the CPR's Hotel Vancouver. Another 400 troops were quarantined at Coquitlam on account of the influenza. See Hertzberg Diary, 2 and 7 October 1918, LAC, Hertzberg Fonds, vol. 1, file 1-18, diary no. 8; Edwin Stephenson Diary, 3 October-11 October 1918, Stephenson Family Collection (private papers); Telegram, 7 October 1918, LAC, RG 9, ser. II-B-12, vol. 2, file "Correspondence – Siberian Force."

69 "C" Company of the 260th Battalion reached Victoria from Regina on 2 October, followed by "D" Company from across British Columbia on 3 October, "A" Company from the Maritimes on 12 October, and "B" Company from Manitoba on 17 October. See Skuce, *CSEF*, 24; McGinnis, "Impact of Epidemic Influenza," 123; Humphries, "Horror at Home," 253-54.

70 "Isolation at Willows Camp" and "City Will Act to Check Epidemic," *Colonist*, 8 October 1918.

71 Victoria, *Annual Reports: Corporation of the City of Victoria* (Victoria: Diggen, 1918), 89.

72 "City Will Act to Check Epidemic," *Colonist*, 8 October 1918; "Spanish Influenza," *Tribune*, 7 October 1918.

73 Victoria, *Annual Reports* (1918), 89; "Marked Decrease of Military 'Flu' Cases," *Colonist*, 22 October 1918; "Field Ambulance Unit Is Kept Busy" and "Epidemic Halts as City Prepares," *Colonist*, 23 October 1918; "Nearly Forty Places under the 'Flu' Ban," *Daily Times*, 24 October 1918; "The Ban," *Tribune*, 14 November 1918.

74 War Diary of 259th Battalion CEF(S), 22 October 1918; Harold to Josie, 22 October 1918, LAC, Harold Steele Fonds, MG 30, E564, file "Correspondence 1 August 1918-23 Nov. 1918"; "Force at Willows Further Augmented," *Colonist*, 24 October 1918.

75 Ron Baird, *Success Story: The History of Oak Bay* (Victoria: Borsman and Heffernan, 1979), 138.

76 Harold to Josie, 2 November 1918, LAC, Harold Steele Fonds, MG 30, E564, file "Correspondence 1 August 1918-23 November 1918."

77 "Siberia Holds Immense Opportunity to Members of Canadian Contingent," *Daily Times*, 17 December 1918, 7.

78 War Diary of 16th Infantry Brigade Headquarters CEF(S), 13 December 1918.

79 See Desmond Morton, "'Kicking and Complaining': Demobilization Riots in the Canadian Expeditionary Force, 1918-19," *Canadian Historical Review* 61, 3 (September 1980): 334-60; Julian Putkowski, *British Army Mutineers, 1914-1922* (London: Francis Boutle, 1998); Julian Putkowski, "The Kinmel Park Camp Riots, 1919," *Flintshire Historical Society Journal* 32 (1989): 55-107; Lawrence James, *Mutiny in the British and Commonwealth Forces, 1797-1956* (London: Buchan and Enright, 1987).

80 Lewis F. Richardson, *Arms and Insecurity* (Chicago: Quadrangle, 1960), 232. See also Jack S. Levy and T. Clinton Morgan, "The War-Weariness Hypothesis: An Empirical Test," *American Journal of Political Science* 30, 1 (February 1986): 26-49; David Garnham, "War-Proneness, War-Weariness, and Regime Type: 1816-1980," *Journal of Peace Research* 23, 3 (September 1986): 279-89; Jeffrey Pickering, "War-Weariness and Cumulative Effects: Victors, Vanquished, and Subsequent Interstate Intervention," *Journal of Peace Research* 39, 3 (September 2002): 313-37; Terry Copp and Bill McAndrew, *Battle Exhaustion: Soldiers and Psychiatrists in the Canadian Army, 1939-1945* (Montreal and Kingston: McGill-Queen's University Press, 1990); Morton, *When Your Number's Up*, 244.

81 Skuce, *CSEF*, 32.

82 Carne to Family, 17 July 1916, UVASC, Carne Fonds, "Letters."

83 War Diary of 259th Battalion CEF(S), 24 October 1918; Elmsley to Mewburn, 31 August 1918, LAC, RG 24, ser. C-1-A, vol. 2557, file HQC-2514 (vol. 1).

84 War Diary of 259th Battalion CEF(S), 16 and 20 November 1918.

85 Ibid., 25 October 1918. The CEFS was initially armed with the notorious Ross rifle, but before leaving the Willows Camp it was equipped with the Short Magazine Lee Enfield (SMLE) rifle, 3,765 of which were transported to Vladivostok, along with 10,746,998 rounds of ammunition, 132 Lewis light machine guns, and 16 Vickers heavy machine guns. See Skuce, *CSEF*, 34.

86 War Diary of 259th Battalion CEF(S), 31 October 1918.

87 Ibid., 1 November 1918.

88 MacLaren, *Canadians in Russia*, 156.

89 Perry to McLean, 29 October 1918, Morrison to Perry, 29 October 1918 (both in LAC, RG 18, vol. 1929, file "RCMP 1918 Siberian Draft Pt. 1").

90 Daily Routine Orders, 6 December 1918, War Diary of Force Headquarters CEF(S); G.S. Worsley Report on "B" Squadron RNWMP, 11 October 1919, LAC, RG 18, vol. 3179, file G 989-3 (vol. 2); Grace Potter Attestation Papers, LAC, RG 150, acc. 1992-93/166, box 7923–16. For the history of the Red Cross in Russia, see Polk, "Canadian Red Cross and Relief in Siberia." See also Floyd Miller, *Wild Children of the Urals* (New York: Dutton, 1965); LAC, Florence Farmer Fonds (hereafter cited as Farmer Fonds), MG 30, ser. C182; Skuce, *CSEF*, 29; S.W. Horrall, "The Force's Siberian Patrol," *RCMP Quarterly* 36, 5 (July 1971): 3-8. The *Monteagle* was previously known as the *Lake Manitoba*, plying the trans-Atlantic crossing. See Hertzberg Diary, 21 April 1919, LAC, Hertzberg Fonds, vol. 1, file 1-18, diary no. 9.

91 Morton and Granatstein, *Marching to Armageddon*, 233.

92 "Enthusiasm Rampant at Peace Celebration" *Colonist*, 12 November 1918.

93 "Labor Men Wouldn't Stand for Red Flag," *Colonist*, 12 November 1918. The unidentified worker had hoisted the Red Flag at the front of the labour column, "the emblem of the workingman throughout the world," which was then flying "in Hungary, Germany, Austria [and] Russia," he said. Other workers shouted insults and persuaded him to surrender the flag and conceal the banner. "The revolution is over, boys," quipped longshoreman Joe Taylor, a socialist who acted as mediator. In the next issue of the *Tribune*, socialist W.E. Peirce, released from Oakalla Prison for publishing the terms of the Allies' secret treaties, defended the action: "The Red Flag is coming here. Of that there can be no doubt. We may help it forward to good ends, or we may oppose it and so cause trouble, but we cannot stop it." See "The Red Flag," *Tribune*, 21 November 1918 and 24 November 1918; "Labour Militant," *Tribune*, 13 January 1919.

94 "Enthusiasm Rampant at Peace Celebration" and "Residents of Mount Tolmie Celebrate," *Colonist*, 12 November 1918; "Entire Population Turns Out for Vast Celebration," *Daily Times*, 12 November 1918.

95 "War Rumours Cause Wild Enthusiasm," *Colonist*, 8 November 1918; "United Press Men Sent False Cable," *New York Times*, 8 November 1918.

96 "Germany Breaks with Bolsheviki," *Colonist*, 7 November 1918; "Soviet Propaganda Is Cause of Break," *Colonist*, 8 November 1918.

97 "Armistice Delegates Arrive in Allied Lines," *Colonist*, 7 November 1918; Dirk Dahnhardt, *Revolution in Kiel: Der Obergang vom Kaiserreich zur Weimarer Republik, 1918-19* (Neumunster: Karl Wachholtz Verbag, 1978).

98 "Revolt Spreads through Germany," *Colonist*, 8 November 1918.

99 "Removal of Wilhelm from Throne Desired" and "German Cities Join in Revolt," *Colonist*, 9 November 1918.

100 "Red Banner Flies over Royal Palace" and "Four More Dreadnought Crews Join in Revolution," *Colonist*, 11 November 1918.

101   "Socialists Overthrow Old German Regime," *Colonist*, 11 November 1918.
102   "Hostilities Are Brought to an End on the Western Front," *Colonist*, 11 November 1918; "Armistice Terms Are Announced," *Colonist*, 12 November 1918; "Germans Say British Want No Bolshevism among German Crews," *Colonist*, 27 December 1918; Richard Garrett, *The Final Betrayal: Armistice, 1918 ... and Afterwards* (Shedfield, Southampton: Buchan and Enright, 1989), 33-41.
103   Douglas Peifer, "Commemoration of Mutiny, Rebellion, and Resistance in Postwar Germany: Public Memory, History, and the Formation of 'Memory Beacons,'" *Journal of Military History* 65 (October 2001): 1013-23; Daniel Horn, *The German Naval Mutinies of World War I* (New Brunswick, NJ: Rutgers University Press, 1969); A.J. Ryder, *The German Revolution of 1918: A Study of German Socialism in War and Revolt* (Cambridge: Cambridge University Press, 1967).
104   "Suffering Russia," *Colonist*, 8 November 1918.
105   "Planning a Great Crime," *Colonist*, 9 November 1918.
106   "Speedy Collapse of the Bolsheviki Regime Expected," *Daily Times*, 12 November 1918.
107   MacLaren, *Canadians in Russia*, 69-70; Swettenham, *Allied Intervention in Russia*, 52 and 68. On 17 September 1918, ninety-two Canadian men sailed from Leith, Scotland, to the Russian port of Murmansk, arriving on 26 September. On 20 September 1918, 469 Canadian troops and eighteen officers sailed from Dundee, Scotland, for Arkhangelsk.
108   Official Press Bureau to Chipress (Ottawa), 15 November 1918, LAC, RG 24, ser. C-1-A, vol. 2566, file. HQC-2698, "Canadian Expedition Force Siberia Censorship."
109   Borden, *Memoirs*, 865.
110   Hopkins, *Canadian Annual Review of Public Affairs* (1918), 154-55.
111   "Parad" [Parade], *Dalekaya Okraina*, 16 November 1918, Vladivostok State Historical Archive; Charles to Family, 15 November 1918, LAC, Hertzberg Fonds, vol. 1, file 1-2, "Personal Correspondence"; MacLaren, *Canadians in Russia*, 151; Hertzberg Diary, 15 November 1918, LAC, Hertzberg Fonds, vol. 1, file 1-18, diary no. 8.
112   A. Steel, "The Present Political Situation in Siberia," 22 November 1918, LAC, Borden Papers, MG 26, H1(a), vol. 103; Ward, *With the "Die-Hards" in Siberia*, 124-39; Connaughton, *Republic of the Ushakovko*, 70-98; Peter Fleming, *The Fate of Admiral Kolchak* (London: Rupert Hart-Davis, 1963); Smele, "White Gold," 1319-21.
113   Connaughton, *Republic of the Ushakovko*, 99.
114   Ward, *With the "Die-Hards" in Siberia*, x.
115   Troopers (London) copied to Elmsley, 20 November 1918, LAC, RG 9, ser. III-A-S, vol. 362, file A3, SEF (file 117).
116   War Diary of Force Headquarters CEF(S), 28 October 1918.
117   *Canada Gazette* (1918), 1804-5 and 1877-8; "Labor Council Asks for Removal of Censorship" and "It Is 'Verboten,'" *BC Federationist*, 15 November 1918.
118   "The Russian Expedition," *Tribune*, 18 November 1918.
119   White to Borden (via Sir Edward Kemp, overseas minister), 14 November 1918, LAC, Borden Papers, MG 6, ser. H1(a), vol. 103. See also CGS (Ottawa) to Troopers (London), 2 November 1918, CGS (Ottawa) to Troopers (London), 14 November 1918 (both in LAC, RG 24, ser. C-1-A, vol. 2557, file HQC-2514 [vol. 1]); MacLaren, *Canadians in Russia*, 158-65. On 2 November 1918, the chief of general staff, Ottawa, had sent an inquiry to the British War Office: "In view of rapid march towards peace, my Minister wishes to know whether dispatch of Force from Canada to Vladivostok should be cancelled or delayed, or whether in any respect existing arrangements should be modified."
120   Borden, *Memoirs*, 779.

121 Borden to White, 24 November 1918, Crerar to White, 22 November 1918, LAC, Borden Papers, MG 26, H1(a), vol. 103.
122 White to Borden, 25 November 1918, LAC, Borden Papers, MG 26, H1(a), vol. 103.
123 "The Siberian Riddle," *Globe*, 3 December 1918. See also "Canadian and Russian Chaos," *Globe*, 29 November 1918.
124 White to Borden, 22 November 1918, Mewburn to Borden (via Kemp), 24 November 1918, Borden to Mewburn, 25 November 1918, White to Mewburn, 28 November 1918, White to Crerar, 28 November 1918, White to Borden, 29 November 1918 (all in LAC, Borden Papers, MG 26, H1[a], vol. 103). See also CGS (Ottawa) to troopers, 24 November 1918, and Major-General for Military Secretary to Naval Secretary, 28 November 1918 (both in LAC, RG 24, vol. 3968, file NSC 1047-14-26 [vol. 1]); Mewburn to Kemp, 22 November 1918, Bickford (Victoria) to Osborne (Ottawa), 26 November 1918, Troopers (London) to CGS (Ottawa), 6 December 1918 (all in LAC, RG 24, ser. C-1-A, vol. 2557, file HQC-2514 [vol. 1]); Adjutant General (Ottawa) to Elmsley, 7 December 1918, LAC, RG 9, ser. III-D-3, vol. 5056, reel T-10950, War Diary of Force Headquarters CEF(S). The decision to proceed with the expedition, subject to the one-year limit on compulsory service, was made on 28 November 1918. "You may regard the matter as closed," White informed Borden.
125 Tompkins, *A Canadian's Road to Russia*, 344.
126 UVACS, Minutes, 27 November 1918; "Labor's Local Parliament," *Tribune*, 28 November 1918. The ban on public gatherings was lifted on 20 November 1918. See Victoria, *Annual Reports* (1918), 89.
127 Sivertz to Mewburn, 6 December 1918, LAC, RG 24, ser. C-1-a, vol. 1993, file 762-11-24, "Queries Relating to CEF (Siberia)." For the government's response, see Deputy Minister of Militia and Defence to Christian Sivertz, 19 December 1918, LAC, RG 24, ser. C-1-a, vol. 1993, file 762-11-24, "Queries Relating to CEF (Siberia)."
128 "Editorial," *BC Federationist*, 29 November 1918.
129 "Carpenters Lose Member," *BC Federationist*, 13 December 1918.
130 Kipp to Chambers, 27 November 1918, Deacon to Kipp, 27 December 1918 (both in LAC, RG 24, ser. C-1-A, vol. 2566, file HQC-2698, "Canadian Expedition Force Siberia Censorship").
131 Bickford (Victoria) to Osborne (Ottawa), 26 November 1918, LAC, RG 24, ser. C-1-A, vol. 2557, file HQC-2514 (vol. 1).
132 "Statement Submitted by 2769509, Rfn. J. Guenard," n.d., Exhibit B, LAC, RG 24, ser. C-1-a, vol. 1992, file H-Q-762-11-10, "Courts Martial in CEF (Siberia)."
133 "Federated Labor Party Launched at Victoria," *BC Federationist*, 13 December 1918; "Crowded Meeting of the Federated Labour Party," *Tribune*, 9 December 1918; "The Protest Meeting," *Tribune*, 12 December 1919; Minutes, 4 and 11 December 1918, UVASC, VLC Fonds, 80-59, box 3. An order-in-council of 30 September 1918 had banned all works by Chicago publisher Charles Kerr and Company from Canada. These included Lewis H. Morgan's *Ancient Society*, Marx's *Capital*, and a pamphlet entitled *The Siberian Expedition*.
134 "Help for Russia," *Daily Times*, 10 December 1918.
135 "Siberia Holds Immense Opportunity to Members of Canadian Contingent," *Daily Times*, 17 December 1918.
136 "Siberians Are in Need of Clothing," *Daily Times*, 16 December 1918.
137 "Organized Attempt to Wreck Mass Meeting," *BC Federationist*, 20 December 1918.
138 Tompkins to Edna, 16 December 1918, reprinted in Tompkins, *A Canadian's Road to Russia*, 355. For a first-hand account of the incident, see George F. Clingan, "Siberian Sideshow:

The Canadian Expeditionary Force, Siberia, 1918-1919," *Legionary* (Ottawa) 30, 1 (June 1955): 10.
139 "Organized Attempt to Wreck Mass Meeting," *BC Federationist*, 20 December 1918.
140 "Help for Russia," *Daily Times*, 10 December 1918; "Organized Attempt to Wreck Mass Meeting," *BC Federationist*, 20 December 1918; "Free Speech," *Tribune*, 19 December 1919; "Soldiers Protect Labor Meeting," *Tribune*, 16 December 1918. At the labour council's next meeting, Joe Taylor suggested the secretary inquire through the press as to the names of those officers who had disrupted the meeting, but his motion was narrowly defeated by the deciding vote of the chair. See Minutes, 18 December 1918, UVASC, VLC Fonds, 80-59, box 3.
141 Barnard to Borden, 4 December 1918, LAC, Borden Papers, MG 26, H1(a), vol. 103.
142 "Labor Council and Censorship of Literature," *BC Federationist*, 22 November 1918. See also "Trades Council to Hold Protest Meeting," *BC Federationist*, 20 December 1918. For labour opposition in nearby Seattle, Washington, see "Protest Siberian Picnic," *Tribune*, 12 December 1918.
143 "Call on Govt. to Withdraw Troops Sent to Siberia," *Ottawa Citizen*, 6 December 1918.
144 "The Siberian Expedition," *Tribune*, 9 December 1918. Developments in Winnipeg are discussed in Norman Penner, ed., *Winnipeg 1919: The Strikers' Own History of the Winnipeg General Strike*, 2nd ed. (Toronto: James Lorimer and Co., 1975), 6-15; Beattie, "Canadian Intervention in Russia," 176-206. Sam Blumenberg advocated a general strike at a trades and labour council meeting in early December.
145 War Diary of 259th Battalion CEF(S), 16 and 20 November 1918. See also Cahan to Deputy Minister of Justice, 8 January 1919, LAC, RG 13, Department of Justice Fonds, ser. A-2, vol. 231, file "43-63 1919"; Comptroller to Secretary, Military Council (Ottawa), 28 January 1919, LAC, RCMP Fonds, RG18, ser. F-1, vol. 3179, file G989-3-24 (vol. 1), pt. 1, "First World War. B Squadron for Service in Siberia."
146 Scott to Borden, 22 October 1918, Borden to Scott, 26 October 1918, Borden to Mewburn, 26 October 1918, Mewburn to Borden, 2 November 1918 (all in LAC, Borden Papers, MG 26, H1[a], vol. 103).
147 Skuce, *CSEF*, 23–28; War Diary of 259th Battalion CEF(S), November and December 1918; Daily Orders, 2 December 1918 to 20 December 1918, LAC, RG 9, ser. II-B-12, vol. 4, file "Part II Daily Orders, 20th Machine Gun Co – Siberia"; "Summary of Evidence in the Case of 2140598, Rifleman Frank Atkinson, 260th Battalion," 9 December 1918, and "Summary of Evidence in the Case of #888039, Rifleman N. Kazakoff," 12 December 1918, LAC, RG 24, ser. C-1-a, vol. 1992, file H-Q-762-11-10, "Courts Martial in CEF (Siberia)."
148 "There Can Be No Peace," *BC Federationist*, 20 December 1918.
149 File 58/19, "Public Safety – Dismissal of Soldiers for Siberia Who Have Shown Bolshevik Tendencies," LAC, RG 13, Department of Justice Fonds, ser. A-2, Public Safety Records, vol. 231, file "43-63 1919."
150 Gouin to Mewburn, 20 December 1918, LAC, RG 24, ser. C-1-a, vol. 1993, file 762-11-24, "Queries Relating to CEF (Siberia)."
151 Gwatkin to Chamber, 22 December 1918, LAC, RG 24, ser. C-1-A, vol. 2566, file HQC-2698, "Canadian Expedition Force Siberia Censorship."
152 "The Siberian Expedition," *Colonist*, 25 December 1918; "Siberia Holds Immense Opportunity to Members of Canadian Contingent," *Daily Times*, 17 December 1918; "Cheered Siberians during Stay Here," *Daily Times*, 28 December 1918.
153 War Diary of 16th Infantry Brigade Headquarters CEF(S), 10 December, 16 December, and 17 December 1918. The sports day, held on 16 December, included field events, hockey, and a boxing match. The YMCA's activities are described in "Expeditionary Force Hears

about Siberia," *Daily Times*, 20 December 1918, 22. The lecture of 17 December was delivered by James W. Davidson, former American consul-general at Shanghai, who had undertaken a detailed study of the resource wealth of the Russian Far East.

154 White to Borden, 7 December 1918, Borden to White, 7 December 1918 (both in LAC, Borden Papers, MG 26, H1[a], vol. 103).

Chapter 5: Departure Day

1 The units aboard the *Teesta* are listed in Daily Routine Orders, Headquarters CEF(S), 14 January 1919, LAC, RG 9, ser. II-B-12, vol. 2, file "Daily Routine Orders, Siberia." See also a telegram from Divisional Transports, Vancouver, to Naval Service, Ottawa, 23 December 1918, LAC, RG 24, vol. 3969, file NSC 1047-12027 (vol. 1). The weather report can be found in the *Colonist* and the *Daily Times*, 21 December 1918.

2 "What a Muddle," *BC Federationist*, 28 February 1919.

3 Censorship in Canada during the war is examined in Jeff Keshen, "All the News that Was Fit to Print: Ernest J. Chambers and Information Control in Canada, 1914-19," *Canadian Historical Review* 73, 3 (September 1992): 315-43.

4 William Rodney reduced the mutiny to "a small number of French-Canadian troops of the 259th Battalion," a claim that is contradicted by contemporary accounts. MacLaren's description of the incident is equally curt: "Following a brief rest halt on Fort Street in Victoria, six declined to march any farther. For their objections, they were promptly arrested and placed on board the ship under guard." He added that "many of the French-speaking soldiers mutely demonstrated that they did not regard service in Siberia as being within the terms of the conscription act." Swettenham quoted a Toronto *Globe* editorial that dismissed "something very like mutiny" on "a Siberia-bound troopship" but that provided no direct reference to the *Teesta*. He is more elaborate in his treatment of a mutiny of Canadian troops on the Murmansk Front in February 1919. Skuce provides the most accurate description of the Victoria mutiny, but, like the others, he offers little detail: "The serious charge of mutiny arose from events on December 22, 1918 [sic] when two companies of the 259th refused to board the transport SS *Teesta* at Victoria." A more thorough treatment can be found in Steuart Beattie's unpublished 1957 MA thesis. See Beattie, "Canadian Intervention in Russia," 167-70; MacLaren, *Canadians in Russia*, 175; Rodney, review of A. Swettenham's *Allied Intervention in Russia*, 186; Skuce, *CSEF*, 19; Swettenham, *Allied Intervention in Russia*, 153, 205.

5 See Granatstein and Hitsman, *Broken Promises*, 24-99.

6 War Diary of 16th Infantry Brigade Headquarters CEF(S), 21 December 1918.

7 War Diary of 20th Machine Gun Company CEF(S), 21 December 1918, LAC, RG 9, series III-D-3, vol. 5057, reel T-11119.

8 Report of Field General Court Martial, Vladivostok, 2 February 1919, LAC, RG 9, ser. III-A-3, vol. 378, file A3, SEF Courts Martial; Bickford to Headquarters CEF(S), 5 April 1919, LAC, RG 9, ser. III-A-3, vol. 373, file A3, SEF Force HQ MSA.

9 Swift to Brigade Headquarters, 8 April 1919, LAC, RG 9, ser. III-A-3, vol. 371, file A3, SEF Force HQ 23.

10 Chambers to General Gwatkin (Chief of General Staff, Ottawa), 31 December 1918, LAC, Department of Justice Fonds, RG 13, ser. A-2, Public Safety Records, vol. 231, file 43-63 1919 (file 57-19).

11 "The Siberian Expedition," *Tribune*, 6 January 1919.

12 "Did Gen. Mewburn Speak the Truth," *Tribune*, 17 March 1919. See also "Remarks of the Owl," *Tribune*, 30 June 1919; Canada, *Report of Debates of the House of Commons*, 10 March 1919, 25 June 1919, 4001.

13 "The Russian Problem," *Colonist*, 27 December 1918, 4; "Siberians Receive Rousing Send-Off," *Colonist*, 27 December 1918. Two weeks later, labour's *Tribune* accused Victoria's daily press of "lying ... to discredit Russia." See "Lying and Lying," *Tribune*, 9 January 1919. See also "Screaming Editorials," *Tribune*, 16 January 1919.

14 "The Siberian Expedition," *Colonist*, 27 December 1918.

15 "The Siberian Expedition," *Globe*, 28 December 1918. See also *Daily Star* (Toronto), 27 December 1918; Beattie, "Canadian Intervention in Russia," 198-206. This alleged mutiny reported in the *Globe* and the *Herald* conflated the *Teesta*'s turbulent departure with problems encountered on the cargo ship *War Charger*, which returned to Vancouver in late December after encountering engine problems.

16 GOC to Chief Censor, 23 December 1918, LAC, RG 24, ser. C-1-A, vol. 2566, file HQC-2698, "Canadian Expedition Force Siberia Censorship."

17 Chambers to Editors, n.d. [23 December 1918]; Chambers to GOC Military District 13, 26 December 1918, LAC, RG 24, ser. C-1-A, vol. 2566, file HQC-2698, "Canadian Expedition Force Siberia Censorship."

18 Mewburn to Chambers, 27 December 1918, LAC, RG 24, ser. C-1-A, vol. 2566, file HQC-2698, "Canadian Expedition Force Siberia Censorship."

19 Chambers to Lyon, 28 December 1918, Chambers to Editor, 28 December 1918 (both in LAC, RG 24, ser. C-1-A, vol. 2566, file HQC-2698, "Canadian Expedition Force Siberia Censorship").

20 "Reasons for Siberian Expedition," *Saturday Night* (Toronto), 28 December 1918.

21 Ford to Department of Militia and Defence, 19 July 1919, LAC, Defence, RG 24, ser. C-1-A, vol. 1994, file HQ-762-11-32, "#2356836 Walter B. Ford declares willingness to support statement that troops were well cared for in Siberia."

22 Tompkins to Edna, 22 December 1918, Washington State Historical Society Archives, MsSC138, Stuart Ramsay Tompkins Papers, box 3, file 3.

23 Richard Garton Holmes to Mother, 21 December 1918, as quoted in Faulstich, "Mail from the Canadian Siberian Expeditionary Force," 20.

24 "The Unemployed Question," *BC Federationist*, 27 December 1918. Though subject to the same regulations as the *Tribune*, the *BC Federationist* appears to have taken a greater risk in reporting details of the mutiny in Victoria. Chief Press Censor Ernest Chambers had visited the Vancouver offices of the newspaper following the Ginger Goodwin general strike of 2 August 1918, threatening to suppress the publication if the directors refused to sign a declaration against "objectionable material," a request with which they complied. Eleven months later, on the night of 30 June 1919, with Vancouver once again tied up in a general strike, members of the RNWMP raided the *BC Federationist* office in the Vancouver Labor Temple, smashing through the front door and seizing a number of documents. See "Censorship," *BC Federationist*, 9 August 1918, and "Mounties Raid Homes and Offices of Labor Men," *BC Federationist*, 4 July 1919.

25 "Editorial," *BC Federationist*, 27 December 1918.

26 "Chewing the Cud," *BC Federationist*, 10 January 1919. General Anton I. Denikin was the leading White general in southern Russia. See Viktor G. Bortnevski, "White Administration and White Terror (The Denekin Period)," *Russian Review* 52 (July 1993): 354–66; A. Denikin, *The White Army*, trans. Catherine Zvegintzov (Gulf Breeze, FL: Academic International, 1973).

27 "Woodsworth Talks to a Capacity House," *BC Federationist*, 17 January 1919.

28 Grace MacInnis, *J.S. Woodsworth: A Man to Remember* (Toronto: Macmillan, 1953), 123.

29 "Verbatim Report of the Calgary Conference, 1919," *Winnipeg One Big Union Bulletin*, 10 March 1927.

30 Hertzberg Diary, 13 January 1919, LAC, Hertzberg Fonds, vol. 1, file 1-18, diary no. 9.

31 "Trial of No. 3167375 Rifleman Onil Boisvert," 25 January 1919, Vladivostok, Russia, LAC, RG 24, ser. C-1-A, vol. 1992, file H-Q-762-11-10, "Courts Martial in CEF (Siberia)."

32 Testimony of Sergeant R. Belleau, "Trial of No. 3040117 Rifleman Edmond Leroux," 28 January 1919, Vladivostok, Russia, LAC, RG 24, ser. C-1-A, vol. 1992, file H-Q-762-11-10, "Courts Martial in CEF (Siberia)."

33 Testimony of Lieutenant T.J. Morin, "D" Company, "Trial of No. 3040117 Rifleman Edmond Leroux," 28 January 1919, Vladivostok, Russia, and "Summary of Evidence for the Trial of No. 3164261, Rfn. Laplante," 1 January 1919 (both in LAC, RG 24, ser. C-1-A, vol. 1992, file H-Q-762-11-10, "Courts Martial in CEF [Siberia]").

34 For the list of charges, consult individual personnel files such as "Casualty Form – Pte. Onil Boisevert," 1918-1919, LAC, RG 150, acc. 92-93/166, vol. 852, file "Boisvert Onil."

35 War Diary of Force Headquarters CEF(S), 15 January 1919; MacLaren, *Canadians in Russia*, 177-76.

36 For biographical information on the occupation, age, and place of origin of the accused, consult the Attestation Papers in LAC, RG 150, acc. 1992-93/166, boxes 8522-20, 852-24, 5392-80, and 5587-64.

37 "Courts Martial," n.d. [c. 11 December 1918]. War Diary of Force Headquarters CEF(S). This stipulation was restated on the eve of the Vladivostok hearings, in Elmsley's General Routine Orders on 27 January 1918: "An opportunity should be given in all cases to the prisoner to have an officer, with legal experience, to act for him as counsel. If necessary, an officer will be detailed for this duty." See General Routine Orders, 27 January 1919, War Diary of Force Headquarters CEF(S). See also "Standing Orders by General Officer Commanding Canadian Expeditionary Force (Siberia), 1918," LAC, RG 24, ser. C-1-A, vol. 1993, file HQ-762-11-19, "Standing Orders – Siberian Expeditionary Force."

38 "Statement submitted by 3164261 Rfn. A. Laplante," n.d, LAC, RG 24, ser. C-1-A, vol. 1992, file H-Q-762-11-10, "Courts Martial in CEF (Siberia)."

39 Ibid.

40 "Trial of No. 3164261, Rifleman Alfred LaPlante, C. Company, 259th Battn. Canadian Rifles, CEFS," 25 January 1919, LAC, RG 24, ser. C-1-A, vol. 1992, file H-Q-762-11-10, "Courts Martial in CEF (Siberia)."

41 Ibid.

42 "Suspension of Sentence," 14 April 1919, LAC, RG 24, ser. C-1-A, vol. 1992, file H-Q-762-11-10, "Courts Martial in CEF (Siberia)."

43 Boisvert to H.C. Hannington, 16 March 1920c, "Trial of No. 3167375 Rifleman Onil Boisvert," 25 January 1919, LAC, RG 24, ser. C-1-A, vol. 1992, file H-Q-762-11-10, "Courts Martial in CEF (Siberia)"; "Case History Sheet," LAC, RG 150, acc. 92-93/166, vol. 852, file "Boisvert Onil."

44 "Trial of No. 3167375 Rifleman Onil Boisvert," 25 January 1919, LAC, RG 24, ser. C-1-A, vol. 1992, file H-Q-762-11-10, "Courts Martial in CEF (Siberia)."

45 "Written statement submitted by 3167375 Rfn. O. Boisvert," LAC, RG 24, ser. C-1-A, vol. 1992, file H-Q-762-11-10, "Courts Martial in CEF (Siberia)."

46 Testimony of Major Guy Boyer, Lieutenant T.J. Morin, Captain G.N. Oliver, Lieutenant L.H.G. Van Boren, Sergeant R. Belleau, Captain S.M. Rapin, "Trial of No. 3312133 Rifleman Arthur Roy," 28 January 1919, "Summary of Evidence for the Trial of No. 3312133, Rfn. Arthur Roy," 27 December 1918, and "Schedule No. 3312133, Rfn. Arthur Roy" (all in LAC, RG 24, ser. C-1-A, vol. 1992, file H-Q-762-11-10, "Courts Martial in CEF [Siberia]"). Chaplain Olivier is identified in the War Diary of 259th Battalion CEF(S), 28 December 1918. See also Olivier Attestation Papers, LAC, RG 150, acc. 1992-93/166, box 7455-42, file "Olivier Jacques."

47   "Schedule, No. 3040117, Rfn. Edmond Leroux," 4 February 1919, "Trial of No. 3040117 Rifleman Edmond Leroux," 28 January 1919 (both in LAC, RG 24, ser. C-1-A, vol. 1992, file H-Q-762-11-10, "Courts Martial in CEF [Siberia]").

48   "Schedule No. 2769509, Rfn. Joseph Guenard," 4 February 1919, "Trial of No. 2769509, Rifleman J. Guenard," "Schedule No. 3173531, Rfn. E. Pauze," and "Trial of #3173531, Rifleman E. Pauze" (all in LAC, RG 24, ser. C-1-A, vol. 1992, file H-Q-762-11-10, "Courts Martial in CEF [Siberia]").

49   "Casualty Form – Active Service," RG 150, acc. 92-93/166, vol. 7663, file "Pauze Edmond."

50   See "No. 206, Property of Prisoners Undergoing Field Punishment," 12 March 1919, War Diary of General Staff CEF(S), Daily Routine Orders, March 1919, app. 41, p. 11.

51   "Schedule No. 2769509, Rfn. Joseph Guenard," 4 February 1919, "Trial of No. 2769509, Rifleman J. Guenard" (both in LAC, RG 24, ser. C-1-A, vol. 1992, file H-Q-762-11-10, "Courts Martial in CEF [Siberia]").

52   Defensor to Elmsley, 1 April 1919, Bickford to Headquarters CEF(S), 5 April 1919, Elmsley to Defensor, 10 April 1919 (all in LAC, RG 9, ser. III-A-3, vol. 373, file A3, SEF Force HQ MSA); Swift to Brigade Headquarters, 8 April 1919, Barclay to Elmsley, 11 April 1918, Barclay to Elmsley, 12 April 1919, "Suspension of Sentence," 14 April 1919 (all in LAC, RG 9, ser. III-A-3, vol. 371, file A3, SEF Force HQ 23); "Courts Martial, CEF (Siberia)," various documents, LAC, RG 9, ser. III-A-3, vol. 378, file A3, SEF Courts Martial; General Routine Orders No. 34 Field General Courts Martial, 11 February 1919, War Diary of General Staff CEF(S), February 1919, app. 48; War Diary of Deputy Judge Advocate General CEF(S), January–February 1919, LAC, RG 9, ser. III-D-3, vol. 5057, reel T-11119. See also "Summary of Events and Information, April 1919," War Diary of Deputy Judge Advocate General CEF(S); Canada, *Report of Debates of the House of Commons*, 1 April 1919, 8 April 1919, 25 June 1919; Beattie, "Canadian Intervention in Russia," 272-86.

53   "Futile Attempt of Military Hooligans to Break Up Assembly," *Tribune*, 23 December 1918.

54   "Cheering Troops Leave for Siberia," *Daily Times*, 26 December 1918; Stuart to Edna, 27 December 1918, reprinted in Tompkins, *A Canadian's Road to Russia*, 362.

55   "Siberian Troops Are Entertained by Local IODE," *Daily Times*, 26 December 1918; "Christmas Cheer Is Enjoyed by Soldiers," *Colonist*, 27 December 1918; War Diary of 16th Infantry Brigade Headquarters CEF(S), 25 December 1918.

56   Elkington interview, June 1980 and January 1986, UVASC, Military Oral History Collection, SC 141, 169 and 170.

57   Tompkins to Edna, 27 December 1918, reprinted in Tompkins, *A Canadian's Road to Russia*, 363.

58   "Cheering Troops Leave for Siberia," *Daily Times*, 26 December 1918; "Takes Out Siberian Force," *Daily Times*, 26 December 1918; Skuce, *CSEF*, 55.

59   Ardagh Diary entry, 26 December 1918, LAC, Harold Vernon Ardagh Fonds (hereafter cited as Ardagh Fonds), MG 30, E-150, file 1/6.

60   Fraser, "Boulion à la SS *Protesilaus*," *Songs of Siberia and Rhymes of the Road*, 21. See also Tompkins to Edna, 6 January 1918, reprinted in Tompkins, *A Canadian's Road to Russia*, 365-66. According to Fraser: "A certain steamship company operating in the Pacific [the Blue Funnel Line], secured a contract from the government to transport the Siberian Expeditionary Forces from Vancouver to Vladivostok in Russia. This contract included the rationing of the Troops en route. War profiteers like so many others they half starved the soldiers for the duration of the voyage, a thin soup or stew being the chief diet for twenty-six days."

61 War Diary of 16th Infantry Brigade Headquarters CEF(S), 30 December 1918; Tompkins to Edna, 30 December 1918, reprinted in Tompkins, *A Canadian's Road to Russia*, 364. See also Ardagh Diary entry, 3 January 1919, LAC, Ardagh Fonds, MG 30, E-150, file 1/6.

62 A Court of Inquiry to investigate the crossing took place at base headquarters in Vladivostok 27 March 1919. See "No. 254 Court of Inquiry," 26 March 1919, War Diary of Force Headquarters CEF(S), Daily Routine Orders, March 1919, app. 41, p. 26; Elmsley to Defensor, 12 January 1919, Elmsley to Defensor, 13 January 1919, Elmsley to Morrisey, 14 January 1919, Elmsley to Troopers, 15 January 1919 (all in War Diary of Force Headquarters CEF[S], January 1919, apps. 24, 26, 27, and 32). See also Naval (Vladivostok) to Naval (Ottawa), 11 January 1919, Naval (Vladivostok) to Naval (Ottawa), 14 January 1919 (both in LAC, RG 24, vol. 3969, file NSC 1047-14-26 [vol. 1]); Tompkins to Edna, 8 January, reprinted in Tompkins, *A Canadian's Road to Russia*, 366-68; "Sgt. Meddie Devarenne Writes Interesting Letter from Vladivostok, Russia," *Sackville Tribune*, 3 March 1919; "Some Impressions of Siberia," *Red Flag* (Vancouver), 12 July 1919; Clingan, "Siberian Sideshow," 10-11; MacLaren, *Canadians in Russia*, 176-77. For a map of ice coverage on Peter the Great Bay, see "The Condition of Ice in the Bay of Peter the Great," 9 February 1919, War Diary of General Staff CEF(S), February 1919, app. 60; Elkington interview, 24 January 1986, UVASC, Military Oral History collection, SC 141, 170.

63 Troopers (London) to Elmsley (Vladivostok), n.d. [c. 18 December 1918], Defensor (Ottawa) to Elmsley (Vladivostok), 18 December 1918 (both in War Diary of Force Headquarters CEF[S], apps. 25 and 26). See also "Strength and Disposition of Units of the Canadian Expeditionary Force, Siberia, and British Units in Siberia as of 31 December 1918," War Diary of Force Headquarters CEF(S), app. 39.

64 The cable from the Privy Council to the War Office read, in part: "Situation everywhere changed since Canada undertook to furnish Contingent; policy of allied and associated Powers not defined; and public opinion strongly opposed to further participation. Therefore, although despatch of Canadian troops will for present continue, they must all return to Canada next spring. Meanwhile Dominion Government cannot permit them to engage in military operations nor, without its express consent, to move up country" (MacLaren, *Canadians in Russia*, 166-67).

65 CGS (Ottawa) to Elmsley, 23 December 1918, War Diary of Force Headquarters CEF(S); Foreign Office to High Commissioner, 14 January 1919, War Diary of Force Headquarters CEF(S), app. 62, p. 14.

66 "Troops May Return from Siberia in Summer Months, or Even during Spring," *Daily Times*, 26 December 1918, 1.

67 "Half of Japanese Force in Siberia Will be Withdrawn," *Daily Times*, 28 December 1918; Edward Coke (Washington) to Gwatkin, 8 January 1919, LAC, RG 24, ser. C-1-A, vol. 2557, file HQC-2514 (vol. 2), "Situation in Russia – Allied Intervention in Russia."

68 CGS Ottawa to Troopers (London), 5 January 1919, Gwatkin to Rowell, 5 January 1919 (both in LAC, RG 24, ser. C-1-A, vol. 2557, file HQC-2514 [vol. 1]); Naval Service, Ottawa to Divisional Transports, Vancouver, 6 January 1919, LAC, National RG 24, vol. 3969, file NSC 1047-14-24 (vol. 1), "Telegraphic Communications Concerning Contingents for Siberia"; Massey, *When I Was Young*, 214-15; F.H. Deacon (Chief Inspector of Accounts, Ottawa) to F.B. Ware (Director of Organization, Ottawa), 20 May 1919, LAC, RG 24, ser. C-1-a, vol. 1993, file 762-11-24, "Queries Relating to CEF (Siberia)."

69 CGS Ottawa to Troopers, 6 January 1919, LAC, Defence, RG 24, vol. 3968, file NSC 1047-14-26 (vol. 2).

70 Troopers (London) to Elmsley, 4 January 1919, Elmsley to Troopers (London), 8 January 1919 (both in War Diary of Force Headquarters CEF[S], January 1919, apps. 11 and 12). See

also CGS (Ottawa) to Troopers (London), 5 January 1919, LAC, RG 24, ser. C-1-A, vol. 2557, file HQC-2514 (vol. 2), "Situation in Russia – Allied Intervention in Russia."

71 High Commissioner (Omsk) to Acting High Commissioner (Vladivostok), 9 January 1919, Lash (Omsk) to Elmsley, 13 January 1919 (both in War Diary of Force Headquarters CEF[S], apps. 19 and 39).

72 Troopers (London) to Ottawa, 11 January 1919, War Diary of Force Headquarters CEF(S), January 1919, app. 28

73 Churchill to Knox, 20 January 1919, War Diary of Force Headquarters CEF(S), January 1919, app. 60.

Chapter 6: Vladivostok, 1919

1 "Lenine's Views Are Proclaimed," *Colonist*, 29 December 1918.

2 G.S. Worsley Report on "B" Squadron RNWMP, 11 October 1919, LAC, RG 18, vol. 3179, file G 989-3 (vol. 2).

3 "Canadians Had Easy Time in Siberia," *Daily Times*, 19 April 1919; Beattie, "Canadian Intervention in Russia," 381.

4 Elkington interview, 24 January 1986, UVASC, Military Oral History Collection, SC 141, 170. For the phrase "backwash of revolution," see Tompkins, *A Canadian's Road to Russia*, vii.

5 Massey, *When I Was Young*, 203; "General Otani Will Command in Siberia," *Colonist*, 10 August 1918; "Allies Forces Move in Siberia," *Colonist*, 22 August 1918.

6 High Commissioner (Omsk) to Acting High Commissioner (Vladivostok), 15 January 1919, War Diary of Force Headquarters CEF(S), January 1919, app. 43; Pares, *My Russian Memoirs*, 508-9 and 515. Bernard Pares cites a discussion with Gondatti, the czar's former governor general in the Russian Far East, who believed Japan had intervened in Siberia "simply to find metals, in order to make themselves independent of supply from America." According to the head of the British Military Mission in Siberia, General Alfred Knox: "Neither the Americans nor the Japanese wish us to go on, the first because President Wilson is advised by Jews who sympathize with Bolshevism and the second because they want a weak Russia rather than a strong one." See Knox to Elmsley, 21 December 1918, as quoted in James Eayrs, *In Defence of Canada*, vol. 1, *From the Great War to the Great Depression* (Toronto: University of Toronto Press, 1964), 35.

7 Memorandum (London) to Vladivostok, 20 December 1918, War Diary of Force Headquarters CEF(S); Wilgress, *Memoirs*, 52.

8 Nash (Irkutsk) to High Commissioner (Vladivostok), 15 December 1918, High Commissioner (Harbin) memo, 12 December 1918, War Diary of Force Headquarters CEF(S). At the end of December 1918, the British high commissioner in Omsk, Sir Charles Eliot, wrote his acting high commissioner in Vladivostok: "Horvat is believed to be in Japanese pay." See High Commissioner (Omsk) to Acting High Commissioner (Vladivostok), 30 December 1918, War Diary of Force Headquarters CEF(S).

9 High Commissioner (Harbin) memo, 12 December 1918, Nash (Irkutsk) to High Commissioner (Vladivostok), 16 December 1918 (both in War Diary of Force Headquarters CEF[S]).

10 Nash (Irkutsk) to High Commissioner (Vladivostok), 3 December 1918, Nash (Irkutsk) to HM Minister, 15 December 1918 (both in War Diary of Force Headquarters CEF[S]).

11 Nash (Irkutsk) to High Commissioner (Vladivostok), 2 December 1918, Greene to HM Minister, 10 December 1918, High Commissioner (Chita) to High Commissioner (Vladivostok), 12 December 1918, Nash (Irkutsk) to High Commissioner (Vladivostok), 15

December 1918, Nash (Irkutsk) to High Commissioner (Vladivostok), 16 December 1918, Green (Tokyo) to High Commissioner (Vladivostok), 7 January 1919, Green (Tokyo) to High Commissioner (Vladivostok), 9 January 1919 (all in War Diary of Force Headquarters CEF[S]). In mid-December, Semyonov cancelled an appointment with an American captain at Chita, who did "not wish to go and fight on the Western Front."

12 Ardagh Diary, 23 March 1919, LAC, Ardagh Fonds, file 2/3.

13 Greene (High Commissioner, Harbin) memo, 12 December 1918, War Diary of Force Headquarters CEF(S), December 1918, app. 13. See also Blair (Vladivostok) to Troopers (London), 4 February 1919, War Diary of General Staff CEF(S), February 1919, app. 27.

14 Massey, *When I Was Young*, 202; Gow (Deputy Minister of Overseas Military Forces of Canada [OMFC], London) to Mewburn, 4 September 1918 and 10 September 1918, Gwatkin to Mewburn, 29 September 1918, Mewburn to Gwatkin, 1 October 1919, CGS (Ottawa) to Elmsley, 8 October 1918 (all in LAC, RG 24, ser. C-1-A, vol. 2557, file HQC-2514 [vol. 1]).

15 Lash was assigned to oversee communication of "strictly Canadian matters," in anticipation of Elmsley's deployment to Omsk. Mewburn saw benefits in granting him status as a commissioner or representative "rather than [as] a mere military appointment." Lash reached Vladivostok with the Advance Party in late October. He left on 9 March 1919, after informing Mewburn that, if the troops were to be recalled by April: "I can be of no further use here and ... propose to return at the earliest opportunity." See Mewburn to Gwatkin, 1 October 1918, LAC, RG 24, ser. C-1-A, vol. 2557, file HQC-2514 (vol. 1); Elmsley to Defensor (Ottawa), 10 March 1919, War Diary of General Staff CEF(S), March 1919, app. 10; Lash to Mewburn, 28 February 1919, LAC, RG 24, ser. C-1-A, vol. 2557, file HQC-2514 (vol. 2), "Situation in Russia – Allied Intervention in Russia"; Timothy C. Winegard, "The Canadian Siberian Expeditionary Force, 1918-1919, and the Complications of Coalition Warfare," *Journal of Slavic Military Studies* 20, 2 (2007): 304. Another intelligence officer, Swedish-born explorer Lieutenant-Colonel Ivor Thord-Gray, served as assistant director of intelligence for the CEFS before being transferred to the Russian army on 15 February 1919. He was appointed to the rank of colonel and commanded the First Siberian Assault Division before serving as Kolchak's chief representative to the Allied Expeditionary Force. He left Vladivostok in February 1920. See Daily Routine Orders, Order No. 143, "Resignation," 22 February 1919, War Diary of General Staff CEF(S), February 1919, app. 49; "Interview with Major-Gen. Thord-Gray," *Voennyi Vestnik* [Military Herald] (Vladivostok), 25 December 1919; also Stellan Bojerud, *Ivor Thord Gray – soldat under 13 fano* [Ivor Thord Gray – A Soldier for 13 Countries] (Stockholm: Sivart, 2008); Joakim Langer, *Mannen som hittade Tarzan* [The Man Who Found Tarzan] (Stockholm: Sivart, 2008).

16 Balfour to High Commissioner (Vladivostok), 30 November 1918, War Diary of Force Headquarters CEF(S)(December 1918), app. 2.

17 Balfour to High Commissioner (Vladivostok), 7 December 1918, War Diary of Force Headquarters CEF(S), app. 10.

18 "Lloyd George Government Put in Power for Another Term by Voters of the United Kingdom," *Daily Times*, 28 December 1918; "Labor's Weapons Not Bombs and Bayonets" and "The British Elections," *BC Federationist*, 13 December 1918. See also "Against Every British Instinct of Honor and Humanity to Leave Russia to Mercies of Bolsheviki," *Ottawa Citizen*, 20 December 1918. Prior to the election, the *BC Federationist* quipped: "Look out for the withdrawal of the troops from Russia if the workers' representatives are returned to power in Britain – and vice versa look out for the iron fist if they don't." See "Carpenters Lose Member," *BC Federationist*, 13 December 1918; Beattie, "Canadian Intervention in Russia," 385-86.

19 Blair (Vladivostok) to Troopers (London), 4 February 1919, High Commissioner (Irkutsk) to High Commissioner (Vladivostok), 12 February 1919 (both in War Diary of General Staff CEF[S], February 1919, apps. 27 and 29).
20 Massey, *When I Was Young*, 211.
21 War Office to Borden, 22 November 1918, as quoted in Swettenham, *Allied Intervention in Russia*, 155.
22 Troopers (London) to Headquarters Battalion CEF(S), 30 November 1918, Troopers (London) to CGS (Ottawa) and General Knox (Vladivostok), 3 December 1918 (both in War Diary of Force Headquarters CEF[S]).
23 Operation Order No. 1, 6 December 1918, War Diary of Force Headquarters CEF(S); Massey, *When I Was Young*, 211; MacLaren, *Canadians in Russia*, 165.
24 Private Edwin Stephenson, an Anglican priest and medic in the Canadian Army Medical Corps, was among the Canadians who travelled to Omsk. He died of small pox the following May, ten days before his scheduled departure from Vladivostok. See W.H. Stephenson to Roy, 16 February 1919, Stephenson Family Collection (private collection); "Nominal Roll – Officers and Other Ranks, CEF (Siberia) Who Have Died," n.d., LAC, RG 9, ser. II-B-12, vol. 2, file "Correspondence – Siberian Force"; "Memorial to Rector," *Canadian Churchman* (Toronto), 12 January 1922, Stephenson Family Collection (private collection).
25 Instructions to Lieutenant-Colonel T.S. Morrisey, 7 December 1918, War Diary of Force Headquarters CEF(S), app. 9.
26 High Commissioner (Chita) to High Commissioner (Vladivostok), 18 December 1918, War Diary of Force Headquarters CEF(S), app. 31; Instructions to Lieutenant-Colonel T.S. Morrisey, 7 December 1918, War Diary of Force Headquarters CEF(S), app. 9; "Operation Order No. 1," 6 December 1918, War Diary of Force Headquarters CEF(S), December 1918, app. 1. See also diary entries, 8 December to 27 December 1918, War Diary of Force Headquarters CEF(S).
27 Elmsley to Chief General Staff (Ottawa) and War Office (London), 6 December 1918; Daily Routine Orders, 14 December 1918, War Diary of Force Headquarters CEF(S).
28 Elmsley to Chief General Staff (Ottawa) and War Office (London), 6 December 1918, War Diary of Force Headquarters CEF(S); Daily Routine Orders, Order No. 114, Strength Decrease, 15 February 1919, War Diary of General Staff CEF(S), February 1919, app. 49. The troops left Vladivostok aboard the SS *Madras* on 15 February 1919.
29 Instruction for OC 1/9th Battalion Hampshire Regiment, 14 December 1918, War Diary of Force Headquarters CEF(S); Elmsley to War Office (London) and CGS (Ottawa), 16 December 1918, War Diary of Force Headquarters CEF(S); Kinvig, *Churchill's Crusade*, 207-9.
30 Elmsley to Knox, 24 December 1918, Neilson (Omsk) to Elmsley, 21 December 1918 (both in War Diary of Force Headquarters CEF[S]).
31 Instructions to Lieutenant-Colonel T.S. Morrisey, 7 December 1918, War Diary of Force Headquarters CEF(S); Daily Routine Orders, 15 December 1918, War Diary of Force Headquarters CEF(S).
32 Elmsley to War Office (London) and CGS (Ottawa), 16 December 1918, War Diary of Force Headquarters CEF(S).
33 Elmsley to Knox, 21 December 1918, LAC, RG 9, ser. III-A-S, vol. 362, file A3, SEF (file 116), "Secret No. 3 Proposed Movement and Composition of Siberian Forces."
34 "Our Stay in Muroran," *Siberian Bugle*, 6 March 1919, War Diary of 259th Battalion CEF(S); Daily Orders, 12 January 1919, LAC, RG 9, ser. II-B-12, vol. 3, file "Part II – Daily Orders 20th Machine Gun Company"; MacLaren, *Canadians in Russia*, 176.

35 The arrival of the *Teesta* and the *Protesilaus* is recorded in Daily Routine Orders, Headquarters CEF(S), 14 and 16 January 1919, LAC, RG 9, ser. II-B-12, vol. 2, file "Daily Routine Orders, Siberia."

36 Conditions aboard the *Teesta* are recorded in the War Diary of ADOS CEF(S), 12 January 1919, LAC, RG 9, series III-D-3, vol. 5057, reel T-11119, and the War Diary of Base Headquarters CEF(S). The procedure for the disembarkation of the *Teesta* can be found in "Secret Administrative Instruction No. 1," 4 January 1919, War Diary of Base Headquarters CEF(S). See also War Diary of 259th Battalion CEF(S), 13 and 14 January 1919. The unloading of the *Teesta* is recounted in War Diary of ADOS CEF(S), 13 January 1919 and War Diary of Base Headquarters CEF(S), 13 January 1919; Hertzberg Diary, 13 January 1919, LAC, Hertzberg Fonds, vol. 1, file 1-18, diary no. 9. Cargo aboard the *Teesta* is itemized by weight in Divisional Transports, Vancouver, to Naval Service, Ottawa, 23 December 1918, LAC, RG 24, vol. 3969, file NSC 1047-14-27 (vol. 1). For the troops' gear, see Skuce, *CSEF*, 25.

37 G.S. Worsley Report on "B" Squadron RNWMP, 11 October 1919, LAC, RG 18, vol. 3179, file G 989-3 (vol. 2); Hertzberg, *Military Engineering with the Canadian Brigade*, 10-13, LAC, Hertzberg Fonds, file 1-4.

38 Richard Garton Holmes to Mother, n.d. [c. January 1919], as quoted in Faulstich, "Mail from the Canadian Siberian Expeditionary Force," 22; Captain W.E. Dunham, "The Canadians in Siberia," *Maclean's* (May 1918), 92-93.

39 George F. Clingan, "Siberian Sideshow," 11; MacLaren, *Canadians in Russia*, 177.

40 Stuart to Edna, 18 January 1919, in Tompkins, *A Canadian's Road to Russia*, 372.

41 Daily Routine Orders, 17 January 1919, Headquarters CEF(S), LAC, RG 9, ser. II-B-2, vol. 2, file "Daily Routine Orders, Siberia."

42 Pares, *My Russian Memoirs*, 498-99. Prior to the departure of the Canadians from Victoria, the daily press had painted a rosy picture of the city, claiming: "Vladivostok is a modern city in every respect." However, an RNWMP member later wrote that Vladivostok's "drainage and water systems were probably the world's worst." See "Siberia Holds Immense Opportunity to Members of Canadian Contingent," *Daily Times*, 17 December 1918; T.B. Caulkin, "Siberia, 1918-1919," *RCMP Quarterly* 9, 2 (October 1941), 196; also Caulkin draft, LAC, RG 18, ser. F, vol. 3179, file 1, "First World War, B Squadron for Service in Siberia." On 19 February 1919, the Canadian command warned of a "water famine" unless the Canadian troops exercised "the strictest economy." This threat was due to a "very limited" water supply at all times, combined with "the small amount of snow" and the fact that the frost had penetrated to "an unusual depth": "The wells are very low and will take longer than usual to fill." See Daily Routine Orders, Order No. 126, Water, 19 February 1919, War Diary of General Staff CEF(S), February 1919, app. 49, p. 17.

43 General Routine Orders, 11 January 1919, Elmsley to Defensor (Ottawa), 19 January 1919, War Diary of Force Headquarters CEF(S), app. 50, p. 3; Polk, "Canadian Red Cross and Relief in Siberia," 59-71.

44 Daily Routine Orders, 8 January 1919, War Diary of Force Headquarters CEF(S).

45 War Diary of Deputy Assistant Director of Supplies and Transport CEF(S), 31 January 1919, LAC, RG 9, series III-D-3, vol. 5057, reel T-11119. See also Hertzberg Diary, 31 January 1919-2 February 1919, 28-29 December 1918, LAC, Hertzberg Fonds, vol. 1, file 1-18, diary no. 9.

46 War Diary of Force Headquarters CEF(S), 17 January 1919. See also Elmsley to Morrisey, 17 January 1919, War Diary of Force Headquarters CEF(S), app. 44, p. 15.

47 War Diary of Force Headquarters CEF(S), 1 January 1919; Wilgress, *Memoirs*, 54; Hertzberg Diary, 1 January 1919, LAC, Hertzberg Fonds, vol. 1, file 1-18, diary no. 9.

48 War Diary of Force Headquarters CEF(S), 26 January 1919.

49 Harold to Josie, 8 March and 19 March 1919, LAC, Harold Steele Fonds, MG 30, E564, file "Correspondence, 1 Dec. 1918-1 May 1919." See also "Letters from Vladivostok, 1918-1923," 497-530.

50 Clingan, "Siberian Sideshow," 40.

51 Pares, *My Russian Memoirs*, 507; Mackintosh Bell, *Side Lights on the Siberian Campaign*, 49.

52 Elkington interview, June 1980, UVASC, Military Oral History Collection, SC 141, 169. Elkington earned his medical degree during the war and, after two decades as a doctor with the British army, opened a medical practice in Duncan. See also Ardagh Diary entry, 16 January and 23 March 1919, LAC, Ardagh Fonds, MG 30, E-150, files 1/6 and 2/6. Ardagh wrote: "Some of the sights are pitiful. One can see that the poor little children are famished." See also LAC, RG 150, acc. 1992-93/166, box 2861-54.

53 Elkington interview, June 1980, UVASC, Military Oral History Collection, SC 141, 169.

54 Ibid., 170. For a slightly different description of this incident, see Pares, *My Russian Memoirs*, 505.

55 Holmes to Mother, n.d., as quoted in Faulstich, "Mail from the Canadian Siberian Expeditionary Force," 22.

56 Elkington interview, June 1980, UVASC, Military Oral History Collection, SC 141, 169.

57 Wilgress, *Memoirs*, 54-55.

58 The SS *Cyclops*, loaded with provisions, brought seven Canadian medics on 14 April 1919. See War Diary of Force Headquarters CEF(S), 3 February and 24 February 1919, app. 40; Daily Routine Orders, Headquarters CEF(S), 28 February 1919, LAC, RG 9, ser. II-B-12, vol. 2, file "Daily Routine Orders, Siberia"; Skuce, *CSEF*, 23-24, 54-55; MacLaren, *Canadians in Russia*, 151, 175. For a description of the *Monteagle's* February crossing, see Pares, *My Russian Memoirs*, 498-99. A total of six officers and three enlisted men reached Vladivostok aboard the *Madras*, while the *Monteagle* carried six officers and nineteen other ranks. See Daily Routine Orders, 4 and 20 February 1919, War Diary of General Staff CEF(S), February 1919, app. 49.

59 Stuart to Edna, 18 February, 22 February and 25 February 1919, in Tompkins, *A Canadian's Road to Russia*, 409; War Diary of Assistant Adjutant (hereafter cited as AA) and Quartermaster General (hereafter cited as QMG) Branch CEF(S), 4 February, 8 February, and 19 February 1919, LAC, RG 9, ser. III-D-3, vol. 5057, reel T-11119; "Daily Routine Orders," 22 February 1919, LAC, RG 9, ser. II-B-12, vol. 2, file "Daily Routine Orders, Siberia"; "Strength of Units of the Canadian Expeditionary Force in Siberia," 8 March 1919, LAC, RG 24, ser. C-1-a, vol. 1992, file HQ-762-11-25, "Returns of Strength CEF (Siberia)"; G.S. Worsley Report on "B" Squadron RNWMP, 11 October 1919, LAC, RG 18, vol. 3179, file G 989-3 (vol. 2). RNWMP Major G.S. Worsley was appointed commanding officer at Second River Barracks on 22 February 1919. See Daily Routine Orders, No. 138, 22 February 1919, War Diary of General Staff CEF(S), February 1919, app. 49, p. 11.

60 "The Roadhouse Minstrels," *Siberian Sapper* (Vladivostok), 8 February 1919, Stephenson Family Collection (private collection); "The Roadhouse Minstrels Present the Following Bill," n.d. [c. January 1919], LAC, RG 9, ser. III-D-3, vol. 5057, file 964; Massey, *When I Was Young*, 214-21.

61 "Vladivostok 28th January 1919," War Diary of Force Headquarters CEF(S), January 1919, app. 78, p. 13. See also General Routine Orders, 23 January 1919, Otani to Elmsley, 24 January 1919, War Diary of Force Headquarters CEF(S), app. 72, p. 7.

62 Captain W.E. Dunham, "The Canadians in Siberia," *Maclean's* (May 1918), 11-12.

63 Dorothy Findlay to Mother, 2 December 1918, in "Letters from Vladivostok," 506-7; Tompkins, *A Canadian's Road to Russia*, 369-404; Elkington interview, June 1980 and January 1986, UVASC, Military Oral History Collection, SC 141, 169 and 170; Massey, *When I Was*

Young, 212-13; Hertzberg Diary, 28 October-5 June 1919, LAC, Hertzberg Fonds, vol. 1, file 1-18, diary no. 8 (10 May 1918-15 November 1918) and diary no. 9 (16 November 1918-22 July 1919); Hertzberg, *Military Engineering with the Canadian Brigade*, 8, LAC, Hertzberg Fonds, file 1-4; Ardagh Diary, January 1919-May 1919, LAC, Ardagh Fonds, MG 30, E-150; MacLaren, *Canadians in Russia*, 198. Interpreters attached to the Canadian force were paid at the rate of five shillings a day, plus room and board. See General Routine Order No. 24, 22 December 1918, Captain Everett memo, 26 December 1918, War Diary of Force Headquarters CEF(S). See also "Siberian Expeditionary Force, Siberia interpreters, c. 1919," LAC, RG 24, ser. c-1-a, vol. 2004.

64 MacLaren, *Canadians in Russia*, 198-99; "Notice," 29 March 1919, War Diary of General Staff CEF(S), Daily Routine Orders, March 1919, app. 41, p. 31. For the activities of the YMCA, see LAC, RG 9, ser. II-B-12, "Part II Daily Orders – Vladivostok – YMCA"; Charles W. Bishop, *The Canadian YMCA in the Great War: The Official Record of the Activities of the Canadian YMCA in Connection with the Great War of 1914-1918* (Toronto: National Council of Young Men's Christian Associations of Canada, 1924), 304-10; I.J.E. Daniel and D.A. Casey, *For God and Country: War Work of Canadian Knights of Columbus Catholic Army Huts* (Ottawa: Knights of Columbia, c. 1922), 167-70. For a description of a Russian Orthodox Church service, see Faulstich, "Mail from the Canadian Siberian Expeditionary Force," 26.

65 "YMCA Notes," *Siberian Sapper* (Vladivostok), 8 February 1919, Stephenson Family Collection (private collection); Daily Routine Order No. 69, 31 January 1919, War Diary of Force Headquarters, CEF(S), app. 92-94, p. 69. See also Stuart to Edna, 15 February 1919, in Tompkins, *A Canadian's Road to Russia*, 402.

66 Polk, "Canadian Red Cross and Relief in Siberia," 65; Faulstich, "Mail from the Canadian Siberian Expeditionary Force," 24-25; MacLaren, *Canadians in Russia*, 198; Stuart to Edna, 25 January 1919, in Tompkins, *A Canadian's Road to Russia*, 378; Ardagh Diary, 31 January 1919, LAC, Ardagh Fonds, MG 30, E-150, file 1/6. For the organization of sporting activities, see "Sports Organization CEF (Siberia)," 4 February 1919, War Diary of General Staff CEF(S), Daily Routine Orders, February 1919, app. 49, pp. 33-34.

67 Ardagh Diary, 29 January 1919, LAC, Ardagh Fonds, MG 30, E-150, file 1/6. For further information on the climate in Vladivostok, see LAC, RG 9, ser. III-A-3, vol. 363, file 125; Skuce, *CSEF*, 35; Hertzberg, *Military Engineering with the Canadian Brigade*, 4-5, LAC, Hertzberg Fonds, file 1-4; Hertzberg Diary, 21 and 22 December 1918, LAC, Hertzberg Fonds, vol. 1, file 1-18, diary no. 9.

68 Elkington interview, June 1980, UVASC, Military Oral History Collection, SC 141, 169; Stuart to Edna, 18 January 1919, in Tompkins, *A Canadian's Road to Russia*, 373.

69 Wilgress, *Memoirs*, 55; Hertzberg Diary, 12 April 1919 and 28 April-2 May 1919, LAC, Hertzberg Fonds, vol. 1, file 1-18, diary no. 9; "Notice – Gymkhana," 26 March 1919, War Diary of General Staff CEF(S), March 1919, Daily Routine Orders, app. 41; "Notice – Gymkhana," 19 April 1919, War Diary of General Staff CEF(S), April 1919, Daily Routine Orders, app. 43, p. 26; "Notice – Gymkhana," 3 May 1919, LAC, War Diary of General Staff CEF(S), May 1919, Daily Routine Orders, app. 55, pp. 5-6; War Diary of General Staff CEF(S), 1 May 1919; G.S. Worsley Report on "B" Squadron RNWMP, 11 October 1919, LAC, RCMP Fonds, RG 18, vol. 3179, file G 989-3 (vol. 2); Clingan, "Siberian Sideshow," 41.

70 Daily Routine Orders, 21 December 1918, p. 82, War Diary of Force Headquarters CEF(S).

71 Massey, *When I Was Young*, 206.

72 Daily Routine Orders, 11 December 1918, War Diary of Force Headquarters CEF(S).

73 General Routine Orders, 23 October 1918, p. 13 and Daily Routine Orders, 20 November and 19 December 1918, p. 78 (all in War Diary of Force Headquarters CEF[S]). See also Suzann Buckley, "The Failure to Resolve the Problem of Venereal Disease among the

Troops in Britain during World War I," in *War and Society: A Yearbook of Military History,* vol. 2, ed. Brian Bond and Ian Roy, 65-85 (London: Croom Helm, 1977).

74   Stephan, *Russian Far East,* 134; MacLaren, *Canadians in Russia,* 201.

75   Elkington interview, June 1980, UVASC, Military Oral History Collection, SC 141, 169.

76   "Shooting of No. 417988 L/Cpl. P. Marchik," 5 February 1919, LAC, RG 9, ser. III-a-3, vol. 378, file A3, SEF Courts of Enquiry, pt. 2, Daily Orders, 10 December 1918, War Diary of Force Headquarters CEF(S). Earlier, Marchik had been convicted of drunkenness and of being absent without leave. See General Routine Orders, 3 January 1919, War Diary of Force Headquarters CEF(S).

77   Elkington interview, June 1980, UVASC, Military Oral History Collection, SC 141, 169.

78   "Typhus Fever – and Its Prevention," *Siberian Sapper* (Vladivostok), 8 February 1919, Stephenson Family Collection (private collection).

79   "No Trade Yet for Canada," *Globe* (Toronto), 3 April 1919.

80   Daily Routine Orders, Order No. 78, Bounds East Barracks, 2 February 1919, War Diary of General Staff CEF(S), February 1919, app. 49, p. 35; Polk, "Canadian Red Cross and Relief in Siberia," 65-69.

81   Polk, "Canadian Red Cross and Relief in Siberia," 210.

82   "Appendix E – Preliminary Report," 9 December 1918, in Canada, *Report of the Canadian Economic Commission (Siberia),* 54.

83   "Vancouver Women Urged to Help Civilians in Siberia," *Vancouver Daily Sun,* 6 November 1918, 4. See also "Aid Is Sought to Siberian Civilians," *Vancouver Daily Sun,* 21 November 1918, 3; Polk, "Canadian Red Cross and Relief in Siberia," 90-91; Floyd Miller, *Wild Children of the Urals* (New York: Dutton, 1965); LAC, Farmer Fonds, MG 30, ser. C182. For the history of nursing matrons in the Canadian military, see G.W.L. Nicholson, *Canada's Nursing Sisters* (Toronto: Hakkert, 1975); E.A. Landells, ed., *The Military Nurses of Canada: Recollections of Canadian Military Nurses* (White Rock, BC: Co-Publishing, 1975). See also Ian Hay, *One Hundred Years of Army Nursing: The Story of the British Army Nursing Services from the Time of Florence Nightingale to the Present Day* (London: Cassell and Co., 1953); Douglas Baldwin, "The American Red Cross in Vladivostok: The Adventures of Nurse Mona Wilson," *Journal of Siberian Studies* 1, 2 (1994-95): 85-107.

84   Polk, "Canadian Red Cross and Relief in Siberia," 60-62 and 67-68; MacLaren, *Canadians in Russia,* 203-5; War Diary of Force Headquarters CEF(S), 9-11 March 1919.

85   According to Mewburn, Dennis was "a very useful man ... the 'handy man' for Elmsley." See Mewburn to Gwatkin, 1 October 1918, LAC, RG 24, ser. C-1-A, vol. 2557, file HQC-2514 (vol. 1); "Col. John S. Dennis, CMG, Is Red Cross Commissioner to Siberia," *Canadian Red Cross Society Bulletin* 40 (18 November 1918), 39-40, CRCR, ser. 1, sec. 2, "Printed Materials."

86   Canada, *Report of the Canadian Economic Commission (Siberia),* 9 and 24. See also "Impression of Vladivostok," *Siberian Sapper* (Vladivostok), 25 January 1919, CRCR, ser. 1, sec. 1, "Archival Documents"; J.P.B. Webster, Vladivostok, to Leslie Urquhart, London, 26 February 1919, CRCR, ser. 1, sec. 1, pt. C, "Royal Bank of Canada."

87   "Zagotovka ogorodnykh semyan" [Stockpiling of Vegetable Seeds], *Dalekaya Okraina* (Vladivostok), 16 November 1918, Vladivostok State Historical Archive; Watson Griffin to A.K. Maclean, 6 February 1919, LAC, Department of Trade and Commerce, RG 20, vol. 1369, file 21916 (vol. 1), "Canadian Economic Commission in Siberia."

88   Wilgress, "From Siberia to Kuibyshev," 367-68.

89   Dennis to Foster, 11 March 1919, LAC, RG 20, vol. 136, file 22804 (vol. 1), "Canadian Economic Commission in Siberia"; War Diary of General Staff CEF(S), 15 March 1919; Beattie, "Canadian Intervention in Russia," 334-68; Hill, *Canada's Salesman to the World,* 210-20.

90 Canada, *Report of the Canadian Economic Commission*, app. F, "Report on Financial Conditions in Siberia," 55-61; William Rodney, "Siberia in 1919: A Canadian Banker's Impression," *Queen's Quarterly* 79, 3 (Autumn 1972): 324-35; D.C. Rea, "Vladivostok, Siberia-in-Russia, Branch" (draft), n.d., 4-5, Royal Bank of Canada Archives (copy in CRCR, ser. 1, sec. 1, pt. B, "Royal Bank of Canada"); O'Hara to Braithwaite, 3 January 1919, Braithwaite to O'Hara, 2 January 1919, LAC, RG 20, vol. 136, file 21916 (vol. 1), "Canadian Economic Commission in Siberia"; Canadians in Siberia," *Globe* (Toronto), 3 December 1918; Stephan, *Russian Far East*, 132.

91 Ardagh Diary, 24 March 1919, LAC, Ardagh Fonds, file 2/6; Faulstich, "Mail from the Canadian Siberian Expeditionary Force," 25; Rodney, "Siberia in 1919," 329; "No. 395 – Russian Currency," 2 May 1919, "No. 405 – Exchange Russian Currency (Kerensky) for Siberian," 7 May 1919, War Diary of General Staff CEF(S), May 1919, Daily Routine Orders, app. 55, pp. 3 and 10.

92 Canada banned the purchase of Russian rubles with Order-in-Council No. 113 on 17 January 1919. See "Clandestine Trading in Russian Rubles," 15 April 1919, LAC, RG 18, ser. A-2, vol. 878, file "Labour Organizations and Communism," reel T-6256.

93 Ward to Blair, 29 January 1919, War Diary of Force Headquarters CEF(S), February 1919, app. 6.

94 "Extra Guards, Fatigues, Etc., Furnished by 16th Inf. Bde.," 28 February 1919, LAC, RG 24, ser. C-1-a, vol. 1992, file 762-11-28, "Guards, Siberian Expeditionary Force"; D.C. Rea, "Vladivostok, Siberia-in-Russia, Branch" (draft), n.d., Royal Bank of Canada Archives (copy in CRCR, ser. 1, sec. 1, pt. B, "Royal Bank of Canada"); "War Diary: Pages from the Chronicle of the Bank's Adventures in Troubled Times," *Royal Bank Magazine* (March 1945), 12-14; "East Remembers Russian Branch," *Interest* (March/April 1979), 20-22; Duncan McDowall, *Quick to the Frontier*, 194-95.

95 Wilgress, "From Siberia to Kuibyshev," 367.

96 Canada, *Report of the Canadian Economic Commission (Siberia)*, 14.

97 "O kanadskoy ekonomichyeskoy missii" [About the Canadian Economic Mission], *Pravityel'stvyenniy vyestnik* [Government Bulletin] (Omsk), 19 January 1919, Khabarovsk State Archives; Canada, *Report of the Canadian Economic Commission (Siberia)*, app. D, "Report of the Joint Meeting Held with the Representatives of the Co-operatives at Vladivostok on Wednesday, March 5, 1919," 47; "Fight against Co-operative Societies," *Siberian Bugle* (Vladivostok), 28 March 1919, War Diary of 259th Battalion CEF(S); J.P.B. Webster, Vladivostok, to Leslie Urquhart, London, 26 February 1919, CRCR, ser. 1, sec. 1, pt. C, "Royal Bank of Canada"; Pares, *My Russian Memoirs*, 505, 519-21; Rodney, "Siberia in 1919," 327-29.

98 Elkington interview, January 1986, UVASC, Military Oral History Collection, SC 141, 170.

99 Resolution passed by Vladivostok Trade-Manufacturers' Assembly, 1 November 1918, as quoted in "K rekvizitsii Pushkinskogo Teatra" [On the Requisition of Pushkinsky Theatre], *Dalekaya Okraina* (Vladivostok), 4 November 1918, Vladivostok State Historical Archive.

100 Elkington interview, June 1980 and January 1986, UVASC, Military Oral History Collection, SC 141, 169 and 170. Ragosin served as an interpreter with the 16th Infantry Brigade Headquarters staff. He was married to renowned ballerina Lydia Kyasht and settled in London after the Russian Civil War.

101 See Hoover Institution Archives, Edith M. Faulstich Collection, Box 7, File "International Military Police and Major Samuel I. Johnson"; "General Becomes Major," *New York Times*, 24 February 1918; Robert L. Willett, *Russian Sideshow: America's Undeclared War, 1918-1920* (Washington: Brassey's, 2003), 192-93. According to Dorothy Findlay, a British citizen who lived in Vladivostok at the time, officers from the HMS *Suffolk* did "some quiet exploring

& investigating" prior to the toppling of the Vladivostok Soviet at the end of June 1918, determining the command structure of the local Bolsheviks. See Dorothy Findlay letter, 1 July 1918, in "Letters from Vladivostok," 500-1; Amir Khisamutdinov interview, 27 March 2008, Vladivostok, Russia; Skuce, *CSEF*, 14.

102 Beattie, "Canadian Intervention in Russia," 316-17, 353; Trade report of L.D. Wilgress, 22 July 1919, Department of Trade and Commerce, *Weekly Bulletin*, 9 September 1919, 487.

103 Nicholson, *Official History of the Canadian Army*, 518; G.S. Worsley Report on "B" Squadron RNWMP, 11 October 1919, LAC, RG 18, vol. 3179, file G 989-3 (vol. 2); MacLaren, *Canadians in Russia*, 197.

104 "Canadians Had Easy Time in Siberia," *Daily Times*, 19 April 1919.

105 William S. Graves, *America's Siberian Adventure, 1918-1920* (New York: Peter Smith, 1941), 101.

106 Captain W.E. Dunham, "The Canadians in Siberia," *Maclean's* (May 1919), 94-95.

107 Williams, *Through the Russian Revolution*, 272.

108 Smith, *Vladivostok under Red and White Rule*, 9-10.

109 Ibid., 9-10; Stephan, *Russian Far East*, 342.

110 Smith, *Vladivostok under Red and White Rule*, 7.

111 The Soviet government changed the name of "Suchan" to "Partizansk" in 1972, vanquishing the Chinese name in the aftermath of the Sino-Soviet border dispute of 1969, which saw Chinese and Russian troops engage in bloody hand-to-hand combat over tiny Damansky (or Zhenboa) Island in the Ussuri River. See Adrian Room, *Placenames of Russia and the Former Soviet Union* (Jefferson, CA: McFarland and Company, 1996), 158; Stephan, *Russian Far East*, 349-54; Andrey Musalov, *Damanskiy i Zhalanashkol': Sovyetsko-kitayskiy vooroozhyenniy konflikt 1969 goda* [Damanski and Zhalanashkol: Sino-Soviet Armed Border Conflict in 1969] (Izdatyel'stvo: Eksprint, 2005).

112 Smith, *Vladivostok under Red and White Rule*, 7-9.

113 Mukhachev, *Dal' nii Vostok Rossii*, 318; "Comrades Workmen and Peasants," n.d., War Diary of General Staff CEF(S), April 1919, app. 38.

114 Smith, *Vladivostok under Red and White Rule*, 7; Graves to Elmsley, 22 March 1919, Elmsley to Eliot, 24 March 1919 (both in War Diary of General Staff CEF[S], March 1919, apps. P[j] and P[l]); "The Siberian Peasant and Koltchak's Regime," *Tribune*, 15 September 1919.

115 "The Train of Death," *Tribune*, 22 May 1919; "The Death Train of Siberia," *Red Flag*, 28 June 1919; Mackintosh Bell, *Side Lights on the Siberian Campaign*, 127.

116 Mukhachev, *Dal' nii Vostok Rossii*, 318.

117 Blair, 24 January 1918, LAC, RG 24, ser. C-1-A, vol. 2557, file HQC-2514 (vol. 2), "Situation in Russia – Allied Intervention in Russia"; Beattie, "Canadian Intervention in Russia," 115-17.

118 Otani to Ivanov Rinov and Horvath, 29 January 1919, War Diary of General Staff CEF(S), Policy Etc. in Case of Uprisings and Disorders in Vladivostok and Vicinity, March 1919, app. P (f).

119 Mackintosh Bell, *Side Lights on the Siberian Campaign*, 125.

120 Clingan, "Siberian Sideshow," 40.

121 "The Canadian Sheriff in Siberia," *Tribune*, 20 January 1919; "A Record Crowd Hears Pritchard," *BC Federationist*, 2 May 1919.

122 Daily Routine Orders, Order No. 172, Attachments, February 1919, War Diary of General Staff CEF(S), February 1919, app. 49, p. 3.

123 Hertzberg Diary, 23 April 1919, LAC, Hertzberg Fonds, vol. 1, file 1-18, diary no. 9

124 Military Intelligence Report No. 1, Vladivostok, 16 January 1919, War Diary of Force Headquarters CEF(S), app. 45, p. 16; Sergey Nikolaevich Shishkin, *Organizatsiya partizanskoi*

bor'by protiv interventov i belogvardeitsev na Dal'nem Vostoke v 1918-1919 [The Organization of Guerrilla Struggle against Interventionists and White Guards in the Far East in 1918-1919] (Moscow: Military publishing house of the Ministry of Defence of the USSR, 1957), 53-70.

125 Report on Military Situation, 28 February 1919, War Diary of General Staff CEF(S), February 1919, app. 45; Elmsley to Defensor (Ottawa), 15 March 1919, "Bolshevik Activity on the Line of Communication," n.d. (c. March 1919), War Diary of General Staff CEF(S), March 1919, apps. 16 and 39; Stephan, *Russian Far East*, 136.

126 *Borba za vlast Sovetov v Primorye* [The Struggle for Soviet Power in Primorye] (Vladivostok 1955), 193, as quoted in Mukhachev, *Dal' nii Vostok Rossii*, 318.

127 Mukhachev, *Dal' nii Vostok Rossii*, 318-19; Report on Military Situation, 28 February 1919, War Diary of General Staff CEF(S), February 1919, app. 45; "Extract of Communication Received from Japanese Headquarters – Bolshevik Movements in the Priamur Province," 1 March 1919, Elmsley to Defensor (Ottawa), 15 March 1919, Intelligence Report re Olga and Suchan Mines, 17 March 1919, Intelligence Report re Situation at Olga Bay, 18 March 1919, "Bolshevik Activity on the Line of Communication," n.d. (c. March 1919) (all in War Diary of General Staff CEF[S], March 1919, apps. 2, 16, 19, 21, and 29, p. 4); Schuyler to Adams, 22 May 1919, "To the Partisan Force Olga District," n.d., LAC, General Staff CEF(S), April 1919, app. O(8).

128 Intelligence Report re Situation at Olga Bay, 18 March 1919, War Diary of General Staff CEF(S), March 1919, app. 21.

129 Intelligence Report on Situation in Vladiromo-Alexandrovka [sic], 11 April 1919, and Intelligence Report, 24 April 1919 (both in War Diary of General Staff CEF[S], April 1919, apps. O[2] and O[22]); Intelligence Communiqué No. 3, 16 April 1919, War Diary of 16th Infantry Brigade Headquarters CEF(S), April 1919, app. 15.

130 Mukhachev, *Dal' nii Vostok Rossii*, 319.

131 Major Jason Adams, "Disturbance in Olga Bay and Suchan Mines Districts," 2 March 1919, War Diary of General Staff CEF(S), March 1919, app. 7.

132 "Report of Lt. Walter F. Resing," 17 March 1919, Graves to Elmsley, 21 March 1919, Elmsley to Eliot, 24 March 1919, Eliot to Elmsley, 25 March 1919 (all in War Diary of General Staff CEF[S], Policy Etc. in Case of Uprisings and Disorders in Vladivostok and Vicinity, March 1919, apps. P[j], P[k], and P[l]); Graves, *America's Siberian Adventure*, 153-56.

133 Smith, *Vladivostok under Red and White Rule*, 10-11; Stephan, *Russian Far East*, 136-37. Stephan attributes the formation of the Military-Revolutionary Staff as part of a Bolshevik manoeuvre to wrest power from the populist and independent partisan commander Gavrila Shevchenko.

134 Intelligence Report, 10 April 1919 and 11 April 1919 (both in LAC, General Staff CEF[S], April 1919, apps. O[1] and O[2]).

135 Report by Lieutenant O.P. Winning Stad of a Trip to Vladimir Alexandrovsky, 14 April 1919, War Diary of General Staff CEF(S), May 1919, app. 53.

136 "Comrades Workmen and Peasants," n.d., War Diary of General Staff CEF(S), April 1919, app. 38.

137 Shishkin, *Organizatsiya partizanskoi*, 53-70.

138 Pares, *My Russian Memoirs*, 505.

139 War Diary of Advance Party, 6th Signal Company, 24 March 1919, CRCR; Skuce, *CSEF*, 19. For an urgent appeal for equipment for wireless communication, see Elmsley to Defensor (Ottawa), 15 March 1919, War Diary of General Staff CEF(S), March 1919, app. 17.

140 War Diary of General Staff CEF(S), 6 February 1919; War Diary of AA and QMG Branch CEF(S), 6 February 1919; Hertzberg, *Military Engineering with the Canadian Brigade*, 9,

LAC, Hertzberg Fonds, file 1-4. The "go-down" garage had been borrowed from White Russian authorities, pending construction of a permanent facility, and the Canadian government provided 300,000 rubles compensation prior to evacuating Vladivostok. See Elmsley to Troopers (London), 5 May 1919, War Diary of General Staff CEF(S), May 1919, app. 27.

141 Clingan, "Siberian Sideshow," 40; Memorandum, Vladivostok, 21 March 1919, LAC, RG 9, ser. III-B-3, vol. 5057; Ardagh Diary, 23 March 1919, LAC, Ardagh Fonds, file 2/3. See also Harold to Josie, 8 March 1919, LAC, Harold Steele Fonds, MG 30, E564, file "Correspondence, 1 Dec. 1918-1 May 1919." See also "Acts of Brutality" and "Official Report – International Commission of Physicians," 15 December 1918, War Diary of General Staff CEF(S), March 1919, app. 36.

142 Massey, *When I Was Young*, 206-7.

143 War Diary of 16th Infantry Brigade Headquarters CEF(S), 12 March 1919; Hertzberg Diary, 9 March 1919, LAC, Hertzberg Fonds, vol. 1, file 1-18, diary no. 9; "Canadians Had Easy Time in Siberia" and "Siberian Lines Being Improved," *Daily Times*, 19 April 1919.

144 Instructions in Case of Riotous Disturbances in Vladivostok Area, 15 March 1919, and Special Operation Orders, 13 March 1919, War Diary of Base Headquarters CEF(S); "Cannot Enter Siberia," *Tribune*, 10 April 1919. Bernard Pares wrote of "an incipient attempt at revolution" in Vladivostok in March 1919. See Pares, *My Russian Memoirs*, 506.

145 Blair to Troopers (London), 13 March 1919, Elmsley to Eliot, 14 March 1919, Eliot to Elmsley, 15 March 1919, Elmsley to Eliot, 15 March 1919, Eliot memorandum, 16 March 1919, Elmsley memorandum, 16 March 1919, Elmsley to War Office, 18 March 1919, Matsudaira to Eliot, 21 March 1919, War Office to Elmsley, 27 March 1919 (all in War Diary of General Staff CEF[S], Policy Etc. in Case of Uprisings and Disorders in Vladivostok and Vicinity, March 1919, app. P); Graves, *America's Siberian Adventure*, 162-74.

146 Hugh Robertson to Mother (from Gornastai Barracks, Vladivostok, Siberia), 16 March 1919, LAC, Hugh Robertson Fonds, MG31, G 17.

147 Instructions in Case of Riotous Disturbances in Vladivostok Area, 15 March 1919, 16th Infantry Brigade Instructions No. 1 and No. 2, 16 March 1919 and 27 March 1919, Commodore J.D. Edwards to Powell (Base Commandant CEFS), 18 March 1919 (all in War Diary of Base Headquarters CEF[S]); McDonnell memorandum, 27 March 1919, "Appendum No. 1," 28 March 1919, "Appendum No. 2," 29 March 1919 (all in War Diary of General Staff CEF [S]), March 1919, app. O [Orders Issued in Case of Uprisings and Disorders in Vladivostok and Vicinity]); War Diary of 16th Infantry Brigade Headquarters, 17 March and 31 March 1919; Elmsley to Blair, 11 April 1919, McDowell to General Staff ADOS, 11 April 1919 (both in War Diary of General Staff CEF[S], April 1919, apps. O[3] and O[4]); Limpton (HMS Kent) to McDonnell, 27 May 1919, Hoover Institution Archives, Geoffrey McDonnell Collection, acc. XX233-10 A-V. The Canadian soldiers were to proceed from Gornostai to East Barracks in "assault kit" (marching gear, with steel helmets and haversacks instead of packs).

148 Commodore J.D. Edwards to Powell (Base Commandant CEFS), 18 March 1919, War Diary of Base Headquarters CEF(S).

149 Elmsley memorandum, 16 March 1919, Elmsley to War Office, 18 March 1919, Elmsley to Otani, 18 March 1919, Elmsley to British High Commissioner (Vladivostok), 22 March 1919, Eliot to Elmsley, 25 March 1919, War Office to Elmsley, 27 March 1919 (all in War Diary of General Staff CEF[S], March 1919, Policy Etc. in Case of Uprisings and Disorders in Vladivostok and Vicinity, apps. P[f] to P[o]); Elmsley to CGS (Ottawa), 24 March 1919, LAC, RG 24, ser. C-1-A, vol. 2557, file HQC-2514 (vol. 2); MacLaren, *Canadians in Russia*,

195-96; G.S. Worsley Report on "B" Squadron RNWMP, 11 October 1919, LAC, RG 18, vol. 3179, file G 989-3 (vol. 2).

150 Memorandum, 21 March 1919, War Diary of Base Headquarters CEF(S); Ardagh Diary, 23 March 1919, LAC, Ardagh Fonds, file 2/3.

151 Ibid.

152 Smith, *Vladivostok under Red and White Rule*, 10-11; Mukhachev, *Dal' nii Vostok Rossii*, 319-20.

153 G.S. Worsley Report on "B" Squadron RNWMP, 11 October 1919, LAC, RG 18, vol. 3179, file G 989-3 (vol. 2); War Diary of General Staff CEF(S), 1 May 1919; Hertzberg Diary, 2 May 1919, LAC, Hertzberg Fonds, vol. 1, file 1-18, diary no. 9.

154 "Operation Plan for Evacuation of Vladivostok," February 1919, War Diary of 259th Battalion CEF(S). See also Major G.F. Worsley Report on "B" Squadron RNWMP, 11 October 1919, LAC, RG 18, vol. 3179, file G 989-3 (vol. 2); Stuart to Edna, 26 March 1919, in Tompkins, *A Canadian's Road to Russia*, 426; "Canadians in Peril in Vladivostok City," *Toronto Globe*, 28 March 1919.

155 General Routine Orders, 10 January 1919, War Diary of Force Headquarters CEF(S).

156 Daily Routine Orders, 21 January 1919, War Diary of Force Headquarters CEF(S).

157 MacLaren, *Canadians in Russia*, 184.

158 Harold to Josie, 19 March 1919, 21 February 1919, LAC, Harold Steele Fonds, MG 30, E564, file "Correspondence, 1 Dec. 1918-1 May 1919." See also Stuart to Edna, 18 February 1919, in Tompkins, *A Canadian's Road to Russia*, 404; General Routine Orders No. 35, Censorship Regulations, 15 February 1919, Elmsley to Morrisey, 19 February 1919, War Diary of General Staff CEF(S), February 1919, apps. 48 and 36. Elmsley's order of 15 February cancelled previous censorship orders but forbade "criticism of operations, of other branches, of Allied troops or of superiors" as well as "statements calculated to bring the enemy or individuals into disrepute." For the prohibition on personal diaries, see Skuce, *CSEF*, 19.

159 Ardagh Diary, 26 January and 29 January 1919, LAC, Ardagh Fonds, MG 30, E-150, file 1/6.

160 Ardagh Diary, 29 January 1919, LAC, Ardagh Fonds, MG 30, E-150, file 1/6.

161 Dunham, "The Canadians in Siberia," *Maclean's* (May 1918), 93.

162 Pares, *My Russian Memoirs*, 506-7; Stuart to Edna, 20 March 1919, as quoted in Tomkins, *A Canadian's Road to Russia*, 421-22; MacLaren, *Canadians in Russia*, 202; War Diary of 16th Infantry Brigade Headquarters CEF(S), 18-19 March 1919.

163 Ireland Diary, March 1919, Erskine Ireland unpublished diary (Toronto), pp. 118-19, as cited in MacLaren, *Canadian in Russia*, 202. See also "Letters," *Morning Albertan* (Calgary), 1 August 1919.

164 "What Are We Doing Here?" *Siberian Sapper* (Vladivostok), 8 February 1919, Gwen Stevenson, personal papers. See also LAC, RG 9, ser. III, vol. 363, file 119, reproduced in Skuce, *CSEF*, 142.

165 "Summary of Events, 1st of March 1919 to 31st of March 1919," 17 March 1919, War Diary of Deputy Judge Advocate General CEF(S); "Charging Sheet," "Summary of Evidence," and "Trial of No. 2014524, Private James Payton, B Company, 260th Battalion," 6 March 1919, LAC, RG 24, ser. C-1-A, vol. 1992, file H-Q-762-11-10, "Courts Martial in CEF (Siberia)." See also "Trial of No. 745 Pte. Mathew Rose, Base Company," 15 February 1919, "No. 197 Field General Court Martial – Pte. William Reginald Newell," 10 March 1919 (both in War Diary of General Staff CEF[S], Daily Routine Orders, March 1919, app. 41, p. 8).

166 Lieutenant-Colonel AQMG to Headquarters CEF(S), 18 May 1919, Gruner to AQMG, 18 May 1919, Elmsley to Grogan, 29 May 1919, Osoll to MCO British Military Mission, 26

May 1919 (all in War Diary of General Staff CEF[S], May 1919, apps. 23 and 47). Kovalchuk Attestation Papers, LAC, RG 150, acc. 1992-93/166, box 5252-26.

167 Graves, *America's Siberian Adventure*, 82.
168 Wilson (London) to CGS (Ottawa), 11 February 1919, CGS (Ottawa) to Elmsley, 12 February 1919, Gwatkin to Wilson, 12 February 1919, Elmsley to Department of Militia and Defence, 19 February 1919, Gwatkin to Wilson, 20 February 1919 (all in LAC, RG 24, ser. C-1-A, vol. 2557, file HQC-2514 [vol. 2] "Situation in Russia – Allied Intervention in Russia").
169 Gwatkin to Troopers (London), 12 February 1919, LAC, RG 24, ser. C-1-A, vol. 2557, file HQC-2514 (vol. 2), "Situation in Russia – Allied Intervention in Russia."
170 Ward, *With the "Die-Hards" in Siberia*, 162-63.
171 Ibid., 163. Ward added: "I am told that Brigadier Pickford [sic] had done his best to maintain order and discipline in his ranks; that he had been compelled to make very awkward promises to his troops which having been made had to be fulfilled ... [T]he proper thing to have done was to send the Canadians home to their farms, and leave the few Britishers who were there to carry on. We had established excellent relations with the Russians which it would have been a thousand pities to spoil."
172 Harold to Josie, 19 March 1919, LAC, Harold Steele Fonds, MG 30, E564, file "Correspondence, 1 Dec. 1918-1 May 1919."
173 Court of Inquiry, 19 March 1919, LAC, RG 9, ser. III-A-3, vol. 378, file "misc."; War Diary of AA and QMG Branch CEF(S), 18 March 1919; War Diary of 16th Infantry Brigade Headquarters CEF(S), 18 March 1919; "Nominal Roll – Officers and Other Ranks, CEF (Siberia) Who Have Died," n.d., LAC, RG 9, ser. II-B-12, vol. 2, file "Correspondence – Siberian Force"; Harold to Josie, 19 March 1919, LAC, Harold Steele Fonds, MG 30, E564, file "Correspondence, 1 Dec. 1918-1 May 1919"; Alfred Henry Thring Attestation Papers, LAC, RG 150, acc. 1992-93/166, box 9683-36; Skuce, *CSEF*, 16-17.
174 Elkington interview, June 1980, UVASC, Military Oral History Collection, SC 141, 169.

Chapter 7: "Up Country" and Evacuation

1 A *verst* was a unit of measurement equal to 1.0668 kilometres, deemed obsolete in 1924 when the Soviet Union adopted the metric system.
2 Elmsley to Knox, 21 December 1918, LAC, RG 9, ser. III-A-S, vol. 362, file A3, SEF (file 116), "Secret No. 3 Proposed Movement and Composition of Siberian Forces."
3 War Diary of Force Headquarters, CEF(S), 27 December 1918; Morrisey (Omsk) to Elmsley (Vladivostok), 28 December 1918, War Diary of Force Headquarters CEF(S). Morrisey informed Elmsley that the arrangements made by Neilson were "satisfactory."
4 "Military Situation, December 31st, 1918," War Diary of Force Headquarters CEF(S), 117.
5 "Twelve Executed for 'Red' Uprising," *BC Federationist*, 3 January 1919.
6 High Commissioner (Omsk) to Acting High Commissioner (Vladivostok), 30 December 1918, War Diary of Force Headquarters CEF(S).
7 Interview with Vladimir Shuldyakov, 4 April 2008, Omsk, Russia.
8 Ward, *With the "Die-Hards" in Siberia*, 155; Jordon (Omsk) to High Commissioner (Vladivostok), 24 December 1918, War Diary of Force Headquarters CEF(S).
9 Jordon (Omsk) to High Commissioner (Vladivostok), 24 December 1918, War Diary of Force Headquarters CEF(S); Ward, *With the "Die-Hards" in Siberia*, 150-55.
10 Ward, *With the "Die-Hards" in Siberia*, 156; Beattie, "Canadian Intervention in Russia," 321-22.
11 War Diary of Force Headquarters CEF(S), 4 and 5 January 1919.
12 War Diary of Force Headquarters CEF(S), 7 January 1919. However, one week later Morrisey wrote to Elmsley: "Please tell me who commands them [the Hampshire and Middlesex

battalions] now. If you do not then what is my position?" See Morrisey to Elmsley, 14 January 1919, War Diary of Force Headquarters CEF(S), app. 38, p. 9.

13 War Diary of Force Headquarters CEF(S), 4 and 5 January 1919; "Pribitiye Kanadskih voysk" [Arrival of Canadian Troops], *Pravityel'stvyenniy vyestnik* (Omsk), 28 December 1918, Khabarovsk State Archives; War Diary of Force Headquarters, CEF(S), 3-11 January 1919; Morrisey to Elmsley, 15 January 1919, War Diary of Force Headquarters, CEF(S), January 1919, app. B8. See also Kinvig, *Churchill's Crusade*, 209-10.

14 War Diary of Force Headquarters CEF(S), 4 January 1919.

15 High Commissioner (Omsk) to Acting High Commissioner (Vladivostok), 9 January 1919, app. 19, Lash to Mewburn (via Elmsley), 13 January 1919, app. 39, Morrisey to Elmsley, 13 January 1919, app. B5 (all in War Diary of Force Headquarters, CEF[S]).

16 For troop totals of Canadian and British forces in Siberia, see "Strength and Disposition of Units of the Canadian Expeditionary Force, Siberia, and British Units in Siberia as of 31 December 1918," War Diary of Force Headquarters CEF(S), December 1918, app. 39.

17 Elmsley to Chief General Staff (Ottawa) and War Office (London), 3 December 1918, LAC, RG 9, ser. III-D-3, vol. 5056, reel T-10950, War Diary of Force Headquarters CEF(S).

18 "Military Situation, December 31st, 1918," War Diary of Force Headquarters CEF(S), p. 117; Ward, *With the "Die-Hards" in Siberia*, 140-43.

19 Instruction for OC 1/9th Battalion Hampshire Regiment, 14 December 1918, War Diary of Force Headquarters CEF(S). For attempts to ease tensions, such as a 9 January meeting between Kolchak, Janin, and Knox, at which Knox was appointed Janin's director of communications, see War Diary of Force Headquarters CEF(S), 9, 15, and 16 January 1919. See also Knox to [Blair, Vladivostok], 12 January 1919, app. 33, p. 3, Knox to [Blair, Vladivostok], 14 January 1919, apps. 35 and 40, pp. 6 and 11, High Commissioner (Omsk) to Acting High Commissioner (Vladivostok), 15 January 1919, app. 63, High Commissioner (Omsk) to Foreign Office (London), 17 January 1919, Elmsley to Defensor (Ottawa), 26 January 1919, app. 73, p. 8 (all in War Diary of Force Headquarters CEF[S], January 1919).

20 War Diary of Force Headquarters CEF(S), 5 and 16 January 1919.

21 Morrisey to Elmsley, 14 January 1919, War Diary of Force Headquarters CEF(S), app. 41, p. 12.

22 Instruction for OC 1/9th Battalion Hampshire Regiment, 14 December 1918, War Diary of Force Headquarters CEF(S).

23 Troopers (London) to Elmsley, 29 January 1919, Elmsley to Trooper (London), 31 January 1919, Elmsley to Morrisey, 31 January 1919 (all in War Diary of Force Headquarters CEF[S], January 1919, apps. 85-87, pp. 21-23). In mid-January, Elmsley had received authorization from Ottawa to move to Omsk once Bickford arrived aboard the *Protesilaus*. He wired Morrisey inquiring "about officers comforts" in that city and prepared a motor car, motorcycle, and several horses to accompany him. However, the Canadian commander noted: "our train [was] difficult to secure." See Defensor (Ottawa) to Elmsley, 17 January 1919, War Diary of Force Headquarters CEF(S), app. 47, p. 18; Elmsley to Morrisey, 16 January 1919, app. 36, p. 7, Elmsley to Morrisey, 20 January 1919 (both in War Diary of Force Headquarters CEF[S], app. 41, p. 13).

4 "Military Situation, December 31st, 1918," War Diary of Force Headquarters CEF(S), December 1919, app. 42.

5 "Military Situation, December 31st, 1918," War Diary of Force Headquarters CEF(S).

6 War Diary of Force Headquarters CEF(S), 18 and 19 January 1919. Elmsley's delayed reply prompted an angry cable from Knox to his Vladivostok deputy, General Blair: "Please ascertain whether Elmsley has had to refer home Morrisey's question about detaching one officer and six men to Orenburg. If he has, this is the limit, and you should wire it

home as a typical instance of the difficulties under which we are working." Elmsley's response, relayed through Blair, demonstrated how Allied ambivalence was hindering military strategy on the ground in Siberia: "Advise you act on your own initiative if urgent pending decision war office. Bear in mind until results peace conference known we cannot reinforce them." However, the British War Office quickly settled the matter: "Regret we cannot agree to any further dispersal of the small British Force in Siberia. You should accordingly refuse to send Company to Orenburg." See Knox (Omsk) to Blair (Vladivostok), 17 January 1919, War Diary of Force Headquarters CEF(S), app. 57, p. 9; Blair to Knox, 19 January 1919, War Diary of Force Headquarters CEF(S), app. 58, p. 10; Troopers (London) to Knox (Omsk), 17 January 1919, War Diary of Force Headquarters CEF(S), app. 59, p. 10; War Diary of Force Headquarters CEF(S), 27 January 1919.

27   Knox to Blair, 29 January 1919, War Diary of Force Headquarters CEF(S), app. 6; Elmsley to Defensor (Ottawa), 10 February 1919, War Diary of General Staff CEF(S), February 1919, app. 25.

28   Dirmilint (London) to Knox (Omsk), 20 January 1919, War Diary of Force Headquarters CEF(S), January 1919, app. 67.

29   Daily Routine Orders, 15 December 1918, War Diary of Force Headquarters CEF(S), December 1918, apps. 1-43, p. 73. See also "Military Situation," Elmsley to Defensor (Ottawa), 30 January 1919, War Diary of Force Headquarters CEF(S), app. 84, p. 20.

30   "Military Situation, December 31st, 1918," War Diary of Force Headquarters CEF(S), p. 117; High Commissioner (Omsk) to Acting High Commissioner (Vladivostok), 30 December 1918, War Diary of Force Headquarters CEF(S). On 6 January 1919, the CEFS Force Headquarters wired the chief of general staff, Ottawa, requesting that the Canadians authorize "an anti-typhus train owing to prevalence of the disease in Siberia." See War Diary of Force Headquarters CEF(S), 6 January 1919. See also Polk, "Canadian Red Cross and Relief in Siberia," 61.

31   "Military Situation, December 31st, 1918," War Diary of Force Headquarters CEF(S), p. 117; High Commissioner (Omsk) to Acting High Commissioner (Vladivostok), 30 December 1918, War Diary of Force Headquarters CEF(S).

32   "Secrete Telegram to Vice Consul, Habarvosk [sic], January 25 1919," British Vice-Consul (Khabarovsk) to Acting High Commissioner (Vladivostok), 25 January 1919, War Diary of Force Headquarters CEF(S), app. 81, p. 17.

33   Ward, *With the "Die-Hards" in Siberia*, 168.

34   Ibid., 169; High Commissioner (Omsk) to Acting High Commissioner (Vladivostok), 26 January 1919, War Diary of Force Headquarters CEF(S), app. 80, p. 16.

35   High Commissioner (Omsk) to Acting High Commissioner (Vladivostok), 1 February 1919 and 2 February 1919, Blair (Vladivostok) to Troopers (London), 4 February 1919, War Diary of General Staff CEF(S), February 1919, apps. 10, 11, and 27.

36   Report on Military Situation, 28 February 1919, War Diary of General Staff CEF(S), February 1919, app. 45.

37   Knox (Omsk) to Blair (Vladivostok), 17 January 1919, War Diary of Force Headquarters CEF(S), app. 68, p. 3; Milner to Governor General, 25 January 1919, LAC, RG 24, ser. C-1-A, vol. 2557, file HQC-2514 (vol. 2), "Situation in Russia – Allied Intervention in Russia."

38   High Commissioner (Omsk) to High Commissioner (Vladivostok), 15 January 1919, War Diary of Force Headquarters CEF(S), app. 37, p. 8.

39   Morrisey to Elmsley, 20 January 1919, War Diary of Force Headquarters CEF(S), app. 69, p. 4.

40   Diary entry, 4 May 1919, LAC, Ardagh Fonds, MG 30, E-150, file 3/6. Information on refugees living in railcars is gleaned from Rodney, "Siberia in 1919," 330.

41 Knox to Blair, 31 January 1919, War Dairy Force Headquarters CEF(S), app. 12; Ward, *With the "Die-Hards" in Siberia*, 161-62.

42 "Sidelights on the Invasion of Russia," *Tribune*, 13 March 1919.

43 High Commissioner (Omsk) to Acting High Commissioner (Vladivostok), 2 February 1919, War Diary of General Staff CEF(S), February 1919, app. 11. In this climate, Elmsley received word from London that the British troops at Omsk would remain under the command of Major-General Knox "for the present." See War Office (London) to Elmsley, 2 February 1919, War Diary of General Staff Siberia CEF(S), February 1919, app. 14.

44 Morrisey to Elmsley, 12 February 1919, War Diary of General Staff Siberia CEF(S), February 1919, app. 33. Morrisey recommended the formation of three self-contained Allied fighting brigades, including aircraft, to lend morale and strength to the New Siberian Army on the Perm, Ufa, and Samara fronts.

45 Sophie Buxhoeveden, *Left Behind: Fourteen Months in Siberia during the Revolution, December 1917-February 1919* (London: Longmans, 1929), 145-46.

46 For discussion of the special Canadian "anti-typhus train," whose purpose was to treat soldiers and civilians with a mobile "bath house and delouser," see Elmsley to Department of Militia and Defence (Ottawa), 10 March 1919, LAC, RG 24, ser. C-1-A, vol. 2557, file HQC-2514 (vol. 2), "Situation in Russia – Allied Intervention in Russia"; Diary of Advanced Hospital Unit Proceeding to Omsk, 11 March 1919, CRCR, ser. 1, sec. 1, pt. A, "Expeditionary Force."

47 War Diary of General Staff CEF(S), 2 March 1919, 10 March 1919, and 11 March 1919; Elmsley to Defensor (Ottawa), 10 March 1919, LAC, RG 24, ser. C-1-A, vol. 2557, file HQC-2514 (vol. 2); Brooke Attestation Papers, LAC, RG 150, acc. 1992-93/166, box 1097-49; Morrison Attestation Papers, LAC, RG 150, acc. 1992-93/166, box 6405-43; Elmsley to Morrisey, 25 February 1919, Knox to Troopers (London), 20 February 1919 (both in War Diary of General Staff CEF[S], February 1919, apps. 41 and 38); Elmsley to Defensor (Ottawa), 1 April 1919, War Diary of General Staff CEF(S), April 1919, app. 1.

48 War Diary of AA and QMG Branch CEF(S), 12 March 1919; Elmsley to Troopers (London), 11 March 1919, Elmsley to Morrisey [sic], 12 March 1919 (both in War Diary of General Staff CEF[S], March 1919, apps. 13 and 14). See also Elmsley to Morrisey [sic], 19 February 1919, War Diary of General Staff CEF(S), February 1919, app. 37. The Canadians evacuated Omsk on 28 March 1919. See Rodney, "Siberia in 1919," 332. Major L.S.W. Cockburn and the British troops at Krasnoyarsk are discussed in Ardagh diary, 20 April 1919 and 12 May 1919, pp. 36 and 47, LAC, Ardagh Fonds, MG 30, E-150, file 3/6; see also Cockburn Attestation Papers, LAC, RG 150, acc. 1992-93/166, box 1829-34; Ward, *With the "Die-Hards" in Siberia*, 103-5 and 193-94; Sir Brian Horrocks, *Escape to Action* (New York: St. Martin's Press, 1960), 52-59.

49 War Diary of AA and QMG Branch CEF(S), 21 March 1919.

50 CGS (Ottawa) to Troopers (London), 14 March 1919, LAC, RG 24, ser. C-1-A, vol. 2557, file HQC-2514 (vol. 2), "Situation in Russia – Allied Intervention in Russia." See also CGS (Ottawa) to Elmsley, 28 February 1919, 22 March 1919, 27 March 1919, Elmsley to Morrisey [sic], 29 March 1919 and 31 March 1919, Troopers (London) to Elmsley, 20 March 1919 and 19 March 1919, Elmsley to Brook, 30 March 1919 (all in War Diary of General Staff CEF[S], March 1919, apps. 5, 26, 28, 30, 31, 32, 333, and 35). At the end of March, the War Office deemed that the "whole Middlesex Regiment should be concentrated at Vladivostok," refusing a request for Elmsley to allow one battalion to remain at Krasnoyarsk.

1 Brook to Elmsley, 25 March 1919, War Diary of General Staff CEF(S), March 1919, app. 29; Elmsley to LeHain, 12 April 1919, War Diary of General Staff CEF(S), April 1919, app. 13; Rodney, "Siberia in 1919," 330.

52 Elmsley to Department of Militia and Defence (Ottawa), 10 March 1919, LAC, RG 24, ser. C-1-A, vol. 2557, file HQC-2514 (vol. 2), "Situation in Russia – Allied Intervention in Russia."

53 High Commissioner (Omsk) to Acting High Commissioner (Vladivostok), 30 December 1918, War Diary of Force Headquarters CEF(S), January 1919, app. 1. See also Richard Orland Atkinson, "Traveling through Siberian Chaos," *Harper's* (November 1918).

54 Wilgress, *Memoirs*, 52; Pares, *My Russian Memoirs*, 515 and 521; "Obituary," *The Times* (London), 11 February 1939.

55 High Commissioner (Omsk) to Acting High Commissioner (Vladivostok), 30 December 1918, War Diary of Force Headquarters CEF(S), January 1919, app. 1.

56 Jacks to Ward, 6 January 1919, War Diary of Force Headquarters CEF(S), app. 17, pp. 2-3. For a contemporary eye-witness account of conditions on the Trans-Siberian Railroad, see Carl W. Ackerman, "Across Siberia from Vladivostok," *New York Times*, 26 January 1919. See also High Commissioner (Omsk) to High Commissioner (Vladivostok), 1 February 1919, War Diary of General Staff CEF(S), February 1919, app. 10.

57 Elmsley to Morrisey, 13 January 1919, War Diary of Force Headquarters CEF(S), January 1919, app. 30, p. 19; Ward, *With the "Die-Hards" in Siberia*, 144-45; "Our Troops Aid on Siberian Railroad," *New York Times*, 17 March 1919. Reflecting ongoing tensions, American troops interned fifteen hundred Cossacks at Khabarovsk in March in response to Japanese intrigue.

58 "Agreement for Operating the Siberian Railways," n.d. [c. January 1920], War Diary of Force Headquarters CEF(S), app. 65, pp. 17-18. See also War Diary of Force Headquarters CEF(S), 20 and 22 January 1919; Green (Tokyo) to Curzon, 21 January 1919, War Diary of General Staff Siberia CEF(S), February 1919, app. 1. American railway engineer John F. "Big Smoke" Stevens, chief engineer of the Panama Canal project from 1905 to 1907, was appointed to head the Inter-Allied Technical Committee in March 1919. See "Our Troops Aid on Siberian Railroad," *New York Times*, 17 March 1919.

59 "Blagozhyelatyel'noye otnoshyeniye Anglii k Rossii" [Goodwill of England to Russia], *Priamoorskaya zhizn'* [Priamursky Life] (Khabarovsk), 15 February 1919, Khabarovsk State Archives.

60 Pavel Aleksandrovich Novikov, "Vyelikoye Iskusstvo Myatyezha" [The Great Art of Mutiny], *Rodina*, 3 (March 2008): 88-92; Pares, *My Russian Memoirs*, 516. See also, S.P. Zviagin, *Kuzbass v gody grazhdanskoi voiny* [Kuzbass during the Civil War Years] (Omsk: Omsk Academy MVD, 2007).

61 Shishkin, *Organizatsiya partizanskoi*, 53-70.

62 Nash (Irkutsk) to High Commissioner (Vladivostok), 26 January 1919, War Diary of Force Headquarters CEF(S), app. 74, p. 14; High Commissioner (Omsk) to Acting High Commissioner (Vladivostok), 22 January 1919, War Diary of Force Headquarters CEF(S), app. 74, p. 9.

63 Nash (Irkutsk) to High Commissoner (Vladivostok), 27 January 1919, War Diary of Force Headquarters CEF(S), January 1919, app. 82.

64 Krasnoyarsk to High Commissioner, 10 February 1919, Elmsley to Defensor (Ottawa), 15 February 1919, Report on Military Situation, 28 February 1919 (all in War Diary of General Staff CEF[S], February 1919, apps. 26, 34, and 45); Elmsley to Defensor (Ottawa), 15 March 1919, "Bolshevik Activity on the Line of Communication," n.d. [c. March 1919], War Diary of General Staff CEF(S), March 1919, apps. 16 and 39.

65 Chelyabinsk to [Elmsley], 11 February 1919, War Diary of General Staff CEF(S), February 1919, app. 28. See also Elmsley to Morrisey, 1 March 1919, War Diary of General Staff CEF(S), March 1919, app. 4.

66 Elmsley to CGS (Ottawa), 7 February 1919, CGS (Ottawa) to Elmsley, 12 February 1919 (both in War Diary of General Staff Siberia CEF[S], February 1919, apps. 21 and 30); T.B. Caulkin, "Siberia, 1918-1919," *RCMP Quarterly* 9, 2 (October 1941) (draft), p. 4, LAC, RCMP, RG 18, ser. F, vol. 3179, file 1, "First World War, B Squadron for Service in Siberia."

67 On his return journey, Braithwaite narrowly escaped injury when a bullet was fired into his railcar. See Rodney, "Siberia in 1919," 331-33.

68 Novikov, "Vyelikoye Iskusstvo Myatyezha"; Novikov, *Grazhdanskaya voina v Vostochnoi Sibiri*, 129-75.

69 Shishkin, *Organizatsiya partizanskoi*, 53-70.

70 "Report – Confidential," 20 February 1919, War Diary of General Staff CEF(S), April 1919, app. 4.

71 Bisher, *White Terror*, 146.

72 Hoyt, *Army without a Country*, 197; Pares, *My Russian Memoirs*, 517-18.

73 Mukhachev, *Aleksandr Krasnoshchekov*, 97.

74 Novikov, "Vyelikoye Iskusstvo Myatyezha."

75 "Wish to Return to Czecho-Slovakia," *Daily Times*, 24 June 1919; Hoyt, *Army without a Country*, 195. See also V.M. Rynkov, "Kolchakovskaia Natsionalizatsiya" [Kolchak's Na-tionalization], *Siberian Zaimka* 2 (2002): 1-31.

76 Ward to Blair, 29 January 1919, War Diary of Force Headquarters CEF(S), February 1919, app. 6.

77 Ward, *With the "Die-Hards" in Siberia*, 96-101; Elmsley to Mewburn, 2 November 1918, LAC, RG 24, ser. C-1-A, vol. 2566, file HG-2738, "Diary GOC Canadians Siberia."

78 Party Archive of the Irkutsk Regional Committee of the CPSU, F 300, file 583, sheet 13; A.G. Solodyankin, *Kommunisty Irkutska v bor'be s kolchakovschinoi* [Communists of Irkutsk in Struggle with the Kolchak Movement] (Irkutsk: East-Siberian Publishing House, 1960), 26-42; *Novaya Sibir'* [New Siberia] (Irkutsk), 15 October 1918.

79 Morrisey to Elmsley, 27 February 1919, War Diary of General Staff CEF(S), March 1919, app. 6; Ward, *With the "Die-Hards" in Siberia*, 170-99; Jonathan D. Smele, *Civil War in Siberia: The Anti-Bolshevik Government of Admiral Kolchak, 1918-1920* (Cambridge: Cam-bridge University Press, 1996), 340.

80 Blair (Vladivostok) to Troopers (London), 4 February 1919, War Diary of General Staff CEF(S), February 1919, app. 27.

81 Beattie, "Canadian Intervention in Russia," 382.

82 Several transport trains proceeded from Vladivostok to Omsk in March and April 1919, with *Echelon 2031* departing on 23 March 1919 and with another ammunition train, under the command of Lieutenant Wallace Webb and carrying eleven soldiers in "C" Company of the 260th Battalion, leaving on 30 March 1919. See War Diary of 16th Infantry Brigade Headquarters CEF(S), 30 March 1919; Stuart Ramsay Tompkins interview with Jane Frede-man, December 1976, Vancouver, as quoted in Tompkins, *A Canadian's Road to Russia*, 427; "Canadians in Peril in Vladivostok City," *Toronto Globe*, 28 March 1919; MacLaren, *Canadians in Russia*, 197.

83 Elkington interview, June 1980 and January 1986, UVASC, Military Oral History Collec-tion, SC 141, 169 and 170.

84 War Diary of Deputy Assistant Director of Supplies and Transport CEF(S), 15 April 1919, "15-4-19. Orders issued to OMSK for final clearing of all Canadian troops West of VLADIVOSTOK. Cable to War Office advising this done and asking for authority to hand over command and Administration of Hants and Middlesex to British Military Mission." See Elmsley to Morrisey, 11 April 1919, Brook to Elmsley, 14 April 1919, Elmsley to Troopers (London), 15 April 1919, Elmsley to Morrisey, 16 April 1919, Elmsley to

Morrisey, 18 April 1919 (all in War Diary of General Staff CEF[S], April 1919, apps. 11, 15, 17, 21, and 23).

85 Ardagh Diary, 23 March 1919-4 May 1919, LAC, Ardagh Fonds, MG 30, E-150, files 2/6 and 3/6. According to Ardagh, Kolchak and his staff left Omsk for the Urals on 5 May 1919. Annoyed, Ardagh commented: "The Russian troops are now clothed in British uniforms. They even have the brass buttons on their jackets. None of us like it at all. The Russians when marching always sing, and they sing well. Their step is only about 80 paces to the minute – slow and easy going, as is everything else."

86 Ardagh Diary, 11 May 1919-1 June 1919, LAC, Ardagh Fonds, MG 30, E-150, file 4/6.

87 "Extract of Communication Received from Japanese Headquarters – Bolshevik Movements in the Priamur Province," 1 March 1919, War Diary of General Staff CEF(S), March 1919, app. 2; Elkington diary, 13 and 14 April 1919, E.H.W. Elkington Collection (private collection).

88 Blair to War Office, 12 April 1919, Elmsley to War Office, 13 April 1919 (both in War Diary of General Staff CEF[S], April 1919, app. O[5]).

89 See intelligence reports and communiqués attached as appendices to War Diary of 16th Infantry Brigade Headquarters CEF(S), April 1919 - in particular, app. 7, "Intelligence Summary No. 1," 17 April 1919; app. 9, "Intelligence Summary No. 2," 19 April 1919; app. 11, "Japanese Organization at Shkotovo," 14 April 1919; app. 17, "'B' Company, 259th Battalion, Canadian Rifles, CEF(S), Detailed for Duty under the Japanese Command at SHKOTOVO, Siberia, on 13th April, 1919"; and app. 18, "For General Circulation." See also "Canadian Detachment, Daily Orders No. 1, Shkotovo Barracks, April 14, 1919," "Instructions to Major M.M. Hart," 13 April 1919, Neda to Elmsley, 20 April 1919, Elmsley to Defensor (Ottawa), 21 April 1919, Elmsley to Defensor (Ottawa), 26 April 1919 (all in War Diary of General Staff CEF[S], April 1919, apps. O[6], O[20], O[21], and O[24]); Hertzberg Diary, 12 April 1919, LAC, Hertzberg Fonds, vol. 1, file 1-18, diary no. 9; Skuce, *CSEF*, 33, 143-44; MacLaren, *Canadians in Russia*, 197; and Swettenham, *Allied Intervention in Russia*, 177.

90 Harold to Josie, 23 April 1919, LAC, Harold Steele Fonds, MG 30, E564, file "Correspondence, 1 Dec. 1918-1 May 1919."

91 Elkington interview, June 1980 and January 1986, UVASC, Military Oral History Collection, SC 141, 169 and 170.

92 Elkington diary, 17 April 1919, Elkington Collection (private collection).

93 Appendix No. 17, "'B' Company, 259th Battalion, Canadian Rifles, CEF (S), Detailed for duty under the Japanese Command at SHKOTOVO, Siberia, on 13th April, 1919," War Diary of 16th Infantry Brigade Headquarters; Elkington diary, 19 and 20 April 1919, Elkington Collection (private collection); Swettenham, *Allied Intervention in Russia*, 177; MacLaren, *Canadians in Russia*, 197.

94 Elmsley to Mewburn, 1 May 1919, LAC, RG 24, ser. C-1-A, vol. 2557, file HQC-2514 (vol. 2), "Situation in Russia – Allied Intervention in Russia."

95 Intelligence report on the American attitude towards the Shkotovo Expedition, 13 April 1919, War Diary of General Staff CEF(S), April 1919, app. O(8).

96 Intelligence report on Shkotova [sic] district, 15 April 1919, LAC, War Diary of General Staff CEF(S), April 1919, app. O(14).

97 Communiqué No. 5, 18 April 1919, War Diary of 16th Infantry Brigade CEF(S), April 1919, app. 15. See also Response of Schevatchenko [sic], 17 April 1919, Maruyan to Elmsley, 16 April 1919, Intelligence Summary, 17 April 1919, Intelligence Report: An Account of the Situation in the Shkotovo Region, 17 April 1919, "Declaration of Japanese Command," 17 April 1919, Isobayashi to Elmsley, 25 April 1919, Elmsley to Isobayashi, 28 April 1919 (all in War Diary of General Staff CEF[S], April 1919, apps. O[13], O[16], O[18], O[25], and

O[26]); Elmsley to Department Militia and Defence (Ottawa), 19 April 1919, LAC, RG 24, ser. C-1-A, vol. 2557, file HQC-2514 (vol. 2), "Situation in Russia – Allied Intervention in Russia"; Stephan, *Russian Far East*, 136.

98 White to Borden, 24 January 1919, LAC, RG 24, ser. C-1-A, vol. 2557, file HQC-2514 (vol. 1); "Insurrection of the Kalmikoff Detachment," 10 May 1919, War Diary of General Staff CEF(S), May 1919, app. 10.

99 "Draft of Interview by Captain Playfair with Admiral Kolchak, Omsk, April 27th, 1919," LAC, Department of Militia and Defence Records, RG 9, ser. III-A-S, vol. 362, file A3, SEF (file 118), "Report – Russian Military and Political Situation, by Canadian Expeditionary Force (Siberia) Vladivostok, June, 1919, Maj-Gen. J.H. Elmsley," p. 57. See also War Diary of General Staff CEF(S), May 1919, app. 52; MacLaren, *Canadians in Russia*, 199-200.

100 "The Beginning of a Turn," 4 May 1919, in Trotsky, *Military Writings and Speeches of Leon Trotsky* vol. 2, *1919: How the Revolution Armed* (London: New Park, 1979), 524, 648. See also Knox (Vladivostok) to CGS (Ottawa), 8 March 1919, Mewburn memorandum, 4 April 1919, LAC, RG 24, ser. C-1-A, vol. 2557, file HQC-2514 (vol. 2), "Situation in Russia – Allied Intervention in Russia"; "Red Rule Totters as Kolchak Wins," *New York Times*, 22 April 1919. See also Intelligence Report, April 1919, "Report – Confidential," 20 February 1919, War Diary of General Staff CEF(S), April 1919, apps. 4 and 42: "From enemy sources it has been ascertained that the Bolsheviks are alarmed at the Siberian successes, and Trotsky has made a special appeal for the restoration of order on this front, and he has stated that it is possible that the fate of Soviet Russia may be decided on this front in the next few weeks."

101 "Capital City Labor Party," *BC Federationist*, 3 January 1919, 8. See also "Local Labor's Parliament," *Tribune*, 23 December 1918.

102 "Capital City Labor Party," *BC Federationist*, 3 January 1919, 8.

103 On 22 December 1918, the Winnipeg Trades and Labor Council and the Socialist Party of Canada local jointly sponsored the mass meeting at the Walker Theatre, where R.B. Russell moved a resolution protesting "the sending of further military forces to Russia" and demanding "the allied troops already there be withdrawn." Other resolutions against the Siberian Expedition were forwarded from mass meetings of workers in Prince Rupert and Morricetown, British Columbia. See R.J.F. Rose to Borden, 6 January 1919, Mr. and Mrs. A. Clay to Borden, 31 March 1919 (both in LAC, Borden Papers, MG 26, H1[a], vol. 103); George A. Clarke to Department of Justice, 8 January 1919, LAC, RG 24, ser. C-1-A, vol. 2557, file HQC-2514 (vol. 2), "Situation in Russia – Allied Intervention in Russia." See also MacLaren, *Canadians in Russia*, 170; Swettenham, *Allied Intervention in Russia*, 153; Beattie, "Canadian Intervention in Russia," 184-86.

104 J.J. Morrison to Mewburn, 4 January 1919, LAC, RG 24, ser. C-1-A, vol. 2557, file HQC-2514 (vol. 2), "Situation in Russia – Allied Intervention in Russia"; Gordon Grey, "Canada and the Siberian Expedition," *The Nation* (New York), 1 February 1919, 162-63.

105 As quoted in Grey, "Canada and the Siberian Expedition," 162-63; "Canadians in Russia," *Hamilton Herald*, 13 December 1918. See also "Canadians for Russia," *Hamilton Spectator*, 13 December 1918.

106 Grey, "Canada and the Siberian Expedition," 162-63. See also "Red Letter Day in History of Labour Movement," *Tribune*, 9 January 1919.

107 Minutes, 8 January 1919, UVACS, VLC Fonds, 80-59, box 3. The meeting also received a letter from the deputy minister of militia and defence, Ottawa, responding to a protest letter from the council. See Deputy Minister of Militia and Defence to Christian Sivertz, 19 December 1918, LAC, RG 24, ser. C-1-a, vol. 1993, file 762-11-24, "Queries Relating to CEF (Siberia)."

108 "Siberian Expedition Must End," *Tribune*, 9 January 1919. See also "Intervention," *Tribune*,
7 April 1919; "Hands Off Russia," *Tribune*, 14 April 1919; "The Mystery of Russia," *Tribune*,
28 April 1919.
109 "Censorship Comes in for Criticism," *Daily Times*, 13 January 1919.
110 Ibid.; "Labor Militant," *Tribune*, 13 January 1919.
111 "Victoria Workers Hold Protest Meeting," *BC Federationist*, 17 January 1919.
112 "Woodsworth Talks to a Capacity House," *BC Federationist*, 17 January 1919.
113 "Chairman Refuses to Fly Red Flag," *Daily Times*, 3 February 1919; "Labor Refused a Hearing" and "Bolshevism and Labour," *Tribune*, 3 February 1919; "Sunday Night Meeting" and
"No Change of Heart," *Tribune*, 6 February 1919; "The Free Speech Deputation," *Tribune*,
10 February 1919. See also "Bolshevism and the Board of Trade," *Tribune*, 30 January 1919.
114 "Chairman Refuses to Fly Red Flag," *Daily Times*, 3 February 1919, 9.
115 Ibid.
116 "Ole Talks," *Tribune* (Victoria), 13 February 1919; "Would Make IWW's in States Outlaws,"
Daily Times, 21 February 1919; "Seattle Is Tied Up in General Strike," *BC Federationist*, 7
February 1919; "Seattle General Strike Called Off," *BC Federationist*, 14 February 1919;
"Seattle Asks for General Strike," *Tribune*, 30 January 1919; "Attempt Fails," *Tribune*, 6
February 1919; "Breaking the Backbone," *Tribune*, 10 February 1919; Robert L. Friedheim,
The Seattle General Strike (Seattle: University of Washington Press, 1964); UVASC, Boiler-
makers Fonds, "Minute Books," 28 January 1919 and 25 February 1919; "Will Seattle Be
Loyal?" *Daily Times*, 11 March 1919. A month earlier, two thousand Seattle workers had
clashed with police during a protest march against their country's intervention in Siberia.
Speakers urged local longshore workers to strike in order to prevent the shipment of war
cargo to Vladivostok. See "Radical Outbreak in Seattle," *Tribune*, 13 January 1919. See also
"Protest Siberian Picnic," *Tribune*, 12 December 1918.
117 F. Henry Johnson, *A History of Public Education in British Columbia* (Vancouver: University
of British Columbia Publications Centre, 1964), 240-42, quoting from H. Charlesworth,
Teachers Institutes, manuscript in possession of BC Teachers' Federation, 4; Rennie Warburton, "The Class Relations of Public School Teachers in British Columbia," *Canadian
Review of Sociology and Anthropology* 23, 2 (1986): 210-29; "The School Teachers," *Tribune*,
13 February 1919. See also "'Scab' Teachers," *Tribune*, 13 February 1919; "The Teachers'
Strike," *Tribune*, 17 February 1919; "Now Teachers Present Ultimatum," *Colonist*, 3 October
1918. See also Alison Prentice, ed., *Women Who Taught: Perspectives on the History of Women
and Teaching* (Toronto: University of Toronto Press, 1991); Allen Seager and David Roth,
"British Columbia and the Mining West: A Ghost of a Chance," in *The Workers' Revolt in
Canada: 1917-1925*, ed. Craig Heron (Toronto: University of Toronto Press, 1998), 252.
118 Minutes, 24 February 1919, UVACS, VLC Fonds, 80-59, box 3.
119 Ibid.; Bent Gestur Sivertz, *The Sivertz Family*, book 1, *Christian Sivertz of Victoria and of
Canada's Early Labor Movement* (Parksville, BC: Arrowmaker, 1984), 41-58. Secretary-
Treasurer Christian Sivertz divided the motions in half, then moved an amendment: "This
Council is in full sympathy with the process of socializing of the means of production,
now in progress in Russia and Germany." The amendment was defeated, and both halves
of the original motion were approved by a vote of seventeen to two. Sivertz and delegate
Dooley voted together in opposing the resolution.
120 "Victoria Central Body and Soviets," *BC Federationist*, 28 February 1919; Minutes, 5 March
1919, UVASC, VLC Fonds, 80-59, box 3. In mid-March, the Victoria Trades and Labor
Council's *Tribune* published the text of the Soviet Constitution. In May, the newspaper
published an interview with Wilfred R. Humphries, an American Red Cross worker in
Russia. See "The Bolshevik Constitution," *Tribune*, 13 March 1919; "Russia under the

Soviets," *Tribune*, 12 May 1919-9 June 1919; "Lenine Gives Interview," *Tribune*, 4 August 1919.

121 "BC Federation of Labor Proceedings," *BC Federationist*, 4 April 1919; "Annual Convention of Alberta Labor," *BC Federationist*, 10 January 1919; A. Ross McCormack, *Reformers, Rebels, and Revolutionaries: The Western Canadian Radical Movement, 1899-1919* (Toronto and Buffalo: University of Toronto Press, 1977), 157.

122 "The Origin of the OBU," *Winnipeg One Big Union Bulletin* , 24 March 1927; Winnipeg Defence Committee, *Saving the World from Democracy: The Winnipeg General Sympathetic Strike, May-June, 1919* (Winnipeg: Defence Committee, 1920), 26-30; "Mass Meeting at Victoria," *BC Federationist*, 18 April 1919; "A Short History of the Canadian OBU," *BC Federationist*, 14 November 1919.

123 *History of the Communist Party of the Soviet Union* (Moscow: Foreign Languages Publishing House, 1960), 311-18. See also Leonard Shapiro, *Communist Party of the Soviet Union* (New York: Random House, 1960) and John S. Reshetar Jr., *A Concise History of the Communist Party of the Soviet Union* (New York: Frederick A. Praeger, 1960).

124 "Soldiers Organize," *Tribune*, 10 February 1919. See also "Doing Things Constitutionally," *Tribune*, 24 February 1919; "Soldiers and Labor," *BC Federationist*, 25 April 1919; "Soldiers and Labor Men Meet at the Avenue," *BC Federationist*, 25 April 1919; "Soldiers Now Fight for Jobs," *BC Federationist*, 8 May 1919; "Returned Soldiers and the Civil Service" and "A Practical Programme," *Tribune*, 19 May 1919; Minutes, 8 January 1919, UVASC, VLC Fonds, 80-59, box 3.

125 "If I Don't Someone Else Will!" *BC Federationist*, 18 April 1919. See also "Refused to Load War Material," *Tribune*, 22 September 1919.

126 "Northwest Mounted Police," *Tribune*, 16 December 1918; "The Ruling Class and Workers Activities," *BC Federationist*, 3 January 1919; "Will Mounted Police Assist Big Interests' Conspiracy," *Tribune*, 5 May 1919; "Certified Copy of a Report of the Committee of the Privy Council Approved by His Excellency the Governor General on the 12 December, 1918," LAC, RG 18, vol. 1930, file "Correspondence Concerning Re-organization and PC 3076 12 Dec. 1918"; Webster (Fort William) to Minister, 20 January 1919, LAC, RG 18, vol. 1930, "Correspondence Concerning Re-organization and PC 3076 12 Dec. 1918."

27 "Arms, Ammunition and Explosives in Victoria District," 7 April 1919, "Federated Labour Party," 8 April 1919, LAC, RG 18, ser. A-2, vol. 878, file "Labour Organizations and Communism," reel T-6256; White to Borden, 28 April 1919, LAC, Borden Papers, MG 26, H1(a), vol. 112, reel 4340. See also Deputy Minister, Department of Naval Service, to MacLean, Comptroller RNWMP, 24 February 1919, LAC, RG 18, ser. A-2, vol. 878, file "Labour Organizations and Communism," reel T-6256.

28 "Russian Workers Union," 25 March 1919 and 3 April 1919, "Clandestine Trading in Russian Rubles," 15 April 1919, LAC, RG 18, ser. A-2, vol. 878, file "Labour Organizations and Communism," reels T-6256 and T-6257.

9 "Theft of High Explosives at Vancouver," 15 April 1919, "Irregularities at the Government Wharf, Vancouver," 19 April 1919 (both in LAC, RG 18, ser. A-2, vol. 878, file "Labour Organizations and Communism," reels T-6256 and T-6257); "That Revolution," *Tribune*, 18 May 1919.

0 Borden to White, 29 April 1919, LAC, Borden Papers, MG 26, H1(a), vol. 112, reel 4340. See also White to Borden, 16 April 1919, Borden to White, 18 April 1919, White to Borden, 22 April 1919, White to Borden, 28 April 1919 (all in LAC, Borden Papers, MG 26, H1[a], vol. 112, reel 4340).

1 Savarie to Militia and Defence, May 1919, LAC, RG 24, ser. C-1-a, vol. 1993, file 762-11-24, "Queries Relating to CEF (Siberia)"; Savarie Attestation Papers, LAC, RG 150, acc. 1992-

93/166, box 8671–58; Suzanne Evans, *Mothers of Heroes, Mothers of Martyrs: World War I and the Politics of Grief* (Montreal and Kingston: McGill-Queen's University Press, 2007).

132   Millson to Mewburn, 27 March 1919, LAC, RG 24, ser. C-1-a, vol. 1993, file 762-11-24, "Queries Relating to CEF (Siberia)."

133   "Inquiry of the Ministry by Mr. Demers, No. 58, Orders of the Day No. 23," 27 March 1919, Proulx to Mewburn, 10 March 1919 (both in LAC, RG 24, ser. C-1-a, vol. 1993, file 762-11-24, "Queries Relating to CEF [Siberia].") Demers, running as an "Opposition" candidate in the 1917 conscription election, won the seat with a commanding 4,271 votes to 363 votes for Borden's Union "Government" candidate. See Chambers, *Canadian Parliamentary Guide* (1918), 220.

134   "Extract of Speech of Dr. Hermas Deslauriers, St-Mary Division, Montreal, 11 March 1919, LAC, RG 24, ser. C-1-A, vol. 2557, file HQC-2514 (vol. 2), "Situation in Russia – Allied Intervention in Russia"; MacLaren, *Canadians in Russia*, 186-89. Deslauriers had been elected by acclamation in the conscription election of 1917. See Chambers, *Canadian Parliamentary Guide* (1918), 220.

135   Order of the House of Commons, 7 April 1919, LAC, RG 24, ser. C-1-a, vol. 1992, file HQ-762-11-27, "Inquiry House of Commons by Mr. Tobin." See also Canada, *Report of Debates of the House of Commons*, 1 April 1919.

136   Defensor to Elmsley, 1 April 1919, Bickford to Headquarters CEF(S), 5 April 1919, Elmsley to Defensor, 10 April 1919 (all in LAC, RG 9, ser. III-A-3, vol. 373, file A3, SEF Force HQ MSA); Swift to Brigade Headquarters, 8 April 1919, Barclay to Elmsley, 11 April 1918, Barclay to Elmsley, 12 April 1919, "Suspension of Sentence," 14 April 1919 (all in LAC, RG 9, ser. III-A-3, vol. 371, file A3, SEF Force HQ 23); "Courts Martial, CEF (Siberia)," LAC, RG 9, ser. III-A-3, vol. 378, file A3, SEF Courts Martial; "Summary of Events and Information, April 1919," War Diary of Deputy Judge Advocate General, CEF(S).

137   Deputy Minister of Militia and Defence to Under-Secretary of State, 1 May 1919, "Return Showing Number of Men who Proceeded to Siberia on or before Nov. 11th 1918," LAC, RG 24, ser. C-1-a, vol. 1992, file HQ-762-11-27 (Inquiry House of Commons by Mr. Tobin).

138   "Appeal for Help of Vladivostok Unions," *Red Flag* (Vancouver), 10 May 1919.

139   "Democracy in Siberia under Kolchak" and "Clippings from the Press," *Red Flag*, 28 June 1919; Beattie, "Canadian Intervention in Russia," 402; "Red Rule Totters As Kolchak Wins," *New York Times*, 22 April 1919.

140   "The Death Train of Siberia," *Red Flag*, 28 June 1919; "Our Siberian Friends" and "Kolchak's Rule in Siberia," *Red Flag*, 21 June 1919; "The White Massacre in Siberia," *Red Flag*, 19 July 1919; "More about Kolchak's Treatment of Jews," *Red Flag*, 11 October 1919; "Bolsheviki Claim Rout of Kolchak," *Red Flag* (Vancouver), 7 June 1919.

141   See "Bolsheviki Claim Rout of Kolchak," *Red Flag* (Vancouver), 7 June 1919; "Our Siberian Friends" and "Kolchak's Rule in Siberia," *Red Flag*, 21 June 1919; "Kolchak: Autocrat and Tyrant," *Tribune*, 17 July 1919; "The White Massacre in Siberia" and "Some Impressions of Siberia," *Red Flag*, 19 July 1919; "Kolchak," *Tribune*, 14 August 1919; "Bolshevist Russia, " *Red Flag*, 23 August 1919; "The Truth about Russia," *Red Flag*, 30 August 1919; "The End of the Koltchak Myth," *Tribune*, 15 September 1919; "Leaving Russia to Its Fate," *Red Flag*, 20 September 1919; "Leon Trotsky on Military Situation," *Red Flag*, 27 September 1919; "Our Poets and Poetry," *Red Flag*, 27 September 1919; "An Attempt to Reach Moscow," *Red Flag*, 4 October 1919; "More about Kolchak's Treatment of Jews," *Red Flag*, 11 October 1919.

142   Wilgress, *Memoirs*, 54. By May 1919, Canadian naval staff in Ottawa had concluded "that Japan is now the enemy." See "Occasional Paper No. 1. Remarks on a Canadian Naval Base in the North Pacific," 29 May 1919, LAC, RG 24, ser. Naval War Staff, vol. 5696, file NS 1017-31-2, as quoted in Roger Sarty, " 'There will be trouble in the North Pacific': The

Defence of British Columbia in the Early Twentieth Century," *BC Studies* 61 (Spring 1984), 26.

143 Borden, *Memoirs*, 888.

144 "The Albert Hall Labor Meeting," *BC Federationist*, 10 January 1919. Shifts in Canadian policy, culminating in the decision to withdraw the troops, are reflected in various correspondence in LAC, Defence, RG 24, Department of Naval Service, Naval Intelligence Records, vol. 3968, file NSC 1047-14-26 (vol. 2). See also August 1918-February 1919, LAC, Borden Papers, MG 26, H1(a), vol. 103. The diverging strategies of the Japanese, American, French, British, Czecho-Slovak, and Canadian forces in Siberia are evident in a report from "British General Staff on Siberian Situation," 22 November 1918, LAC, Borden Papers, MG 26, H1(a), vol. 103. See also "Memorandum on the Subject of United States Intentions as to Siberia," n.d., LAC, Borden Papers, MG 26, H1(a), vol. 103; Skuce, *CSEF*, 6–10; Swettenham, "Allied Intervention in Siberia," 5-25.

145 Beattie, "Canadian Intervention in Russia," 385-86.

146 War Diary of Force Headquarters CEF(S), 23 January 1919; Admiralty to Elmsley, 22 January 1919, War Diary of Force Headquarters CEF(S), app. 70, p. 5; Elmsley to Morrisey, 23 January 1919, War Diary of Force Headquarters CEF(S), app. 71, p. 6. The *Monteagle* had been slated to leave Canada on 23 January while the *Empress of Japan* was scheduled to depart on 10 February. See White to Borden, 24 January 1919, LAC, RG 24, ser. C-1-A, vol. 2557, file HQC-2514 (vol. 1).

147 Borden, *Memoirs*, 886.

148 "Bolsheviki Send Peace Proposals," *Colonist*, 28 December 1918.

149 Borden, *Memoirs*, 889.

150 Ibid.

151 War Diary of Force Headquarters CEF(S), 14 January 1919; War Diary of Force Headquarters, 17 January 1919, p. 15.

152 Borden, *Memoirs*, 903-4. See also Silverlight, *Victors' Dilemma*, 143-48; Swettenham, "Allied Intervention in Siberia," 19.

153 Silverlight, *Victors' Dilemma*, 147; War Diary of Force Headquarters CEF(S), 20 January 1919. Days earlier, Denikin had been recognized as commander-in-chief of all White Russian forces in the south. A rival White general, Krasnov, consented to Denikin's supreme authority while retaining operational command of the Don Army. See Dirmilint (London) to Blair (Vladivostok), 15 January 1919, War Diary of Force Headquarters CEF(S), app. 64, p. 16.

154 High Commissioner (Irkutsk) to High Commissioner (Vladivostok), 12 February 1919, High Commissioner (Omsk) to High Commissioner (Vladivostok), 3 February 1919, Elmsley to Militia and Defence (Ottawa), 7 February 1919 (all in LAC, RG 24, ser. C-1-A, vol. 2557, file HQC-2514 [vol. 2], "Situation in Russia – Allied Intervention in Russia"); High Commissioner (Omsk) to Acting High Commissioner (Vladivostok), 29 January 1919, War Diary of Force Headquarters CEF(S), February 1919, apps. 29, 25, 2; High Commissioner (Omsk) to Acting High Commissioner (Vladivostok), 26 January 1919, War Diary of Force Headquarters CEF(S), January 1919, app. 80; Silverlight, *Victors' Dilemma*, 146-47.

155 Silverlight, *Victors' Dilemma*, 143-48; Ward, *With the "Die-Hards" in Siberia*, 157-59.

156 "Soviet Official Thrown in Jail," *BC Federationist*, 2 May 1919.

157 CGS (Ottawa) to Elmsley, 31 January 1919, LAC, RG 9, War Diary of General Staff CEF(S), February 1919, app. 5. See also Morrisey to Elmsley, 19 February 1919, Knox to War Office, 20 February 1919 (both in LAC, War Diary of General Staff CEF[S], February 1919, apps. 37 and 38); Hertzberg Diary, 4 February 1919, LAC, Hertzberg Fonds, vol. 1, file 1-18, diary no. 9.

158 Borden, *Memoirs*, 2:188-90; Borden to Lloyd George, 13 February 1919, Borden to Mewburn (via White), 13 February 1919, CGS (Ottawa) to War Office (London), 16 February 1919, Borden to Lloyd George, 7 February 1919 (all in LAC, Borden Papers, MG 26, H1[a], vol. 103); Memo from Major-General for Military Secretary (Naval and Military Committee) to Naval Secretary (Naval and Military Committee), 27 February 1919, RG 24, Naval Intelligence Records, Department of Naval Service, vol. 3968, file NSC 1047-14-26 (vol. 2); Mewburn to Borden, 13 February 1919, LAC, Borden Papers, MG 26, H1[a], vol. 103, reel C-4449, p. 173355; CGS (Ottawa) to Troopers (London), 16 February 1919, LAC, RG 24, ser. C-1-A, vol. 2557, file HQC-2514 (vol. 2), "Situation in Russia – Allied Intervention in Russia"; "Russian Policy of No Intervention," *Tribune*, 10 February 1919; Swettenham, *Allied Intervention in Russia*, 182.

159 See Mewburn to Maclean, 25 March 1919, Memorandum of Agreement, 1919, Mewburn and Maclean to Governor-in-Council, 4 April 1919, R.M. Stephens, "Memo: For the Military Secretary, Naval and Military Committee," 27 March 1919 (all in LAC, Defence, RG 24, Department of Naval Service, Naval Intelligence Records, vol. 3778, file 1048-61-2).

160 CGS (Ottawa) to Troopers, London, 13 March 1919, LAC, RG 24, Department of Naval Service, Naval Intelligence Records, vol. 3698, file NSC 1047-14-26 (vol. 2).

161 Werner to Borden, 16 February 1919, LAC, Borden Papers, MG 26, H1[a], vol. 103; Borden, *Memoirs*, 2:188; MacLaren *Canadians in Russia*, 193-94 and 206.

162 Elmsley to Militia and Defence (Ottawa), 11 March 1919, LAC, RG 24, ser. C-1-A, vol. 2557, file HQC-2514 (vol. 2), "Situation in Russia – Allied Intervention in Russia."

163 Churchill to Borden, 17 March 1919, LAC, Borden Papers, MG 26, H1[a], vol. 103; "Canadians to Quit Siberia," *New York Times*, 9 April 1919.

164 Churchill to Borden, 1 May 1919, Sifton to Borden, 5 May 1919, Borden to Churchill, 5 May 1919, Creighton to Yates, 7 May 1919, Borden to Churchill, 18 May 1919 (all in LAC, Borden Papers, MG 26, H1[a], vol. 103); Kinvig, *Churchill's Crusade*, 209-10; "Churchill and Russia," *Tribune*, 21 July 1919.

165 Massey, *When I Was Young*, 212; "Embarkation Orders SS *Monteagle*," n.d., War Diary of General Staff CEF(S), April 1919, app. 25.

166 "Troops Forced to Keep Below Decks on the *Monteagle*," *Ottawa Citizen*, 6 May 1919; General Officer Commander to Quartermaster General (Ottawa), 1 May 1919, Cablegram from Victoria to Adjutant General (Ottawa), 3 May 1919 (both in LAC, RG 24, ser. C-1-a, vol. 1992, file 762-11-13, "Conducting and Clearing Procedure Troops and Their Documents Siberian Expeditionary Force"); Elmsley to Defensor (Ottawa), 27 April 1919, War Diary of General Staff CEF(S), April 1919, app. 30; Defensor to Elmsley, 18 May 1919, War Diary of General Staff CEF(S), May 1919, app. 26. When the *Monteagle* left Vladivostok, only seventeen soldiers were sick. See Major Deputy Acting Adjutant General Demobilization to General Officer Commanding Military District No. 11 (Victoria), 22 April 1919, LAC, RG 24, ser. C-1-a, vol. 1992, file 762-11-13 (Conducting and Clearing Procedure Troops and Their Documents Siberian Expeditionary Force).

167 Elmsley to Defensor (Ottawa), 16 May 1919, Gruner to AQMG, 18 May 1919, Elmsley to Defensor (Ottawa), 18 May 1919, Brook to Blair, 18 May 1919, Elmsley to Grogan, 29 May 1919, Osoll to MCO British Military Mission, 26 May 1919, "No. 432 – Strength Decrease," 11 May 1919 (all in War Diary of General Staff CEF[S], May 1919, apps. 8, 23, 24, 47, and 55, p. 18); War Diary of General Staff CEF(S), 2 June 1919; MacLaren, *Canadians in Russia*, 207-8. The *Empress of Japan* arrived in Victoria on 21 May 1919, but only those officers and enlisted men who had signed on in Victoria were permitted to disembark. The remainder sailed for Vancouver.

168 Worsley to Commissioner, 25 May 1919, LAC, RG 18, vol. 1929, file "RCMP 1918 Siberian Draft Pt. 1"; Defensor to Elmsley, 22 May 1919, LAC, War Diary of General Staff CEF(S), May 1919, app. 34; "Nominal Roll – Officers and Other Ranks, CEF (Siberia) Who Have Died," n.d., LAC, RG 9, ser. II-B-12, vol. 2, file "Correspondence – Siberian Force"; "Memorial to Rector," *Canadian Churchman* (Toronto), 12 January 1922, Stephenson Family Collection (private collection).

169 Elkington interview, June 1980 and January 1986, UVASC, Military Oral History Collection, SC 141, 169 and 170. Elkington also stated: "We left in the spring." See Elmsley to Defensor (Ottawa), 20 May 1919 and "No. 480 Strength Decrease," 22 May 1919 (both in War Diary of General Staff CEF(S), May 1919, apps. 30 and 55, p. 32).

170 General Officer Commanding to Adjutant-General (Ottawa), 27 May 1919 and 29 May 1919, Lieutenant-Colonel AAG Demobilization to D. of S. and T. (Militia and Defence), 14 May 1919, Instructions and Procedure to Be Carried Out on Disembarkation M.D. 11, n.d. [May 1919], LAC, RG 24, ser. C-1-a, vol. 1992, file 762-11-13; MacLaren, *Canadians in Russia*, 207-8; Tompkins, *A Canadian's Road to Russia*, 449.

171 Embarkation Instructions SS *Monteagle*, 5 June 1919, War Diary of General Staff CEF(S), June 1919, app. 51; Hertzberg Diary, 5 June 1919, LAC, Hertzberg Fonds, vol. 1, file 1-18, diary no. 9; Ardagh Diary, 5 and 12 June 1919, LAC, Ardagh Fonds, MG 30, E-150, file 4/6. The *Monteagle* crossed the 180th degree longitude – the International Date Line – on Friday, 13 June 1919. "We will have two Friday the 13ths in unison," Lieutenant Harold Ardagh wrote: "However, we are not superstitious."

172 James H. Elmsley, "Report – Russian Military and Political Situation," June 1919, 47, LAC, RG 9, ser. III-A-S, vol. 362, file A3, SEF (file 118).

173 "Treaty of Peace between the Allies and Associated Powers and Germany, Signed at Versailles, June 28, 1919," in Canada, *Sessional Papers* 55, 1 (1919): 55; Margaret MacMillan, *Paris, 1919: Six Months That Changed the World* (New York: Random House, 2002).

174 Fifty-three Canadian officers and enlisted men were transferred to the British Military Mission and British Railway Mission in May, along with the remaining supplies of the Canadian force. They returned with British forces in autumn 1919. The Canadian "Rear Party," consisting of thirty-three troops, returned to Canada via Yokohama on 29 August 1919. See "Officers and Other Ranks, CEF (Siberia), Seconded and 'On Command' to British Military Mission," LAC, RG 24, ser. C-1-a, vol. 1992, file HQ-762-11-25; "No. 446 Service with British Railway Mission on Evacuation of CEF from Siberia," 15 May 1919, "No. 447 Service with British Military Mission on Withdrawal of CEF(S) from Siberia," 15 May 1919 (both in War Diary of General Staff CEF[S], May 1919, Daily Routine Orders, app. 55, pp. 23-41); "Handing over of CASC supplies by the CASC Siberia to the British Military Mission at Vladivostok," n.d., LAC, RG 24, ser. C-1-a, vol. 2007, file pt. 1; "Statement According to Record of Siberian Expeditionary Force," and "Nominal Roll – Rear Party, CEF(S)," n.d., LAC, RG 9, ser. II-B-12, vol. 2, file "Correspondence – Siberian Force"; Cablegram, Britmis (Vladivostok) to CGS (Ottawa), 13 August 1919, LAC, RG 24, ser. C-1-A, vol. 2557, file HQC-2514 (vol. 2), "Situation in Russia – Allied Intervention in Russia"; MacLaren, *Canadians in Russia*, 207 and 211.

175 MacLaren, *Canadians in Russia*, 180; "No. 224, Appointments," 15 March 1919, War Diary of General Staff CEF(S), Daily Routine Orders, March 1919, app. 41, p. 16; LAC, John Whiteman Warden Fonds, MG 30, E192.

176 "Diary of Echelon. 2209," May-June 1919; Constable G.H. Pilkington to RNWMP Commissioner, n.d. [1919]; Captain Montague Smith to Commissioner RNWMP, 11 August 1919 (all in LAC, RCMP Fonds, RG 18, vol. 3179, file G 989-3 [vol. 2]); Cablegram to CGS

(Ottawa), 11 June 1919, LAC, RG 24, ser. C-1-A, vol. 2557, file HQC-2514 (vol. 2), "Situation in Russia – Allied Intervention in Russia." See also Vladivostok to Canadian General Staff (Ottawa), 11 June 1919, LAC, Borden Papers, MG 26, H1(a), vol. 103; T.B. Caulkin, "Siberia, 1918-1919," *RCMP Quarterly* 9, 2 (October 1941) (draft), p. 3, LAC, RCMP, RG 18, ser. F, vol. 3179, file 1, "First World War, B Squadron for Service in Siberia"; S.W. Horrall, "The Force's Siberian Patrol," *RCMP Quarterly* 36, 5 (July 1971): 3-8; See also *RCMP Quarterly* 7, 3 (January 1940): 229; Skuce, *CSEF*, 32; "Bolshevik Forces Have Retaken Ufa," *Red Flag* (Vancouver), 14 June 1919. Two RNWMP officers, Farrier Sergeant J.E. Margetts and Corporal P.S. Bossard, were awarded service medals for their role in rescue efforts following the ambush. In his description of the journey, RNWMP constable G.H. Pilkington wrote: "this is claimed on good authority to be the longest journey ever undertaken and completed by any British horses."

177 Wilgress, *Memoirs*, 55.

178 The commission's final meeting in Ottawa took place on 5 July 1919. See "Canadian Economic Mission, Siberia," *Citizen* (Ottawa), 7 July 1919; Canada, *Report of the Canadian Economic Commission (Siberia)*; Hill, *Canada's Salesman to the World*, 210-20. Despite the withdrawal of the Canadian Siberian Economic Commission, the Department of Militia and Defence received a request from Nova Scotia businessman J. Edward Jones in August 1919 regarding whether it was possible to "reach Moscow or other points in Central Russia" and whether it was "probable that trade relations [would] shortly be resumed between Great Britain and Russia." He also requested "authentic information regarding the liquor traffic in Russia at present – whether total prohibition still obtain[ed] or whether the sale of vodka, wines, etc., [was] permitted." Jones to Department of Militia and Defence, 15 August 1919, LAC, RG 24, ser. C-1-a, vol. 1993, file 762-11-24, "Queries Relating to CEF (Siberia)."

179 Wilgress, *Memoirs*, 55-59; Wilgress, "From Siberia to Kuibyshev," 368-75; McDowall, *Quick to the Frontier*, 195.

180 Memorandum, 4 June 1919, War Diary of General Staff CEF(S), June 1919; Skuce, *CSEF*, 33. See also Elmsley to Troopers (London), 8 March 1919, War Diary of General Staff CEF(S), March 1919, app. 9; War Diary of General Staff CEF(S), 11 and 12 April 1919, apps. O(3) and O(4).

181 "Memorial Service Unveiling Ceremony, CEF (Siberia)," 1 June 1919, LAC, RG 9, ser. II-B-12, vol. 2, file "Correspondence – Vladivostok"; "Officers and Others Ranks, CEF (Siberia) Who Have Died," LAC, Defence, RG 24, ser. C-1-a, vol. 1992, file HQ-762-11-25; Defensor to Elmsley, 21 May 1919, War Diary of General Staff CEF(S), May 1919, app. 32; War Diary of General Staff CEF(S), 1 June 1919. The Privy Council authorized the acquisition of land in Russia, at public expense, for the burial of bodies when it was "considered impracticable to transfer [them] to Canada." On 30 April, Elmsley informed the Department of Militia and Defence: "Officers and Other Ranks CEF (Siberia) unanimously agree that bodies should not be disturbed and express strong wish to erect cemetery memorial here." The commanding officer requested $5,000, which the department approved; a Czech sculptor carved the granite cross and other Czech soldiers erected a wooden fence. Preparations at the cemetery are described in Charles Hertzberg's diary, 28 December 1918, 20 March 1919, and 15 May 1918-1 June 1919, LAC, Hertzberg Fonds, vol. 1, file 1-18, diary no. 9; Privy Council Report, 20 March 1919, LAC, RG 9, ser. II-B-12, vol. 2, file "Correspondence – Siberian Force"; "Memorial Stone," 5 March 1919, War Diary of General Staff CEF(S), Daily Routine Orders, March 1919, app. 41; Elmsley to Defensor (Ottawa), 30 April 1919, War Diary of General Staff CEF(S), April 1919, app. 36; Defensor (Ottawa) to Elmsley, 8 May 1919, War Diary of General Staff CEF(S), May 1919, app. 35.

182 Imperial War Graves Commission, *Cemeteries and Memorials in British North Borneo, Ceylon, China, Cochin China, Hong Kong, Japan, Malaya, the Philippine Islands, and Siberia: Asia I-50* (London: His Majesty's Stationery Office, 1931), 23-25; Stephenson Family Collection (private collection); Skuce, *CSEF*, 16-17.

183 "Nominal Roll – Deserters CEF (Siberia)," n.d. [1919], LAC, RG 24, ser. C-1-a, vol. 1992, file 762-11-25, "Returns of Strength CEF Siberia." See Attestation Papers, RG 150, acc. 1992-93/166, box 1023-92, box 7380-41, box 7774-46, box 3362-21, and box 8888-28.

Afterword

1 "General Says Reds Menace Empire," *Colonist*, 19 February 1921.

2 See Gregory S. Kealey, "State Repression of Labour and the Left in Canada, 1914-20: The Impact of the First World War," *Canadian Historical Review* 73, 3 (1992): 281-314; Rodney, "Russian Revolutionaries in the Port of Vancouver," 31; MacLaren, *Canadians in Russia*, 185-86.

3 Borden, *Memoirs*, 972.

4 "Stowaways Believed to Be Bolshevik Agents," *Daily Times*, 20 June 1919; "Canadians Troops Back from Siberia," *Daily Times*, 19 June 1919. One of the stowaways, a young Russian named Nicholai Demotrovich, was adopted by Sergeant Charleston of Brandon, Manitoba, who had helped him hide aboard the *Monteagle*. Demotrovich ended up becoming the director of the Metro-Goldwyn-Mayer property department in Hollywood, California. See MacLaren, *Canadians in Russia*, 208. See also LAC, RG 24, ser. C-1-A, vol. 1994, file 762-11-33, "Complaints of Immigration Dept. That Russian Boys Are Being Brought into Canada with SEF Returning."

5 "Longshoremen Shy at Overland Cargo," *Colonist*, 20 June 1919. As the longshore workers struck, the last troops from the CEFS landed at Victoria's Outer Wharves aboard the *Monteagle*. Major-General J.H. Elmsley, commander of the Canadians in Siberia, was aboard the ship. See "Canadian Troops Back from Siberia," *Daily Times*, 19 June 1919.

6 "Longshoremen Have Declared Walk-Out," *Daily Times*, 20 June 1919; "Metal Trades Council Calls Strike Monday," *Colonist*, 21 June 1919. Conflicting reports appeared on the cause of the dispute, with the *Colonist* reporting that the longshore workers' secretary denied the strike was in support of the seamen.

7 UVASC, Boilermakers, "Minute Books," 20 June 1919.

8 "Big Walk-Out Started in City To-Day When Boilermakers Struck," *Daily Times*, 21 June 1919. The sentiment to strike "was very greatly intensified by the developments at Winnipeg," the *Daily Times* reported, and metal-trades workers were incensed over the dissolution of the Victoria Strike Committee.

9 "Metal Trades Council Calls Strike Monday," *Colonist*, 21 June 1919.

10 "Big Walk-Out Started in City To-Day When Boilermakers Struck," *Daily Times*, 21 June 1919. For details of the Victoria General Strike, see Chrow to Ackland, 1 August 1919, LAC, RG 7, Department of Labour Fonds, vol. 315, "Strikes and Lockouts File." See also "Workers Threw Down Tools When Strike Order Went Forth," *Daily Times*, 23 June 1919.

11 The sympathetic strikes of spring 1919 are examined in Gregory S. Kealey, "1919: The Canadian Labour Revolt," *Labour/Le Travail*, 13 (Spring 1984): 11-44; Craig Heron, "National Contours: Solidarity and Fragmentation," in Heron, *Workers' Revolt in Canada*, 268-304; Nolan Reilly, "The General Strike in Amherst, NS, 1919," *Acadiensis* 9, 2 (1980): 56-77; Elaine Bernard, "Last Back: Folklore and the Telephone Operators in the 1919 Vancouver General Strike," in *Not Just Pin Money: Selected Essays on the History of Women's Work in British Columbia*, ed. Barbara K. Lantham and Roberta J. Pazdro, 279-86 (Victoria: Camosun College, 1984); Allen Seager and David Roth, "British Columbia and the Mining West: A

Ghost of a Chance," in Heron, *Workers' Revolt in Canada*, 231-67; David Bright, *The Limits of Labour: Class Formation and the Labour Movement in Calgary, 1883-1929* (Vancouver: UBC Press, 1998), 145-61; James Naylor, *The New Democracy: Challenging the Social Order in Industrial Ontario, 1914-25* (Toronto: University of Toronto Press, 1991), 42-71; and Gerald Friesen, "Yours in Revolt: Regionalism, Socialism, and the Western Canadian Labour Movement," *Labour/Le Travail* 1 (1976): 141-57. International dimensions of the postwar labour conflict are discussed in Larry Peterson, "The One Big Union in International Perspective: Revolutionary Industrial Unionism, 1900-1925," *Labour/Le Travail* 7 (Spring 1981): 41-66 and "Revolutionary Socialism and Industrial Unionism in the Era of the Winnipeg General Strike: The Origins of Communist Labour Unionism in Europe and North America," *Labour/Le Travail* 13 (Spring 1984): 115-31.

12 Alan Phillips, *The Living Legend: The Story of the Royal Canadian Mounted Police* (Toronto and Boston: Little, Brown, 1954), 86; Major G.F. Worsley Report on "B" Squadron RNWMP, 11 October 1919, LAC, RG 18, RCMP, vol. 3179, file G 989-3 (vol. 2). RNWMP comptroller A.A. McLean insisted: "I gave no instructions to Siberian Squadron to remain in Vancouver. If delayed there I assume by order Military Authorities [of District No. 11]. I was not consulted." Perry to Ottawa (telegram), 24 June 1919, Worsley to Commissoner, 21 June 1919, McLean to Commissioner, 7 June 1919 (all in LAC, RG 18, RCMP, vol. 1929, file "RCMP 1918 Siberian Draft Pt. 1"). On 30 June, McLean advised Newton Rowell, president of the Privy Council, of "discontent which ha[d] developed in 'B' Squadron owing to detention at Vancouver," with RNWMP commissioner Perry advising "demobilization without delay." See McLean to Rowell, 30 June 1919, Perry to McLean, 29 June 1918 (both in LAC, RCMP Fonds, RG 18, vol. 3179, file G 989-3-24 [vol. 2]).

13 Telegram "Empress of Russia," n.d. [c. June 1919], Hoover Institution Archives, Geoffrey McDonnell Collection, acc. XX233-10 A-V.

14 The role of the RNWMP and Canadian military in the Winnipeg Strike is explored in Norman Penner, ed., *Winnipeg 1919: The Strikers' Own History of the Winnipeg General Strike*, 2nd ed. (Toronto: James Lorimer and Co., 1975).

15 "The Swedish Portent," *BC Federationist*, 8 June 1917.

16 "Think Police Acted beyond Their Power," *Daily Times*, 2 July 1919; "Red-Coats Busy," *Tribune*, 30 June 1919. See also "Red Guards Again," *Tribune*, 18 August 1919. Taylor was named in a warrant issued by Alfred E. Andrews, special counsel for Manitoba of the federal Department of Justice and envoy of the Citizens Committee of 1000. The warrant read, in part: "There is reason to suspect that certain books, papers, letters, documents, [and] writings ... afford ample evidence ... of the indictable offense of seditious conspiracy, [and] are concealed in ... the place of abode, office and premises of J. Taylor."

17 "Mounties Raid Home and Offices of Labor Men," *BC Federationist*, 4 July 1919; "Vancouver Labor Temple Raided by Police," *Daily Times*, 30 June 1919; "Tons of Bolshevik Papers Seized in Raids Made by 130 Montreal Police" and "Further Raids Made in Winnipeg," *Daily Times*, 2 July 1919. The national dimensions of labour radicalism were illuminated months later with the release of a list of police targets, a virtual who's who of British Columbia's socialist movement. See "Andrews' List of Undesirable Citizens," *BC Federationist*, 30 January 1920.

18 Gregory S. Kealey and Reg Whitaker, *RCMP Security Bulletins: The Early Years, 1919-1929* (St. John's: Canadian Committee on Labour History, 1994), 679.

19 Ibid., 451; "Police Amalgamation," *Tribune*, 25 August 1918.

20 As quoted in Kealey and Whitaker, *RCMP Security Bulletins*, 693. In the by-election, Barnard was defeated by incumbent MP Simon Fraser Tolmie, 5,085 votes to 7,219 votes. See Canada, *Sessional Papers*, 56, no. 4 (1920): 369-70; Chambers, *Canadian Parliamentary*

Guide (1919), 278; "Barnard Has 'Em on the Run in Victoria," *BC Federationist*, 17 October 1919; "Grave Election Irregularities," *Tribune*, 30 October 1919; "Barnard Defeated in Victoria Election," *BC Federationist*, 31 October 1919; "Sore and Sorry," *Tribune*, 6 November 1919; "Dirtiest Fight Ever Known," *BC Federationist*, 17 November 1919.

21 Kealey and Whitaker, *RCMP Security Bulletins*, 708-9.

22 Ibid., 706.

23 "The SP of C and the Third International," *Western Clarion* (Vancouver), 16 January 1921; "Vote Was in Favour of Third," *BC Federationist*, 27 January 1922; "Third International Referendum," *Western Clarion*, 16 November 1921; Peter Campbell, "'Making Socialists': Bill Pritchard, the Socialist Party of Canada, and the Third International," *Labour/Le Travail* 30 (Fall 1992): 42-65; Peter Campbell, *Canadian Marxists and the Search for a Third Way* (Montreal and Kingston: McGill-Queen's University Press, 2000), 99; Ross Alfred Johnson, "No Compromise – No Political Trading: The Marxian Socialist Tradition in British Columbia" (PhD diss., University of British Columbia, 1975), 357; Benjamin Isitt, "The Search for Solidarity: The Industrial and Political Roots of the Co-operative Commonwealth Federation in British Columbia, 1913-1928" (MA thesis, University of Victoria, 2003), 97-141.

24 "V Kanada" [In Canada], *Bednota* [The Poor] (Moscow), 2 March 1921, Khabarovsk State Archives; *The Communist* (Toronto), 1921; William Rodney, *Soldiers of the International: The First Ten Years of the Communist Party of Canada* (Toronto: University of Toronto Press, 1968); Ian Angus, *Canadian Bolsheviks: The Early Years of the Communist Party of Canada* (Montreal: Vanguard, 1981); John Manly, "Does the International Labour Movement Need Salvaging? Communism, Labourism, and the Canadian Trade Unions, 1921-1928," *Labour/Le Travail* 41 (Spring 1998): 147-80.

25 Sean Griffin, *Fighting Heritage: Highlights of the 1930s Struggle for Jobs and Militant Unionism in British Columbia* (Vancouver: Tribune Publishing Company, 1985); John Manley, "'Starve, Be Damned!': Communists and Canada's Urban Unemployed, 1929-1939," *Canadian Historical Review* 79 (September 1998): 467-73.

26 See Ivan Avakumovic, *The Communist Party in Canada* (Toronto: McClelland and Stewart, 1975); Norman Penner, *Canadian Communism: The Stalin Years and Beyond* (Toronto: Methuen, 1988); Anonymous, *Canada's Party of Socialism: History of the Communist Party of Canada, 1921-1976* (Toronto: Progress Books, 1982).

27 Chambers, *Canadian Parliamentary Guide* (1921), 280-498.

28 Kenneth McNaught, *A Prophet in Politics: A Biography of J.S. Woodsworth* (Toronto: University of Toronto Press, 1959); Chambers, *Canadian Parliamentary Guide* (1922), 212 and 285.

29 Beattie, "Canadian Intervention in Russia," 372.

30 "Cities Recaptured by the Bolsheviki," *Red Flag* (Vancouver), 26 July 1919; "Leaving Russia to Its Fate," *Red Flag*, 20 September 1919; Swettenham, *Allied Intervention in Russia*, 186; Bisher, *White Terror*, 192-215. The Middlesex regiment left Vladivostok on 8 September 1919, while the Hampshires pulled out on 1 November 1919.

31 "Wish to Return to Czecho-Slovakia," *Daily Times*, 24 June 1919; Hoyt, *Army without a Country*, 195. See also "President Masaryk on Russian Intervention," *Tribune*, 31 July 1919.

32 In November, Czech general Gaida – aged twenty-seven and once a loyal fighter for the White Russian cause – led a revolt in Vladivostok, which was suppressed. Gaida fled Vladivostok en route to Czechoslovakia. In the 1930s, he became the leader of the Czechoslovak Fascist movement. See "Revolt Put Down at Vladivostok," *New York Times*, 20 November 1918; Dorothy Findlay to Family, 18 November 1919, Dorothy Findlay to Mother and Father, 30 September 1919 (both in "Letters from Vladivostok, 508-10, 511-22); Pereira,

White Siberia, 148-50; Smele, *Civil War in Siberia*, 667; and Swettenham, *Allied Intervention in Russia*, 246.

33 Pereira, *White Siberia*, 142-59; Connaughton, *Republic of the Ushakovko*, 147; Muirden, *Diggers Who Signed on for More*, 27; Kinvig, *Churchill's Crusade*, 300-2.

34 Mackintosh Bell, *Side Lights on the Siberian Campaign*, 125-26; Luckett, *White Generals*, 346-47; Pereira, *White Siberia*, 148-50; David Footman, *The Last Days of Kolchak* (Oxford: St Anthony's College, 1953); Fleming, *Fate of Admiral Kolchak*; Smele, *Civil War in Siberia*, 667; Swettenham, *Allied Intervention in Russia*, 246.

35 Smele, *Civil War in Siberia*, 667; Smele, "White Gold," 1334. According to one interpretation, a portion of the Russian gold reserve never returned to Moscow. Some was transported to Japan and other remnants were smuggled to Europe by returning members of the Czecho-Slovak Legion. See "The Japanese and the Russian Gold," *Izvestia* (Moscow), 17 June 2004.

36 Williams, *Through the Russian Revolution*, 280; Luckett, *White Generals*, 343-84; Alexis Wrangel, *General Wrangel: Russia's White Crusader* (London: Hippocrene, 1987).

37 "Will Attempt to Lower the Standard of Living," *BC Federationist*, 28 May 1920; "Czecho-Slovaks Pass through City," *BC Federationist*, 11 June 1920; "Note and Comment," *Winnipeg One Big Union Bulletin*, 19 June 1920; "A Masterly Retreat," *Vancouver Western Clarion*, 16 June 1920; Aloysius Balawyder, "The Czechoslovak Legion Crosses Canada, 1920," *East European Quarterly* 6, 2 (June 1972): 177-91. A proposal that the Czecho-Slovaks be employed as railway labourers in Canada, and also a tense exchange between Canadian and British officials over the cost of transporting and provisioning the Legion, can be found in correspondence from April to June 1920, LAC, Borden Papers, MG 26, ser. H1(a), vol. 103. As the *BC Federationist* reported, the Czecho-Slovaks arrived in Vancouver amid fears from organized labour that they would be employed by the city's economic leaders to drive down wages and break the power of the unions.

38 "Czecho-Slovaks Pass through City," *BC Federationist*, 11 June 1920.

39 MacLaren, *Canadians in Russia*, 212; Swettenham, *Allied Intervention in Russia*, 246.

40 Smith, *Vladivostok under Red and White Rule*, 6.

41 Ibid., 6-7. See also "Revolt Put Down at Vladivostok," *New York Times*, 20 November 1918.

42 Smith, *Vladivostok under Red and White Rule*, 16.

43 Polk, "Canadian Red Cross and Relief in Siberia," 170-201; Young to Robertson, 8 March 1921, as quoted in Polk, "Canadian Red Cross and Relief in Siberia," 223-25; CGS (Ottawa) to Blair, 21 May 1919, Elmsley to Defensor (Ottawa), 30 May 1919 (both in War Diary of General Staff CEF[S], May 1919, apps. 36 and 49).

44 MacLaren, *Canadians in Russia*, 277-78; "Deportation of Gregorie Semenoff – Hearings before the Committee on Education and Labor," United States Senate, Sixty-Seventh Congress, Second Session, April 12-18, 1922, pt. 1, Washington, Government Printing Office; "Semenoff, Cossack Chief, Is Arrested on Arrival Here," *New York Times*, 7 April 1922; "Move to Deport Semenoff Begun," *New York Times*, 9 April 1922; "New Bail Bond or Jail for Semenoff," *New York Times*, 13 April 1922; "Can't Exile Semenoff Authorities Decide," *New York Times*, 30 May 1922. Shortly after his return to Canada, Lieutenant-Colonel T.S. Morrisey described Semyonov as "the most disreputable outlaw to be found." See "An Address to the Members of the University Club of Montreal by Lt. Col. T.S. Morrisey, December 9, 1919," T.S. Morrisey private papers, as quoted in Beattie, "Canadian Intervention in Russia," 320; Bisher, *White Terror*.

45 John Findlay to Foreign Office (London), 26 October 1922, Dorothy Findlay to Mother, 21 November 1923 (both in "Letters from Vladivostok," 522-26, 526-30); Pereira, *White Siberia*, 153 and 156; Smith, *Vladivostok under Red and White Rule*, 17-174; "Japanese Prevent

Vladivostok Fight," *New York Times*, 30 May 1921; Henry Kittredge Norton, *The Far Eastern Republic in Siberia* (London: Allen and Unwin, 1923); Novikov, *Grazhdanskaya voina v Vostochnoi Sibiri*, 209-17.

46　Ward, *With the "Die-Hards" in Siberia*, 9; Bernard Pares, "John Ward: Obituary," *Slavonic and East European Review* 13, 39 (April 1935): 680-83.

47　Graves, *America's Siberian Adventure*, 108.

48　"Canadians Had Easy Time in Siberia," *Daily Times*, 19 April 1919. Playfair was attached to the CEFS headquarters in December 1918 and wrote reports that appeared in newspapers in Vancouver, Winnipeg, Toronto, and Montreal in spring 1919. He does not appear to have produced a more detailed history of the expedition. See Daily Routine Orders, 6 December 1918, War Diary of Force Headquarters CEF(S); MacLaren, *Canadians in Russia*, 199-200; Mackintosh Bell, *Side Lights on the Siberian Campaign*, 127; Stephan, *Russian Far East*, 137; "Obituary: James Mackintosh Bell," *Geographical Review* 24, 3 (July 1934): 535. Mackintosh Bell described Kolchak's notorious "death train" and also the alleged massacre of five thousand White Russians and Japanese civilians at the Far Eastern town of Nikolaevsk after it fell to Bolsheviks in 1920.

49　Ward, *With the "Die-Hards" in Siberia*, x-xi.

50　Ibid., xii. The Red Scare of the post-1917 period gave way to the Cold War after the Second World War. Soviet Communism was isolated and outspent in an international arms race that contributed to its undoing. See Richard Rhodes, *Arsenals of Folly: The Making of the Nuclear Arms Race* (New York: Knopf, 2007). See also Keith Neilson, *Britain, Soviet Russia and the Collapse of the Versailles Order, 1919-1939* (Cambridge: Cambridge University Press, 2006).

51　Novikov, *Grazhdanskaya voina v Vostochnoi Sibiri*; see also Trotsky, *Military Writings and Speeches*, vols. 1-5.

52　Emma Goldman, *My Disillusionment in Russia* (New York: Doubleday, Page and Company, 1923); Peter Arshinov, *Istoriya Maknovskogo Dvizheniya* [History of the Makhnovist Movement] (Berlin: Gruppa Russkikh Anarkhistov v Germanii, 1923).

53　James Hughes, *Stalin, Siberia, and the Crisis of the New Economic Policy* (Cambridge: Cambridge University Press, 1991), 21-23; Novikov, *Grazhdanskaya voina v Vostochnoi Sibiri*, 267-79. In 1922, Soviet grain procurements from Siberia accounted for 27 percent of the Russian total.

54　Aleksei Karvop to the Editors of Pravda, 23 October 1928, as quoted in Vladlen S. Izmozik, "Voices fom the Twenties: Private Correspondence Intercepted by the OGPU," *Russian Review* 55, 2 (April 1996): 293.

55　See Lynne Viola, *The Unknown Gulag: The Lost World of Stalin's Special Settlements* (New York: Oxford University Press, 2007); Amir Khisamutdinov interview, 27 March 2008, Vladivostok, Russia; Aleksander I. Solzhenitsyn, *The Gulag Archipelago, 1918-1956: An Experiment in Literary Investigation* (New York: Harper and Row, 1974).

56　Naomi Klein, *The Shock Doctrine: The Rise of Disaster Capitalism* (Toronto: Knopf, 2007), 262-308; "Russian Life Expectancy on Downward Trend," *St. Petersburg Times*, 17 January 2003.

57　"Vladivostok: Russia's Wild Far East," *New York Times*, 12 September 1993.

58　Ibid. See also Arnold Smith, "Siberia: Land of Promise," *The Geographical* (May 1965), 36-57.

59　Pavel Minakir and Gregory Freeze, *The Russian Far East: An Economic Survey* (Khabarovsk: RIOTIP, 1996). See PrimStat, www.primstat.ru; Amir Khisamutdinov, "The Russian Far East Today," in his *The Russian Far East: Historical Essays* (Honolulu: Center for Russia in Asia, 1993), 151-63; "Russian Front," *Business in Vancouver*, 13-19 November 2007.

60 "Vladivostok: Russia's Wild Far East," *New York Times*, 12 September 1993; "TV Journalist Beaten to Death in Russian City of Vladivostok," *International Herald Tribune*, 22 January 2007.

61 For scientific data on air, water, and soil pollution, see Vladivostok Ecocenter Report (1998), http://www.fegi.ru/ecology/e_inter/khrist_e.htm (viewed 29 August 2007). See also Judith Thornton and Charles E. Ziegler, eds., *Russia's Far East: A Region at Risk* (Seattle and London: National Association for Asiatic Research and University of Washington Press, 2002).

62 "Vladivostok Falls from a Pristine Beach to a Coastal Ruin," *International Herald Tribune*, 19 September 2006.

63 Ecocenter report, (1998), http://www.fegi.ru/ecology/e_inter/khrist_e.htm (viewed 29 August 2007).

64 "Vladivostok Falls from a Pristine Beach to a Coastal Ruin," *International Herald Tribune*, 19 September 2006.

Conclusion

1 "Lessons to Be Learned," *BC Federationist*, 17 October 1919, 4.

2 Jonathan F.W. Vance, *Death So Noble: Memory, Meaning, and the First World War* (Vancouver: UBC Press, 1997).

3 Matthews to Duguid, 27 March 1928, LAC, RG 24, vol. 1741, file DHS 4-18.

4 Duguid to Morrow, 28 March 1931, Matthews to Duguid, 27 March 1928 (both in LAC, RG 24, vol. 1741, file DHS 4-18).

5 Duguid to Evans, 28 March 1931, LAC, RG 24, vol. 1741, file DHS 4-18. Duguid compiled a summary from the Americans "to preserve the entente cordiale on the Niagara frontier." See Memorandum from Duguid to CGS (Ottawa), 28 March 1931, LAC, RG 24, vol. 1741, file DHS 4-18.

6 See Wes Gustavson, "'Fairly Well Known and Need Not Be Discussed': Colonel A.F. Duguid and the Canadian Official History of the First World War," *Canadian Military History* 10, 2 (2001): 41-54; Tim Cook, *Clio's Warriors: Canadian Historians and the Writing of the World Wars* (Vancouver: UBC Press, 2006).

7 Nicholson, *Official History of the Canadian Army*, 517-23.

8 Imperial War Graves Commission, *Cemeteries and Memorials in British North Borneo, Ceylon, China, Cochin China, Hong Kong, Japan, Malaya, the Philippine Islands and Siberia: Asia I-50* (London: His Majesty's Stationery Office, 1931), 23, Stephenson Family Collection (private collection). See also Commonwealth War Graves Commission, "Cemetery Details – Churkin Russian Naval Cemetery," http://www.cwgc.org (viewed 22 February 2008).

9 Wilgress, *Memoirs*, 51.

10 Williams, *Through the Russian Revolution*, 280.

11 Nicholson, *Official History of the Canadian Army*, 523.

12 I.K. Kautsky, "Preface: The Moscow Trial and the Bolsheviki," in W. Woytinsky, *The Twelve Who Are to Die: The Trial of the Social Revolutionists in Moscow* (Berlin: Delegation of the Party of Socialists-Revolutionists, 1922), 8.

13 American historian Clarence Manning observed: "The movement was commenced by ignorance, continued in folly, and fortunately, by the successful withdrawal, did not end in disaster." See Clarence A. Manning, *The Siberian Fiasco* (New York: Library Publishers, 1952), 1.

14 Canada, *Report of Debates of the House of Commons*, 10 June 1919, p. 3298. See also MacLaren, *Canadians in Russia*, 213-14; Jonathan F. Vance, "Dr. Henri Beland: Nobody's Darling," *American Review of Canadian Studies* 28, 4 (Winter 1998): 469-87.

15 Mewburn to Borden, 6 December 1918, Borden to White, 7 December 1918, Lash to Mewburn, 3 December 1918 (all in LAC, RG 24, ser. C-1-A, vol. 2557, file HQC-2514 [vol. 1]).

16 Beattie, "Canadian Intervention in Russia," iii.

17 Morton, *When Your Number's Up*, 250-52; Desmond Morton, "The Supreme Penalty: Canadian Deaths by Firing Squad in the First World War," *Queen's Quarterly* 79, 3 (Autumn 1972): 345-52.

18 "Siberian Expedition Cost Canada $2,823,960," *Toronto Globe*, 30 March 1926; Canada, *Report of Debates of the House of Commons*, 29 March 1926, p. 1985, 7 April 1920, p. 995; Canada, *Debates of the Senate of the Dominion of Canada: Session 1919*, 25 June 1919, p. 736. For the cost-sharing agreement between Canada and the British government, see "Memorandum Respecting the Organization and Status of the Proposed Canadian Siberian Expeditionary Force," n.d. (c. 9 November 1918), LAC, RG 24, ser. C-1-A, vol. 2557, file HQC-2514 (vol. 1). Between March 1917 and March 1919, Britain gave 184,000,000 pounds sterling to various White Russian governments. See "Britain's Aid to 'Democracy,'" *BC Federationist*, 31 October 1919; "$350,000,000 Spent to Enslave Russia," *Tribune*, 2 October 1919; "Statement of Expenditure on Naval and Military Operations in Russia, from the Date of the Armistice to the 31st March 1920," 1920, LAC, Defence, ser. C-1-A, vol. 2013, file HQ-11-762-36.

19 The poor condition of the Canadian graves in Vladivostok came to the attention of Canada's standing committee on foreign affairs in the mid-1990s. The committee received evidence for the following: "There are Canadian graves left in Vladivostok that are in a terrible shambles. Headstones have been stolen or knocked over. Graffiti has been painted on some of the headstones. It seems a shame that we forget about those." Shortly after the condition of the Allied plot came to light, the Commonwealth War Graves Commission embarked on a restoration of the site. See Canada, Department of Foreign Affairs, "Evidence," 30 May 1995, DEFA 25 Block 101, http://www.parl.gc.ca/35/Archives/committees351/defa/evidence/25_95-05-30/defa25_blk101.html (viewed 14 July 2008).

20 Aloysius Balawyder, *Canadian-Soviet Relations between the Wars* (Toronto: University of Toronto Press, 1972).

21 See George F. Clingan, "Siberian Sideshow: The Canadian Expeditionary Force, Siberia, 1918-1919," *Legionary* (Ottawa) 30, 1 (June 1955): 9-11, 40-41; Robert Nielson, "Combatting the Cold in Siberia," *Maclean's* (October 1972), 47-65; "The Canadians Who Got Home Too Late for the Celebrations," *Weekend Magazine*, 23 February 1974; "Last Wartime Corps CO Once Served in Siberia," *Saint John Telegraph-Journal*, 27 December 1978; "Cambridge Man May Be Last Survivor of Canadian Force Sent to Siberia," *Ottawa Citizen*, 11 March 1987; Michael Westaway McCue, "Robert Borden's Siberian Adventure," *The Beaver* 81, 6 (December 2001/January 2002): 25-30; Nathan Greenfield, "War on the Reds: Canada Joined Others in Trying to Overthrow the Bolshevik Revolution," *Maclean's* (26 January 2004), 35-36; "5,000 'Forgotten' Canadians," *Toronto Star*, 10 November 2007; Ian C.D. Moffat, "Forgotten Battlefields: Canadians in Siberia, 1918-1919," *Canadian Military Journal* 8, 3 (Autumn 2007): 73-86.

2 Beattie, "Canadian Intervention in Russia," 409.

3 See "History Teaching All Wrong," *Tribune*, 22 September 1919: "So we grow up thinking there were no struggles to engage in, no obstacles to be overcome. We suppose now that the new text books will tell children that the world was set free in 1914-1918 – with no hint that autocracy is not yet out of the saddle, no suggestion that there are other fields to be won."

Bibliography

Archival Sources

British Columbia Archives (Victoria, British Columbia)
  British Columbia Federation of Labour Fonds
  Christian Sivertz Fonds
Centre for Research on Canadian-Russian Relations (Barrie, Ontario)
  Siberian Expedition records
E.H.W. Elkington Collection (private collection) (Ladysmith, British Columbia)
  Eric Elkington Papers
Hoover Institution Archives, Stanford University (Palo Alto, California)
  Edith M. Faulstich Collection
  Geoffrey McDonnell Collection
Khabarovsk State Historical Archives (Khabarovsk, Russia)
  Bednota [The Poor] (Moscow)
  Pravityel'stvyenniy vyestnik [Governmental Bulletin] (Omsk)
  Priamoorskaya zhizn' [Priamursky Life] (Khabarovsk)
Library and Archives Canada (LAC) (Ottawa, Ontario)
  Charles Sumner Lund Hertzberg Fonds
  Department of Employment and Immigration Fonds
  Department of Justice Fonds
  Department of Labour Fonds
  Department of Militia and Defence Fonds
  Department of National Defence Fonds
  Department of Trade and Commerce Fonds
  Dorothy I. Perrin Fonds
  Florence Farmer Fonds
  George Addison McHaffie Fonds
  Harold Steele Fonds
  Harold Vernon Ardagh Fonds
  Hugh Robertson Fonds
  Imperial Oil Collection
  James Mackintosh Bell Fonds
  Leolyn Dana Wilgress Fonds
  Record Group 150 (Personnel files)
  Robert Borden Papers
  Royal Canadian Mounted Police Fonds
McMaster Archives and Research Collection, McMaster University (Hamilton,
  Ontario)
  Canadian Siberian Expeditionary Force Fonds
Public Archives of Manitoba (Winnipeg)
  One Big Union Collection

Robert Patterson Aitchison McNay Collection (private collection) (Katrine, Ontario)
    Robert McNay Papers
Sidney Rodger Collection (private collection) (Beamsville, Ontario)
    Sidney Rodger Papers
Stephenson Family Collection (private collection) (Burlington, Ontario)
    Edwin Stephenson Papers
University of British Columbia Special Collections
    Eugene S. Woodward Fonds
    One Big Union Fonds
University of Victoria Archives and Special Collections (UVASC) (Victoria)
    Boilermakers Fonds
    Frederick Carne Fonds
    Military Oral History Collection
    Victoria Labour Council Fonds
Viateur Beaulieu Family Collection (Private Collection) (Cacouna, Quebec)
    259th Battalion Photographs
Vladivostok State Historical Archives (Vladivostok, Russia)
    Dalekaya Okraina [Far Suburb] (Vladivostok)
    Primorskaya Zhizn' [Primorsky Life] (Vladivostok)
    Voennyi Vestnik [Military Herald] (Vladivostok)
Washington State Historical Archive (Tacoma, Washington)
    Stuart Ramsay Tompkins Papers

Newspapers

Bednota [The Poor] (Moscow), 1921
Business in Vancouver, 2007
British Columbia Federationist (Vancouver), 1914-20
The Communist (Toronto), 1921
Daily Colonist (Victoria), 1914-19
Daily Province (Vancouver), 1917-19
Daily Star (Toronto), 1918
Daily Sun (Vancouver), 1917-19
Daily Times (Victoria), 1914-19
Dalekaya Okraina [Far Suburb] (Vladivostok), 1918-19
Echo (Vladivostok), 1919
Globe (Toronto), 1918-19
The Guardian (London), 2001
Halifax Herald, 1917
Hamilton Herald, 1918-19
Hamilton Spectator, 1918-19
International Herald Tribune, 1905, 2006-7
Izvestia (Moscow), 2004
Montreal Gazette, 1918-19
Montreal Star, 1918
Morning Albertan (Calgary), 1919
The Nation (New York), 1918-19
New York Times, 1917-20
Novaya Sibir' [New Siberia] (Irkutsk), 1918
One Big Union Bulletin (Winnipeg), 1919-27

Ottawa Citizen, 1940, 1978
Pravda [Truth] (Petrograd), 1917; (Moscow), 1928
Pravityel'stvyenniy vyestnik [Governmental Bulletin] (Omsk), 1918-19
Priamoorskaya zhizn' [Priamursky Life] (Khabarovsk), 1919
Primorskaya Zhizn' (Primorsky Life] (Vladivostok), 1918
Red Flag (Vancouver), 1918-19
Sackville Tribune (New Brunswick), 1919
Saint John Telegraph-Journal, 1978
Saturday Night (Toronto), 1918
Semi-Weekly Tribune (Victoria), 1918-19
Siberian Bugle (Vladivostok), 1919
Siberian Sapper (Vladivostok), 1919
Socialist Party Bulletin (Chicago), 1917
St. Peterburg Times, 2003
Toronto Star, 2007
Voennyi Vestnik [Military Herald] (Vladivostok), 1919
Week (Victoria), 1918, 1920
Western Clarion (Vancouver), 1920-22
The Worker (Toronto), 1922, 1933

Government Sources
Canada. *Canada Gazette.* Ottawa: J. de Labroquerie Taché, 1917-19.
–. *Debates of the Senate of the Dominion of Canada: Session 1919.* Ottawa: J. de Labroquerie Taché, 1919.
–. Department of External Affairs. *Documents on Canadian External Relations.* Vol. 1: *1909-1918.* Ottawa: Department of External Affairs, 1967.
–. Department of Trade and Commerce. *Report of the Canadian Economic Commission (Siberia).* Ottawa: J. de Labroquerie Taché, 1919.
–. Department of Trade and Commerce. *Weekly Bulletin.* Vol. 21. 9 September 1919.
–. *Labour Gazette.* Ottawa: J. de Labroqueire Taché, 1917-19.
–. *The Military Service Act, 1917.* Ottawa: J. de Labroquerie Taché, 1917.
–. *Report of Debates of the House of Commons.* Ottawa: J. de Labroquerie Taché, 1919-26.
–. Machin, H.A.C. *Report from the Director of the Military Service Branch to the Honourable Minister of Justice on the Operation of the Military Service Act, 1917.* Ottawa: J. de Labroquerie Taché, 1919.
–. *Sessional Papers* 56: 4 (1920).
–. "Treaty of Peace between the Allied and Associated Powers and Germany and Protocol," *Sessional Papers*, vol. 55, no. 1, special session 1919. Ottawa: J. de Labroquerie Taché, 1919.
Imperial War Graves Commission. *Cemeteries and Memorials in British North Borneo, Ceylon, China, Cochin China, Hong Kong, Japan, Malaya, the Philippine Islands, and Siberia: Asia I-50.* London: His Majesty's Stationery Office, 1931.
Victoria. *Annual Reports: Corporation of the City of Victoria.* Victoria: Diggen, 1918.
United States of America, *Foreign Relations of the United States.* Vol. 2: *1918 Russia.* Washington: United States Government Printing Office, 1932.

Contemporary Sources
Ackerman, Carl W. *Trailing the Bolsheviki: Twelve Thousand Miles with the Allies in Siberia.* New York: Scribner, 1919.

Arshinov, Peter. *Istoriya Maknovskogo Dvizheniya* [History of the Makhnovist Movement]. Berlin: Gruppa Russkikh Anarkhistov v Germanii, 1923.

Bishop, Charles W. *The Canadian YMCA in the Great War: The Official Record of the Activities of the Canadian YMCA in Connection with the Great War of 1914-1918.* Toronto: National Council of Young Men's Christian Associations of Canada, 1924.

Borden, Robert. *Canada at War: A Speech Delivered in Parliament by Rt. Hon. Sir Robert Børden.* Ottawa: 1917. CIHM no. 76128.

–. *Extension of the Term of Parliament,* 17 July 1917, CIHM reel 76107.

–. *Robert Laird Borden: His Memoirs.* Ed. Henry Laird Borden and Heath MacQuarrie. Toronto: McClelland and Stewart, 1969.

Brunker, H.M.E. *Story of the Russo-Japanese War, 1904-05.* London: Forster Groom, 1909.

Buxhoeveden, Sophie. *Left Behind: Fourteen Months in Siberia during the Revolution, December 1917-February 1919.* London: Longmans, Green, 1929.

Cahan, C.H. *Socialistic Propaganda in Canada: Its Purposes, Results and Remedies.* Address delivered to St. James Literary Society, Montreal, 12 December 1918. Montreal: n.d. (c. 1918). CIHM no. 87228.

Chambers, Ernest J., ed. *Canadian Parliamentary Guide.* Ottawa: Mortimer, 1918-1922.

Cocks, F. Seymour, ed., *The Secret Treaties and Understandings.* London: Union of Democratic Control, n.d. (c. 1918).

Daniel, I.J.E., and D.A. Casey. *For God and Country: War Work of Canadian Knights of Columbus Catholic Army Huts.* Ottawa: Knights of Columbus, c. 1922.

Denikine, A. *The White Army.* Trans. Catherine Zvegintzov. Gulf Breeze, FL: Academic International, 1973.

Fraser, Dawn. *Songs of Siberia and Rhymes of the Road.* Glace Bay, NS: Eastern Publishing, c. 1919.

Goldman, Emma. *My Disillusionment in Russia.* New York: Doubleday, Page and Company, 1923.

Graves, William S. *America's Siberian Adventure, 1918-1920.* New York: Peter Smith, 1931.

Hopkins, J. Castell. *Canadian Annual Review of Public Affairs.* Toronto: Canadian Annual Review, 1918-19.

Kautsky, I.K. "Preface: The Moscow Trial and the Bolsheviki." In W. Woytinsky, *The Twelve Who Are to Die: The Trial of the Social Revolutionists in Moscow.* Berlin: Delegation of the Party of Socialists-Revolutionists, 1922.

Kavanagh, J. *The Vancouver Island Strike.* Vancouver: BC Miners' Liberation League, c. 1913.

Knox, Alfred W.F. *With the Russian Army, 1914-1917.* New York: Arno, 1971.

Kollontai, Alexandra. *The Autobiography of a Sexually Emancipated Communist Woman.* Trans. Salvator Attanasio. New York: Herder and Herder, 1971 [1927].

Lenin, V.I. *Collected Works.* Vol. 27. 3rd English ed. Moscow: Progress Publishers, 1965.

Mackintosh Bell, James. *Side Lights on the Siberian Campaign.* Toronto: Ryerson, n.d. [1922].

Norton, Henry Kittredge. *The Far Eastern Republic in Siberia.* London: Allen and Unwin, 1923.

Pares, Bernard. *My Russian Memoirs.* London: Jonathan Cape, 1931.

Roy, Ferdinand. *L'appel aux armes et la réponse canadiennne-française: Étude sur le conflit des races.* Québec: Garneau, 1917.

Simpson, James Young. *Side-Lights on Siberia: Some Account of the Great Siberian Railroad, the Prisons and Exile System.* Edinburgh and London: William Blackwood and Sons, 1897.

Shvittau, G.G. *Revolutsiya i Narodnoe Khoziaistvo v Rossii, 1917-1921* [The Revolution and the National Economy in Russia, 1917-1921]. Leipzig: Tsentral'noe kooperativnoe izdatel'stvo, 1922.

Trotsky, Leon. *The Military Writings and Speeches of Leon Trotsky.* Vol. 1: *1918: How the Revolution Armed.* London: New Park, 1979.

–. *The Military Writings and Speeches of Leon Trotsky.* Vol. 2: *1919: How the Revolution Armed.* London: New Park, 1979.

–. *My Life: An Attempt at an Autobiography.* New York: Charles Scribner's Sons, 1930.

–. *Socheneniya* [Collected Works]. Moscow: State Publishing House, 1924.

–. *V Plenu u Anglichan* [In British Captivitiy] (Petrograd, n.d.), reprinted as "In British Captivity," *The Class Struggle* (New York), 2, 4 (December 1918): 542-47.

Ward, John. *With the "Die-Hards" in Siberia.* London: Cassell, 1920.

Williams, Albert Rhys. *Through the Russian Revolution.* New York: Boni and Liveright, 1921.

Winnipeg Defence Committee. *Saving the World from Democracy: The Winnipeg General Sympathetic Strike, May-June, 1919.* Winnipeg: Defence Committee, 1920.

Books

Angus, Ian. *Canadian Bolsheviks: The Early Years of the Communist Party of Canada.* Montreal: Vanguard, 1981.

Anon. *Canada's Party of Socialism: History of the Communist Party of Canada, 1921-1976.* Toronto: Progress Books, 1982.

–. *History of the Communist Party of the Soviet Union.* Moscow: Foreign Languages Publishing House, 1960.

Anweiler, Oskar. *The Soviets: The Russian Workers, Peasants, and Soldiers Councils, 1905-1921.* New York: Pantheon, 1974.

Armstrong, Elizabeth H. *Le Québec et la crise de la conscription, 1917-1918.* Montréal: VLB Éditeur, 1998.

Avakumovic, Ivan. *The Communist Party in Canada.* Toronto: McClelland and Stewart, 1975.

Baird, Ron. *Success Story: The History of Oak Bay.* Victoria: Borsman and Heffernan, 1979.

Balawyder, Aloysius. *Canadian-Soviet Relations between the Wars.* Toronto: University of Toronto Press, 1972.

Barratt, Glynn. *Russian Shadows on the British Northwest Coast of North America, 1810-1890.* Vancouver: UBC Press, 1983.

Belikova, L.I., and S.A. Ivanov, eds. *Bor ba za vlast Sovetov v Primor e (1917-1922): Sbornik dokumentov* [The Struggle for Control of the Soviets in the Primor'ye (1917-1922): A Collection of Documents]. Vladivostok: Primorskoe knizhnoe izd-vo, 1955.

Bercuson, David, J. *Confrontation at Winnipeg: Labour, Industrial Relations, and the General Strike.* Montreal and Kingston: McGill-Queen's University Press, 1974.

–. *Fools and Wise Men: The Rise and Fall of the One Big Union.* Toronto: McGraw-Hill Ryerson, 1978.

Bisher, Jamie. *White Terror: Cossack Warlords of the Trans-Siberian.* London: Routledge, 2005.

Bojerud, Stellan. *Ivor Thord Gray: Soldat under 13 Fano* [Ivor Thord Gray: A Soldier for 13 Countries]. Stockholm: Sivart, 2008.

Bradley, John. *Allied Intervention in Russia.* Lantham, New York, and London: University Press of America, 1968.

–. *The Czechoslovak Legion in Russia, 1914-1920.* Boulder: East European Monographs, 1991.

Bright, David. *The Limits of Labour: Class Formation and the Labour Movement in Calgary, 1883-1929.* Vancouver: UBC Press, 1998.

Brinkley, George A. *The Volunteer Army and Allied Intervention in South Russia, 1917-1921: A Study in the Politics and Diplomacy of the Russian Civil War.* Notre Dame: University of Notre Dame Press, 1966.

Brookfield, Tarah. "Divided by the Ballot Box: The Montreal Council of Women and the 1917 Election." *Canadian Historical Review* 89, 4 (December 2008): 473-501.

Brown, Robert Craig, and Ramsey Cook. *Canada, 1896-1921: A Nation Transformed.* Toronto: McClelland and Stewart, 1974.

–. *Robert Laird Borden: A Biography.* Vol. 2: *1914-1937.* Toronto: Macmillan, 1980.

Buck, Tim. *Canada and the Russian Revolution: The Impact of the World's First Socialist Revolution on Labor and Politics in Canada.* Toronto: Progress Books, 1967.

Bulygin, Paul. *Murder of the Romanovs: The Authentic Account.* London: Hutchinson, 1935.

Campbell, Peter. *Canadian Marxists and the Search for a Third Way.* Montreal and Kingston: McGill-Queen's University Press, 2000.

Carley, Michael J. *Revolution and Intervention: The French Government and the Russian Civil War, 1917-1919.* Montreal and Kingston: McGill-Queen's University Press, 1983.

Chen, Vincent. *Sino-Russian Relations in the Seventeenth Century.* The Hague: Martinus Nijhoff, 1966.

Connaughton, R.M. *The Republic of the Ushakovko: Admiral Kolchak and the Allied Intervention in Siberia, 1918-20.* London and New York: Routledge, 1990.

Cook, Tim. *Clio's Warriors: Canadian Historians and the Writing of the World Wars.* Vancouver: UBC Press, 2006.

Copp, Terry. *The Brigade: The Fifth Canadian Infantry Brigade.* Stoney Creek: Fortress, 1992.

–, and Bill McAndrew. *Battle Exhaustion: Soldiers and Psychiatrists in the Canadian Army, 1939-1945.* Montreal and Kingston: McGill-Queen's University Press, 1990.

Dahnhardt, Floyd. *Revolution in Kiel: Der Obergang vom Kaiserreich zur Weimarer Republik, 1918-19.* Neumunster: Karl Wachholtz Verbag, 1978.

Dansereau, Bernard. *Le mouvement ouvrier montréalais et la crise de la conscription, 1916–1918.* Montréal: Université du Québec à Montréal, 1994.

Deeg, Lothar. *Kunst & Albers Wladiwostok: Die Geschichte eines deutschen Handelshauses im russischen Fernen Osten 1864-1924.* Essen: Klartext-Verlagsges, 1996.

Dobson, Christopher, and John Miller, *The Day They Almost Bombed Moscow: The Allied Intervention in Russia, 1918-1920.* New York: Atheneum, 1986.

–, and Bill McAndrew. *Battle Exhaustion: Soldiers and Psychiatrists in the Canadian Army, 1939-1945.* Montreal and Kingston: McGill-Queen's University Press, 1990.

Eayrs, James. *In Defence of Canada.* Vol. 1: *From the Great War to the Great Depression.* Toronto: University of Toronto Press, 1964.

Evans, Suzanne. *Mothers of Heroes, Mothers of Martyrs: World War I and the Politics of Grief.* Montreal and Kingston: McGill-Queen's University Press, 2007.

Fic, Victor M. *The Bolsheviks and the Czechoslovak Legion: The Origin of Their Armed Conflict, March-May 1918.* New Delhi: Abhinav Publications, 1978.

Filteau, Gérard. *Le Québec, le Canada et la guerre, 1914-1918.* Montréal: L'Aurore, 1977.

Fleming, Peter. *The Fate of Admiral Kolchak.* New York: Harcourt, Brace and World, 1963.

Foglesong, David S. *America's Secret War against Bolshevism: US Intervention in the Russian Civil War, 1917-1920.* Chapel Hill and London: University of North Carolina Press, 1995.

Footman, David. *The Last Days of Kolchak.* Oxford: St. Anthony's College, 1953.

Friedheim, Robert L. *The Seattle General Strike.* Seattle: University of Washington Press, 1964.

Frost, Orcutt. *Bering: The Russian Discovery of America.* New Haven, CT: Yale University Press, 2003.

Garrett, Richard. *The Final Betrayal: Armistice, 1918 ... and Afterwards.* Shedfield, Southampton: Buchan and Enright, 1989.

Gibbon, John Murray. *Steel of Empire: The Romantic History of the Canadian Pacific, the
Northwest Passage of Today.* Toronto: McClelland and Stewart, 1935.

Granatstein, J.L., and J.M. Hitsman. *Broken Promises: A History of Conscription in Canada.*
Toronto: Copp Clark Pitman, 1985.

Griffin, Sean, ed. *Fighting Heritage: Highlights of the 1930s Struggle for Jobs and Militant
Unionism in British Columbia.* Vancouver: Tribune Publishing Company, 1985.

Hardy, George. *Those Stormy Years: Memories of the Fight for Freedom on Five Continents.*
London: Lawrence and Wishart, 1956.

Hay, Ian. *One Hundred Years of Army Nursing: The Story of the British Army Nursing Services
from the Time of Florence Nightingale to the Present Day.* London: Cassell and Co., 1953.

Heron, Craig, ed. *The Workers' Revolt in Canada, 1917-1925.* Toronto, Buffalo, and London:
University of Toronto Press, 1998.

Hill, O. Mary. *Canada's Salesman to the World: The Department of Trade and Commerce,
1892-1939.* Toronto and Montreal: Institute of Public Administration and McGill-Queen's
University Press, 1977.

Horn, Daniel. *The German Naval Mutinies of World War I.* New Brunswick, NJ: Rutgers
University Press, 1969.

Horrocks, Sir Brian. *Escape to Action.* New York: St. Martin's Press, 1960.

Hoyt, Edwin P. *The Army without a Country.* New York: Macmillan, 1967.

Hughes, James. *Stalin, Siberia, and the Crisis of the New Economic Policy.* Cambridge:
Cambridge University Press, 1991.

Iarocci, Andrew. *Shoestring Soldiers: The 1st Canadian Division at War, 1914-1915.* Toronto: University of Toronto Press, 2008.

James, Lawrence. *Mutiny in the British and Commonwealth Forces, 1797–1956.* London:
Buchan and Enright, 1987.

Johnson, F. Henry. *A History of Public Education in British Columbia.* Vancouver: University
of British Columbia Publications Centre, 1964.

Kealey, Gregory S., and Reg Whitaker. *RCMP Security Bulletins: The Early Years, 1919-1929.*
St. John's: Canadian Committee on Labour History, 1994.

Kenez, Peter. *The Defeat of the Whites: Civil War in South Russia, 1919-1920.* Berkeley:
University of California Press, 1977.

Kennan, George. *Siberia and the Exile System.* New York: Century Company, 1891.

Kerensky, Alexander. *The Catastrophe: Kerensky's Own Story of the Russian Revolution.*
New York: D. Appleton and Co., 1927.

Kettle, Michael. *The Allies and the Russian Collapse, March 1917-March 1918.* London:
Deutsch, 1981.

–. *The Road to Intervention: March-November 1918.* London and New York: Routledge, 1988.

Khisamutdinov, Amir. *The Russian Far East: Historical Essays.* Honolulu: Center for Russia
in Asia, 1993.

Kinvig, Clifford. *Churchill's Crusade: The British Invasion of Russia, 1918-1920.* London:
Continuum, 2006.

Klein, Naomi. *The Shock Doctrine: The Rise of Disaster Capitalism.* Toronto: Knopf, 2007.

Landells, E.A., ed. *The Military Nurses of Canada: Recollections of Canadian Military Nurses.*
White Rock, BC: Co-Publishing, 1975.

Langer, Joakim. *Mannen som hittade Tarzan* [The Man Who Found Tarzan]. Stockholm:
Sivart, 2008.

Leier, Mark. *Where the Fraser River Flows: The Industrial Workers of the World in British
Columbia.* Vancouver: New Star Books, 1990.

Lessner, Erwin. *Cradle of Conquerors: Siberia*. Garden City, NY: Doubleday and Company, 1955.

Luckett, Richard. *The White Generals: An Account of the White Movement and the Russian Civil War*. Edinburgh: Longman, 1971.

McCormack, A. Ross. *Reformers, Rebels, and Revolutionaries: The Western Canadian Radical Movement, 1899-1919*. Toronto and Buffalo: University of Toronto Press, 1977.

MacMillan, Margaret. *Paris, 1919: Six Months that Changed the World*. New York: Random House, 2002.

McDowall, Duncan. *Quick to the Frontier: Canada's Royal Bank*. Toronto: McClelland and Stewart, 1993.

McNaught, Kenneth. *A Prophet in Politics: A Biography of J.S. Woodsworth*. Toronto: University of Toronto Press, 1959.

MacLaren, Roy. *Canadians in Russia, 1918-19*. Toronto: Macmillan, 1976.

Maddox, Robert J. *The Unknown War with Russia: Wilson's Siberian Intervention*. San Rafael, CA: Presidio, 1977.

Madsen, Chris. *Another Kind of Justice: Canadian Military Law from Confederation to Somalia*. Vancouver: UBC Press, 1999.

Mandel, David. *The Petrograd Workers and the Fall of the Old Regime*. London: Macmillan, 1983.

–. *The Petrograd Workers and the Soviet Seizure of Power*. London: Macmillan, 1984.

Manning, Clarence A. *The Siberian Fiasco*. New York: Library Publishers, 1952.

Mantle, Craig Leslie, ed. *The Apathetic and the Defiant: Case Studies of Canadian Mutiny and Disobedience, 1812-1919*. Kingston: Canadian Defence Academy Press/Dundurn, 2007.

Marks, Steven G. *Road to Power: The Trans-Siberian Railroad and the Colonization of Asian Russia, 1850-1917*. London: Taurus, 1991.

Martin, Christopher. *The Russo-Japanese War*. London: Abelard-Schuman, 1967.

Massey, Raymond. *When I Was Young*. Toronto: McClelland and Stewart, 1976.

Mawdsley, Evan. *The Russian Civil War*. Boston: Allen and Unwin, 1987.

Mayse, Susan. *Ginger: The Life and Death of Albert Goodwin*. Madeira Park, BC: Harbour, 1990.

Miller, Floyd. *Wild Children of the Urals*. New York: Dutton, 1965.

Miller, Ian Hugh Maclean. *Our Glory and Our Grief: Torontonians and the Great War*. Toronto: University of Toronto Press, 2002.

Minakir, Pavel and Gregory Freeze, *The Russian Far East: An Economic Survey*. Khabarovsk: RIOTIP, 1996.

Morley, James. *The Japanese Thrust into Siberia, 1918*. New York: Columbia University, 1957.

Morton, Desmond. *Canada and War: A Military and Political History*. Scarborough: Butterworths, 1981.

–. *When Your Number's Up: The Canadian Soldier in the First World War*. Toronto: Random House of Canada, 1993.

–, and J.L. Granatstein. *Canada and the Two World Wars*. Toronto: Key Porter Books, 2003.

–, and J.L. Granatstein. *Marching to Armageddon: Canadians and the Great War, 1914–1919*. Toronto: Lester and Orpen Dennys, 1989.

Muirden, Bruce. *The Diggers Who Signed on for More: Australia's Part in the Russian Wars of Intervention, 1918-1919*. Kent Town, Australia: Wakefield, 1990.

Mukhachev, Boris I. *Aleksandr Krasnoshchekov: Istoriko-biograficheskii ocherk* [Aleksandr Krasnoshchekov: A Historico-Biographic Study]. Vladivostok: Far Eastern Division of the Russian Academy Sciences, 1999.

–, ed. *Dal' nii Vostok Rossii v period revoliutsii 1917 goda i grazhdanskoi voi ny* [The Far East of Russia in the Period of the Revolutions of 1917 and Civil War]. Vladivostok: Dal'nauka, 2003.

– et al., eds. *Kolchak i interventsiia na Dal'nem Vostoke: Dokumenty i materialy* [Kolchak and the Intervention in the Far East: Documents and Materials]. Vladivostok: Institute of History, Archeology and Ethnography of the Far Eastern People, Russian Academy of Sciences, 1995.

– et al., eds. *Podgotovka i nachalo interventsii na Dal'nem Vostoke Rossii: Oktiabr 1917-oktiabr 1918: Dokumenty i materialy* [Preparation and Beginning of the Intervention in the Far East of Russia, October 1917 to October 1918: Documents and Materials]. Vladivostok: Institute of History, Archeology and Ethnography of the Far Eastern Peoples, Russian Academy of Science, 1997.

Musalov, Andrey. *Damanskiy i Zhalanashkol': Sovyetsko-kitayskiy vooroozhyenniy konflikt 1969 goda* [Damanski and Zhalanashkol: Sino-Soviet Armed Border Conflict in 1969]. Izdatyel'stvo: Eksprint, 2005.

Naylor, James. *The New Democracy: Challenging the Social Order in Industrial Ontario, 1914-25*. Toronto: University of Toronto Press, 1991.

Neilson, Keith. Britain, *Soviet Russia and the Collapse of the Versailles Order, 1919-1939*. Cambridge: Cambridge University Press, 2006.

Nicholson, G.W.L. *Canada's Nursing Sisters*. Toronto: Hakkert, 1975.

–. *Official History of the Canadian Army in the First World War: Canadian Expeditionary Force, 1914–1919*. Ottawa: Queen's Printer and Controller of Stationery, 1962.

Nordlander, David J. *For God and Tsar: A Brief History of Russian America, 1741–1867*. Anchorage: Alaska Natural History Association, 1994.

Novikov, Pavel Aleksandrovich. *Grazhdanskaya voina v Vostochnoi Sibiri* [The Civil War in Eastern Siberia]. Moscow: Tsentrpoligraf, 2005.

Pearson, Michael. *The Sealed Train*. New York: Putnam, 1975.

Penner, Norman. *Canadian Communism: The Stalin Years and Beyond*. Toronto: Methuen, 1988.

–, ed. *Winnipeg 1919: The Strikers' Own History of the Winnipeg General Strike*. 2nd ed. Toronto: James Lorimer and Co., 1975.

Pereira, N.G.O. *White Siberia: The Politics of Civil War*. Montreal and Kingston: McGill-Queen's University Press, 1996.

Pedroncini, G. *Les mutineries de 1917*. Paris: Presses universitaires de France, 1967.

Phillips, Alan. *The Living Legend: The Story of the Royal Canadian Mounted Police*. Toronto and Boston: Little, Brown, 1954.

Phillips, Howard, and David Killingray, eds. *The Spanish Flu Pandemic of 1918: New Perspectives*. London and New York: Routledge, 2003.

Phillips, Paul A. *No Power Greater: A Century of Labour in British Columbia*. Vancouver: Boag Foundation, 1967.

Pipes, Richard. *The Russian Revolution*. New York: Vintage Books, 1990.

Poliakov, U.A., ed. *Antisovetskaia interventsiia i ee krakh, 1917-1922* (The Anti-Soviet Intervention and Its Break-Up, 1917-1922] (Moscow: Izd-vo polit. lit-ry, 1987).

Prang, Margaret. *N.W. Rowell: Ontario Nationalist*. Toronto: University of Toronto Press, 1975.

Prentice, Alison, ed. *Women Who Taught: Perspectives on the History of Women and Teaching*. Toronto: University of Toronto Press, 1991.

Preston, Diana. *The Boxer Rebellion: The Dramatic Story of China's War on Foreigners that Shook the World in the Summer of 1900*. New York: Berkeley Books, 2001.

Putkowski, Julian. *British Army Mutineers, 1914-1922*. London: Francis Boutle, 1998.

Reshetar, John S. Jr. *A Concise History of the Communist Party of the Soviet Union*. New York: Frederick A. Praeger, 1960.

Rhodes, Richard. *Arsenals of Folly: The Making of the Nuclear Arms Race*. New York: Knopf, 2007.

Richardson, Lewis F. *Arms and Insecurity*. Chicago: Quadrangle, 1960.

Robin, Martin. *Radical Politics and Canadian Labour, 1880-1930*. Kingston: Industrial Relations Centre, Queen's University: 1968.

Rodney, William. *Soldiers of the International: The First Ten Years of the Communist Party of Canada*. Toronto: University of Toronto Press, 1968.

Rudé, George. *The Crowd in History: A Study of Popular Disturbances in France and England, 1730-1848*. New York: Wiley, 1964.

Ryder, A.J. *The German Revolution of 1918: A Study of German Socialism in War and Revolt*. Cambridge: Cambridge University Press, 1967.

Shapiro, Leonard. *Communist Party of the Soviet Union*. New York: Random House, 1960.

Shishkin, Sergey Nikolaevich. *Organizatsiya partizanskoi bor'by protiv interventov i belogvardeitsev na Dal'nem Vostoke v 1918-1919* [The Organization of Guerrilla Struggle against Interventionists and White Guards in the Far East in 1918-1919]. Moscow: Military Publishing House of the Ministry of Defence of the USSR, 1957.

Sidwell, Walter. *The Island I Can't Forget*. Deroche, BC: Sidwell, 2002.

Silverlight, John. *The Victors' Dilemma: Allied Intervention in the Russian Civil War*. London: Barrie and Jenkins, 1970.

Sivertz, Bent Gestur. *The Sivertz Family*. Book 1: *Christian Sivertz of Victoria and of Canada's Early Labor Movement*. Parksville, BC: Arrowmaker Graphics, 1984.

–. *The Sivertz Family*. Book 2: *Elinborg*. Canby, OR: Copy Rite, 1982.

Skuce, J.E. *CSEF: Canada's Soldiers in Siberia, 1918-1919*. Ottawa: Access to History Publications, 1990.

Smele, J.D. *Civil War in Siberia: The Anti-Bolshevik Government of Admiral Kolchak, 1918-1920*. Cambridge: Cambridge University Press, 1996.

–, ed. *The Russian Revolution and Civil War, 1917-1921: An Annotated Bibliography*. London and New York: Continuum, 2003.

Smith, Canfield F. *Vladivostok under Red and White Rule: Revolution and Counterrevolution in the Russian Far East, 1920-1922*. Seattle: University of Washington Press, 1975.

Smith, Gaddis G. *Nation and Empire: Canadian Diplomacy during the First World War*. New Haven, CT: Yale University Press, 1969.

Smith, L.V. *Between Mutiny and Obedience: The Case of the French Fifth Infantry Division during World War I*. Princeton: Princeton University Press, 1994.

Smith, S.A. *Red Petrograd: Revolution in the Factories, 1917-1918*. Cambridge: Cambridge University Press: 1983.

Snow, Russell E. *The Bolsheviks in Siberia, 1917-1918*. Cranbury, New Jersey: Associated University Presses, 1977.

Solodyankin, A.G. *Kommunisty Irkutska v bor'be s kolchakovschinoi* [Communists of Irkutsk in Struggle with the Kolchak Movement]. Irkutsk: East-Siberian Publishing House, 1960.

Solzhenitsyn, Aleksander I. *The Gulag Archipelago, 1918-1956: An Experiment in Literary Investigation*. New York. Harper and Row, 1974.

Steeves, Dorothy G. *The Compassionate Rebel: Ernest Winch and the Growth of Socialism in Western Canada*. Vancouver: Boag Foundation, 1977.

Stephan, John J. *The Russian Far East: A History*. Stanford: Stanford University Press, 1994.

Stonebanks, Roger. *Fighting for Dignity: The Ginger Goodwin Story*. St. John's: Canadian Committee on Labour History, 2004.

Strakhovsky, Leonid I. *Intervention at Archangel: The Story of Allied Intervention and Russian Counter-Revolution in North Russia, 1918-1920*. New York: Princeton University Press, 1944.

Svetachev, M.I. *Imperialisticheskai'a' intervent's'ii'a' v Sibiri i na Dal'nem Vostoke* [The Imperialistic Intervention in Siberia and the Far East]. Novosibirsk: Nauka, Siberian Division, 1983.

Swettenham, John. *Allied Intervention in Russia, 1918-19, and the Part Played by Canada*. Toronto: Ryerson Press, 1967.

Thornton, Judith, and Charles E. Ziegler, eds. *Russia's Far East: A Region at Risk*. Seattle and London: National Association for Asiatic Research and University of Washington Press, 2002.

Tompkins, Stuart Ramsey. *A Canadian's Road to Russia: Letters from the Great War Decade*. Ed. Doris H. Pieroth. Edmonton: University of Alberta Press, 1989.

Turner, Arthur J. *Somewhere: A Perfect Place*. Vancouver: Boag Foundation, 1981.

Unterberger, Betty Miller. *America's Siberian Expedition, 1918-1920: A Study of National Policy*. Durham, NC: Duke University Press, 1956.

–. *The United States, Revolutionary Russia, and the Rise of Czechoslovakia*. Chapel Hill: University of North Carolina Press, 1989.

Vance, Jonathan F. *Death So Noble: Memory, Meaning, and the First World War*. Vancouver: UBC Press, 1997.

Viola, Lynne. *The Unknown Gulag: The Lost World of Stalin's Special Settlements*. New York: Oxford University Press, 2007.

Wheeler-Bennett, Sir John. *Brest-Litovsk: The Forgotten Peace, March 1918*. London: Macmillan, 1938.

White, John Albert. *The Siberian Intervention*. New York: Princeton University Press, 1950.

Wilgress, Leolyn Dana. *Memoirs*. Toronto: Ryerson, 1967.

Willett, Robert L. *Russian Sideshow: America's Undeclared War, 1918-1920*. Washington: Brassey's, 2003.

Wrangel, Alexis. *General Wrangel: Russia's White Crusader*. London: Hippocrene, 1987.

Xiang, Lanxin. *The Origins of the Boxer War*. New York: Routledge, 2003.

Zviagin, S.P. *Kuzbass v gody grazhdanskoi voiny* [Kuzbass during the Civil War Years]. Omsk: Omsk Academy MVD, 2007.

Articles and Book Chapters

Akers, David. "Rebel or Revolutionary? Jack Kavanagh and the Early Years of the Communist Movement in Vancouver, 1920-1925." *Labour/Le Travail* 30 (Fall 1992): 9-44.

Auger, Martin F. "On the Brink of Civil War: The Canadian Government and the Suppression of the 1918 Quebec Easter Riots." *Canadian Historical Review* 89, 4 (December 2008): 503-40.

Balawyder, Aloysius. "The Czechoslovak Legion Crosses Canada, 1920." *East European Quarterly* 6, 2 (June 1972): 177-91.

Baldwin, Douglas. "The American Red Cross in Vladivostok: The Adventures of Nurse Mona Wilson." *Sibirica: Journal of Siberian Studies* 1, 2 (1994-95): 85-107.

Bercuson, David. "Labour Radicalism and the Western Industrial Frontier, 1897-1919." *Canadian Historical Review* 57 (June 1977): 154-77.

Bernard, Elaine. "Last Back: Folklore and the Telephone Operators in the 1919 Vancouver General Strike." In *Not Just Pin Money: Selected Essays on the History of Women's Work in British Columbia*, ed. Barbara K. Lantham and Roberta J. Pazdro, 279-86. Victoria: Camosun College, 1984.

Bortnevski, Viktor G. "White Administration and White Terror (The Denekin Period)." *Russian Review* 52 (July 1993): 354–66.

Buckley, Suzanne. "The Failure to Resolve the Problem of Venereal Disease among the Troops in Britain during World War I." In *War and Society: A Yearbook of Military History.* Vol. 2, ed. Brian Bond and Ian Roy, 65-85. London: Croom Helm, 1977.

Campbell, Peter. "'Making Socialists': Bill Pritchard, the Socialist Party of Canada, and the Third International." *Labour/Le Travail* 30 (Fall 1992): 42-65.

Carley, Michael J. "The Origins of the French Intervention in the Russian Civil War, January-May 1918: A Reappraisal." *Journal of Modern History* 48, 3 (September 1976): 413-39.

Caulkin, T.B. "Siberia, 1918-1919." *RCMP Quarterly* 9, 2 (October 1941): 195-99.

Clingan, George. "Siberian Sideshow: The Canadian Expeditionary Force, Siberia, 1918-1919." *Legionary* 30, 1 (June 1955): 10-14, 40-41.

Davies, David. "The Pre-1917 Roots of Canadian-Soviet Relations." *Canadian Historical Review* 70, 2 (June 1989): 180-205.

Dugas, Gaston. "Le Québec et la crise de la conscription, 1917-1918." *L'Action nationale* 9 (November 1999): 139–41.

"East Remembers Russian Branch." *Interest* (Montreal [Royal Bank]) (March/April 1979): 20-22.

Eskridge-Kosmach, Alena N. "Russia in the Boxer Rebellion." *Journal of Slavic Military Studies* 21, 1 (January 2008): 38-52.

Farnsworth, Beatrice Brodsky. "Bolshevism, the Woman Question, and Aleksandra Kollontai." *American Historical Review* 81, 2 (April 1976): 292-317.

Faulstich, Edith M. "Mail from the Canadian Siberian Expeditionary Force." *Postal History Journal* 12, 1 (January 1968): 3-33.

Florinsky, Michael. "Twilight of Absolutism: 1905." *Russian Review* 8, 4 (October 1949): 322-33.

Frank, V.S. "The Territorial Terms of the Sino-Russian Treaty of Nerchinsk, 1689." *Pacific Historical Review* 1, 3 (August 1947): 265-70.

Friesen, Gerald. "Yours in Revolt: Regionalism, Socialism, and the Western Canadian Labour Movement." *Labour/Le Travail* 1 (1976): 141-57.

Garnham, David. "War-Proneness, War-Weariness, and Regime Type: 1816-1980." *Journal of Peace Research* 23, 3 (September 1986): 279-89.

Griezic, Foster J.K. "The Honourable Thomas Alexander Crerar: The Political Career of a Western Liberal Progressive in the 1920s." In *The Twenties in Western Canada: Papers of the Western Canadian Studies Conference, March 1972*, ed. S.M. Trofimenkoff, 107-37 (Ottawa: National Museum of Man, 1972).

Gustavson, Wes. "'Fairly Well Known and Need Not Be Discussed': Colonel A.F. Duguid and the Canadian Official History of the First World War." *Canadian Military History* 10, 2 (2001): 41-54.

Horrall, S.W. "The Force's Siberian Patrol." *RCMP Quarterly* 36, 5 (July 1971): 3-8.

Humphries, Mark Osborne. "The Horror at Home: The Canadian Military and the 'Great' Influenza Pandemic of 1918." *Journal of the Canadian Historical Association* 16, 1 (2005): 235-60.

Izmozik, Vladlen S. "Voices fom the Twenties: Private Correspondence Intercepted by the OGPU," *Russian Review* 55, 2 (April 1996): 287-308.

Kautsky, I.K. "Preface: The Moscow Trial and the Bolsheviki." *The Twelve Who Are to Die* (Berlin: Delegation of the Party of Socialists-Revolutionists, 1922): 7-18.

Kealey, Gregory S. "1919: The Canadian Labour Revolt." *Labour/Le Travail* 13 (Spring 1984): 11-44.

–. "State Repression of Labour and the Left in Canada, 1914-20: The Impact of the First World War." *Canadian Historical Review* 73, 3 (1992): 281-314.

Keshen, Jeff. "All the News that Was Fit to Print: Ernest J. Chambers and Information Control in Canada, 1914-19." *Canadian Historical Review* 73, 3 (1992): 315-43.

Knight, Amy. "Female Terrorists in the Russian Socialist Revolutionary Party." *Russian Review* 38, 2 (April 1979): 139-59.

Koekner, Diane, and William G. Rosenberg. "Skilled Workers and the Strike Movement in Revolutionary Russia." *Journal of Social History* 19, 4 (Summer 1986): 605-29.

Kukushkin, Vadim. "Protectors and Watchdogs: Tsarist Consular Supervision of Russian-Subject Immigrants in Canada, 1900-1922." *Canadian Slavonic Papers*, 44, 3-4 (September/December 2002), 209-32.

Lackenbauer, P. Whitney. "The Military and 'Mob Rule': The CEF Riots in Calgary, February 1916." *Canadian Military History* 1, 10 (2001): 31-43.

–. "Under Siege: The CEF Attack on the RNWMP Barracks in Calgary, October 1916." *Alberta History* 49, 3 (2001): 2-12.

–, and Nikolas Gardner. "Soldiers as Liminaries: The CEF Soldier Riots of 1916 Reassessed." In *Canadian Military History since the 17th Century*, ed. Yves Tremblay, 164-74. Ottawa: National Defence, 2001.

Lamb, W. Kaye. "Building Submarines for Russia in Burrard Inlet." *BC Studies* 7 (Autumn 1986): 3-26.

Lensen, George Alexander. "The Attempt on the Life of Nicholas II in Japan." *Russian Review* 20, 3 (July 1961): 232-53.

"Letters from Vladivostok, 1918-1923." *Slavonic and East European Review* 45, 105 (July 1967): 497-530.

Levy, Jack S., and T. Clinton Morgan. "The War-Weariness Hypothesis: An Empirical Test." *American Journal of Political Science* 30, 1 (February 1986): 26-49.

Lyandres, Semion. "The 1918 Attempt on the Life of Lenin: A New Look at the Evidence." *Slavic Review* 48, 3 (Autumn 1989): 432-48.

McCue, Michael Westaway. "Robert Borden's Siberian Adventure." *The Beaver* 81, 6 (December 2001/January 2002): 25-30.

McGinnis, Janice P. Dickin. "The Impact of Epidemic Influenza: Canada, 1918-1919." *Historical Papers of the Canadian Historical Association* 12, 1 (1977): 120-40.

McGuire, C.R., and R.F. Narbonne. "A Siberian Expeditionary Force Discovery." *BNA Topics* 58, 2 (April-June 2001): 42-49.

Manly, John. "Does the International Labour Movement Need Salvaging? Communism, Labourism, and the Canadian Trade Unions, 1921-1928." *Labour/Le Travail* 41 (Spring 1998): 147-80.

–. "'Starve, Be Damned!': Communists and Canada's Urban Unemployed, 1929-1939." *Canadian Historical Review* 79, 3 (September 1998): 467-73.

Moffat, Ian C.D. "Forgotten Battlefields: Canadians in Siberia, 1918-1919." *Canadian Military Journal* 8, 3 (Autumn 2007): 73-86.

Morton, Desmond. "'Kicking and Complaining': Demobilization Riots in the Canadian Expeditionary Force, 1918-19." *Canadian Historical Review* 61, 3 (September 1980): 334-60.

–. "The Supreme Penalty: Canadian Deaths by Firing Squad in the First World War." *Queen's Quarterly* 79, 3 (Autumn 1972): 345-52.

Murby, Robert N. "Canadian Economic Commission to Siberia, 1918-1919." *Canadian Slavonic Papers* 11, 3 (1969): 374-93.

Norcross, Elizabeth. "Mary Ellen Smith: The Right Woman in the Right Place at the Right Time." In *Not Just Pin Money: Selected Essays on the History of Women's Work in British Columbia*, ed. Barbara K. Lantham and Roberta J. Pazdro, 357-64. Victoria: Camosun College, 1984.

Novikov, Pavel Aleksandrovich. "Vyelikoye Iskusstvo Myatyezha" [The Great Art of Mutiny]. *Rodina* 3 (March 2008): 88-92.

"Obituary: James Mackintosh Bell." *Geographical Review* 24, 3 (July 1934): 535.

Owen, Thomas C. "Chukchi Gold: American Enterprise and Russian Xenophobia in the Northeastern Siberia Company." *Pacific Historical Review* 77, 1 (February 2008): 49-85.

Pares, Bernard. "John Ward: Obituary." *Slavonic and East European Review* 13, 39 (April 1935): 680-83.

Peifer, Douglas. "Commemoration of Mutiny, Rebellion, and Resistance in Postwar Germany: Public Memory, History, and the Formation of 'Memory Beacons.'" *Journal of Military History* 65 (October 2001): 1013-23.

Peterson, Larry. "The One Big Union in International Perspective: Revolutionary Industrial Unionism, 1900-1925." *Labour/Le Travail* 7 (Spring 1981): 41-66.

−. "Revolutionary Socialism and Industrial Unionism in the Era of the Winnipeg General Strike: The Origins of Communist Labour Unionism in Europe and North America." *Labour/Le Travail* 13 (Spring 1984): 115-31.

Pickering, Jeffrey. "War-Weariness and Cumulative Effects: Victors, Vanquished, and Subsequent Interstate Intervention." *Journal of Peace Research* 39, 3 (September 2002): 313-37.

Putkowski, Julian. "The Kinmel Park Camp Riots 1919." *Flintshire Historical Society Journal* 32 (1989): 55-107.

Reichman, Henry. "The 1905 Revolution on the Siberian Railroad." *Russian Review* 47, 1 (January 1988): 25-48.

Reilly, Nolan. "The General Strike in Amherst, Nova Scotia, 1919." *Acadiensis* 9, 2 (1980): 56-77.

Richard, Carl J. "'The Shadow of a Plan': The Rationale behind Wilson's 1918 Siberian Intervention." *Historian* 49 (November 1986): 64–84.

Robin, Martin. "British Columbia: The Company Province." In *Canadian Provincial Politics: The Party Systems in the Ten Provinces*, ed. M. Robin, 2nd ed., 28-60. Scarborough: Prentice-Hall, 1978.

−. "Registration, Conscription, and Independent Labour Politics, 1916-1917." In *Conscription 1917*, ed. Ramsay Cook, 60-77. Toronto: University of Toronto Press, 1969.

Rodney, William. "Broken Journey: Trotsky in Canada, 1917." *Queen's Quarterly* 74, 4 (Winter 1967): 649-65.

−. "Russian Revolutionaries in the Port of Vancouver, 1917." *BC Studies* 16 (Winter 1972-73): 25-31.

Rosenberg, William G., and Diane P. Koekner. "The Limits of Formal Protest: Worker's Activism and the Social Polarization in Petrograd and Moscow, March to October, 1917." *American Historical Review* 92, 2 (April 1987): 296-326.

Rynkov, V.M. "Kolchakovskaia Natsionalizatsiya" [Kolchak's Nationalization]. *Siberian Zaimka* 2 (2002): 1-31.

Sarty, Roger. "'There will be trouble in the North Pacific': The Defence of British Columbia in the Early Twentieth Century." *BC Studies* 61 (Spring 1984): 3-29.

Seager, Allen, and David Roth. "British Columbia and the Mining West: A Ghost of a Chance." In *The Workers' Revolt in Canada, 1917-1925*, ed. Craig Heron, 231-67. Toronto, Buffalo, and London: University of Toronto Press, 1998.

Smele, J.D. "White Gold: The Imperial Russian Gold Reserve in the Anti-Bolshevik East, 1918-? (An Unconcluded Chapter in the History of the Russian Civil War)." *Europe-Asia Studies* 46, 8 (1994): 1317-47.

Smith, Gaddis. "Canada and the Siberian Intervention, 1918–1919," *American Historical Review* 64 (July 1959): 866-77.

Smith, Robert C. *A Canadian in Siberia, 1918-1921: BNAPS Exhibitor's Series No. 12*. Saskatoon: British North American Philatelic Soviety, 1999.

–. "Markings of the Canadian Expeditionary Force (Siberia)." *Postal History Society of Canada Journal* 36 (December 1983): 4-10.

Strakhovsky, L.I. "The Canadian Artillery Brigade in North Russia, 1918-1919." *Canadian Historical Review* 39, 2 (1958): 125-46.

Tirado, Isabel A. "The Socialist Youth Movement in Revolutionary Petrograd." *Russian Review* 46, 2 (April 1987): 135-56.

Unterberger, Betty Miller. "The Russian Revolution and Wilson's Far-Eastern Policy." *Russian Review* 16, 2 (April 1957): 35-46.

Vance, Jonathan F. "Dr. Henri Beland: Nobody's Darling." *American Review of Canadian Studies* 28, 4 (Winter 1998): 469-87.

Warburton, Rennie. "The Class Relations of Public School Teachers in British Columbia." *Canadian Review of Sociology and Anthropology* 23, 2 (1986): 210-29.

Wilgress, Dana. "From Siberia to Kuibyshev: Reflections on Russia, 1919-1943." *International Journal* 22, 3 (Summer 1967): 364-75.

Winegard, Timothy C. "The Canadian Siberian Expeditionary Force, 1918-1919, and the Complications of Coalition Warfare." *Journal of Slavic Military Studies* 20, 2 (2007): 283-328.

Wiren, Alexis R. "The Lessons of Port Arthur," *Russian Review*, 1, 2 (April 1942): 40-43.

Wood, H.F. "Adventure in North Russia." *Canadian Army Journal* 11, 4 (1957): 112-24.

Woodward, David R. "The British Government and Japanese Intervention in Russia during World War I." *Journal of Modern History* 46 (December 1974): 663-85.

Wrong, George M. "Canada and the Imperial War Cabinet," *Canadian Historical Review* 1, 1 (1920): 3-25.

Theses, Dissertations, and Papers

Beattie, Steuart. "Canadian Intervention in Russia, 1918-1919." MA thesis, McGill University, 1957.

Bennet, Joshua. "Canadian National Security: Legislations vs. Practices, 1919-1946." Paper presented to the Conference of Defence Associations 6th Annual Graduate Defence Symposium. October 2003.

Grantham, Ronald. "Some Aspects of the Socialist Movement in British Columbia." MA thesis, University of British Columbia, 1942.

Isitt, Benjamin. "Battling Bolshevism from Victoria to Vladivostok: The Canadian Siberian Expeditionary Force and Class Warfare in Canada, 1917-1919." BA honours thesis, University of Victoria, 2001.

Johnson, Ross Alfred. "No Compromise – No Political Trading: The Marxian Socialist Tradition in British Columbia." PhD diss., University of British Columbia, 1975.

Lacroix, Ronald A. "Problems of Plant Closures and Worker Relocation: A Case Study of James Island, BC." MA thesis, University of Victoria, 1981.

Lalande, Jean-Guy. "'Russia and the Soviets as Seen in Canada': Une analyse de l'opinion politique de la presse canadienne, de 1914 à 1921." PhD diss., McGill University, 1981.

Meenan, Mary Ann. "The Canadian Intervention in Siberia, 1918-1919." MA thesis, Dalhousie University, 1989.

Murby, Robert Neil. "Canada's Siberian Policy 1918-1919." MA thesis, University of British Columbia, 1969.

Polk, Jennifer Ann. "The Canadian Red Cross and Relief in Siberia, 1918-1921." MA thesis, Carleton University, 2004.

Ricard, Jeffrey. "Bringing the Boys Home: A Study of the Canadian De-Mobilization Policy after the First and Second World Wars." MA thesis, University of New Brunswick, 1999

Warrian, Peter. "The Challenge of the One Big Union Movement in Canada, 1919-1921." MA thesis, University of Waterloo, 1971.

Online and Multimedia Sources

Canada, Department of Foreign Affairs, "Evidence" (Churkin Russian Naval Cemetery), 30 May 1995, DEFA 25 Block 101, http://www.parl.gc.ca/35/Archives/committees351/defa/evidence/25_95-05-30/defa25_blk101.html (viewed 14 July 2008).

Commonwealth War Graves Commission. "Cemetery Details – Churkin Russian Naval Cemetery." http:// www.cwgc.org (viewed 22 February 2008).

Lackenbauer, P. Whitney. "Why Siberia? Canadian Foreign Policy and Siberian Intervention, 1918-1919." *Canadian Military History Project* (1998). http://www/rootsweb.com/~canmil/siberia/siberia1.html (viewed 21 January 2008).

Primorsky Statistiks. http://www.primstat.ru (viewed 14 June 2008).

Rodney, William, narrated by Leigh Taylor. *Canada and the Siberian Intervention, 1918–1919*, CBC Radio documentary, tape reel, n.d. (ca. 1970), University of Victoria Archives and Special Collections, range 43, ID no. 416, 006.

Swettenham, J.A. "Allied Intervention in Siberia 1918-1919." Report No. 83, Historical Section (G.S.) Army Headquarters, 20 October 1959. http://www.forces.ca/dhh/downloads/ahq/ahq083.pdf (viewed May 2005).

Vladivostok Ecocenter Report (1998). http://www.fegi.ru/ecology/e_inter/khrist_e.htm (viewed 29 August 2007).

Index

rubles: banning of, 123, 150, 231n92; from Canada to Vladivostok civil authorities, 234n140; cost of Trans-Siberian Railroad, 37; in Imperial Russian Gold Reserve, 8, 41, 63, 82, 162, 191n38; payment to White Russians, 54; and Siberian commerce, 40, 122, 199n24; value of, 49, 123; and war loans, 7, 26, 57, 93. *See also* Imperial Russian Gold Reserve

Russian Civil War: Allied intervention in, 5, 137, 144, 168; beginnings of, 22, 23, 54; British expenses in, 183; and Canadian press, 27, 147; and execution of Romanovs, 47; horror and legacy of, 29, 163, 164, 169; and Trans-Siberian Railroad, 140, 143; in Vladivostok, 36. *See also* Allies; Bolshevik Party; Red Army; Red Terror; Russian Revolution (1917); Soviet Russia; White Russian forces; White Terror

Russian Far East: Allied intervention in, 54, 57, 59-62, 64; American evacuation from, 162; Bolsheviks in, 125-26, 127, 129, 131; Canadian evacuation from, 5, 152, 154, 158; Canadian troops in, 4, 9, 80, 144, 170; and Canadian sovereignty, 65; colonization of, 36-37, 197n3; commerce in, 7, 39, 76, 123; Czarist administration of, 224n6; Czecho-Slovak Legion in, 59; geography of, 197n1; governments of, 180; and gulag, 165; immigration to, 40; labour relations in, 143, 151; Japanese forces in, 55, 88, 106, 112, 163; in 1905 revolution, 37; in 1917 revolution, 41-52; partisans in, 124, 128, 135; railworkers in, 143; refugees in, 111, 122; resource wealth of, 219n153; strategic importance of, 36, 82; White Russians in, 59, 81. *See also* Far Eastern Republic; Goldbreikh, S.M.; Gondatti, Nikolai Lvovich; Horvath, Dmitri; Ivanov-Rinov, Pavel; Kalmykov, Ivan; Khabarovsk; Krasnoshchekov, Aleksandr; Lazo, Sergei; Olga; Rozanov, Sergei N.; Russian Island; Semyonov, Grigori; Shevchenko, Gavrila; Shkotovo; Suchan; Sukhanov, Konstantin; Ussuri Railroad; Vladivostok

Russian Island, officer's training school: ammunition at, 130, 157; British role in, 114; Canadian role in, 126, 156, 213n52; preparation of, 80

Russian Orthodox Church, 229n64

Russian Revolution (1905): and Russian Far East, 36, 37-39, 125, 143, 198n10; in St. Petersburg, 17; in Vladivostok

Russian Revolution (March 1917): Canadian responses, 26-35; and Czecho-Slovak Legion, 60, 189n27; and foreign trade, 7, 77, 123, 156; and Gregorian calendar, 193n38; in Petrograd, 17-20; and Russian émigrés from America, 44-45; and Soviets, 21; in Vladivostok and Russian Far East, 41-51. *See also* soviets

Russian Revolution (November 1917): and Allied intervention, 4, 53, 55, 62, 168-69; anniversary of, 86, 87; and Bolsheviks, 53, 87, 164; and Canadian elite, 8, 23, 35, 69-71, 76-77, 171; and Canadian workers, 5, 26-34, 149, 160, 179; and co-operative societies, 201n79; and Czecho-Slovak Legion, 60; historiography of, 3, 9; and partisan movement, 181-82; in Petrograd, 23-26; refugees from, 111; and Russian Civil War, 164; and trade, 7, 123, 156, 166; and Trotsky, 21; and White movement, 59, 82, 213n52; in Vladivostok and Russian Far East, 36, 51-52, 56-57, 80, 166. *See also* Bolshevik Party; Lenin, Vladimir; Trotksy, Leon

Saanich (district near Victoria, BC), 86
Samara (city in Russia): military front at, 138, 239n44; seizure by Czecho-Slovaks, 60, 80
Sea of Japan, 36, 37, 44, 197n1
Sea of Okhotsk, 36, 44
Seattle General Strike, 149, 244n116
Second River, Canadian barracks: *plate* 13, 116, 118, 129; commanding officer at, 228n59; hospital at, 117, 211n36; munitions at, 130; recreation at, 120; RNWMP quarters at, 119. *See also* Gornostai Bay barracks
secret service. *See* MI5
secret treaties, 6, 55, 67, 215n93

John Griffith Armstrong, *The Halifax Explosion and the Royal Canadian Navy: Inquiry and Intrigue*

Andrew Richter, *Avoiding Armageddon: Canadian Military Strategy and Nuclear Weapons, 1950-63*

William Johnston, *A War of Patrols: Canadian Army Operations in Korea*

Julian Gwyn, *Frigates and Foremasts: The North American Squadron in Nova Scotia Waters, 1745-1815*

Jeffrey A. Keshen, *Saints, Sinners, and Soldiers: Canada's Second World War*

Desmond Morton, *Fight or Pay: Soldiers' Families in the Great War*

Douglas E. Delaney, *The Soldiers' General: Bert Hoffmeister at War*

Michael Whitby, ed., *Commanding Canadians: The Second World War Diaries of A.F.C. Layard*

Martin Auger, *Prisoners of the Home Front: German POWs and "Enemy Aliens" in Southern Quebec, 1940-46*

Tim Cook, *Clio's Warriors: Canadian Historians and the Writing of the World Wars*

Serge Marc Durflinger, *Fighting from Home: The Second World War in Verdun, Quebec*

Richard O. Mayne, *Betrayed: Scandal, Politics, and Canadian Naval Leadership*

P. Whitney Lackenbauer, *Battle Grounds: The Canadian Military and Aboriginal Lands*

Cynthia Toman, *An Officer and a Lady: Canadian Military Nursing and the Second World War*

Amy J. Shaw, *Crisis of Conscience: Conscientious Objection in Canada during the First World War*

James G. Fergusson, *Canada and Ballistic Missile Defence: Déjà Vu All Over Again*

Serge Marc Durflinger, *Veterans with a Vision: Canada's War Blinded in Peace and War*

James Wood, *Militia Myths: Ideas of the Canadian Citizen Soldier, 1896-1921*

Printed and bound in Canada by Friesens

Set in Minion and Helvetica Condensed by Artegraphica Design Co. Ltd.

Copy editor: Joanne Richardson

Proofreader: Jean Wilson

Cartographer: Eric Leinberger